Renaissance Ethnography and the Invention of the Human

Giants, cannibals and other monsters were a regular feature of Renaissance illustrated maps, inhabiting the Americas alongside other indigenous peoples. In a new approach to views of distant peoples, Surekha Davies analyses this archive alongside prints, costume books and geographical writing. Using sources from Iberia, France, the German lands, the Low Countries, Italy and England, Davies argues that mapmakers and viewers saw these maps as careful syntheses that enabled viewers to compare different peoples. In an age when scholars, missionaries, native peoples and colonial officials debated whether New World inhabitants could – or should – be converted or enslaved, maps were uniquely suited for assessing the impact of environment on bodies and temperaments. Through innovative interdisciplinary methods connecting the European Renaissance to the Atlantic world, Davies uses new sources and questions to explore science as a visual pursuit, revealing how debates about the relationship between humans and monstrous peoples challenged colonial expansion.

SUREKHA DAVIES is a cultural historian and historian of science at Western Connecticut State University. Her interests include exploration, observational sciences, monstrosity and the history of mentalities c.1400–1800.

CAMBRIDGE SOCIAL AND CULTURAL HISTORIES

Series editors
Margot C. Finn, *University College London*
Colin Jones, *Queen Mary, University of London*
Robert G. Moeller, *University of California, Irvine*

Cambridge Social and Cultural Histories publishes works of original scholarship that lie at the interface between cultural and social history. Titles in the series both articulate a clear methodological and theoretical orientation and demonstrate clearly the significance of that orientation for interpreting relevant historical sources. The series seeks to address historical questions, issues or phenomena which – although they may be located in a specific nation, state or polity – are framed so as to be relevant and methodologically innovative to specialists of other fields of historical analysis.

A list of titles in the series can be found at:
www.cambridge.org/socialculturalhistories

Renaissance Ethnography and the Invention of the Human

New Worlds, Maps and Monsters

SUREKHA DAVIES
Western Connecticut State University

CAMBRIDGE
UNIVERSITY PRESS

University Printing House, Cambridge CB2 8BS, United Kingdom

One Liberty Plaza, 20th Floor, New York, NY 10006, USA

477 Williamstown Road, Port Melbourne, VIC 3207, Australia

4843/24, 2nd Floor, Ansari Road, Daryaganj, Delhi - 110002, India

79 Anson Road, #06-04/06, Singapore 079906

Cambridge University Press is part of the University of Cambridge.

It furthers the University's mission by disseminating knowledge in the pursuit of education, learning and research at the highest international levels of excellence.

www.cambridge.org
Information on this title: www.cambridge.org/9781108431828

First published 2016
First paperback edition 2017

A catalogue record for this publication is available from the British Library

Library of Congress Cataloging in Publication data
Names: Davies, Surekha, 1974- author.
Title: Renaissance ethnography and the invention of the human : new worlds, maps and monsters / Surekha Davies.
Description: New York : Cambridge University Press, 2016. | Series: Cambridge social and cultural histories ; 24 | Includes bibliographical references and index.
Identifiers: LCCN 2016000905 | ISBN 9781107036673 (Hardback)
Subjects: LCSH: Cartography–Europe–History–16th century. | Cartography–Europe–History–17th century. | Western Hemisphere–Maps. | Geography–Sociological aspects.
Classification: LCC GA781 .D38 2016 | DDC 912.09–dc23 LC record available at http://lccn.loc.gov/2016000905

ISBN 978-1-107-03667-3 Hardback
ISBN 978-1-108-43182-8 Paperback

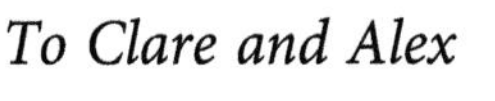

To Clare and Alex

Contents

Figures

Acknowledgements

It is a pleasure and a privilege to acknowledge the friends, colleagues, mentors and family who have helped to bring this project to fruition. Early supporters in the History and Philosophy of Science Department at the University of Cambridge were Michael T. Bravo and Liba Taub; at Robinson College, Cambridge, I am grateful for the mentorship of Martin Brett. This book began life in a very different form as a doctoral dissertation completed at the Warburg Institute, University of London, under the patient and conscientious tutelage of Jill Kraye and Elizabeth McGrath and careful examination by Jean Michel Massing and Joan-Pau Rubiés.

The book, which has expanded considerably since the dissertation, would not have been possible without generous support from numerous institutions. During my doctoral research, I was supported by a Short-Term Fellowship in the History of Cartography at the Newberry Library; the Warburg Charitable Trust and Student Travel Grant Fund; the University of London Scholarship Fund; a Fellowship from the Society for Renaissance Studies; The British Library; and an Education Grant from the Letchworth Garden City Heritage Foundation. A three-year Leverhulme Early Career Fellowship then provided me with the opportunity to join the faculty at Birkbeck, University of London. This enabled me to place this book aside for a while and research a fresh project while teaching; to travel widely collecting further material for this book; and to organize an interdisciplinary workshop, *Rethinking Encounters, Ethnography and Ethnology: Continuities and Ruptures* and a major international conference, *The Global Dimensions of European Knowledge, 1450–1700*, which expanded this project in exciting new ways. These events were supported by The Leverhulme Trust, Birkbeck College, the Royal Historical Society, the Society for Renaissance Studies and the *Journal of Early Modern History*.

In the United States, a two-month fellowship at the John Carter Brown Library in Providence, RI provided an idyllic and creative setting for re-immersing myself in a book that had gone cold after a transatlantic move. The final period of (re)writing and research was made possible by a four-month Jay I. Kislak Fellowship at the John W. Kluge Center of the Library of Congress and a three-month Hardison Fellowship at the Folger

Shakespeare Library. Essential transatlantic research travel was supported by a Franklin Research Grant from the American Philosophical Society and a Bernadotte E. Schmitt Grant from the American Historical Association. I also received generous research and travel support from Western Connecticut State University via CSU-AAUP Research Grants, Faculty Development Grants and Minority Retention Grants.

The staff at numerous libraries have been patient, welcoming and informative. I benefited from collections and expertise at: the Bibliothèque nationale de Paris; the Bibliothèque du Service historique de l'armée de terre at the Château de Vincennes, where Marie-Anne de Villèle graciously allowed me to see, *in situ* in the vault, the original manuscript of Guillaume Le Testu's *Cosmographie universelle*, and staff granted me library access even outside opening hours; the John Rylands Library, Manchester, where Anne Young and the conservation staff granted me studio space in which to consult the enormous Rylands planisphere of 1546; the Warburg Institute Library and Photographic Collection, the British Library, Lambeth Palace Library and the Royal Geographical Society, London; the Caird Library at the National Maritime Museum, Greenwich; Cambridge University Library and Trinity College Library, Cambridge; St John's College Library and the Bodleian Library, Oxford; the Huntington Library, San Marino, CA; the Newberry Library, Chicago, IL; the Library of Congress and the Folger Library, Washington, DC; the John Carter Brown Library and the John Hay Library, Providence, RI; the Beinecke Library, New Haven, CT; the New York Public Library, the Pierpont Morgan Library and the Butler Library at Columbia University, New York, NY; Princeton University Library, Princeton, NJ; the Archivos de las Indias, Seville; the Biblioteca Nacional de España, Madrid; the CRAI Biblioteca de Reserva, Universitat de Barcelona, Barcelona; the Bayerische Staatsbibliothek, Munich; the Biblioteca Nazionale di Firenze, Florence; the Vatican Library, where the staff graciously agreed to lock me into an underground vault with a security guard and the Ribeiro 1529 planisphere, Vatican City; Leiden University Library, Leiden, the Netherlands; and Ghent University Library, Ghent, Belgium.

This transnational, transdisciplinary and transimperial project has benefitted immensely from the interlocutors who have listened to me work through material that felt, in the early days, like a parade of men on maps wearing skirts. Many institutions have invited me to present portions of my research. I thank them for their generous sponsorship and stimulating discussion of work in progress. These seminar papers and invited conference papers were delivered at the Ashmolean Museum, Oxford; the John

Carter Brown Library, Brown University; Columbia University; the Folger Shakespeare Library; Indiana University; Georgetown University; The George Washington University; Harvard University; the Huntington Library, the Library of Congress; Ludwig-Maximilians-Universität, Munich; New York University; Oriel College, Oxford; Princeton University; Université Paris Diderot – Paris 7; the University at Buffalo (SUNY); the University of London; the University of Maryland College Park; and the University of Saskatoon, Saskatchwan. Special thanks are due to Brad Gregory and to my fellow participants of the *Afterlife of the Reformation* Folger Institute Seminar (Spring 2015) for intellectual stimulation and thoughtful suggestions: Gregory Erickson, Christopher P. Gillett, Lauren Robertson, Kyle B. Robinson, Rachel B. Stevenson and Kelly Whitford. For valuable suggestions and questions, I thank the audiences of the conferences at which I have spoken, which include meetings of the American Historical Association, the Renaissance Society of America, the Sixteenth Century Society and The History of Science Society.

Parts of Chapter 1 are adapted by permission of the Publishers from 'The Unlucky, the Bad and the Ugly: Categories of Monstrosity from the Renaissance to the Enlightenment', in *The Ashgate Research Companion to Monsters and the Monstrous*, ed. Asa Simon Mittman with Peter J. Dendle (Farnham and Burlington, VT: Ashgate, 2013), 49–75. Copyright © 2013. Chapter 4 is an expanded version of 'Depictions of Brazilians on French Maps, 1542–1555', *The Historical Journal*, 55:2 (2012), 217–48.

For reading the entire book twice I thank the anonymous readers for Cambridge University Press (including the no-longer-anonymous Rebecca Earle); they encouraged me to hack my way through routes that continue to challenge and enchant me. I am deeply grateful to Ralph Bauer, Felipe Fernández-Armesto, Alison Sandman and Camille Serchuk who also read the entire manuscript along the way, and who have been loyal friends, generous mentors and founts of excellent advice. For reading chapters, I thank Leah Chang, Nandini Das, Caroline Duroselle-Melish, Andrea Frisch, Carina L. Johnson, Christine Johnson, Hal Langfur, Stephanie Leitch, Lia Markey, Asa Simon Mittman, Marcy Norton, Carol Pal and Nicholas Popper. At an earlier stage, various dissertation chapters received thoughtful comments from Charles Burnett, Tony Campbell, Charlotte Coffin, Chet Van Duzer, Kristine Haugen, Peter Hulme, Michael Gaudio, Michiel van Groesen, Elisabeth Offer, Marcus Offer, Fernanda Peñaloza, Alessandro Scafi and Jennifer Spinks. Any errors that remain are, of course, my own.

Travellers' lives are greatly improved by good companions along their journeys. Many friends have generously welcomed me into their homes at all manner of busy times, and made complicated research trips so much more pleasurable. For almost two decades of friendship and hospitality in Paris and beyond, I cannot thank Charlotte Coffin and Laurent Perron enough. Marika Leino and James Frost provided an idyllic base in Oxfordshire on numerous occasions; Debbie Hall and Joe Andrews provided the same in central Oxford. For multiple hostings in New York City, I thank: Christine Hegel and Luke Cantarella; Ximena Gallardo C. and C. Jason Smith; Dániel Margócsy and Ania Cieslik; and Asa and Michele Mittman. Mary Fuller generously hosted visits to Cambridge, MA; Alison Sandman, a visit to Seville; Neil Safier and Iris Montero Sobrevilla hosted me repeatedly in Providence, RI; Ralph Bauer and Grace Crussiah continue to offer a wonderful home away from home from which to explore the libraries of Washington, DC. Other generous hosts I thank here for conversation and support include Andrew S. Curran, Nandini Das, Jenny Rampling and Camille Serchuk.

My fellow Fellows at various institutions provided advice, scintillating academic debate, friendship and laughter. They include Claire Byrne, Clare Carroll, Scott Cave, Elia Andrea Corazza (who even provided piano composition masterclasses), Lara Dodds, Emma Doubt, Derek Dunne, Alan Galey, Joe Genetin-Pilawa, Gail Gibson, Nathan Hofer, Adam Jasienski, Donald Johnson, Erika Lin, Nicole Lindenberg, Fabio Luppi, César Manrique, Craig Martin, Jeffrey Moser, Andrea Nate, Guadeloupe Pinzón, Tamara Walker and Daniel Webb. Pepa Hernández and, in particular, Amanda Crompton were delightful fellowship comrades and later wonderful people with whom to write while being connected via live video feed – the only way to survive a New England winter or focused morning writing blitzes.

I have benefited greatly from advice and encouragement from friends, mentors and colleagues over the years. These include Sunil Amrith, John Arnold, Peter Barber, Carlos Bern, Josiah Blackmore, David Boruchoff, Hugh Glenn Cagle, Mary Baine Campbell, Daniel Carey, Erica Charters, Danielle Carrabino, Marcia Chatelain, Hal Cook, Stephen Clucas, Jenny Davis, Catherine Delano-Smith, Filippo De Vivo, Whitney Dirks-Schuster, Anne Goldgar, Paula E. Findlen, Linford Fisher, Malick Ghachem, Touba Ghadessi, Anthony Grafton, Alfred Hiatt, Catherine Hofmann, Eva Johanna Holmberg, Chloë Houston, Michael Hunter, Claire Jowitt, Natasha Korda, Virginia Krause, Kay Dian Kriz, Karen Ordahl Kupperman, Evelyn Lincoln, Jeremy Ravi Mumford, Joseph Loh, Christina Normore, Tara Nummedal, Brian W. Ogilvie, Katharine Park, Sandra Sáenz-López

Pérez, Ayesha Ramachandran, Jan Rüger, David Harris Sacks, Hilary Sapire, Jyotsna Singh, Benjamin Schmidt, Gary Shaw, Claudia Swan, Phiroze Vasunia, Nicolás Wéy Gomez, Neil L. Whitehead, Kären Wigen, Wes Williams and Rebecca Zorach.

The advice and assistance of Ann M. Blair and Samantha Wesner facilitated an intensive summer of research in Harvard's libraries. Writing accountability, camaraderie, enthusiasm and empathy from the Facebook group #theGraftonline has been a tremendous catalyst for energy and discipline. For advice concerning translations, thanks are due to Rembrandt Duits, Michiel van Groesen and Sjoerd Levelt for Dutch; Edouard Kopp and François Quiviger for French; Susanne Meurer, Magnus Ryan and Hanna Vorholt for German; Guido Giglioni, Jill Kraye and Elizabeth McGrath for Latin; and Joanne Harwood and Lisa Voigt for Portuguese. At Western Connecticut State University, Kelli Custer, Marcy May, Burt Peretti and – most especially – Helena Prieto and Rachel Prunier helped me to flourish in the New World; the flexible thinking of Missy Alexander, Jennifer Duffy and Wynn Gadkar-Wilcox leveraged fellowships into a year in Washington, DC. At Cambridge University Press, I thank Elizabeth Friend-Smith, Rosalyn Scott, Rebecca Taylor and Michael Watson for transmuting the manuscript into this book, and series editors Margot C. Finn, Colin Jones and Robert G. Moeller for believing that it could be done. Roystone Fernandez at SPi Global patiently coordinated the production process. For making the index, I thank Michael W. Phillips Jr.

Books – and people – stand or fall on the way they weather the worst storms they face. I am especially grateful to those friends and mentors who helped to control the sails when my trajectory looked less than certain. I owe a particular debt of gratitude to Alex Offer and Clare Offer (née Carpenter), to whom I dedicate this book. Alex was in the vanguard of my support as I learned to stop trying to become an astronaut and to start hanging out with the really cool people doing history and literature; Clare shepherded me through the years of self-doubt in which I wondered whether I was smart enough to get a Ph.D., and supplied extraordinary gooseberry tarts along the way. In recent years I have also had the support of Julian Swann – a rock of reassurance in the interminable final year of the dissertation. Julian's support for my postdoctoral project was instrumental in providing the mental space in which I completed my interdisciplinary circlings and confirmed that I was indeed a historian, and all the more so in consuming methods from every which way. Andrew S. Curran helped to soften the landing in the New World.

Washington, DC, March 2016

Preface and note on the text

I have normalized *i* and *j* and *u* and *v* in Latin quotations. I have occasionally modified punctuation and capitalization in Latin and other languages for ease of reading. Unless otherwise stated, all translations are my own. In all languages, contractions have been expanded.

What I mean by 'ethnography' in this book is descriptive writing or picturing of peoples and cultures. By 'comparative ethnology' I mean, loosely, analytical and comparative reflection on human diversity and its causes. There is clearly an overlap between these two terms; neither is meant to imply any particular methodological or theoretical standpoint, but rather to indicate the description and analysis of the world's peoples via text, image or diagram.

What I refer to science in this volume, I do so in the Renaissance sense of *scientia*, or knowledge, particularly about the natural world, of which human civilization was a part. Renaissance science encompassed a broader range of topics, disciplines and practitioners than are commonly associated with modern science.

'America' refers to the combined landmasses of North and South America. The terms 'Virginia', 'Florida', 'Peru', 'Guiana', 'Brazil' and 'Patagonia' are used to designate general regions identified and named on maps and in texts during the period under study. Since these maps did not draw boundaries between areas, their dimensions were not precisely determined. These places are not intended to be taken as co-extensive with the eponymous modern regions. 'Amerindians' refers to peoples of either North or South America.

Abbreviations

AEM: Hans Wolff, ed., *America: Early Maps of the New World*, trans. Hugo Beyer et al. (Munich: Prestel, 1992).

Americae Pars II: René de Laudonnière, Jacques Le Moyne de Morgues, et al., *Brevis narratio eorum quae in Florida Americae provincia Gallis acciderunt . . .. Quae est secunda pars Americae. . .*, ed. Theodor de Bry (Frankfurt am Main, 1591).

Americae Pars III: Hans Staden, Jean de Léry and Nicolas Barré, *Americae tertia pars memorabile provinciae Brasiliae historiam . . .*, ed. Theodor de Bry (Frankfurt am Main, 1592).

Americae Pars IV: Girolamo Benzoni, *Americae pars quarta. Sive, insignis et admiranda historia de reperta primum Occidentali India a Christophoro Columbo anno MCCCCXCII . . .*, ed. Theodor de Bry (Frankfurt am Main, 1594).

Americae Pars V: Girolamo Benzoni, *Americae pars quinta. Nobilis et admiratione plena Hieronymi Benzoni Mediolanensis, secundae sectionis Historia. . .*, ed. Theodor de Bry (Frankfurt am Main, 1595).

Americae Pars VI: Girolamo Benzoni and Nicolas Challeux, *Americae pars sexta, sive historiae ab Hieronymo Benzono Mediolanense scriptae, sectio tertia . . .*, ed. Theodor de Bry (Frankfurt am Main, 1596).

Americae Pars IX: José de Acosta, Barent Jansz and Olivier van Noort, *Americae nona et postrema pars. Qua de ratione elementorum: de Novi Orbis natura. . .copiose pertractatur . . .*, [ed. widow and sons of Theodor de Bry] (Frankfurt am Main, 1602).

Americae Pars XII: Antonio de Herrera, Pedro Ordóñez de Cevallos [and Petrus Bertius], *Novi orbis pars duodecima.*

	Sive descriptio Indiae Occidentalis . . ., ed. Johannes Theodor de Bry (Frankfurt am Main, 1624).
Americae Pars XIII:	John Smith et al., *Decima tertia pars historiae Americanae. . .*, ed. Matthias Merian (Frankfurt am Main, 1634).
ARC-MM:	Asa Simon Mittman with Peter J. Dendle, eds., *The Ashgate Research Companion to Monsters and the Monstrous* (Farnham and Burlington, VT: Ashgate, 2012).
BA:	Joseph Sabin, *Bibliotheca Americana: A Dictionary of Books Relating to America*, 19 vols. (New York: Joseph Sabin, 1868–1936).
BAV:	Henry Harrisse and Carlos Sanz, *Bibliotheca Americana vetustissima: A Description of Works Relating to America, Published Between the Years 1492 and 1551* (New York: G. P. Philes, 1866).
BL-Mss:	British Library, Manuscript Collections.
BLCH:	Juan Friede and Benjamin Keen, eds., *Bartolomé de Las Casas in History: Toward an Understanding of the Man and His Work* (DeKalb, IL: Northern Illinois University Press, 1971).
BNF-Cartes:	Bibliothèque nationale de France, Département des Cartes et plans.
BNF-Mss:	Bibliothèque nationale de France, Département des Manuscrits.
CCB:	George Watson Cole, *A Catalogue of Books Relating to the Discovery and Early History of North and South America Forming a Part of the Library of E. D. Church*, 5 vols. (New York: Dodd, Mead & Co., 1907).
Circa 1492:	Jay A. Levenson, ed., *Circa 1492: Art in the Age of Exploration* (New Haven, CT and London: Yale University Press, 1991).
CV-ADG:	Vincennes, Château de Vincennes, Service historique de l'armée de terre, Archives du Dépôt de la guerre.
EA:	John Alden and Dennis C. Landis, eds., *European Americana: A Chronological Guide to Works printed*

	in Europe relating to the Americas, 1493–1776, 6 vols. (New York: Readex Books, 1980–97).
HC1:	J. B. Harley and David Woodward, eds., *The History of Cartography Volume 1: Cartography in Prehistoric, Ancient and Medieval Europe and the Mediterranean* (Chicago, IL etc.: University of Chicago Press, 1987).
HC3:	David Woodward, ed., *The History of Cartography Volume 3: Cartography in the European Renaissance*, 2 vols. (Chicago, IL and London: University of Chicago Press, 2007).
IM:	*Imago Mundi: The International Journal for the History of Cartography.*
HL:	San Marino, Henry E. Huntington Library.
JRM-SC:	Manchester, John Rylands Library, Department of Special Collections.
KB:	The Hague, Koninklijke Bibliotheek.
MC:	F. C. Wieder, *Monumenta Cartographica*, 5 vols. (The Hague: M. Nijhoff, 1925–33).
MCN:	Günter Schilder, *Monumenta Cartographica Neerlandica*, 9 vols. (Alphen aan den Rijn: Uitgeverij Canaletto, 1986–2013).
NRC:	*Nuova Raccolta Colombiana*, English edition.
NRC-V:	Amerigo Vespucci, *[Writings]*, ed. Ilaria Luzzana Caraci, 2 vols. (Rome: Istituto poligrafico e Zecca dello Stato, 1996–99).
NRC-XI:	Gaetano Ferro et al., *Columbian Iconography*, trans. Luciano F. Farina and Carla Onorato Wysokinski (Rome: Istituto poligrafico e Zecca dello Stato, 1992).
PMC:	Armando Cortesão and Avelino Teixeira da Mota, *Portugaliae Monumenta Cartographica*, 6 vols. (Lisbon, [s.n.], 1960).
RC:	Repertorium Columbianum.
RC vi, SE:	Christopher Columbus, *A Synoptic Edition of the Log of Columbus's First Voyage*, ed. Francesca Lardicci (Turnhout: Brepols, 1999).
RC v, PM:	Pietro Martire d' Anghiera, *Selections* . . ., ed. and trans. Geoffrey Eatough (Turnhout: Brepols, 1998).

RC x, LD:	Geoffrey Symcox, ed., *Italian Reports on America, 1493–1533: Letters, Dispatches, and Papal Bulls* (Turnhout: Brepols, 2001).
RC xii, AC:	Geoffrey Symcox and Luciano Formisano, eds., *Italian Reports on America, 1493–1533: Accounts by Contemporary Observers* (Turnhout: Brepols, 2002).

Introduction

Renaissance maps and the concept of the human

For the late medieval friar and chronicler Paolino Veneto, without a world map (*map[p]a mundi*), 'it is not just difficult but impossible to make [oneself] an image of, or even for the mind to grasp, what is said of the children and grandchildren of Noah and of the Four Kingdoms and other nations and regions, in both divine and human writings'. In Paolino's view, a history of the world needed a map composed of text and image: 'Nor will you deem one sufficient without the other, because painting without writing does not indicate regions or nations clearly, [and] writing without the support of painting truly does not mark the boundaries of the provinces of a region sufficiently clearly for them to be seen almost at a glance'.[1] For Paolino, illustrated maps were far from being mere decoration; instead, they were vital tools for understanding the relationship between geography and Biblical history. The arrangement of words and pictures in a geographical setting gave illustrated maps a particular explanatory power.

This book demonstrates how maps illustrated human variation across the globe in new ways in the sixteenth and early seventeenth centuries, in the mid- to late Renaissance.[2] In this period, scholars, geographers and mapmakers investigated the relationship between information garnered from westward voyages and ideas about the distant east and south that had long circulated in classical, Biblical and medieval sources. By analyzing images and descriptions of peoples on maps alongside contemporary

[1] Paolino Veneto, Vat. Lat. 1960, f.13 (Biblioteca Apostolica Vaticana): 'que dicuntur de filiis ac filiis filiorum Noe et que IIIIor monarchis ceterisque regnis atque provincias tam in divinis quam in humanis scripturis, non tam difficile quam impossibile . . . ymaginari aut mente posse concipere. . ..Nec unum sin altero putes sufficere, quia pictura sine scriptura provincias seu regna confuse demonstrat, scriptura vero non tamen sufficienter sine adminiculo picture provinciarum confinia per varias partes celi sic determinat, ut quasi ad oculum conspici valeant', transcribed and translated in Juergen Schulz, 'Jacopo de' Barbari's View of Venice: Map Making, City Views, and Moralized Geography before the Year 1500', *The Art Bulletin*, 60 (1978), 425–74, at 452. I have made minor amendments to the translation.

[2] I use the term 'Renaissance' in its broadest sense to refer to a period rather than to the philological rediscovery of classical antiquity. Nevertheless, many cartographers and geographers who devised illustrated maps, and the scholars and literate audiences who consulted their work, did so in dialogue with the writings of classical antiquity.

prints, costume books, natural histories, encyclopedias and travel literature I show how maps made arguments about the relationship of human societies, bodies and cultures to their environments. Mapmakers used particular rhetorical devices and formal layouts to encourage their audiences to consider their works as containing reliable knowledge. Seemingly fantastic images of, for example, Brazilian cannibals or Patagonian giants were carefully devised syntheses that helped mapmakers to market these works as uniquely suited for comparing environmental influences on bodies and temperaments.

Many Renaissance readers were fascinated by the customs and manners of distant peoples. The traveller Pieter de Marees, in his foreword to the first Dutch illustrated account of Africa which was printed by the prolific travel and map printer Cornelis Claesz, noted that he decided to 'adorn [his account] with some handsome plates, so that one might see of what shape or character the men and women are there in Guinea; and also what clothes and ornaments they use there, [and] what religious ideas and feelings they have'.[3] Readers consulted maps and atlases alongside travel editions in order to locate and contextualize such texts. In what distinctive ways, then, did maps constitute ethnographic knowledge and thereby inflect the ways in which readers understood human variety? This book explores the emergence of iconic representations on maps with this question in mind. My argument is that maps were key artefacts in the fluctuating shape of the human in the European imaginary in an era of transformative, often catastrophic, cultural contacts.

Mapping human variety

The Renaissance world map placed information about the world's peoples within a two-dimensional grid in which the location of cultures was fundamental to understanding human variety. As mapmakers increasingly used the latitudinal and longitudinal coordinate system of the second-century CE Greco-Egyptian geographer Ptolemy's *Geographia* for their

[3] Pieter de Marees, *Beschryvinghe ende historische verhael van het Gout Koninckrijck van Guinea* (Amsterdam, 1602), dedicatory epistle to Ian Sandra: 'met sommighe fraeye Fygueren te vercieren, daermen in sien moeghte van wat ghestaltenisse ofte gedaente dat de Mans ende Vrouw persoonen aldaer in Guiana zijn, ende ooc wat cleedinghe ende ciraet dat sy daer ghebruycken, ende wat opinien ende gevoelen dat sy in haer ghelooff hebben'; Pieter de Marees, *Description and Historical Account of the Gold Kingdom of Guinea (1602)*, trans. and ed. Albert van Dantzig and Adam Jones (Oxford: Oxford University Press, 1987), 1.

world maps and atlases, the relationship between geography, climate and humans became more precisely intertwined. Since geography was thought to influence human customs, temperaments and physiques, placing ethnographic images within a gridded spatial system was tantamount to providing viewers with a shortcut for extrapolating the civility of a people.[4]

New mapping techniques and oceanic expansion prompted scholars and artisans to rethink the boundaries of the human. Readers versed in classical humoral theory expected extreme environments to cause the degeneration of humans into peoples who were physically or behaviourally monstrous.[5] In works of natural history, ancient authors such as Pliny the Elder had argued that regions to the far south and east of the Greek world had such hostile climates that they engendered monstrous peoples.

Iconic map illustrations and captions delineating peoples of the world effectively made epistemological claims about the proper way to make ethnographic knowledge, and ontological ones about the concept of the human and the boundaries between humans and monstrous peoples. The maps' illustrations emblematized what a region's people had in common and what made them distinguishable from those of other regions. Mapmakers across regional cartographic traditions – from Amsterdam to Seville – shared certain visual codes, as we shall see. By selecting and devising images, mapmakers did not merely reflect the ethnographic and natural historical contents of their sources, but also constituted it in new ways. Mapmakers' map inscriptions, atlas prefaces and other writings illuminate how readers were expected to decode the imagery, thus establishing an interpretative collaboration between mapmaker, illustrator, commentator and viewer.[6]

4 For a similar point, see Jacqueline Duvernay-Bolens, *Les Géants patagons: voyage aux origines de l'homme* (Paris: Éditions Michalon, 1995), 39. For Ptolemy in the Renaissance, see Patrick Gautier Dalché, 'The Reception of Ptolemy's *Geography* (End of the Fourteenth to Beginning of the Sixteenth Century)', *HC3*, I, 285–364.

5 For colonial contexts, see Jorge Cañizares-Esguerra, 'New World, New Stars: Patriotic Astrology and the Invention of Indian and Creole Bodies in Colonial Spanish America, 1600–1650', *American Historical Review*, 104:1 (1999), 33–68; Joyce Chaplin, 'Natural Philosophy and an Early Racial Idiom in North America: Comparing English and Indian Bodies', *William and Mary Quarterly*, Third Series, 54 (1997), 229–52; Karen Ordahl Kupperman, 'Fear of Hot Climates in the Anglo-American Colonial Experience', *William and Mary Quarterly*, 3rd ser., 41 (1984), 215–40.

6 I have adopted the phrase 'interpretative collaboration' from Arnold Hunt, *The Art of Hearing: English Preachers and their Audiences* (Cambridge: Cambridge University Press, 2010), 292. For the ways in which the interplay of illustrations and captions shaped reading practices and served mnemonic functions, see Christian Jacob, *The Sovereign Map: Theoretical Approaches in Cartography throughout History*, trans. Tom Conley, ed. Edward H. Dahl (Chicago, IL: University of Chicago Press, 2006), 167–72.

Collectively, these mapmakers created imagined communities. Benedict Anderson defined the nation as 'an imagined political community – and imagined as both inherently limited and sovereign', quoting the philosopher and social anthropologist Ernest Gellner: 'Nationalism is not the awakening of nations to self-consciousness: it invents nations where they do not exist.'[7] We can also talk about communities made in the imaginations of others, invented as inherently distinctive ethnic groups and located in particular geographical spaces. Renaissance maps were central to how Europeans fashioned this type of imagined community.

Maps illustrated with distant peoples were, in effect, both 'contact zones' between cultures and 'representational machines' in the sense that they were analytical tools with which Europeans made sense of human diversity.[8] They reveal a key part of the history of Renaissance ethnography, by which I mean descriptions of distant peoples in words or images.[9] In comparison, geographical compendia, although rich in textual information about peoples, were largely unillustrated. Costume books offered few depictions of Amerindians, did not begin to appear until the 1560s, and do not survive in the same numbers as maps. Illustrations within travel editions were far more dependent on specific narratives. In travel writing, descriptions of the peoples are scattered across the narratives. Illustrated maps, by contrast, were a genre in which information about a range of peoples was synthesized in one place, offering a unique medium that invited the comparative contemplation of human civilizations.

European maps depicting Amerindian peoples allow us to trace responses to human diversity across regions with varying relationships to the New World in the long sixteenth century: the Spanish and Portuguese empires; the French proto-empire; the Low Countries; and the German lands of the financial backers of many Iberian voyages of exploration. During the period

7 Benedict Anderson, *Imagined Communities: Reflections on the Origin and Spread of Nationalism* (London: Verso, 1991), 6; Ernest Gellner, *Thought and Change* (London: Weidenfeld and Nicolson, 1964), 168.

8 For contact zones, see Mary Louise Pratt, *Imperial Eyes: Travel Writing and Transculturation* (London: Routledge, 1992 [2008 printing]), 7; for representational machinery, see Stephen Greenblatt, *Marvelous Possessions: The Wonder of the New World* (Oxford: Clarendon Press, 1991), 4.

9 Here I expand upon James Clifford and George E. Marcus's classic formulation of ethnography as writing about fieldwork that also lends itself to disciplines beyond anthropology (*Writing Culture: The Poetics and Politics of Ethnography* (Berkeley and Los Angeles, CA: University of California Press, 1986)). I define ethnography more broadly, as is generally the case with scholars of Renaissance encounters, to include all manner of descriptive writing and of the making of images and artefacts intended to represent peoples.

covered by this book, roughly 1492–1650, the production of maps depicting and describing distant peoples reached its widest extent, flourishing in centres across Iberia, France, the German lands, the Low Countries and eventually England. This was also an era in which numerous travel accounts of European explorers became available via print to a broader reading public. Mapmakers in Europe drew on travel and geographical writing in order to incorporate new regions into their maps, atlases and geographies.

To explore the questions that drive this book I have drawn on new directions in the history of science, art history, literary studies and the history of cartography. The book is in essence a cultural history underpinned by methods from *l'histoire des mentalités* or historical anthropology articulated in the now classic works of Peter Burke, Natalie Zemon Davis, Robert Darnton and Carlo Ginzburg, among others. It is informed by the anthropological and psychological tradition for the interdisciplinary study of artefacts and culture elaborated by medieval and Renaissance scholars such as Michael Baxandall. I have also drawn on the writings of ethnohistorians, most notably the work of Neil L. Whitehead, who have pioneered ways of recovering indigenous agency, events on the ground and historical realities in the structures and motifs of European colonial texts. Historical anthropologists – those historians whose work is informed by sociology and anthropology – have demonstrated that details that are seemingly irrelevant to modern eyes cannot be assumed to be so, and how the very incomprehensibility of such details gestures towards a route to new historical insights. The strangeness of Renaissance maps to our eyes is one such signal.[10]

Geography, environment and the colonial project

In the history of the development of analytical languages for understanding other peoples, the issue of geography was paramount.[11] For European

[10] See, e.g., Robert Darnton, *The Great Cat Massacre and Other Episodes in French Cultural History* (New York, NY: Basic Books, 1984); Carlo Ginzburg, *The Cheese and the Worms: The Cosmos of a Sixteenth-Century Miller* (Baltimore, MD and London: Johns Hopkins University Press, 1980); Natalie Zemon Davis, *The Gift in Sixteenth-Century France* (Oxford: Oxford University Press, 2000); Michael Baxandall, *The Limewood Sculptors of Renaissance Germany* (New Haven, CT and London: Yale University Press, 1980); *The Discoverie of the Large, Rich, and Bewtiful Empyre of Guiana by Sir Walter Ralegh*, transcribed, annotated and introduced by Neil L. Whitehead (Norman, OK: University of Oklahoma Press, 1997).

[11] For the development of an analytical discourse on human variety between the late Middle Ages and the Renaissance, see especially Joan-Pau Rubiés, *Travel and Ethnology in the Renaissance: South India through European Eyes 1250–1625* (Cambridge: Cambridge University Press, 2000).

readers in the sixteenth and early seventeenth centuries, human variety was a function of place, a tenet that took on a visually persuasive form on illustrated maps. Interpretative cruxes that emerged – the fact that Amerindians at the same latitude as Ethiopians were not black, for instance – raised questions about whether social customs could affect mental capacities, and, by implication, the likely impact of American climates on European settlers.

Geographical discourses about the nature of the peoples of the Americas informed scholarly and juridical reflections on how the New World should be administered.[12] In order to better understand the colonial enterprises of the early decades of European oceanic expansion, we need to pay attention to changes to the intellectual foundations of colonialism and expansion across multiple European states in response to colonial experiences. This book contributes to scholarship on the nexus of climate, geography and colonialism by showing how geographical thinking underpinned by maps shaped ideas about indigenous bodies and temperaments. These issues were of paramount importance for safeguarding the continuing health and civility of European colonists and their descendants.[13] Multiple epistemologies of ethnology and geography – crucially shaped by maps – fed wide-ranging debates about the justifications for conquest, colonial policies and the methods of proselytizing to different peoples.

A central topic of this book is the impact of maps on viewers' perceptions of human diversity. I argue that maps contained visual codes that made claims about the civility/barbarism of the communities they mapped, claims that had implications for subsequent cultural encounters and, to an extent, for colonial administration. Imperial officials, particularly those based in European metropolises rather than in the field, were dependent on the information in circulation. Renaissance scholars like the former Jesuit Giovanni Botero argued that multiple approaches were needed to

[12] See, e.g., Nancy E. van Deusen, *Global Indios: The Indigenous Struggle for Justice in Sixteenth-Century Spain* (Durham, NC and London: Duke University Press, 2015); Sabine MacCormack, *On the Wings of Time: Rome, The Incas, Spain, and Peru* (Princeton, NJ: Princeton University Press, 2007); Anthony Pagden, *The Fall of Natural Man: The American Indian and the Origins of Comparative Ethnology*, reprinted with corrections and additions (Cambridge: Cambridge University Press, 1986); Anthony Pagden, *European Encounters with the New World: From Renaissance to Romanticism* (New Haven, CT and London: Yale University Press, 1993).

[13] Rebecca Earle, *The Body of the Conquistador: Food, Race and the Colonial Experience in Spanish America, 1492–1700* (Cambridge: Cambridge University Press, 2012); Mark Harrison, *Medicine in an Age of Commerce and Empire: Britain and its Tropical Colonies, 1660–1830* (New York, NY: Oxford University Press, 2010).

Christianize heathen peoples with different levels of civility.[14] A glance at a seventeenth-century Dutch map speckled with peoples of contrasting attributes would also suggest that successful evangelization and colonization required a plurality of approaches. Maps offered statesmen and scholars what one might anachronistically call a panoptic view on the world.

As Joyce E. Chaplin has reminded us, human history was unproblematically part of natural history until the nineteenth century.[15] Classical and medieval texts such as the fifth-century BCE Hippocratic work *Airs, Waters and Places* had fostered a tradition of conceiving differences in human cultures as the product of place. The thirteenth-century *De natura loci* (*On the Nature of Places*) by Albertus Magnus connected place explicitly with political theory. The southernness of the bulk of the early, documented and widely published voyages had great significance since late medieval scholarly traditions argued that hot climates produced inhabitants of more feeble mental capacities than temperate ones; this theory implicitly justified the enslavement and dominion of such peoples. The Renaissance re-invention of the 'torrid zone', as Nicolás Wey Gómez has argued, had a crucial impact on the shaping of early modern colonialism c.1450–1750.[16] The present book shows how ideas about monstrous peoples in southern latitudes were elaborated on maps and taken up by their readers.

Also important for the concept of the human was the eastward destination of those expeditions to the Americas by virtue of the circumnavigatory potential of a round earth. The Magellan-Elcano expedition's circling of the world in the 1520s marked for the first time the sewing together of two vectors of travels east and west of Europe.[17] The circumnavigation also marked an ontological seam between two discourses from classical antiquity for understanding human cultural and physical variation: the

[14] Giovanni Botero, *Relationi universali* ... (Brescia, 1599). The New World section contains a chapter entitled 'Concerning the diversity of barbarous peoples, and of the manner of preaching the Gospel' ('Della varietà de' barbari, e del modo di predicar l'Euangelio') in *Parte Quarta*, lib. III, 60–9.

[15] Joyce E. Chaplin, 'Ogres and Omnivores: Early American Historians and Climate History', *William and Mary Quarterly*, 72:1 (2015), 25–32.

[16] Nicolás Wey Gómez, *The Tropics of Empire: Why Columbus Sailed South to the Indies* (Cambridge, MA and London: MIT Press, 2008), xiii.

[17] By contrast, the corresponding northerly vector to the Far East – the fabled Northwest Passage – was not traversed until the eighteenth century, and the South Pole resisted human attempts to peer around it well beyond the era in which it marked a meaningful juncture in conceptions of human variety.

discourse of monstrous peoples, who fell beyond the purview of regular humanity and civility; and the discourse of contingent human variance in temperament, appearance and capacities in relation to local climatic conditions.[18]

Too much to know

One challenge of making knowledge about the New World was the multifariousness of its witnesses. Travellers of varying reliability had each seen only a small part of the story. Problems of credibility were also acute for the editors, printers, cosmographers and mapmakers who repackaged travel information in new formats. These cultural arbiters deployed distinctive rhetorical strategies to imbue their works with authority.[19] Renaissance mapmakers sought to convince their readers of their powers of analysis and synthesis in order to garner authority for maps of regions that they had not seen for themselves. Many maps articulate this rhetorically with titles along the lines of 'the most accurate map made from the newest, best information', which claim that their makers had evaluated and synthesized information from many eyewitnesses. In an era in which there was 'too much to know', there was also a de-centring of eyewitnesses by mapmakers who, at the same time, sought to bask in their glow.[20]

With the advent of the moveable type printing press and the availability of paper manufactured within Europe, an ever-increasing number of books began to pour off the presses in editions of hundreds or thousands of copies, at a price that brought individual copies within the reach of a much wider range of people.[21] This led to an avalanche of potential reading matter. Perhaps nowhere was the consequent information overload and

[18] For monstrous peoples, see especially John Block Friedman, *The Monstrous Races in Medieval Art and Thought*, 2nd ed. (Syracuse, NY: Syracuse University Press, 2000). For classical theories of climate and human difference, see Clarence J. Glacken, *Traces on the Rhodian Shore: Nature and Culture in Western Thought from Ancient Times to the End of the Eighteenth Century* (Berkeley and Los Angeles, CA: University of California Press, 1967).

[19] For the notion of cultural arbiters, see Christine R. Johnson, 'Buying Stories: Ancient Tales, Renaissance Travelers, and the Market for the Marvelous', *Journal of Early Modern History*, 11 (2007), 405–46.

[20] For the expansion of knowledge-making genres in the early modern period, see Ann M. Blair, *Too Much to Know: Managing Scholarly Information Before the Modern Age* (New Haven, CT and London: Yale University Press, 2010).

[21] For two influential and contrasting views of the impact of printing, see Elizabeth L. Eisenstein, *The Printing Press as an Agent of Change: Communications and Cultural Transformations in Early-Modern Europe* (Cambridge: Cambridge University Press, 1979); Adrian Johns, *The*

fracturing of knowledge categories more disruptive than in the arena of geography.[22] As the seventeenth-century English geographer Peter Heylyn put it in an aside about the invention of the printing-press, 'this most excellent invention hath been much abused, and prostituted to the lust of every foolish and idle paper-blurrer: the treasury of learning being never so full, and yet never more empty; over-charged so with the froth and scumme of foolish and unnecessary discourses'. What was more, Heylyn continued, the Dutch were the worst offenders since they would print their works not only in Dutch but also in Latin, and 'send them twice a year to the publick marts, though neither worth the reader's eye, nor the printer's hand'.[23]

Renaissance and early modern readers attempted to keep up with the increasing pace of book publishing by collecting and organizing salient excerpts. The era saw the emergence of 'a new attitude toward note-taking'; printed compendia of excerpts were the earliest reference books.[24] The early modern atlas, the world map and the map of a continent also served to manage the barrage of new geographical information. Such works, intended for consultation in libraries, studies, parlours and state rooms alongside other works, were reference genres for those seeking to understand distant peoples comparatively. Renaissance mapmakers promoted their works as a way of garnering a wider perspective without the dangers of travelling. The geographer Georg Braun described it thus in the 1581 preface to the *Civitates orbis terrarum*: 'Can one . . . imagine anything more pleasant than to be in one's own home, a place far from all danger, to see, thanks to these books, the entire shape of the world . . . embellished by

Nature of the Book: Print and Knowledge in the Making (Chicago, IL: University of Chicago Press, 1998).

22 Anthony Grafton et al., *New Worlds, Ancient Texts: The Power of Tradition and the Shock of Discovery* (Cambridge, MA and London, 1992); Wolfgang Haase and Meyer Reinhold, eds., *The Classical Tradition and the Americas* (Berlin: Walter de Gruyter, 1994). This movement began with the southward voyages around the west African coast in the fifteenth century; see, e.g., Andrew Gow, 'Fra Mauro's World View: Authority and Empirical Evidence on a Venetian Mappamundi', in *The Hereford World Map: Medieval World Maps and their Context*, ed. P.D.A. Harvey (London: The British Library, 2006), 405–14. Recent literature has challenged the 'blunted impact' thesis of J. H. Elliott, *The Old World and the New, 1492–1650* (Cambridge: Cambridge University Press, 1972).

23 Peter Heylyn, *Cosmographie in foure bookes containing the Chorographie and Historie of the whole World* (London, 1657), 865. For an overview of the range of responses to printing and to the widening of audiences in the early decades of the printed book, see Elizabeth L. Eisenstein, *Divine Art, Infernal Machine: The Reception of Printing in the West from First Impressions to the Sense of an Ending* (Philadelphia, PA and Oxford: University of Pennsylvania Press, 2011), 4–33.

24 Blair, *Too Much to Know*, 63.

the beauty and splendour of towns and cities, and to see by examining the images and reading the account . . . that which could scarcely be seen but by long and difficult journeys?' [25] While world maps and other large maps at small scales only offered an overview, this was exactly what a policy-maker needed. The summarizing character of maps, far from being seen as something that made them superficial and inferior, was in fact a selling point.

Harnessing the eyewitness: artefactual epistemology and science as a visual pursuit

There was not one early modern scientific epistemology, but many.[26] The present book examines interlocking epistemologies that emerged out of the problem of how to authenticate eyewitness testimony about distant places. The interpretation of testimony was – and arguably still is – not solely based on the experiential knowledge of a witness but also on social and ethical relationships, such as those between a witness and their interlocutor, and on the rhetorical structures of their testimony.[27] Andrea Frisch has excavated the shift from 'ethical' to 'epistemic' modes of witnessing between the late Middle Ages and the Renaissance. Medieval travel writers attempted to construct their *ethos* in their texts in ways that highlighted the shared ethical and social backgrounds of writer and audience: their claims to authority were ethical (tied to personal relationships), rather than epistemic (independent of their social context). When witnesses addressed audiences through the medium of the printed word, the relationship between witness and judge of testimony was no longer an ethical one: rather, the communication was between a physically absent first-hand eyewitness and an anonymous audience; their relationship was protean and unknown. The paradigm of the ethical witness, stretched to its limit, was largely transformed into that of the epistemic eyewitness whose

[25] Georg Braun and Franz Hogenberg, *Theatre des principales villes de tout l'vniuers*, 6 vols. (Cologne, 1579–1625), III, preface, sig. F.3*r*.: 'que pouroit on . . . imaginer plusplaisant, qu'en quelque lieu seur hors de tout danger en sa maison propre, veoir par moyen & ayde de ces liures, . . . ornée par la beaute & splendeur des villes & citez, & veoir par l'inspection de la peincture, & lecture du recit ce qu'aultres ont a grand peine oncques poeult veoir par voiages longs & difficilz?'

[26] Dániel Margócsy, *Commercial Visions: Science, Trade, and Visual Culture in the Dutch Golden Age* (Chicago, IL: University of Chicago Press, 2014), 6.

[27] For a classic formulation of this point, see Steven Shapin, *A Social History of Truth: Civility and Science in Seventeenth-Century England* (Chicago, IL and London: University of Chicago Press, 1994).

authority emerged out of first-hand experience. As Frisch observed, travel accounts were 'writings that most consistently raised, confronted, and discussed issues of what made a testimonial account believable'.[28]

In this book, I argue that late medieval and Renaissance maps were early adopters of the epistemic paradigm over the ethical one precisely *because* these mapmakers were not themselves eyewitnesses. Just as humanist philologists, theologians and historians needed to develop methods for evaluating information in a text without relying on its (often long dead) author's reputation for truth, Renaissance mapmakers needed to develop methods for selecting reliable information from travellers' accounts, and to convince their own readers of their authority.[29] Mapmakers developed what we may call an artefactual mode of testimony, one which fused ethical and epistemic modes of 'being there' with the mode of synthesizing multiple sources into a particular type of artefact. Maps containing images of distant peoples were thus embedded with a distinct ethnographic authority.

This book contributes to the understanding of early modern science as a visual pursuit in two ways. It elucidates the ways in which the epistemological rhetoric of maps encouraged viewers to think about new peoples in comparative terms. It also shows how the concept of the monster as a being that broke the category of the human is essential for understanding the long history of the concept of the human and the pre-history of the concept of race. I ask new questions of illustrated maps in order to uncover two related histories: the challenges posed to conceptions of the human by European encounters with peoples of the Americas; and the emergence of a visual, artefactual epistemology that bestowed authority on workshops rather than on eyewitnesses. Putting the ethnographic information on maps at the centre of an analysis of the reception and reconstitution of information about distant peoples allows us to see previously unnoticed aspects of the ways in which science in this period was a visual pursuit.

28 Andrea Frisch, *The Invention of the Eyewitness: Witnessing and Testimony in Early Modern France* (Chapel Hill, NC: University of North Carolina Press, 2004), 13.

29 For Renaissance humanist scholarship, see, e.g., Anthony Grafton, 'The Jewish Book in Christian Europe: Material Texts and Religious Encounters', in Andrea Sterk and Nina Caputo, eds., *Faithful Narratives: Historians, Religion, and the Challenge of Objectivity* (Ithaca, NY and London: Cornell University Press, 2014), 96–114; Anthony Grafton, *Defenders of the Text: The Traditions of Scholarship in an Age of Science, 1450–1800* (Cambridge, MA: Harvard University Press, 1991); Nicholas Popper, *Walter Ralegh's History of the World and the Historical Culture of the Late Renaissance* (Chicago, IL: University of Chicago Press, 2012); Nicholas Popper, 'An Ocean of Lies: The Problem of Historical Evidence in the Sixteenth Century', *Huntington Library Quarterly*, 74 (2011), 375–400.

I suggest that the epistemological ambitions of the makers of illustrated Renaissance maps were bound up with their distinct depictions of inhabitants of different regions of the New World.

Scholars have recently explored the participation of artists in the practice of early modern science, and the rise of a visual rhetoric of empiricism in ethnographic and natural historical illustration.[30] For mapmakers in European workshops, however, the 'drawn from life' card of the on-the-spot observer had limited value. In order to underline the authority of their syntheses, mapmakers needed a different epistemology. Art historians and literary scholars who have examined ethnographic imagery on maps have generally focused on identifying visual models and establishing the generic conventions within which map images were devised.[31] Here I focus on the epistemological purposes for which these images were devised. By parsing the differences between, for example, multiple images of Patagonian giants and the significance of these differences, we can uncover the cultural work done by these representations.

The maps in this study were produced in workshops where transnational groups of scholars and artisans worked together and drew on books, prints and of course maps, both printed and manuscript. In *The Body of the Artisan*, Pamela H. Smith noted that alchemy was one of the few disciplines in which practitioners worked with both texts and their hands. She argued that this combination was central to the articulation of a new relationship between scholars and artisans, and that the decades around the turn of the sixteenth century were 'crucial in the development of a new relationship between scholars and craftspeople'.[32] Smith showed the importance of naturalistic representations in artisanal knowledge

30 See, e.g., Michael Gaudio, *Engraving the Savage: The New World and Techniques of Civilization* (Minneapolis, MN: University of Minnesota Press, 2008); Susan Dackerman, ed., *Prints and the Pursuit of Knowledge in Early Modern Europe* (Cambridge, MA, New Haven, CT and London: Yale University Press, 2011). For the ways in which Spanish natural history practitioners conceptualized nature in the Americas through a visual epistemology, see Daniela Bleichmar, *Visible Empire: Botanical Expeditions and Visual Culture in the Hispanic Enlightenment* (Chicago, IL: University of Chicago Press, 2012). For the visual practices of sixteenth-century university-educated physicians, see Sachiko Kusukawa, *Picturing the Book of Nature: Image, Text, and Argument in Sixteenth-Century Human Anatomy and Medical Botany* (Chicago, IL and London: University of Chicago Press, 2012).

31 See, e.g., Elizabeth A. Sutton, *Early Modern Dutch Prints of Africa* (Farnham and Burlington, VT: Ashgate, 2012); Valerie Traub, 'Mapping the Global Body', in *Early Modern Visual Culture: Representation, Race, and Empire in Renaissance England*, ed. Peter Erickson and Clark Hulse (Philadelphia, PA: University of Pennsylvania Press, 2000), 44–97.

32 Pamela H. Smith, *The Body of the Artisan: Art and Experience in the Scientific Revolution* (Chicago, IL: University of Chicago Press, 2004), 142.

claims in the contexts of alchemy, metalworking and painting. This mingling of social and educational backgrounds also took place in mapmakers' workshops. In contrast to the settings explored by Smith, the subsequent synthesis of empirical observation and textual exegesis led mapmakers to make epistemological claims that de-centred the eyewitness, and to develop a visual epistemology that was not naturalistic but diagrammatic.

While the emergence of authenticating institutions for methods of seeing, documenting and processing empirical information are of course important in the history of science, also vital for the construction of socially acceptable knowledge were the processes by which the experiences of eyewitnesses were synthesized, transformed and re-circulated by non-witnesses. In their classic work of historical sociology, Steven Shapin and Simon Schaffer analysed the nature of experiment, its intellectual products and their reception through the case study of knowledge-making practices surrounding the air-pump in the seventeenth century.[33] One might say that Renaissance mapmakers who consulted travel literature were examining the results of empirical activity in the form of geographical forays into regions that had yet to be mapped by Europeans. Maps were intellectual products that could legitimate the experimental process of travel.

For travel to produce matters of fact, certain things needed to be written down in particular forms, and one of these forms was the map. This book looks at the story of how one set of cultural arbiters – the scholars, printers and artisans of the mapmaking world – used particular analytical and rhetorical processes to make knowledge about distant worlds that they had not visited and which, by definition, were expected to differ from regions closer to home. When the object of inquiry was embedded in a distant world, the process of bringing portions of it home disrupted it in as many ways as it facilitated analysis.[34]

Thick descriptions of strange things: Thinking with maps and monsters

Lorraine Daston and Katharine Park's seminal *Wonders and the Order of Nature* showed that 'to tell the history of the study of nature from the

[33] Steven Shapin and Simon Schaffer, *Leviathan and the Air-Pump: Hobbes, Boyle, and the Experimental Life* (Princeton, NJ: Princeton University Press, 1985).

[34] For these issues in the practice of natural history, see Bleichmar, *Visible Empire*; Margócsy, *Commercial Visions*.

standpoint of wonders is to historicize the order of nature and thereby to pose new questions about how and why one order succeeds another'.[35] The present book historicizes the order of human variety by telling that history, at times, from the standpoint of monsters. The sixteenth century saw the rise of debates about the nature of the peoples in the Americas as travellers, humanists, editors and publishers attempted to parse Amerindian peoples in relation to monstrous peoples and human beings. The question of whether monstrous peoples were human, a matter of some hermeneutic anxiety in the Middle Ages, moved from the world of theory to that of empirical inquiry during the Renaissance. A history of European representations of distant peoples must thus also incorporate the history of shifting collective perceptions of the concept of the human and the nature of its boundaries.

One thematic field that has taken to heart the study of that which appears strange to our eyes is the interdisciplinary field of monster studies, a vibrant critical intervention in history, history of science, art history and literary studies. As one scholar put it, 'monsters do a great deal of cultural work, but they do not do it *nicely*'.[36] In the broadest sense, monsters are beings that fall outside the viewer's ontological categories in some way; a two-headed calf and a new animal species both constitute monsters in this sense. Monsters, and our own puzzlement about them, are thus entry-points to a deeper understanding of a culture's ways of thinking. Each of the monstrous peoples explored in this book offers a route into a different challenge posed by distant peoples to European epistemological structures and to ideas about the order of nature. While the historiography on medieval monstrous peoples and on medieval and Renaissance monstrous (individual) births is rich, Renaissance monstrous peoples in distant places have received only limited scholarly attention.[37]

Attempts to understand the causes of monsters were efforts to understand physical and cultural differences among people, and have a very long history. In the Middle Ages, commentators frequently drew causal links

[35] Lorraine Daston and Katharine Park, *Wonders and the Order of Nature, 1150–1750* (New York, NY: Zone Books, 1998), 14.

[36] Asa Simon Mittman, 'Introduction: Impact of Monsters and Monster Studies', in *ARC-MM*, 1-14, at 1.

[37] For medieval monstrous peoples, see especially Friedman, *Monstrous Races*; Asa Simon Mittman, *Maps and Monsters in Medieval England* (New York, NY and London: Routledge, 2006). The classic work on early modern monsters, in which monsters are shown to be part of a broader discourse on wonder from the High Middle Ages to the Enlightenment, is Daston and Park, *Wonders*. For an extensive treatment of monsters and monstrosity, see *ARC-MM*.

between physical monstrosity, faith and lifestyle. In the late-thirteenth century Christian history *Cursor mundi*, four dog-headed, dark-skinned Saracens are physically transformed when they beg to see the wood that would become the True Cross. Not only did their skin become 'white as milk', but 'their shape was entirely made new'.[38] In other words, the distinction between monster and human could be conceived as one of active choice, in the manner of Adam and Eve's fall from grace, rather than a fixed category. Another tradition posited extreme climates as the cause of monsters. This too raised problems for the stability of the human: what might happen to colonists and their descendants in a region whose climate had brought forth monsters? Each point on the human–monster graph performed different cultural work. The blurriness of the human–monster boundary could be cause for optimism; a civilizing or evangelizing mission, for example, might well eradicate monstrosity, as proper belief and behaviour wrought a physical transformation on monstrous peoples.

Maps have enjoyed the emergence of a revisionist historiography in recent decades. Art historians, literary scholars and historians have offered correctives to the long tradition of positivist narratives focused on the increase in cartographic accuracy over time; instead, they have analysed the cultural significances of the delineation of space.[39] Much has been written about Renaissance and early modern maps as artefacts that construct or symbolize power, and about maps as decoration in the sense of works intended to generate an aesthetic or emotional response or to provoke admiration for technical and artistic skill.[40] Renaissance maps

[38] Richard Morris et al., eds., *Cursor mundi* (London, 1874), lines 8120–2; Karl Steel, 'Centaurs, Satyrs, and Cynocephali: Medieval Scholarly Teratology and the Question of the Human', in *ARC-MM*, 257–74.

[39] Two classic examples are Jacob, *Sovereign Map*; Sveltana Alpers, *The Art of Describing: Dutch Art in the Seventeenth Century* (Chicago, IL: University of Chicago Press, 1983).

[40] On gender and power on maps, see Traub, 'Mapping the Global Body'; Stephanie Pratt, 'From the Margins: The Native American Personage in the Cartouche and the Decorative Borders of Maps', *Word & Image*, 12 (1996), 349–65. On mapping and the construction of empire, see Ricardo Padrón, *The Spacious Word: Cartography, Literature and Empire in Early Modern Spain* (Chicago, IL and London: University of Chicago Press, 2004); Matthew H. Edney, *Mapping an Empire: The Geographical Construction of British India, 1765–1843* (Chicago, IL and London: University of Chicago Press, 1997). On art and symbolic power, see Mark Rosen, *The Mapping of Power in Renaissance Italy: Painted Cartographic Cycles in Social and Intellectual Context* (New York: Cambridge University Press, 2015); Francesca Fiorani, *The Marvel of Maps: Art, Cartography and Politics in Renaissance Italy* (New Haven, CT and London: Yale University Press, 2005). On cartographic knowledge and power, see the influential articles reprinted in J. B. Harley, *The New Nature of Maps: Essays in the History of Cartography*, ed. Paul Laxton (Baltimore, MD and London: John Hopkins University Press, 2001); David Buisseret, ed., *Monarchs, Ministers and Maps: The Emergence of Cartography as a*

have not, however, been seen as a genre in which ethnographic knowledge making was a significant goal.[41]

By bringing approaches from the histories of science and art, from history, ethnohistory, literary studies and from the field of monster studies to bear on the analysis of ethnographic imagery, I advance new methods for analyzing map images that may appear, at first glance, to be evidence of ignorance or fabrication.[42] Thus in scope, questions posed and methods, this book differs from those works on illustrated cartography aimed at popular audiences which have described, for example, sea monsters on maps.[43] Instead, my starting point is the view that pre-modern diagrammatic conventions and uses of the term 'monster' are entry-points into earlier epistemologies. My larger historiographical argument is that analyzing images on maps must go beyond tracking their sources and derivatives, and beyond their political, symbolic, allegorical and decorative uses, important though these aspects are. I invite readers to ask new questions of map imagery that help to uncover experiences of making and reading maps rather than merely questions that reflect our current sensibilities.

Art historians have uncovered the assumptions that underlie seemingly aesthetic or conventional choices in painting, reminding us that a lifelike image is not a self-evidently straightforward one but rather something that has been crafted and is a product of a visual convention.[44] The converse is also true: what appears unrealistic to us (such as a creature which appears to modern eyes as an imaginary sea monster on a map) might have been intended and read very differently by those makers and viewers who were familiar with its particular visual language, and to have been consciously crafted in a diagrammatic way to make a point. In order to understand such images we must analyse them through their makers' and viewers' contexts. The limited space on maps for descriptive material meant that

Tool of Government in Early Modern Europe (Chicago, IL and London: University of Chicago Press, 1992).

41 An important exception is Stephanie Leitch, *Mapping Ethnography in Early Modern Germany: New Worlds in Print Culture* (New York, NY: Palgrave MacMillan, 2010).

42 These and other value judgements of pre-modern illustrations are endemic in the continuing cartobibliographical and popular traditions in the history of cartography. See, e.g., *MCN*, I-IX; Ronald Rees, 'Historical Links between Cartography and Art', *Geographical Review*, 70 (1980), 60–78. An influential example from literary studies is Walter D. Mignolo, *The Darker Side of the Renaissance: Literacy, Territoriality, and Colonization* (Ann Arbor, MI: University of Michigan Press, 1995), chap. 6.

43 Chet Van Duzer, *Sea Monsters on Medieval and Renaissance Maps* (London: The British Library, 2013); Joseph Nigg, *Sea Monsters: A Voyage around the World's Most Beguiling Map* (Chicago, IL: University of Chicago Press, 2013).

44 Alpers, *Art of Describing*.

mapmakers had to make careful selections from their sources. Old images used in new works were not merely copied, but were adopted into new settings and genres where they make new points. As Peter Burke has noted, such images 'are first decontextualized and then recontextualized, domesticated or "localized"'.[45] Mapmakers' choices, and the processes of translating material from one mode to another, had epistemological ramifications, and offer us a way into the mentalities in which these processes of looking, observing and recording were bound up. What is seen by the eyes, noted by the mind and annotated by the hand is conditioned by what viewers already know, and what they have learned to regard as significant. In order to uncover these facets, we must develop a 'period eye'.[46]

One can either debate the possibility of the history of ethnographic material on maps, or one can get the job done.[47] I have chosen the latter option. This book demonstrates how these map illustrations were freighted with ontological significance, how mapmakers made knowledge claims through ethnographic illustrations, and how and why their readers would have examined such images and descriptions on maps.

Scope of the book

This book traverses a broad swathe of ground: six regional European mapping traditions; seven New World regions; visual, print and manuscript culture c.1450–1650; and classical, medieval and Renaissance cultural and intellectual traditions. In order to delve deeply into the most fruitful arenas of inquiry, this book is not exhaustive in its examples of European maps illustrated with peoples of the Americas, although it is distilled from just such a brew.[48] The arguments presented here rest on an examination of over 2,000 cartographic works, drawn from numerous libraries and archives, alongside texts, images and artefacts.[49] Around

[45] Peter Burke, 'Translating Knowledge, Translating Cultures', in Michael North, ed., *Kultureller Austausch in der Frühen Neuzeit* (Cologne: Böhlau, 2009), 69–77, at 70. See, more generally, Peter Burke, *Eyewitnessing: The Uses of Images as Historical Evidence* (London: Reaktion, 2001).

[46] Baxandall, *Limewood Sculptors*, chap. VI, 'The Period Eye'.

[47] I adapt here a phrase from Shapin and Schaffer, *Leviathan and the Air-Pump*, 15.

[48] For analyses of a much larger number of examples, see Surekha Davies, 'Representations of Amerindians on European Maps and the Construction of Ethnographic Knowledge, 1506–1642', Ph.D. dissertation, 2 vols. (University of London: Warburg Institute, 2009).

[49] I derived my sample of maps containing ethnographic information beyond indistinct stick figures from some 2,000 maps and atlases c.1492–1650 that I consulted. The foundation collections for my research were the British Library (London), The Bibliothèque Nationale de

two hundred European world maps, maps of the continents and atlases with distinctive images of Amerindians survive for the period 1500–1650, from across a range of print and manuscript mapmaking centres in Iberia, the German lands, the Low Countries, France, England and Italy, all regions which feature in the pages that follow.

Since I am concerned here with the emergence of iconic visions of relatively large areas – Brazil, Patagonia, Peru and so on – I do not analyse maps of smaller regions, such as those in the *relaciones geográficas* produced in Spanish America that represented areas as small as villages.[50] Local and indigenous manuscript maps made for local legal and administrative purposes in the Americas were not, in the main, part of the visual landscape from which European mapmakers drew when devising maps of the parts of the world that we now term continents. In order to understand the processes by which lands found by sailing west acquired an ontology distinct from that of Asia, Africa and Europe, and in order not to overload the reader with a tome that is indigestibly large, diffuse and convoluted, this book focuses on questions that emerge from the fashioning of imagery of Amerindians, although it draws on European thinking about the Old World. The peoples of Asia and Africa did not receive the same iconographic attention, innovation or geographical specificity on Renaissance maps. The story of European constructions of the peoples of Asia and Africa in the pre-modern era begins in a period for which far fewer maps exist, and is less about maps than it is about classical and medieval geographical writing.[51]

France (Paris) and the Library of Congress (Washington, DC). Further materials were consulted at institutions including: the John Carter Brown Library (Providence, RI); the Folger Library (Washington, DC); the Beinecke Library (New Haven, CT); the New York Public Library, the Pierpont Morgan Library and the Butler Library at Columbia University (New York, NY); the Huntington Library (San Marino, CA); the Newberry Library (Chicago, IL); Princeton University Library (Princeton, NJ); the Bodleian Library and St John's College Library (Oxford); Cambridge University Library and Trinity College Library (Cambridge); the John Rylands Library (Manchester); the Archivos de las Indias (Seville); the Biblioteca Nacional de España (Madrid); the CRAI Biblioteca de Reserva, Universitat de Barcelona (Barcelona); the Château de Vincennes (Vincennes); the Bayerische Staatsbibliothek (Munich); the Biblioteca Nazionale di Firenze (Florence); the Vatican Library (Vatican City); Leiden University Library (Leiden, the Netherlands); and Ghent University Library (Ghent, Belgium).

50 For the *relaciones geográficas*, see Barbara E. Mundy, *The Mapping of New Spain: Indigenous Cartography and the Maps of the Relaciones Geográficas* (Chicago, IL: University of Chicago Press, 1996). For indigenous local mapping, see also Rolena Adorno, *The Polemics of Possession in Spanish American Narrative* (New Haven, CT and London: Yale University Press, 2007), chap. 2.

51 Francesc Relaño, *The Shaping of Africa: Cosmographic Discourse and Cartographic Science in Late Medieval and Early Modern Europe* (Aldershot: Ashgate, 2002); Marianne O'Doherty, *The*

Nor does this book attempt to cover the work done by textual, narrative geographies and cosmographies that mapped peoples in spaces through words. Such a treatment would require many books. As Denis Cosgrove has noted, cartographic and narrative forms of geographical description evolved from the two interlinked classical traditions of Ptolemy and Strabo.[52] Geographies and cosmographies by Sebastian Münster, Giovanni Battista Ramusio and other textual geographers are treated here at times, but are not a focus.[53] Finally, while an account of the impact of maps on the literary imagination resides in the corners of this book, that is not the one I have written. A wide-ranging study of Renaissance map imagery from postcolonial and gender studies perspectives also remains to be written. The focus here is on a set of interrelated questions about how maps functioned as ways of making knowledge and of thinking about the peoples of the Americas, and on their impact on genres that were primarily concerned with making knowledge.

I hope this book will be of interest not only to historians, historians of science and scholars of the Atlantic world, but also to art historians, literary scholars, global historians, environmental historians, ethnohistorians and historians of cartography. The emphasis here on close readings points out new directions via which to bring to light the cultural work that Renaissance maps performed.

The route ahead

The chapters that follow tell three overlapping stories. First, they reveal how maps illustrated with ethnographic material worked, and propose

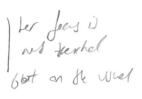

Indies and the Medieval West: Thought, Report, Imagination (Turnhout: Brepols, 2013). Mapmakers did not begin mapping America with a pre-existing iconography, whereas in Asia and Africa, which had had long traditions of particular monsters hopping their way across maps, the traditional repertoire of images was hard to shift during the golden age of European map illustration. Thus, although preconceptions about distant lands informed Renaissance mapmakers' responses, the ethnography of the Americas on maps emerged in very direct relation to contemporary travel writing. The words 'new world' appear very early in the post-Columbian cartographic record. The construct was unstable, sometimes including elements of what we now call Asia and Africa, but it was a meaningful one.

52 Denis Cosgrove, *Geography and Vision: Seeing, Imagining and Representing the World* (London: I. B. Tauris, 2008), 7. For textual geographies, see also Padrón, *Spacious Word*; Margaret Small, 'Displacing Ptolemy? The Textual Geographies of Ramusio's *Navigazione e viaggi*', in *Mapping Medieval Geographies: Geographical Encounters in the Latin West and Beyond, 300–1600*, ed. Keith D. Lilley (Cambridge: Cambridge University Press, 2013), 152–72.

53 For Münster, see Surekha Davies, 'America and Amerindians in Sebastian Münster's *Cosmographiae universalis libri VI*, 1550', *Renaissance Studies*, 25:3 (2011), 351–73; for Ramusio, see, e.g., Small, 'Displacing Ptolemy?', 152–72.

period readings. Second, they tell an epistemological story about how maps participated in making knowledge about the nature of the human. Third, they show why the relationship between the human and the classical concept of monstrous peoples mattered for European colonialism. Maps were part of the mental architecture through which jurists, administrators and scholars debated the fundamental effects of environmental and innate causes for human diversity, and made claims about ontological differences between peoples.

Chapters 1 and 2 lay out the ethnographical and geographical contexts for the rest of the book. Chapter 1 outlines the interpretative frameworks available c.1500 for thinking about human diversity. It introduces the main classical and Biblical traditions that shaped late medieval conceptions of monstrosity, wildness, civility and barbarism, and illuminates some of the ways in which they were applied on maps. I argue that while there had always been seams at which these traditions overlapped uneasily, these intersections multiplied in the age of oceanic exploration. Chapter 2 surveys the regions of cartographic production in which maps depicting Amerindians were most commonly made: Portugal, Seville, the German lands around the Rhine, Normandy, Antwerp and Amsterdam. These centres encompassed manuscript and printed cartographic traditions, but artists, mapmakers, travellers and their maps and books circulated widely, facilitating the development of a shared visual language. I outline some of the reasons why scholars, burghers, courtiers and royalty used large, decorative maps, and the ways in which mapmakers generated authority for maps of distant regions.

As mapmakers read travel and geographical literature, selected ethnographic material and made decisions about where to place information on their maps, they made choices that amounted to the invention of distant communities. Brazil, the first region of the Americas to acquire a distinctive ethnographic motif and the one that was illustrated most prolifically, is the subject of Chapters 3 and 4. In Chapter 3, I analyse comparatively the ways in which mapmakers across printed and manuscript mapping regions devised the concept of the Brazilian cannibal from travel writing about Caribbean islands. I argue that neither the elements of the motifs nor the fact that it was cannibalism that came to emblematize Brazil was inevitable. The association of northern South America with cannibalism – a practice that the Iberian crowns considered a justification for enslaving the region's people – took place against a backdrop of colonial debates about the proper administration of the region and the nature of its inhabitants.

In the mid-sixteenth century, an outpouring of extraordinarily ornate maps and atlases emanated from Normandy. In Chapter 4, I seek to understand the reasons behind the iconography of Brazil, a region of particular commercial interest for the French. Norman examples highlight peaceful relations, particularly the dyewood trade. By analysing the maps alongside travel accounts and examples of visual culture, I establish the extent to which Norman representations of Brazilians had a basis in experience. By investigating the use of these maps as gifts to French kings, I suggest that the mapmakers' selective use of trading imagery also played a persuasive role in the Norman maritime world's disputes with the Portuguese Crown over the extent of Portugal's Atlantic empire.

Motifs of physical monstrosity form the subject of Chapters 5 and 6. In Chapter 5, I investigate the ways in which mapmakers extrapolated creatively but also reasonably from the travel accounts from the 1520s that detailed the presence of giants in a region that came to be known as Patagonia. The translation of a written description of an encounter with giants to the space of Patagonia on a map shaped the ontology of these giants in the minds of map viewers, and redrew the boundary between human and monster. Subsequent writers reflected on the significance of the Patagonians' size and location for knowledge about how tropical climates worked on bodies and temperaments.

Printed maps depicting New World peoples developed a visual epistemology for wondrous ethnography that was diagrammatic rather than naturalistic. This is clear in the Dutch mapping of Guiana at the turn of the seventeenth century which gave rise to an iconic, if fleeting pair of motifs for the region's peoples: headless men and Amazons. In Chapter 6, I analyse the wondrous peoples of Sir Walter Ralegh's 1596 account of his expedition to Guiana, and the ways in which a group of Amsterdam map printers devised and discussed them. I argue that headless beings and Amazons were intrinsically credible, and that it was an extrinsic quality – the ethical relationship between the witness of such beings and the reader or viewer – that determined plausibility.

Images of Amerindians on maps were not uniformly violent or monstrous. In Chapter 7, I analyse the iconographic traditions for depicting cities and leaders that emblematized Mexico and Peru. I argue that mapmakers chose indicators of civility rather than elements of idolatry, sodomy and human sacrifice with which to emblematize these regions not only to limit confessional anxieties and the likelihood of censorship but also to offer new motifs that helped their viewers to tell distinguish these regions from Brazil, a place which had already been emblematized by cannibalism.

The development around the turn of the seventeenth century of Dutch wall maps with large, decorated borders containing images of peoples was a direct response to the new genres of the costume book and the illustrated travel book. In Chapter 8, I explore the ways in which cartographical and ethnographical modes that described and pictured the peoples of the world multiplied and cross-fertilized one another in this period. Treating together a range of ethnographic modes reveals that Dutch wall maps with decorated borders signal the culmination of the cartographic genre's claim for ethnographic authority based on an epistemology that was at once artefactual, cartographical and exegetical. This mapmaking strategy meant, however, that these wall maps lost their ability to simplify and synthesize travellers' views on the world's peoples. Mapmakers soon ceased to try to compete with texts for ethnographic authority.

Taken together, these chapters reveal some of the ways in which illustrated maps functioned within discourses of knowledge and science. The questions posed are intended to be exemplary of new directions waiting to be pursued, not exhaustive. They suggest that new world epistemologies were specific to particular genres, and that a particular cartographic epistemology led map viewers to read scenes of peoples on maps as knowledge-bearing images.

1 | Climate, culture or kinship? Explaining human diversity c.1500

It was my hint to speak...
... of the Cannibals that each other eat,
The Anthropophagi, and men whose heads
Do grow beneath their shoulders....
(Shakespeare, *Othello*, I, iii, 141–4)

When Othello courted Desdemona, he wooed her with tales of his adventures in distant lands and the marvellous beings who lived there, stories that Desdemona would 'with a greedy ear devour'.[1] European travellers to the Caribbean basin had introduced the 'Cannibals' to European audiences in the late fifteenth century; the *anthropophagi* of writings from classical antiquity had also consumed human flesh. Other travellers claimed to have encountered beings who were physically monstrous, such as those with no heads but with faces in their chests, who had also long populated travel and geographical writing. Othello's words reveal some of the views on distant peoples that Shakespeare could expect his audience – who ranged from the humbler sort among the groundlings to royalty in the best seats – to recognize at the turn of the seventeenth century.

From the late fifteenth century, oceanic expansion spawned ever-increasing numbers of travel accounts revealing the inhabitants of regions that had either never been described or that had previously been known through a fixed corpus of texts. The textual traditions of classical antiquity and Biblical scripture underlay Renaissance explanations for the diversity of human (and quasi-human) appearance and behaviour. These traditions encompassed multiple interpretative frameworks that explained the variation of habitats across the globe, the paths by which these habitats were populated, and the impact of environment on human bodies and behaviour.

The fault-lines at which these frameworks met required expert arbitration as the number of intersections between them expanded sharply in the age of Atlantic expansion: latitudes and longitudes thought to deform

[1] William Shakespeare, *Othello*, ed. Kenneth Muir (London: Penguin, 1996), I, iii, 148–9.

physiques, behaviours and even souls, or to be uninhabitable, turned out to be inhabited. These intersections prompted two sets of intellectual problems. One concerned the practices of making knowledge: what authoritative status should be ascribed to information garnered from recent voyages compared to the works of ancient authorities, and who was qualified to arbitrate between contradictory sources? The second concerned the nature of human distinctiveness (or lack thereof) from monstrous peoples and even animals. Where did the land of rational men formed in God's own image become regions populated by monstrous peoples? On what basis could the proper interpretative framework for understanding the inhabitants of a region be chosen? How might distant beings be correctly identified as humans, animals or monsters? And were monstrous peoples fundamentally different from humans?

These conundrums surface vividly in naval administrator and diarist Samuel Pepys's diary-entry for 24 August 1661. Pepys, who would later become president of the Royal Society, one of the earliest private societies devoted to the advancement of natural knowledge, described how he had come face-to-face with a monster:

> We are called to Sir W. Battens to see the strange creature that Captain Holmes hath brought with him from Guiny; it is a great baboone, but so much like a man in most things, that (though they say there is a species of them) yet I cannot believe but that it is a monster got of a man and she-baboone. I do believe that it already understands much English, and I am of the mind it might be tought to speak or make signs.[2]

For Pepys, this 'baboone' was so monstrous that the notion that it was a previously unknown animal – and thus one of many such creatures whose offspring were just like them – was untenable. It was more plausible, in his view, that the creature was a singular, monstrous individual born of unnatural behaviour. The epistemological problem that Pepys faced was how to ascertain whether something was unique or representative based on a limited number of exemplars. The ontological problem with which he grappled was that of determining whether an individual was human, animal or monster and, if a monster, then precisely what sort of monster.

In this chapter, I lay out the influential ethno-geographical frameworks c.1500, the expectations they raised concerning the nature of humanity

[2] Samuel Pepys, *The Diary of Samuel Pepys: A New and Complete Transcription*, ed. Robert Latham and William Matthews, 11 vols. (London: HarperCollins, 2000 [reissue of 1970–83 ed.]), II, 160, no. 24. Robert Holmes had returned from West Africa the previous month. He may have brought back a chimpanzee or a gorilla.

beyond Europe, and their implications for understanding the shifting boundaries between conceptions of humans and of monstrous peoples. Renaissance cartography cracked the thin conceptual walls that had separated discourses for making sense of peoples who were distant and monstrous from those for explaining cultural diversity and individual monstrous errors closer to home.

Humoralism

Renaissance European ideas about the body originated in classical Greece and Rome and in the Islamic world. A theory of bodily humours underpinned several interpretative frameworks and offered two interconnected approaches for explaining the disposition of bodies and the temperament of individuals: a theory of internal humours, and one of how outside influences influenced these humours. Late medieval geographers and other scholars drew on humoralism to interpret the differences among individuals and among groups as the result of a combination of innate and environmental factors.[3]

Classical humoralism was based on writings of the so-called Hippocratic corpus, dating from the fifth century BCE to the first century CE and associated with the fifth century BCE physician Hippocrates.[4] Later authors often drew on these writings through the forms known as *On the Nature of Man* and *On Airs, Waters and Places*. The Hippocratic paradigm was adopted and adapted by subsequent authors, notably Aristotle, the second century BCE physician Galen, and scholars across the Islamic world whose works would cross-fertilize western European medicine, particularly in Spain.[5] Authors of humoral works posited that all bodies were composed of a balance of four humours: blood, phlegm, black bile and yellow bile. Each humour was associated with one of the four elements (air, water, earth and fire, respectively), and was either hot (blood and yellow bile) or cold (phlegm and black bile).[6]

3 For late medieval arguments about geography and human variety, see Wey Gómez, *Tropics of Empire*, 74–86 and *passim*; for humoralism, see Mary Floyd-Wilson, *English Ethnicity and Race in Early Modern Drama* (Cambridge and New York, NY: Cambridge University Press, 2003), chap. 1.

4 For humoral theory in ancient Greek thought, see Nancy G. Siraisi, *Medieval and Early Renaissance Medicine: An Introduction to Knowledge and Practice* (Chicago, IL and London: University of Chicago Press, 1990), 102–6; Glacken, *Traces on the Rhodian Shore*, chap. 2.

5 Earle, *Body of the Conquistador*, 33.

6 Siraisi, *Medieval & Early Renaissance Medicine*, 104–6; Joyce E. Chaplin, *Subject Matter: Technology, the Body, and Science on the Anglo-American Frontier, 1500–1676* (Cambridge, MA and London: Harvard University Press, 2001), 120.

The humours were associated with macro-environmental categories, such as the constellations and seasons.[7] An environment's impact on its inhabitants thus went beyond the contingencies of local climate and lay in the region's geographical position. Humoral theory connected the nature of individual bodies to their environment. In this tradition, hypotheses concerning the extreme physical or behavioural variation of peoples who lived in very different climates were reasonable.[8] Such reasoning parallels that of today's astrobiologists as they extrapolate from the nature of life in the most extreme environments on earth – the deepest oceans, volcanos and polar regions – in order to determine upon which types of planets to concentrate their search for extraterrestrial life.

Physical activities and medicaments could also shape the humours. Human variation was thus also a matter of individual experiences, and a person's complexion – the overall cast of their character and physique – could vary over time. The idea that dietary practices and cultural choices produced physical difference was prevalent from at least the Middle Ages, and would become an important element in the definition of indigenous *vs.* creole (persons of European ancestry) populations in colonial Latin America.[9]

The balance of a person's humours was known as their complexion, a concept that encompassed physical appearance, personality and even mental aptitude and character. Complexion was thought to result from the interaction of climate (ambient sunlight, temperature and the qualities of the air, water and terrain) and the bodily humours (blood, bile, phlegm and choler); a person's complexion, therefore, would change if s/he moved to a different climate. Human difference was thus mutable, the function of changing and changeable external elements such as food and environment. Identifying and interpreting it in the Atlantic world, and determining its limits, was a subjective practice contingent on fluctuating colonial conventions and such practical considerations as the legitimation of slavery.[10]

Maps were important tools with which this mutability was articulated. They made visible the latitudinal grounding of humoral theory as they emblematized the peoples of different regions by their levels of urbanity, dietary practices, costumes and physiques. Late medieval readers had contradictory options for predicting the habitability of distant parts of

[7] Earle, *Body of the Conquistador*, 88–9.

[8] For examples of analyses of human variety underpinned by humoralism, see Chaplin, *Subject Matter*, 121–3.

[9] Earle, *Body of the Conquistador*, 26–8.

[10] Van Deusen, *Global Indios:*, chap. 6; Earle, *Body of the Conquistador*, 7, chap. 4.

the world.[11] In the context of some elements of classical and Biblical traditions, finding populated lands west of the Atlantic or south of the Equator was problematic. Advocates of the traditions of classical zonal theory – who included Ptolemy, Pliny and Aristotle among Greco-Latin authors, and Albertus Magnus and Pierre d'Ailly among the medieval scholastics – divided the spherical earth into five latitudinal zones: two uninhabitable polar zones, two temperate zones and an uncrossable equatorial torrid zone, too hot for human habitation. Medieval and Renaissance authors may have come across this view on a zonal map. Two examples appear in a 1483 edition of Pierre d'Ailly's *Imago Mundi* (Fig. 1.1).[12] Here, 'Figure Six' (*Sexta figura*) lays out the five zones. 'Figure Seven' (*Septima figura*) shows schematically the zones in which various parts of the known world appear, and subdivides the northern temperate zone into its seven climates (*climata*). Those regions that approached the polar and equatorial limits of the temperate zone were thought to be incapable of sustaining civil societies, or even of properly formed humans. In the literal interpretation of Scripture in the writings of St Augustine, the early fifth-century theologian and bishop of Hippo in Numidia, the Roman province in North Africa, since all men were descended from Adam and the apostles had preached to all men, but the antipodean lands were forever separate from the known world or *oikoumene*, those lands must be uninhabited.[13]

Nonetheless, variant traditions left room for the tropics to be universally uninhabitable and yet accidentally inhabited due to, for example, rivers. As early as Strabo (at the turn of the Common Era), alternatives to an uninhabited torrid zone were posited. As varied texts re-circulated in the Latin West in the mid-thirteenth century, some Christian authors, beginning with the scholar and bishop Albertus Magnus, also suggested that both the torrid and southern zones were fertile, temperate and capable of sustaining life.[14]

[11] For theoretical models for the globe, prior to oceanic voyages, see Davies, 'America and Amerindians', 352–3.

[12] Left: *Sexta figura. Hec figura servit nono capitulo pro divisione terre per climata.* Right: *Septima figura. Hec figura servit xiiii. capitulo pluribus aliis pro divisione terre in tres partes . . .* in Pierre d'Ailly, [Ymago Mundi], ([Louvain?], [1483?]). For zonal theory and the climatic zones, see Wey Gómez, *Tropics of Empire*, 71–86; David Woodward, 'Geography', in *The Cambridge History of Science: Volume 3: Early Modern Science*, ed. Katharine Park and Lorraine Daston (New York, NY: Cambridge University Press, 2006), 548–68, 550. The tradition owed much to Aristotle; for his delineation of the zones, see his *Meteorologia*, ed. and trans. H. D. P. Lee (London: William Heinemann; Cambridge: Harvard University Press, 1952), II.v.362a.33–362b.12.

[13] Relaño, *Shaping of Africa*, 24–6; Hiatt, *Terra Incognita*, 6.

[14] Wey Gómez, *Tropics of Empire*, 162–3, 231, 233.

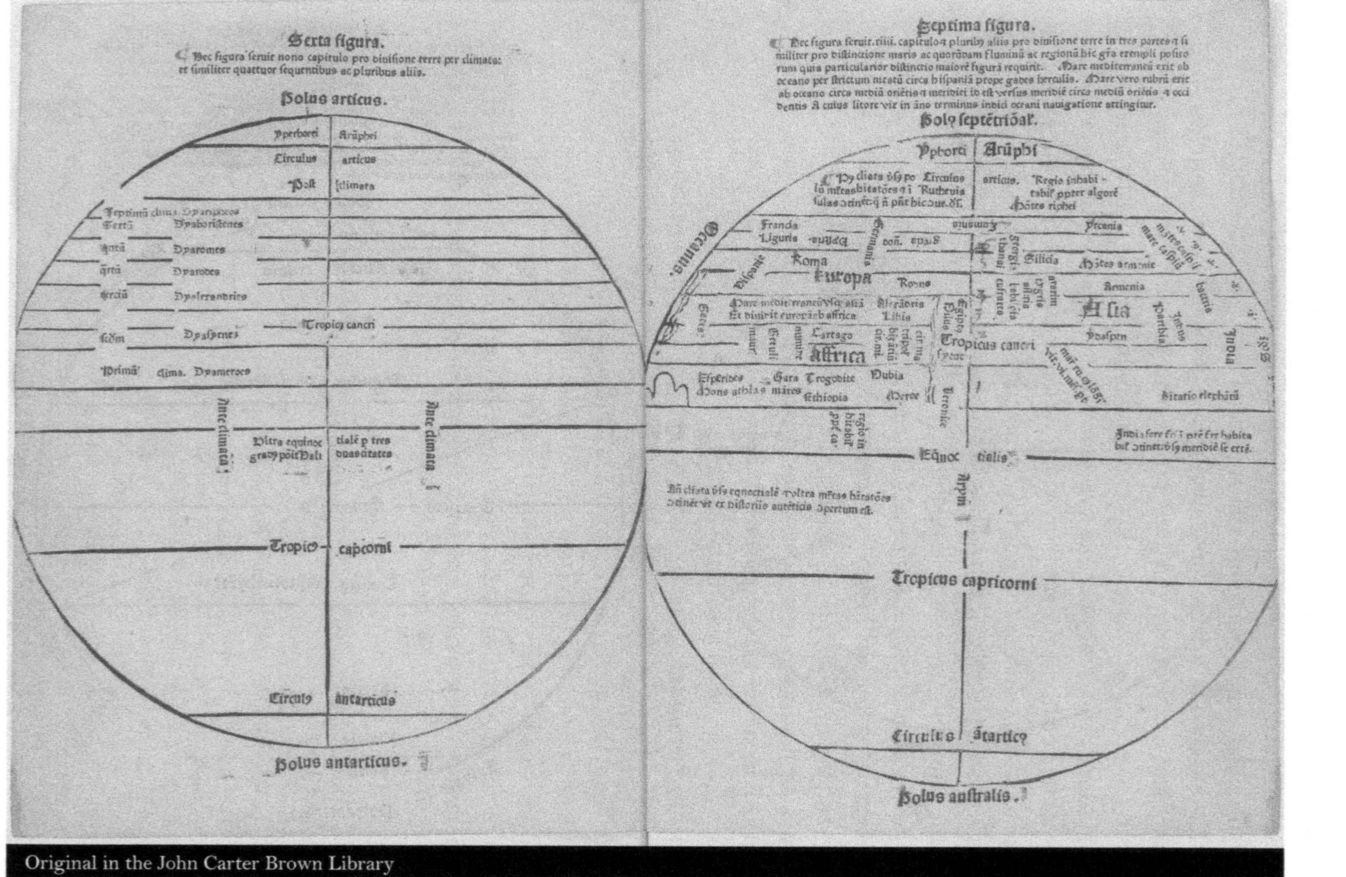

Original in the John Carter Brown Library

1.1 Left: *Sexta figura. Hec figura servit nono capitulo pro divisione terre per climata.* Right: *Septima figura. Hec figura servit xiiii. capitulo pluribus aliis pro divisione terre in tres partes* . . . in Pierre d'Ailly, [Ymago Mundi], ([Louvain?], [1483?]).
Courtesy of the John Carter Brown Library at Brown University, A483 A293i/1-SIZE.

At the end of the twelfth century, the world map form known as the *mappamundi* began to structure the world along socio-political lines according to Biblical traditions.[15] *Mappaemundi* depicted the inhabited portion of the spherical world as a circle dissected into three portions by the Mediterranean Sea, the Black Sea or River Don, and the Nile, which together form a T-shape. East was usually placed at the top of these maps.[16] This tripartite world view was commonly associated with the idea that, after the Biblical Flood, the children of each of the sons of Noah had populated a different part of the world.[17]

For ancient Greek geographers and their heirs, latitude played a critical role in shaping the nature of living things. Ptolemy had noted that 'all animals and plants that are on the same parallels . . . equidistant from either pole ought to exist in similar combinations in accordance with the similarity of their environments.'[18] This view persisted in the Renaissance. Fifteenth- and early sixteenth-century manuscripts of Ptolemy's *Geography* marked latitudes and climatic zones (*climata*) on each map.[19] A mid-seventeenth century manuscript handbook to geography and hydrography by a Spanish military engineer laid out the types of people who lived at different parallels.[20] Spanish chroniclers devised geographies that were structured through latitude and longitude descriptions; and printed editions of Ptolemy displayed the climatic zones prominently, marking them out by latitude.[21]

[15] Hiatt, *Terra Incognita*, 4; Margriet Hoogvliet, *Pictura et scriptura: textes, images et herméneutique des 'mappae mundi' (XIIIe-XVIe siècles)* (Turnhout: Brepols, 2007). More generally, see P. D. A. Harvey, ed., *The Hereford World Map: Medieval World Maps and Their Context* (London: The British Library, 2006); David Woodward, 'Medieval *Mappaemundi*', in *History of Cartography Volume 1: Cartography in Prehistoric, Ancient and Medieval Europe and the Mediterranean*, ed. J. B. Harley and David Woodward (Chicago, IL and London: University of Chicago Press, 1987), 286–370.

[16] For these, see Edson, *World Map*.

[17] For the historical evolution of this idea, see Benjamin Braude, 'The Sons of Noah and the Construction of Ethnic and Geographical Identities in the Medieval and Early Modern Periods', *William and Mary Quarterly*, 54:1 (1997), 103–42.

[18] Claudius Ptolemy, *Ptolemy's Geography: An Annotated Translation of the Theoretical Chapters*, eds. and trans. J. Lennart Berggren and Alexander Jones (Princeton, NJ and Oxford: Princeton University Press, 2000), 1:9, 69, cited and discussed further in Wey Gómez, *Tropics of Empire*, 49.

[19] Renaissance manuscripts of Ptolemy's *Geographia* that show the climatic zones include John Carter Brown Library, Codex Latin 1. Henricus Glareanus, 'De geometriae principiis ad sphaerae astronomicae noticiam necessariis', c.1513, ff. 25*v*-26*r*.

[20] Barcelona, Universitat de Barcelona, CRAI Biblioteca de Reserva, MS 1557. Sebastián Fernández de Medrano, Guia Geografica y Hidrografica, 17th century, 138–43.

[21] For Spanish geographies, see Padrón, *Spacious Word*.

Monstrous peoples and the edges of humanity

> ...when you meet anything that's going to be human and isn't yet, or used to be human once and isn't now, or ought to be human and isn't, you keep your eyes on it and feel for your hatchet.
>
> (C. S. Lewis, *The Lion, The Witch and The Wardrobe*)

Samuel Pepys's musings on the baboon, with which this chapter began, point us towards the three interpretative traditions of early modern teratology. Each of these traditions was based on textual prototypes from classical antiquity.[22] One tradition may be traced to Aristotle's *Generation of Animals* (c.350 BCE).[23] It considered monsters as occasional errors in nature, brought about as a result of the working of nature on the brute, occasionally unresisting substance of matter. Anything that did not resemble its parents, particularly its father, was a monster in Aristotle's view.[24] A second tradition existed within a discourse of omens and prodigies founded by Cicero's *On Divination* (44 BCE).[25] Cicero perceived monstrous births as signs of impending calamity, and many later classical and Christian authors continued this tradition.[26] Authors writing in the medieval chronicle tradition interpreted a range of prodigies, from comets to floods to conjoined twins, as general signs of impending political upheaval or war.[27]

The third tradition, largely based on Pliny the Elder's *Historia naturalis* (c.77–9 CE), was of monsters as wonders of nature, and dealt specifically with monstrous peoples in distant places. Authors in this tradition posited

22 See, e.g., Zakiya Hanafi, *The Monster in the Machine: Magic, Medicine, and the Marvelous in the Time of the Scientific Revolution* (Durham, NC: Duke University Press, 2000), 7–14; Lorraine Daston and Katherine Park, 'Unnatural Conceptions: The Study of Monsters in Sixteenth- and Seventeenth-Century France and England', *Past and Present*, 92 (1981), 20–54, at 22–3; Jean Céard, *La Nature et les prodiges: l'Insolite au XVIe siècle*, 2e édition revue et augmentée (Geneva: Droz, 1996), 3–20.

23 Aristotle, *Generation of Animals*, with trans. by A. L. Peck (London and Cambridge, MA: Harvard University Press, 1963).

24 Ibid., II.iii and IV.iii-iv. See also Hanafi, *Monster in the Machine*, 8; Marie-Hélène Huet, *Monstrous Imagination* (Cambridge, MA: Harvard University Press, 1993), 3–4. Thus even women, who lacked the perfection of men, were a kind of monster although they did not, for Aristotle, illustrate or portend anything, apart from showing that female generative secretions had triumphed over male seed and caused a departure from a normal male child.

25 Cicero, *De senectute; De amicitia; De divinatione*, with trans. by William Armistead Falconer (London and Cambridge, MA: Harvard University Press, 1971).

26 Hanafi, *Monster in the Machine*, 8; Céard, *Nature et les prodiges*, 3.

27 For positive interpretations of prodigious births in pre-Reformation Germany, see Jennifer Spinks, *Monstrous Births and Visual Culture in Sixteenth-Century Germany* (London: Pickering & Chatto, 2009), chaps. 1 and 2.

that entire species of monstrous peoples – beings characterized by physical or behavioural abnormalities such as having one leg rather than two, or living on an exclusive diet of smells – dwelt in the far corners of the earth. Many were believed to be the consequence of extreme climates and environments. Particularly fertile regions could lead to beings with exaggerated attributes, such as Giants or *Panotii* (beings with very large ears); the inhabitants of desert regions might be lacking in some way, like pygmies (who lacked height); or, as in the case of troglodytes (cave-dwellers), they might attempt to avoid their environment.[28]

Two features separated monstrous peoples in the classical tradition from one-off monstrous individuals. First, the deviations of a monstrous people were found across a population and passed down the generations, rather than being restricted to a few unnatural individuals.[29] Second, monstrous peoples occurred at the edges of the known world. In theory, these elements distinguished monstrosity close to home – the occasional two-headed baby, for example – from distant forms. For the ancient Greeks, distance was measured from the Mediterranean; in medieval Europe, monsters and marvels increased with distance from Jerusalem, the spiritual centre of the Christian world. While Pliny had remarked that 'India and parts of Ethiopia especially teem with marvels',[30] the far north and west were also associated with monstrosity, a fact that Anglo-Saxon and medieval English chroniclers and mapmakers made clear by regularly placing monstrous peoples in Britain.[31]

In the Middle Ages, Biblical scripture offered indirect explanations for the monstrous peoples.[32] Some strands suggested that these beings were the result of degeneration. Cain (who committed fratricide when he killed Abel) and Ham (who jeered when he came upon his father Noah's drunken stupor) were thought to have prompted divine curses that

[28] For these points, see Relaño, *Shaping of Africa*, 33; Céard, *Nature et les prodiges*, 52–4.

[29] For the ontological difference between anomalous, portentous, alarming monstrous individuals and wondrous but natural monstrous peoples in medieval thought, see Daston and Park, *Wonders*, 48–50.

[30] Pliny the Elder, *Natural History*, trans. H. Rackham, 10 vols. (Cambridge, MA: Harvard University Press, 1969), VII:ii.21: 'Praecipue India Aethiopiumque tractus miraculis scatent.'

[31] Asa Simon Mittman, *Maps and Monsters in Medieval England* (New York, NY and London: Routledge, 2006), 12–5. For monsters and 'symbolic extremes' in the East, see Mary W. Helms, *Ulysses' Sail: An Ethnographic Odyssey of Power, Knowledge and Geographical Distance* (Princeton, NJ: Princeton University Press, 1988), 213–7.

[32] For extensive bibliography and examples, see Chet Van Duzer, '*Hic sunt dracones*: The Geography and Cartography of Monsters', in *ARC-MM*, 385–433. For monstrous peoples in medieval art and maps, see Friedman, *Monstrous Races*.

deformed their kin.[33] A legend in northeast Asia on the thirteenth-century Hereford Map recounts that in this region live 'exceedingly savage people who eat human flesh and drink blood, the accursed sons of Cain'. God was said to have sent earthquakes that brought mountains down on top of mountains around them; Alexander closed off the area lacking mountains by means of a wall.[34]

While most accounts also conceded that Cain's kin did not survive the Flood, a post-diluvian curse in the *Book of Genesis* allowed for the persistence of the monstrous in human ancestry. After Ham told his brothers that he had seen his father Noah naked and in a drunken sleep, his father cursed him so that his descendants would carry the mark of Ham's shame. After the floods had subsided, Noah divided the world among his sons. The Scriptures do not specify which son received which part. Nevertheless, the idea that God gave Africa to Ham and that Ham's descendants, starting with his grandson Nimrod, had black skin as a mark of his shame, began to circulate during the fifteenth century.[35]

Even if monstrous peoples were comfortably confined to the edges of the earth in classical and medieval natural history, there remained the question of their precise relationship to the rest of humanity. St Augustine of Hippo attempted to wrestle the natural history of monstrous peoples into a Christian framework. In his *De civitate dei* (*On the City of God*), St Augustine suggested that 'either the written accounts of certain races are completely unfounded or, if such races do exist, they are not human; or, if they are human, they are descended from Adam'.[36] This statement clarified little, but it did raise the stakes of identifying beings as *homines*: Adam's descendants were by definition human and thus rational beings, and remained that way regardless of their outward appearance.[37] Since humans

33 David N. Livingstone, *Adam's Ancestors: Race, Religion, and the Politics of Human Origins* (Baltimore, MD: The Johns Hopkins University Press, 2008), 13–4.

34 Scott D. Westrem, *The Hereford Map: A Transcription and Translation of the Legends with Commentary* (Turnhout: Brepols, 2001), Text 141: 'homines truculenti nimis, humanis carnibus vescentes, cruorem portantes, fili Caim maledicti'.

35 See Braude, 'Sons of Noah'. For the emergence of humoral and moral explanations of black skin, see also Earle, *Body of the Conquistador*, 191–200.

36 St Augustine, *The City of God Against the Pagans*, trans. Eva Matthews Sanford and William McAllen Green, 7 vols. (London and Cambridge, MA: Harvard University Press, 1965), V, XVI. viii (for text and translation): 'Aut illa quae talia de quibusdam gentibus scripta sunt, omnino nulla sunt; aut si sunt, homines non sunt; aut ex Adam sunt, si homines sunt.' Earlier in this section, Augustine had asserted that any human being, i.e., a 'rational mortal creature' ('animal rationale mortale'), must be descended from Adam, no matter how strange they might be in appearance, custom or nature.

37 For this point, see Livingstone, *Adam's Ancestors*, 14–5.

were the only animals capable of rational thought in medieval theology, if a monstrous people turned out to be rational beings, they must share ancestry with all of humanity and be of the same kind ontologically. Such monstrous peoples would also be capable of salvation. The tympanum above an entrance to the nave of the twelfth-century cathedral at Vézelay in Burgundy depicts monstrous peoples among the inhabitants of pilgrimage routes, thus suggesting that these beings were in need of – and capable of receiving – Christianity.[38]

In the early seventh century the bishop, historian and encyclopedist Isidore of Seville paraphrased and rearranged material from St Augustine's *De civitate dei* and other sources in an encyclopedic work known as the *Etymologiae*. Isidore clarified the difference between monstrous races and monstrous individuals thus: 'Just as, in individual nations, there are instances of monstrous people, so in the whole of humankind there are certain monstrous races, like the giants, the *Cynocephali* [dog-headed people], the *Cyclopes*, and others.'[39]

The influential thirteenth-century Dominican theologian and natural philosopher Albertus Magnus espoused the opposite view: rational souls were to be found in perfect bodies; highly unusual bodies were signs of sub-human souls and mental capacities.[40] Now there was an ontological elephant in the room: Since the nature of the human body was not fixed but varied with climate, what might that mean for the state of the soul? Could humans transmute into non-rational beasts or monsters? What constituted an ontologically significant level of physical deviance or monstrosity, the sort that signified an irrational and therefore subhuman or bestial soul?[41]

For the early fourteenth-century polymath and theologian Nicolas Oresme, since it was not known at what point in the generative process God infused a body with a soul, it was impossible to know at which point the physical variation of a monstrous being was so great that the creature lacked a rational soul. For Oresme, judging whether such an individual could use reason was a better test of their rationality than their physical appearance.[42]

38 Friedman, *Monstrous Races*, 77–9.

39 Isidore of Seville, *The Etymologies of Isidore of Seville*, ed. and trans. Stephen A. Barney et al. (Cambridge: Cambridge University Press, 2006), XI.iii.12; also quoted in Céard, *Nature et les prodiges*, 43. For medieval ideas about human diversity, see, e.g., Hodgen, *Early Ethnology*, chap. 2.

40 Albertus Magnus, *De natura locorum*, II.2–4 in *Opera omnia*, ed. Auguste Borgnet, 38 vols. (Paris: apud Ludovicum Vivès, 1890–95), IX, 560–65.

41 Fernández-Armesto, *So You Think You're Human?*, 70.

42 Nicole Oresme, *Nicole Oresme and the Marvels of Nature: A Study of his De causis mirabilium with Critical Edition, Translation, and Commentary*, ed. Bert Hanson (Toronto, ON: Pontifical Institute of Mediaeval Studies, 1985), 232–5.

Such questions needed to be answered not only through the discourse of monstrosity but also through traditions for making sense of the soul. Renaissance psychology at the turn of the sixteenth century was built on Aristotelian and other classical foundations.[43] These had been re-worked in the Middle Ages by Islamic and early Christian authors, and fifteenth- and sixteenth-century commentators continued to transform and diversify the traditions. The human soul was thought to comprise a number of different faculties of which two – the intellect and the will – were incorporeal and immortal. Most aspects of the soul were closely tied to the body and its organs. While the intellect and the will did not need the body directly, they depended on sensory information relayed through organs. Physical problems in the brain could prevent the rational human soul from interpreting sensory information correctly. External conditions, illness or injury could impair the highest mental faculties and the practice of reason.[44] Extreme environments were thus potentially capable of deforming souls or their capacity to understand nature or the divine. If a people were no longer capable of reason, they were not governed by natural law and, being little more than beasts, were arguably natural slaves.[45]

Although scepticism about the reality of monstrous peoples appears to be as old as ideas about them, since God's powers were believed to be infinite, such wonders were intrinsically credible.[46] Consequently, treatises about monsters were often bound with works on the regular workings of nature. The three tenth- to twelfth-century Anglo-Saxon and Anglo-Norman recensions of the *Marvels of the East*, an encyclopedia of monstrous beings derived from classical sources, are bound with such non-monstrous texts as those by the English monk Bede (late eighth and early ninth centuries) and by the late antique author Macrobius. Classical sources and Germanic folklore intermingled in the Anglo-Latin *Liber monstrorum*, first composed in the British Isles in the seventh or eighth centuries but comprising a composite of earlier works.[47]

[43] See especially Aristotle, *On the Soul*, with English trans. by W. S. Hett (London: William Heinemann; Cambridge, MA: Harvard University Press, 1957).

[44] For Renaissance conceptions of the soul, see Katharine Park, 'The Organic Soul', in *The Cambridge History of Renaissance Philosophy*, ed. Charles B. Schmitt et al. (Cambridge: Cambridge University Press, 1988), 464–84 and Katharine Park, 'The Intellective Soul', 485–534 in the same volume.

[45] For Castilian debates about the nature of the Amerindians and those arguments made to legitimate indigenous slavery, see Van Deusen, *Global Indios*, 3–9 and Chapter 7 in this book.

[46] Daston and Park, *Wonders*, 39–40, 44–5. For late medieval approaches to eyewitness and encyclopedic accounts of wondrous geography, see Gow, 'Fra Mauro's World View'.

[47] Mittman, *Maps and Monsters*, 67; Daston and Park, *Wonders*, 26, 48–9.

The geographical distribution of monstrous peoples received a diagrammatic form on medieval *mappaemundi* or world maps.[48] The *mappaemundi* tradition portrayed human (particularly Biblical) history and Christian theology within a geographical framework.[49] On surviving exemplars from the thirteenth to the fifteenth centuries, these peoples were placed as far away as possible from Jerusalem, the spiritual centre of the Christian universe.[50] On the English Psalter map (c.1265) (Fig. 1.2), the outer rim corresponding to the African regions south of the western Nile includes such beings as troglodytes, *anthropophagi*, *blemmyae*, *cynocephali* and a *sciapod* (a person with one giant foot usually raised as a sunshade).[51] Locating monsters may have formed part of processes of identity formation: in order to know oneself, one must know how others are different, and one must understand where one lives in relation to others. This was particularly important for those medieval Europeans who saw themselves as dwelling in the margins of what had been the classical world – such as Britain – and at a great distance from Jerusalem.[52]

Mappaemundi were perceived in the Middle Ages as appropriate sources for learned contemplation and reference. The thirteenth-century bishop of Acre and longtime resident of the Near East Jacques de Vitry consulted *mappaemundi* alongside the works of Pliny, Solinus, St Augustine and Isidore of Seville while writing his *Historia orientalis*.[53] The Minorite friar Paolino Veneto linked the purpose of maps explicitly to understanding human diversity and the earliest history of humanity.[54]

During the first two centuries of printed books, beings such as apple-smellers, troglodytes, *anthropophagi* and *sciapodes*, who had sniffed, huddled, chomped or hopped their way across medieval manuscripts of the *Marvels of the East* and Pliny the Elder's *Historia naturalis* continued to pass through the hands and minds of European writers, readers and

[48] Hoogvliet, *Pictura et scriptura*, 202–19; Kline, *Maps of Medieval Thought*, 150–3; Woodward, 'Medieval *Mappaemundi*', 330–3 (includes list of peoples found on various *mappaemundi*); Friedman, *Monstrous Races*, 37–58. For monstrous peoples on maps the Middle Ages, see Mittman, *Maps and Monsters*; Relaño, *Shaping of Africa*, 28–41 (overview), 84–6 (Africa).

[49] Woodward, 'Medieval *Mappaemundi*', 286–370; Edson, *World Map*, 11–32.

[50] Mittman, *Maps and Monsters*, 34–42.

[51] BL-MS, Add.Ms. 28681, f. 9*r*.

[52] For this argument, and for examples of medieval writers in Britain seeing themselves as inhabiting the edge of the world, see Mittman, *Maps and Monsters*, 11–26.

[53] Friedman, *Monstrous Races*, 42.

[54] See p. 1 above.

1.2 Psalter map, c.1265. MS Add. 28681, f. 9*r*.

viewers. In the decades around 1500, ideas about monstrous peoples at the rim of the world culled from travel accounts, encyclopedias, Biblical works and other sources appeared in geographies, maps and globes. These works, which selected and reformulated information to suit the space constraints and intellectual vision of the geographers and mapmakers, illuminate the intrinsic credibility of monstrous peoples. Of the sources cited in maps and geographies in the long sixteenth century, Pliny was the most widely cited authority among the classical sources on monstrous peoples. Also popular were medieval encyclopedic texts such as St Augustine's *De civitate dei* and Isidore's *Etymologiae*.[55] The books attributed to Marco Polo and John Mandeville were printed widely into the seventeenth century. The fictional narrative attributed to Mandeville, for instance, was one of the earliest of all works to be printed, and the most popular incunable by a medieval prose writer.[56] The *Book of John Mandeville* outlined his alleged pilgrimage to the Holy Land, and had appeared in at least seventy-two printed editions by the end of the sixteenth century.[57] While the majority of the vellum-inches in Marco Polo and Mandeville manuscripts were devoted to folk who were not monstrous, the *Book of John Mandeville* in particular was frequently cited on monstrous peoples dwelling in the furthest parts of the world.[58] The circulation of these works informed conceptions of the wondrous inhabitants of Asia.[59]

Late medieval expectations about lands reached by sailing south or west across the Atlantic mirrored ideas about Asia. What was new about monstrous peoples during the long sixteenth century was the nature of their march across the globe. The mid-fifteenth century had heralded the age of oceanic expansion: European navigators began to sail south along the coast of west Africa and around it to India, and west across the Atlantic to what became known as the Americas. As the span of the world laid out by scholars was traversed by men in ships, the possibility of meeting monstrous peoples theoretically became increasingly likely. Contemporary travel literature became an important new source for monstrous peoples; texts and the maps that drew upon them helped to re-shape their interpretation.

55 Isidore, *Etymologies*, XI.iii.12–30. For late medieval wonder books, see Daston and Park, *Wonders*, chap. 1.

56 Mary B. Campbell, *The Witness and the Other World: Exotic Eastern Travel Writing 400–1600* (Ithaca, NY and London: Cornell University Press, 1988), 122.

57 Rosemary Tzanaki, *Mandeville's Medieval Audiences: A Study on the Reception of the Book of Sir John Mandeville (1371–1550)* (Aldershot: Ashgate, 2003), 1, n. 1; this study focuses on manuscripts.

58 See also Braham, 'The Monstrous Caribbean', in *ARC-MM*, near n. 8.

59 See Davies, *Wondrous East*; Daston and Park, *Wonders*, 25–43.

A key question in the minds of travellers and their readers was the relationship between the monstrous peoples they expected to see and the beings newly observed in the field. Their expectations were informed by broad ethno-geographical ideas. One related to the roundness of the world.[60] If you sailed west for long enough, you would eventually reach the east. Thus Columbus and other travellers to America considered the peoples they encountered in the light of their expectations about the easternmost parts of Asia: gold, the Great Khan, and monstrous peoples.[61] Similarly, exploration of the southernmost reaches of South America suggested that Tierra del Fuego (in southern Patagonia) was the edge of a great antipodean region, another site previously associated with monstrous peoples.[62] These ideas provided the theoretical basis for expecting monstrous peoples in the Americas.

Pre-modern monstrosity inspired a multitude of different emotions; physical or behavioural difference did not immediately correlate to a particular level of fear or disgust. Some of the illuminations of monstrous peoples in an early fifteenth-century English manuscript of the *Book of John Mandeville* exemplify monstrosity as pleasurable wonder.[63] The manuscript describes, for example, a people with flat faces. The corresponding illumination shows two naked figures with the schematic features of the modern smiley-face emoticon: two dots for eyes and a semi-circle mouth. Distant monstrous peoples merely appeared to go against nature but were wonders of God's creation, not unnatural portents of doom.[64] Distance was not the only determinant of nastiness, as the treatment of peoples all along the pilgrim route in the *Book of Mandeville* makes clear. The author directs far greater censure at the Jews than at people, monstrous or otherwise, who live further away, such as the dog-headed cannibals of southeast Asia.[65] Over time, the concerns that Christian writers

[60] Contrary to popular belief, medieval scholars were well aware that the earth was spherical. See Louise M. Bishop, 'The Myth of the Flat Earth', in Stephen J. Harris and Bryon L. Grigsby, eds., *Misconceptions about the Middle Ages* (London and New York, NY: Routledge, 2008), 97–101.

[61] For late medieval travel writing about India, see Rubiés, *Travel and Ethnology*, chap. 2. Columbus also sailed south: see Wey Gómez, *Tropics of Empire*, chap. 6; for the large and fluid geographical concept of India in this period, see chap. 3 in the same volume.

[62] Jacqueline Duvernay-Bolens, *Géants patagons*, 44–6; for the antipodes, see Hiatt, *Terra Incognita*, 54–60, 80–1, 236–43.

[63] BL-Mss, Harley MS 3954, Travels of Mandeville. East Anglia, c.1430, f.42*r*.

[64] For the positive emotions engendered by distant monstrous peoples, see Daston and Park, *Wonders*, 50–1.

[65] For Jews in Mandeville, see Iain Macleod Higgins, *Writing East: The "Travels" of Sir John Mandeville* (Philadelphia, PA: University of Pennsylvania Press, 1997), 178–88.

found most worrisome changed. While religious practices were the most pressing indicators of difference in the Middle Ages, indicators of civility/savagery, and of physical monstrosity, became increasingly important in the sixteenth century.[66] By the late seventeenth century, skin colour began to be investigated as the primary determinant of human difference.[67]

Although the classical typology of prodigious, natural and distant monsters (and their medieval variants) continued to inform expectations in the Renaissance, in practice, the three categories overlapped. Monstrous births and monstrous peoples began to converge in several discourses, particularly in the context of natural history.[68] Voyages of exploration were one of the drivers of this conversion. When physically unusual individuals (from the point of view of European sailors) were encountered in distant regions, ascertaining whether or not they were a monstrous people or merely monstrous individuals was not straightforward, for monsters of all causes *looked* the same: unnatural. There was no consensus on whether (say) dog-headed beings were one-off errors or members of a monstrous people. Not only was the interpretation of monsters within Europe a contested enterprise, as many scholars have shown, but so too was the interpretation of distant monsters.

Wildness, savagery and civility

The alternative to establishing the limits of the human by physique was to establish it by observing actions. In classical antiquity, human diversity in behaviour, like variation in physique, was also understood via several conceptual schemes. In the fourth century BCE, in his *Nicomachean Ethics*, the Greek philosopher Aristotle maintained that there were different degrees of humanity from god-like individuals imbued with 'superhuman virtue, or goodness on a heroic or divine scale' at one end of the scale, to bestial persons at the other. In between were normal human beings, whose

[66] For interpretations of human difference through religious difference, see Carina L. Johnson, Cultural Hierarchy in Sixteenth-Century Europe: The Ottomans and *Mexicans* (New York, NY etc.: Cambridge University Press, 2011), 24–32; Rebecca Anne Goetz, *The Baptism of Early Virginia: How Christianity Created Race* (Baltimore, MD: Johns Hopkins University Press, 2012).

[67] For late seventeenth- and eighteenth-century experiments and philosophical arguments, see Andrew S. Curran, *The Anatomy of Blackness: Science and Slavery in an Age of Enlightenment* (Baltimore, MD: Johns Hopkins University Press, 2011); for Enlightenment literature, see Roxann Wheeler, *The Complexion of Race: Categories of Difference in Eighteenth-century British Culture* (Philadelphia, PA: University of Pennsylvania Press, 2000).

[68] For these shifting boundaries, see Surekha Davies, 'The Unlucky, the Bad and the Ugly: Categories of Monstrosity from the Renaissance to the Enlightenment', in *ARC-MM*, 49–75.

actions were characterized by vice and virtue.[69] The degrees on the scale were distinguished by particular behaviours that indicated mental capacities. In a bestial person, the higher faculties of thought were entirely absent, as in an animal. While this state was less evil than vice – since it was the result of an intellect that was insufficient to practice virtue – its associated behaviour was more horrible, closer to those of beasts.[70]

Near the lower end of the scale was the barbarian – literally someone unable to speak Greek and who babbled instead, but effectively an outsider who possessed insufficient reason to speak, to act like Greeks or to form a civil society. As Anthony Pagden and others have pointed out, the Aristotelian distinction between Greeks and *barbaroi* was in essence a distinction between those who were fully human and those who were not. While all humans were biologically the same beings for the ancient Greeks, their different behaviours were indicative of fundamental differences. *Barbaroi* might well never achieve the full human potential of reason, happiness and virtue. Christian Europeans understood as barbarians anyone who did not live as they did. Those who did not believe in Christ and therefore demonstrated their inability to use reason properly were barbarians, a word that would become synonymous with pagans during the Middle Ages.[71]

Aristotle's degrees of humanity were related to his ideas about social organization. In his *Politics*, which began re-circulating in Latin Christendom in the 1260s, Aristotle aimed to explicate how people might conduct themselves and be governed so as to live the best life and thus achieve happiness.[72] He argued that the organization of communities had a direct bearing on their members' potential for happiness; moreover, those who were unable by nature to live in a city – the ideal community – lacked higher levels of intellect.[73] Aristotle listed six classes of people who were essential for an ideal community: farmers, craftsmen, soldiers, the wealthy (to purchase goods and finance wars), priests and judges.[74] Early modern writers and mapmakers often used variations of these classes when describing Amerindians.

In his *Politics*, Aristotle compared the peoples of northern Europe and Asia to the Greeks. He considered the latter, who occupied 'the middle

[69] Aristotle, *The Nicomachean Ethics*, trans. H. Rackham (London and Cambridge, MA: Harvard University Press, 1928), VII:i.1–3.

[70] Ibid., VII: vi.7. For an extensive elaboration of Aristotle's notion of the barbarian and its circulation in Latin Christendom, see Pagden, *Fall*, 15–24.

[71] Aristotle, *Nic. Ethics*, VII:i.3; Pagden, *Fall*, 16–19.

[72] For the re-introduction of Aristotle's *Politics* in the Latin West, see Johnson, *Cultural Hierarchy*, 23, n. 7.

[73] Aristotle, *Politics*, I:i.8–12.

[74] Ibid.,VII:vii.5.

position geographically', to be 'both spirited and intelligent', and to possess the best balance of the characteristics of both Europeans and Asians.[75] He then provided an extended description of the ideal state, using many of the same attributes later employed by Renaissance authors.[76]

The boundaries of the category of the human were murky in classical antiquity and continued to be so for its heirs. In the Greek and Christian traditions, all living beings existed in a hierarchy, sometimes called the Great Chain of Being. Not only were species arranged according to their complexity and capabilities, but so were individuals among them. The thirteenth-century Dominican theologian and philosopher Thomas Aquinas, among others, suggested that the lowest members of one category might resemble the highest members of the category below them.[77] For St Augustine's followers, observing behaviour for signs of rational thought – sophisticated social life, clothing or weaponry, for example – was the way to establish whether or not a people had rational souls.[78]

The wild man in European thought has roots in several traditions. Greek and Roman mythology contributed Hercules and Cyclopes.[79] Christian traditions contained hermit saints and wild giants.[80] Wild men were frequently characterized by extreme hairiness covering their bodies (generally apart from their faces, hands, knees and elbows).[81] They might be naked, wear skins of animals or merely dress in skimpy foliage around their waists. They were 'monstrous' in their behaviour, but could be civilized through exposure to other lifestyles. Wild men bore tree trunks or clubs as weapons, and lived in the woods, away from civil people.[82] They were sometimes depicted with shields, clubs or staffs, and this imagery

75 Ibid., VII:vi.1.

76 Ibid., VII:vii.5; Louis Le Roy, *De la vicissitude ou variété des choses in l'vnivers* (Paris, 1579).

77 Pagden, *Fall*, 22. See also Rhodri Lewis, 'William Petty's Anthropology: Religion, Colonialism, and the Problem of Human Diversity', *Huntington Library Quarterly*, 74:2 (June 2011), 261–88, at 264–6.

78 Fernández-Armesto, *So You Think You're Human?*, 96.

79 For wild men in Greek and Roman works, see Roger Bartra, *Wild Men in the Looking Glass: The Mythic Origins of European Otherness*, trans. Carl T. Berrisford (Ann Arbor, MI: University of Michigan Press, 1997), chaps. 1–2.

80 Merry Wiesner-Hanks, *The Marvelous Hairy Girls: The Gonzales Sisters and Their Worlds* (New Haven, CT and London: Yale University Press, 2009), 32–55; Leitch, *Mapping Ethnography*, 39; Walter Stephens, *Giants in Those Days: Folklore, Ancient History, and Nationalism* (Lincoln, NE and London: University of Nebraska Press, 1989), 60–1; Bartra, *Wild Men*, 26–8.

81 Bartra, *Wild Men*, 88.

82 Susi Colin, 'The Wild Man and the Indian in Early 16th-Century Book Illustration', in *Indians and Europe: An Interdisciplinary Collection of Essays*, ed. Christian F. Feest (Aachen: Edition Herodot, 1987), 5–36, at 6–7.

sometimes decorated heraldic devices.[83] Other common characteristics included great strength, hairy bodies and living in forests.[84] In the late medieval period, traditional folkloric views of the wild man seem to have shifted from negative to positive.[85]

At the turn of the sixteenth century, the earliest printed imagery of the Amerindians conflated these peoples with the ancient, wild ancestors of the Germanic peoples. The recently re-discovered text of the Roman senator and historian Tacitus' *Germania*, first printed in the 1470s, contrasted the urban and civilized Romans with the tribes of the *Germanii* who inhabited fields and forests and had neither laws nor written language. German humanists like Conrad Celtis turned the lack of the trappings of civilization into a virtue by identifying their own sylvan ancestors with the mythological wild man, and championed them as simple and unspoiled. Celtis used this interpretation to argue against Italian and papal influence on German affairs.[86] The earliest German woodcuts of Amerindians 'began life', as art historian Stephanie Leitch put it, 'in the boots of the invented and conventional persona of the wild man'.[87] Illustrations to early editions of Vespucci's letters depicted these peoples with little or no clothing and long, curly hair and beards when, in fact, these peoples typically had straight hair and no beards.[88]

Conclusion: Continuities and ruptures from the late middle ages to the sixteenth century

Late medieval scholars stitched together their views on the nature of humanity at the earth's climatic fringes using multiple authorities and

[83] Richard Bernheimer, *Wild Men in the Middle Ages: A Study in Art, Sentiment, and Demonology* (Cambridge, MA: Harvard University Press, 1952), chap. 6. For illustrations, see Bartra, *Wild Men*, Figs 2, 4–5, 33–4, 48–50, 51–3, 57, 83–8, 90–3. The shields are usually in the form of coats of arms, flanked by wild men or women.

[84] Bernheimer, *Wild Men*, 23. For types of wild men, see Hayden White, 'The Forms of Wildness: Archaeology of an Idea', in *The Wild Man Within: An Image in Western Thought from the Renaissance to Romanticism*, ed. Edward Dudley and Maximillian E. Novak (Pittsburgh: University of Pittsburgh Press, 1972), 3–38, at 10–28.

[85] Stephens, *Giants*, 59.

[86] This movement is analysed in detail in Leitch, *Mapping Ethnography*, 41–53. My overview draws on 41–5. For the rediscovery of Tacitus's *Germania* and constructions of 'Germanness', see also Ulinka Rublack, *Dressing Up: Cultural Identity in Renaissance Europe* (Oxford: Oxford University Press, 2010), 127–39.

[87] Leitch, *Mapping Ethnography*, 38–9.

[88] See Vespucci, *De novo mundo* (Rostock, 1505), title-page; idem, *Van den nyge[n] Insulen und landen* (Magdeburg, 1506) and idem, *Diss büchlin sagt*... (Strasbourg, 1509), sigs B.i.*v*, D.iiii.*r* and E.iiii.*v*.

interpretative frameworks for understanding the nature of the human, the reasons for human variation, and the boundaries between human, monster and animal. While this bricolage of interpretative tools intersected with and at times blended into one another, they did not always overlay one another smoothly. During the course of late Renaissance and the early modern period (c.1450–1750), multiple and sometimes contradictory meanings emerged for such concepts as blackness, savagery and tropicality, sometimes in the same text. The humanist and physician Hartmann Schedel, for example, in his influential Christian cosmography known as the *Nuremberg Chronicle* (1493), described a people who lived by the River Ganges, opposite the Earthly Paradise, who ate nothing, but drank through a straw and sustained themselves on the smells of apples and flowers, thus illuminating the extremes thought to co-exist in the east.[89] As Stephanie Leitch has shown, the world map in the *Chronicle* integrated Christian chronology, ancient secular geography and information from recent travels along the west coast of Africa.[90] Monstrous individuals in Europe, such as dwarves and hirsutes, might find themselves on retainer at princely courts where, hovering somewhere between subjects and objects, they could find themselves listed amongst a prince's retainers or 'inventoryed' in a catalogue.[91]

Sixteenth-century scholars inherited from the Middle Ages a framework for understanding human difference that was environmental, social and malleable, rather than biological and fixed. Classical writings about airs, waters and places allowed readers of travel and geographical literature to draw connections between a region's location, climate, environment, foodstuffs and the physical, mental and moral states of its inhabitants, but these works also raised problems of ontology. Christian bodies and behaviours might change under the influence of new geographical spaces; questions were asked about possible threats to their bodies. Those who wished to encourage colonists might point out similarities between the climate of a region and some part of Europe.[92] Could one mitigate against undesirable

[89] Hartmann Schedel, *Chronicle of the World: The Complete and Annotated Nuremberg Chronicle of 1493*, introduction and appendix by Stephan Füssel (Cologne and London: Taschen, 2001), Blatten XII*r*-XIII*r*. For discussion, see ibid., 636–7 and Christoph Reske, . . . *The Production of Schedel's Nuremberg Chronicle* (Wiesbaden: Harrassowitz, 2000).

[90] For a discussion of the map's ethnography in the context of the *Chronicle*, see Leitch, *Mapping Ethnography*, chap. 2. See also Timothy Husband, *The Wild Man: Medieval Myth and Symbolism* (New York, NY: Metropolitan Museum of Art, 1980), 48.

[91] Touba Ghadessi, 'Inventoried Monsters: Dwarves and Hirsutes at Court', *Journal of the History of Collections*, 23:2 (2011), 267–81.

[92] For English examples, see Chaplin, *Subject Matter*, 133–7.

changes, and even change the local population's temperament for the better?[93] Just as those places that were extreme in geography were believed to engender monsters, so were those that were extreme in terms of climate. What, then, was the nature of the boundary between normal space and monster space?

The ramifications of what I shall call spatial thinking – conceptions of space and through space – about human difference were extensive. Ultimately, the natures of human souls and intellects and their capacities for improvement were determined through observations of their bodies, behaviours and environments. Competing interpretative frameworks raised questions about the relative influence of polity, environment and immutable physiological qualities; and about people's natures as products of the political systems and social environments in which they lived, as the mutable results of the interaction between their humours and their environments, and as beings fixed into particular mental capacities and physical attributes for one of a variety of reasons, such as the alleged curse of Ham.

As Nicolás Wey Gómez has shown, late medieval European cosmological thinking brought together geography and politics in a unified knowledge system, whereby 'natural places were thought to assign nations their unique positions in a hierarchy of polities as well as their roles in a teleological history'.[94] The relative southerliness of the western lands reached by Spanish oceanic travellers in the decades around 1500, and the elaboration of a political philosophy of tropicality, underwrote European juridical and scholastic elaborations of the nature of the inhabitants of the Americas and the proper administration of empire.[95] By implication, political – and colonial – administration had to be tuned to suit the humours exhibited by the local inhabitants. In this way, geography and politics were intricately intertwined in the machine of the world.[96]

These analyses were inflected by what we might call the Renaissance gridding of the world: the wider application to world maps of a coordinate system devised by Ptolemy, the second century CE Greco-Egyptian geographer and mathematician. This system made geographical relationships between distant peoples visible in a new way, enabling viewers to see at a glance the relative latitudes of different regions. When combined with

[93] For environmental aspects of native health and temperament, see, e.g., José Pardo-Tomás, '"Antiguamente vivían más sanos que ahora": Explanations of Native Mortality in the *Relaciones Geográficas de Indias*', in *Medical Cultures of the Early Modern Spanish Empire*, ed. John Slater et al. (Farnham and Burlington, VT: Ashgate, 2014), 41–65.

[94] Wey Gómez, *Tropics of Empire*, 69. [95] Ibid.

[96] For colonial geopolitics, see ibid., 61, 69.

geohumoral thinking, this map projection made implicit claims about life in different parts of the world, assumptions that underlay spatial thinking in a variety of geographical genres.[97] Maps depicting iconic types for the inhabitants of different parts of the world made this approach to human variance visible in distinct ways.

Commentators on the Americas wrestled with the challenge of selecting the appropriate framework for its peoples. The nudity of the inhabitants on northeast South America on maps might be read as a sign that they either lived in paradise or that they were barbarous and lacked the most elementary foundations of civilized life. While the distance of Peru from Europe, and its latitude, suggested the presence of a barbarous society, the city of Cuzco was at high altitude, and thus had a temperate climate. Similarly, despite the presence of impressive architecture in Tenochtitlàn (present-day Mexico City), the inhabitants were, from a Christian perspective, idolaters and pagans. Although a classical proverb that was well known in the Renaissance asserted that to wash an Ethiopian white was to labour in vain, if Ethiopians were to migrate to cooler climes then could not their blackness be 'washed' away across generations? The history of early modern ethnological writing is, to an extent, the history of competing ethnological frameworks, sometimes utilized by individual authors to promote a particular agenda.

Scholars and travellers reflecting on the inhabitants of new worlds instituted changes to their knowledge-making practices and representational genres while, simultaneously, sustaining interpretative traditions as they sought to see and to read new peoples through these traditions. This was not an either/or binary, but one in which numerous possibilities were ever-present in the artefacts, images, and texts with which travellers, scholars, and artisans framed worlds. Richard Krautheimer, writing about the iconography of medieval architecture, famously proposed that multiple interpretations 'all "vibrated" simultaneously in the mind of educated Early Christian and medieval men', a vibration that he termed 'medieval "multi-think"'.[98] Krautheimer argued that this vibration settled in the era of the

[97] For geohumoralism or 'regionally framed humoralism', see Floyd-Wilson, *English Ethnicity and Race*, 2. For the reception of Ptolemy in the Renaissance, Patrick Gautier Dalché, 'The Reception of Ptolemy's *Geography*'.

[98] For a similar point in relation to early modern science, see Surekha Davies, 'Science, New Worlds, and the Classical Tradition: An Introduction', *Journal of Early Modern History*, 18:1–2 (2014), 1–13, at 4. For medieval multi-think, see Richard Krautheimer, *Studies in Early Christian, Medieval, and Renaissance Art* (New York, NY/London: New York University Press/University of London Press, 1969), 149–50.

Renaissance. Similarly, in the traditional meta-narratives in the history of science, the notion of such a march towards certainty has held similar sway. Recent scholarship on early modern science, however, has revealed the protean nature of knowledge-making in this period.[99] Multiple interpretations of new knowledge were possible for Renaissance Europeans as a whole, and one might say that individual actors continued to practise 'multi-think'.

How then did Renaissance 'multi-think' shape frameworks for thinking about human diversity? Scholars, travellers and readers frequently engaged deeply and reflexively with empirical information and textual authorities in their attempts to better understand the natural world. This could lead to the breaking of existing categories and intellectual assumptions. At the same time, the existing frameworks were not – and probably never were – ossified frames that could not be molded or expanded without collapsing. Rather, the classical tradition was a living tradition in this period. Renaissance 'multi-think' was a necessity born of social, religious, political, cultural, and intellectual shifts that unfolded independently of one another. The shock of the new lay, at times, in its capacity to add fuel to old world flames.

[99] See especially Pamela H. Smith, 'Science on the Move: Recent Trends in the History of Early Modern Science', *Renaissance Quarterly*, 69:2 (2009), 345–75.

2 | Atlantic empires, map workshops and Renaissance geographical culture

Renaissance illustrated maps were devised in cosmopolitan workshops where artisans and scholars drew from printed and manuscript travel accounts, images and other maps. These maps were often intended for international and even transimperial audiences. The maps in this book were not used by mariners but rather by scholars, merchants, nobility and royalty, and often by individuals who had an interest in trade or empire. Analyzing evidence for the readership of these works across Europe would constitute a book in itself. In this chapter, after outlining the transnational settings in which maps were produced and viewed, I focus on examples of map viewers in two settings: the Low Countries – the locus of the most prolific producers and viewers of illustrated maps – and England – the least prolific sixteenth-century mapmaking locale featured in this book but one in which map consumption was enthusiastic and extensive. World maps and maps of the parts of the world (eventually known as continents) that these viewers consulted functioned as organizing devices that helped them to compare the world's regions and peoples.

Regions of production

The Iberian powers dominated oceanic exploration in the first half of the sixteenth century.[1] The Treaty of Tordesillas (1494), based in part on papal bulls and signed between Spain and Portugal, divided the new discoveries between the two kingdoms. Incursions into these regions by other European nations were forbidden, although often unpreventable in practice.

[1] The literature is extensive. For an introduction to the Portuguese empire, see Anthony R. Disney, *A History of Portugal and the Portuguese Empire*, 2 vols., I (New York, NY: Cambridge University Press, 2009); Francisco Bethencourt and Diogo Ramada Curto, eds., *Portuguese Oceanic Expansion, 1400–1800* (Cambridge: Cambridge University Press, 2007). For the Spanish empire, see J. H. Elliott, *Spain, Europe, and the Wider World, 1500–1800* (New Haven, CT and London: Yale University Press, 2009); Hugh Thomas, *Rivers of Gold: The Rise of the Spanish Empire, from Columbus to Magellan* (New York, NY: Weidenfeld & Nicolson, 2003); Henry Kamen, *Empire: How Spain Became a World Power, 1492–1763* (London: HarperCollins, 2003).

Maps were crucial for constructing these (imaginary) empires on paper. In the 1410s, the Portuguese Crown had established the Casa da Ceuta, an institution for regulating overseas trade and supporting the technical skills necessary for oceanic travel. By the sixteenth century this institution was called the Casa da Índia, and was based in Lisbon.[2] From around the 1480s, Portuguese official chartmaking was regulated by a separate body eventually known as the Armazém da Guiné, Mina e Índia. Access to sensitive information was controlled: government officials regularly ordered the destruction of certain categories of map and restricted the ownership of maps and globes by private individuals.[3]

In Spain, the state attempted to regulate mapmaking, exploration and trade via the Casa de la Contratación, or Board of Indies Trade, in Seville, which supervised activities in the Americas and also in the Canary Islands, Barbary and Spanish stations on the coast of Africa. Founded in 1503 and modelled on the Portuguese Armazém, the Casa administered ships and supplies for voyages, and distributed the booty that returned. The Casa's Hydrographic Office and School of Navigation were established in 1508. As in Portugal, these institutions attempted to protect and standardize cartography and navigational techniques by training pilots and by establishing processes for improving charts and navigational instruments in the light of the experiences of each returning voyage.[4] Accurate geographical information was also important for the practices of diplomacy through which the Crown laid claim to new lands and refuted the claims of others, particularly of the Portuguese.[5]

2 Harald Kleinschmidt, *Ruling the Waves: Emperor Maximilian I, the Search for Islands and the Transformation of the European World Picture c.1500* (Utrecht: 't Goy-Houten, 2008), 102, 110–14; *RC x, LD*, 12 and, for the papal bulls, see documents 5–7 and 12.

3 Maria Fernanda Alegria et al., 'Portuguese Cartography in the Renaissance', in *HC3*, I, 975–1068, at 1003–5; Avelino Teixeira da Mota, 'Some Notes on the Organization of Hydrographical Services in Portugal Before the Beginning of the Nineteenth Century', *IM*, 28 (1976), 51–60, at 51; José Manuel Garcia and Max Justo Guedes, *Tesouros da cartografia portuguese* (Lisbon: Edições Inapa, 1997), 15–17 and 129–30.

4 Antonio Barrera-Osorio, *Experiencing Nature: The Spanish American Empire and the Early Scientific Revolution* (Austin, TX: University of Texas Press, 2006), esp. chaps. 2–3; Alison Sandman, 'An Apologia for the Pilots' Charts: Politics, Projections and Pilots' Reports in Early Modern Spain', *IM*, 56:1 (2004), 7–22 at 7–10; Belén Rivera Novo and Luisa Martín-Merás, *Quatro siglos de cartografía en América* (Madrid: Mapfre, 1992), 65; 96–102; Alison Sandman, 'Spanish Nautical Cartography in the Renaissance', in *HC3*, I, 1095–142; María M. Portuondo, *Secret Science: Spanish Cosmography and the New World* (Chicago, IL and London: University of Chicago Press, 2009).

5 For illustrated maps as diplomatic gifts and political instruments, see Ricardo Cerezo Martínez, *La cartografía náutica española en los siglos XIV, XV, y XVI* (Madrid: CSIC, 1994), 180 and 258–60; Sandman, 'Spanish Nautical Cartography', 1096–7; Sandman, 'Mirroring the World: Sea

Iberian cartographers had privileged access to information from early voyages of exploration.[6] This made them attractive experts to foreign powers, and many Iberians worked outside their country of origin.[7] The master chart from which maps were made for Magellan's voyage (which left from Seville) was made by the Reinels of Portugal; the pilots' charts and navigational instruments were made by Diogo Ribeiro, another Portuguese cartographer.[8] Indeed, Ribeiro advised the Spanish delegation to the Treaty of Zaragoza negotiations with Portugal on the rightful ownership of the Moluccas, which took place at Badajoz, Spain and Elvas, Portugal between 1524 and 1529.[9]

Despite the fact that mapmaking took place in settings with particular imperial and mercantile concerns, the international traffic in maps and their makers brought about a common set of iconographic themes. Since foreign mapmakers often used local assistants for the illumination, lettering and even copying of maps, cartographic workshops were transnational and transimperial in nature in the strict sense of crossing political boundaries. For example, while the cartographers of the Norman manuscript works known as the Vallard and Hague atlases may have been Portuguese, their illuminators were probably French. Some maps drawn in Spain were printed elsewhere; Diego Gutiérrez's 1562 map of America rolled off the presses at Antwerp and was engraved by Hieronymous Cock, a Flemish artist.[10] Collaborative enterprises were rarely recorded in

Charts, Navigation, and Territorial Claims in Sixteenth-Century Spain', in Pamela H. Smith and Paula Findlen, eds., *Merchants & Marvels: Commerce, Science and Art in Early Modern Europe* (New York, NY and London: Routledge, 2002), 83–108, at 97–101. For royal interest in cartography, see Luisa Martín Merás, 'La cartografía de los descubrimientos en la epoca de Carlos V', in *Carlos V: La náutica y la navegación* (Barcelona: Lunwerg Editores, 2000), 75–94, at 91–3.

6 See Manuel Garcia and Justo Guedes, *Tesouros*, 146–7. For attempts to control knowledge, see Alison Sandman, 'Controlling Knowledge: Navigation, Cartography, and Secrecy in the Early Modern Spanish Atlantic', in *Science and Empire in the Atlantic World*, ed. James Delbourgo and Nicholas Dew (New York, NY and London: Routledge, 2008), 31–51.

7 For cartographers of maps discussed in this book, see e.g., L. A. Vigneras, 'The Cartographer Diogo Ribeiro', *IM*, 16 (1962), 76–83, at 76; Alegria et al., 'Portuguese Cartography', 987–9; Alison Sandman and Eric S. Ash, 'Trading Expertise: Sebastian Cabot between Spain and England', *Renaissance Quarterly*, 57 (2004), 813–46; Michel Mollat du Jourdin et al., *Sea Charts of the Early Explorers*, trans. L. le R. Dethan (New York, NY: Thames & Hudson, 1984), 226–7 (for Jean Rotz).

8 Barrera-Osorio, *Experiencing Nature*, 43.

9 See Surekha Davies, 'The Navigational Iconography of Diogo Ribeiro's 1529 Vatican Planisphere', *IM*, 55 (2003), 103–12, at 105.

10 Diego Gutiérrez, *Americae sive quartae orbis partis nova et exactissima descriptio* (Antwerp, 1562).

signatures on manuscript maps. While the master mapmaker signed some maps, unsigned ones from the same workshop may have been produced by assistants to be sold more cheaply.[11]

In the first half of the sixteenth century, centres of map printing in the German lands had fewer direct contacts with overseas regions than the Atlantic port cities of Portugal, Spain and France.[12] In the German-speaking regions, most maps illustrated with the world's peoples were produced in the area around the middle and upper Rhine from Duisburg in the north to Freiburg in the south. German explorers were few in number during this period, and the princes had little involvement in colonization.[13] Nevertheless, there was sufficient interest in the Americas and in the spices of the Far East for German merchants to help finance Portuguese expeditions in the early sixteenth century.[14] Travel narratives and artefacts from around the world flowed to the city of Augsburg, the base of the Fugger and Welser merchant families. Their factors or agents returned home not just with silks and spices, but also with marvellous *naturalia* and even with local inhabitants.[15] German princes both received Iberian manuscript maps as gifts and actively acquired them; Rhenish mapmakers used these manuscripts to devise their own, printed maps.[16] Although mapmakers from the Rhenish regions had few connections with colonial expansion or maritime circles, they did have close ties with humanist learning and the book trade. Through the medium of print, mapmakers from the German lands and the Low Countries encountered a broad range of ethnographic writing and picturing, not just of the Americas but also of Africa and Asia. The map publisher Cornelis Claesz also printed travel accounts, navigational works and

11 Corradino Astengo, 'The Renaissance Chart Tradition in the Mediterranean', in *HC3*, I, 174–262, at 189–90. For assistants, see Vincenç Roselló Verger, 'Cartes i atles portolans de les col•leciones espanyoles', in *Portolans procedents de col•leciones espanyoles, segles XV-XVII*, ed. Vincenç Roselló Verger and M. Carme Montaner i García (Barcelona: Institut Cartogràfic de Catalunya, 1995), 9-59, at 47, 363; for illuminations by different miniaturists, see Peter Barber, *The Queen Mary Atlas: Commentary* (London: Folio Society, 2005), 39; for map copyists, see Peter Barber, 'Review of Facsimile Edition of the Portolan Atlas of 1546 of Battista Agnese from the Russian National Library, St Petersburg', *IM*, 47 (1995), 196–7, at 197.

12 For overview, bibliography and a study of regional maps, see Peter H. Meurer, 'Cartography in the German Lands, 1450–1650', in *HC3*, II, 1172–245.

13 Meurer, 'Cartography in the German Lands', 1245.

14 See especially Christine R. Johnson, *The German Discovery of the World: Renaissance Encounters with the Strange and Marvelous* (Charlottesville, VA and London: University of Virginia Press, 2008) and also Kleinschmidt, *Ruling the Waves*, 182–4.

15 Leitch, *Mapping Ethnography*, 2.

16 For an example, see Chapter 3 in this book, near n. 101.

illustrated maps, running a workshop in which all of these modes cross-fertilized one another.[17]

In the first half of the sixteenth century, the Low Countries had similarly little direct involvement in transatlantic exploration, trade or imperial projects.[18] Many exotic goods arrived over land, and Dutch merchants collaborated with Iberian ones, financing ships that sailed under Portuguese and Spanish flags. By 1560, Antwerp had become one of the most populous cities in Europe, as well as an important commercial port and one of the foremost centres of cartography.[19] While only a few maps depicting Amerindians were printed there,[20] several prolific Amsterdam mapmakers began their careers in Antwerp.[21] From the 1580s, the mapmakers of Antwerp and Amsterdam produced a profusion of mostly printed world maps and maps of America for commercial printers rather than for official institutions. After the fall of Antwerp in 1585 to Spanish forces in the course of the Dutch Revolt (1565–1648), many Protestant map publishers, engravers and artists emigrated from Antwerp to Amsterdam.[22] These included Petrus Bertius, Cornelis Claesz, Jodocus Hondius the Elder and his sons Jodocus and Henricus, Pieter van den Keere and Petrus Plancius. Some, including Bertius, Van den Keere and the Hondius family, settled in England before moving to Amsterdam,[23] strengthening contacts and markets in England.[24] From the 1590s, Amsterdam produced the greatest number of illustrated maps of anywhere in Europe.[25]

Mapmakers were not, of course, a hermetically sealed group of artisans and scholars, but rather an amorphous body that intersected and collaborated with practitioners of other knowledge-making endeavours, including

[17] For Claesz, see *MCN*, VIII; Sutton, *Dutch Prints.*

[18] Kees Zandvliet, 'Mapping the Dutch World Overseas in the Seventeenth Century', *HC3*, II, 1433–62, at 1449.

[19] Jonathan Israel, *The Dutch Republic: Its Rise, Greatness, and Fall, 1477–1806* (Oxford: Clarendon Press, 1998), 114–8; Cornelis Koeman et al., 'Commercial Cartography and Map Production in the Low Countries, 1500–ca.1672', *HC3*, II, 1296–383, at 1299.

[20] Koeman et al., 'Commercial Cartography', appendix 44.4 lists six world maps and two maps of America published in Antwerp c.1540–1576.

[21] Cartographers who published illustrated works at Antwerp include Petrus Plancius, Abraham Ortelius and Gerard and Cornelis de Jode.

[22] Ibid., 1299–1300. For a political overview, see Graham Darby, 'Narrative of Events', in Graham Darby, *The Origins and Development of the Dutch Revolt*, ed. Graham Darby (London: Routledge, 2001), 8–28, at 16–27.

[23] *MCN*, VIII, 23: both Bertius and Van den Keere were linked to the Hondius family by marriage; Van den Keere's sister Colette married Jodocus Hondius the Elder.

[24] For Low Countries maps in England, see Laurence Worms, 'The London Map Trade to 1640', in *HC3*, II, 1693–721, at 1694–5.

[25] Koeman et al., 'Commercial Cartography', 1305; *MCN*, III, 3–7.

artists and naturalists.[26] A letter that the Antwerp-based cartographer Ortelius wrote to the Flemish naturalist Carolus Clusius illuminates the protean character of cartographic authorship and the connections between cartography and other disciplines. Clusius had played a crucial part in the collation of information for Ortelius's 1571 wall map of Spain, a service for which Ortelius felt much gratitude. Ortelius attached much importance to the precise citation of cartographic agency and empirical observation. Ortelius sent Clusius an addition he wished to add to the map: 'by the care and from the travels of Carolus Clusius of Arras'.[27] He also noted that he wished to include Clusius in the atlas's *Catalogus auctorum* or list of authors for his 1570 atlas, *Theatrum orbis terrarum*, 'for the title will be absolutely true since you are indeed the maker and frankly speaking you have also enriched and published the map and without you this map would be far less complete'.[28]

Ortelius's decision to claim as author the traveller who added eyewitness emendations to Ortelius's existing map was a creative way of claiming the authority of the eyewitness and the authority of the mapmaker were one and the same. It throws up the anxieties inherent in the epistemology of mapmaking: how much of the land depicted had been traversed by someone whose knowledge was embodied in the map? At what level of detail had this area been surveyed? How precisely had the eyewitnesses' experiences been represented on the map?

Users of illustrated maps

In an era when exploration through geographical space and, through classical archaeology, time, were throwing up large quantities of people, ideas and things for perusal by antiquarians, humanists, geographers and students of the natural world, classificatory genres exploded in many formats, from atlases to *Wunderkammern*.[29] Dedicatory epistles to the reader in contemporary manuscript and printed maps and atlases reveal that patrons and intended users fall into three broad and sometimes overlapping groups: scholars, burghers (particularly merchants and town

[26] For artists as knowledge-makers, see Dackerman, ed., *Prints*. For artists' contributions to maps, see Rosen, *Mapping of Power*, *passim*.

[27] 'ex diligentia et peregrinatione Caroli Clusii Atreb'. For this letter, see Schilder, *MCN*, II, 99.

[28] The letter was first published in F. W. T. Hunger, 'Vier onuitgegeven brieven van Abraham Ortelius aan Carolus Clusius', in *De Gulden Passer*, 3 (1925), 208–11. The original is Leiden, Universiteitsbibliotheek, letter of 14 October 1569. The letter is illustrated in MCN, II, 102.

[29] For genres of reference texts, see Blair, *Too Much To Know*.

officials) and landed and courtly viewers, including royalty. Evidence for the uses and users of maps and atlases is scattered among wills, official documents, paintings, inventories, published texts and the maps themselves.[30]

Readers in the Low Countries had both good access to a wide variety of early printed *Americana* and high urban literacy rates (up to 50 percent among men in Antwerp in the sixteenth century and in Amsterdam in the early seventeenth). More than half the oldest private libraries in the northern provinces held works about the Americas, which were twice as common as works on Asia.[31] This contrasts with France, where there were twice as many geography books on Turkey as on America, as well as more books on the Caribbean, Portuguese colonies, Asian nations and the Holy Land, than on mainland America.[32] Additionally, from the late sixteenth century, ships from the northern provinces of the Low Countries increasingly travelled beyond Europe: the Dutch East India Company was founded in 1602; the Dutch West India Company, in 1621.[33] Dutch map-viewing audiences thus became increasingly engaged in global imperial and trading concerns.

Printed maps from the Rhenish area, Antwerp and Amsterdam were produced in large numbers for the open market. Most large wall maps survive in very few copies, and some are completely lost.[34] Maps hung on walls were typically replaced as newer maps appeared, or as they became battered under the onslaught of soot and passing bodies. Such maps, when replaced, would sometimes circulate in less wealthy households.[35] The storage methods in scholarly libraries have preserved a few wall maps that would otherwise be completely lost to us. The sole surviving copies of Martin Waldseemüller's gigantic 1507 and 1516 wall maps, for example, come from the library of the contemporary globe-maker Johannes Schöner, where both maps had been folded and bound into a folio which protected them from the wear and tear normally suffered by wall maps.[36]

30 Tolias, 'Maps in Renaissance Libraries and Collections', *HC3*, I, 637-60, at 643: purchased works may also be traced to collectors via the provenance notes of the libraries that hold them today. See ibid., *passim* for more examples.

31 Benjamin Schmidt, *Innocence Abroad: The Dutch Imagination and the New World, 1570–1670* (Cambridge: Cambridge University Press, 2001), 5–8; for Dutch-American interactions and the publication of American travel narratives, see 12–54.

32 Lucien Febvre and Henri-Jean Martin, *The Coming of the Book: The Impact of Printing 1450–1800*, trans. David Gerard (London: Foundations of History Library, 1976), 282.

33 Zandvliet, 'Mapping the Dutch World', 1433–4.

34 *MCN*, VII, 329; Koeman et al., 'Commercial Cartography', 1342.

35 Woodward, 'Maps as Prints', 75–102.

36 John W. Hessler and Chet Van Duzer, *Seeing the World Anew: The Radical Vision of Martin Waldseemüller's 1507 & 1516 World Maps* (Delray Beach, FL: Levenger Press in association with the Library of Congress, 2012); S. J. Fischer and R. Wieser, *The Oldest Map with the Name*

From the early seventeenth century, there was a large market for printed maps in Amsterdam.[37] Large, illustrated wall maps hung in the houses of wealthy burghers, merchants and governmental and commercial offices.[38] By the 1660s, each office of the Dutch East India (VOC) and West India Companies (WIC) might have had as many as sixty wall maps and landscape paintings on display.[39] For those who lacked the space to unfurl a whole map across a wall, methods of dissecting,[40] storing and displaying maps were developed.[41] One traveller to Amsterdam commented that even Dutch cobblers and tailors possessed wall-maps, and through them knew the history of the New World.[42]

Written evidence of precisely what map viewers wanted out of large illustrated maps at small scales – maps that could not be used for way-finding – is scattered, but consistently suggests that viewers expected such maps to facilitate comparative analysis. At times, the design of manuscript and printed maps was shaped by a patron. Archival sources and inscriptions on maps show how these works were sometimes illustrated in ways that served the construction of political power and identities. In 1556, the Privy Council of Mechlin gave the mapmaker Hendrik Terbruggen, also known as Pontanus, a patent:

> to print and engrave a world map in the form of an imperial eagle, adorned with the names of princes, potentates, dignitaries and offices concerning the said empire, with ancient and modern imperial cities, organized in alphabetical order to facilitate their finding thereof, together [with] the escutcheons and coats of arms of each, with personifications of the seven planets and a border in the grotesque style.[43]

America of the Year 1507 and the Carta Marina of the Year 1516 (Innsbruck: Wagner'sche Universitäts-Buchhandlung, 1903), 4–5.

37 Koeman et al., 'Commercial Cartography', 1306.

38 Ibid., 1342.

39 Kees Zandfliet, *Mapping for Money: Maps, Plans and Topographic Paintings and Their Role in Dutch Overseas Expansion during the 16th and 17th Centuries* (Amsterdam, 1998), 227, with more examples on 217–27; Zandvliet, 'Mapping the Dutch World', 1458.

40 Cutting a large map into sections and mounting them on linen or boards.

41 Koeman et al., 'Commercial Cartography', 1343–4.

42 Kurt Schottmüller, 'Reiseeindrücke aus Danzig, Lübeck, Hamburg und Holland 1636. Nach dem neuentdeckten II Teil von Charles Ogiers Gesandtschaftstagebuch', *Zeitschrift des westpreussischen Geschichtsverein*, 52 (1910), 199–273, at 260, noted in Alpers, *Art of Describing*, 159.

43 Brussels, Algemeen Rijksarchief, Geheime Raad, Reg. 56, f.46*r*, transcribed in Schilder, *MCN*, II, 32: '. . .pour imprimer et graver une mappe du monde, en forme d'un aigle de l'empire, aorné des noms des princes, potentatz, dignitez et offices concernans ledict empire, avec les villes imperiales anchiennes et modernes, colloquées selon l'ordre de l'alphabeth, pour les trouver plus aysément, ensemble les blasons et armoyeries de chascune d'icelles, avec figuraige des sept planètes et d'une bordure crotesque'.

Such a map would facilitate the comparison of the world's empires, their administrative structures and the antiquity of their cities. The alphabetical order suggests that this information was gathered together in a list, perhaps along the borders of the map, indicating that the patron intended for the map to be an aid to reflection on the diversity of human civilization. The escutcheons and coats of arms would have helped viewers to better visualize and retain the salient differences between empires.

A contract dated 19 November 1598, between the Amsterdam cartographer Henricus van Langren and a certain Lenert Rens, betrays an almost authorial competitiveness in a client's stipulations for an illustrated map. Van Langren's task was:

> to make and to engrave .... a map of the whole world, as large as the large map of Petrus Plancius ...; further that the same [map] shall be engraved better and more correctly, and cut deeper, than the aforesaid largest map of Petrus Plancius and, moreover, shall be adorned more copiously with curious figures than any map hitherto published.[44]

The deeper cuts would have necessitated thicker and more expensive plates, which could then be re-used to make more impressions. The contract stipulated that 2,000 copies were to be delivered to Rens; that Van Langren was permitted to keep 400 copies; and that Rens 'reserved the right to take the plates for himself against the payment to Van Langren of an indemnity of 1,100 florins'.[45] In addition to specifying a particular model – a map by Plancius that does not survive – the contract suggests an atmosphere of commercial rivalry in which the more elaborate the iconography the better. Curiosity, moreover, was a habit of mind that could be turned into commercial success for purveyors of maps as much as of natural curiosities.[46] A further requirement was that 'the person of Lenert Rans aforesaid... shall be portrayed, in as lifelike a manner as possible, on the same map'.[47]

44 The document is partially transcribed and translated in *MC*, II, 41: 'te maecken ende snyden .... een caerte van de geheele werelt, zoo groot als de groote caerte van Petro Plancio .... item dat d'selve beter, correcter ende dieper sal gesneden wesen, als die voors. grootste caerte van Petro Plancio, ende mede verciert met veelder curieuse figueren, als eenige die tot noch toe int licht zijn geweest'. Here and elsewhere, I have made small revisions to the translation. See also *MCN*, III, 28–31 for a discussion and a reproduction of the document.

45 *MC*, II, 41; the terminology is Wieder's. The 2,400 promised copies survived to the early twentieth century only in an incomplete original of four damaged sheets, all of which were destroyed in the Second World War.

46 For the part played by curiosity and commerce in natural history, see Margócsy, *Commercial Visions*.

47 *MC*, II, 41: 'Sal oock den persoon van Lenert Rans voorn. soo veel doenlijck is nae t'leven inde zelve caerte geconterfeyt zijn.'

When maps were produced for specific commissions, parts played by clients and mapmakers in the final shape and content of the maps cannot be easily disentangled.[48] A contract for the production of four *mappae-mundi* in Barcelona in 1399–1400 reveals that Baldassare degli Ubriachi, a Florentine ivory and jewel merchant, stipulated how they should be made by two cartographers, Jacme Riba and Francesco Becaria. Riba was to work on them first. They were then to be collected by Simone d'Andrea Bellandi, a Florentine banker based in Barcelona. Bellandi was to pass them to Becaria to add the illustrations.[49] The terms of the agreement and records of a subsequent dispute indicate that the maps were the work of two separate workshops and that Becaria costed every illustrative detail, for which he demanded payment. Moreover, Ubriachi's reply suggests that, despite his detailed instructions (which included the provision of a model map), the maps were not executed to his satisfaction: he claimed that the maps contained errors.[50]

For sixteenth-century English geographers and promoters of oceanic exploration, maps were vital reading tools with which to make sense of travel and geographical literature and to agitate for greater English participation in voyages of exploration. As Lesley B. Cormack put it, '[t]he study of geography was essential to the creation of an ideology of imperialism in early modern England'.[51] The Elizabethan polymath and enthusiast for English imperial activity John Dee observed that maps were used by:

> some, to beautifie their halls, parlers, chambers, galeries, studies, or libraries with, other some, for thinges, past, as battels fought .... Some other, presently to vewe the large dominion of the Turke, the wide empire of the Moschouite, and the litle morsell of ground, where Christendome (by profession) is certainly knowen.... some, for one purpose, and some, for another, liketh, loueth, getteth, and vseth, mappes, chartes, & georaphicall globes. Of whose vse, to speake sufficiently, would require a booke peculier.[52]

Such observations reveal that maps led viewers to think about their own kingdoms, and about Europe itself, in a broader, comparative context. Dee,

48 Astengo, 'Renaissance Chart Tradition', 178. For Venetian examples, see Barber, 'Facsimile Edition', 197.

49 R. A. Skelton, 'A Contract for World Maps at Barcelona, 1399–1400', *IM*, 22 (1968), 107–13, at 107–8.

50 Ibid., 108–9.

51 Lesley B. Cormack, *Charting an Empire: Geography at the English Universities, 1580–1620* (Chicago, IL: University of Chicago Press, 1997), 1.

52 John Dee, *The Elements of Geometrie of Euclide* (London, 1570), preface, sig. A4*r*.

and perhaps many other readers, reflected on the differences between the world's kingdoms and empires, and on the relatively minor political reach of European kingdoms in the first two decades of the sixteenth century. Wall maps allowed one to gain knowledge of the entire world at a glance, and their selections of information were authoritative.

In England, the use of maps for the teaching of geography, history and scripture, and as political and military aids, was encouraged.[53] In his treatise on the education of a monarch, Thomas Elyot, former secretary to the Privy Council under Cardinal Wolsey, wrote the following of 'cosmographie by materiall figures and instrumentes':

> what pleasure is it in one houre to beholde those realmes, cities, sees, ryuers and mountaynes, that vneth in an olde mannes life can nat be iournaide and pursued. What incredible delite is taken in beholding the diuersities of people, beastis, foules, fisshes, trees, fruites and herbes; to knowe the sondry maners and conditions of people and the varietie of their natures, and that in a warme studie or perler, without perill of the see or daunger of longe and paynfull iourneys. I cannot tell what more pleasure should happen to a gentle wit, than to behold in his own house everything that within all the world is contained.[54]

For both Dee and Elyot, maps facilitated what one might call a panoptical view of the globe, one which would have been impractical for a scholar or statesman to seek safely or speedily in person. Instead, maps provided an authoritative selection of information, facilitating the painless and pleasant comparison of the world's flora, fauna and human folk. Since seeing and reflecting on the whole world with one's own eyes was a practical impossibility, works of reference allowed viewers to extend their knowledge beyond their physical grasp; giving over some of the decision-making to someone else was a necessary compromise.

Some maps illustrated 'thinges, past, as battels fought'.[55] Here, Dee echoes a common view among early modern scholars: the centrality of geography for the comprehension of history. On the frontispiece of Abraham Ortelius's atlas of the classical world, *Parergon*, appears the motto 'Geography is the eye of history'. Ortelius elaborated this point in the title he devised for his 1571 wall map of Spain: 'A new map of Spain, more correct than others, and enriched in very many places; and with the ancient

[53] See esp. Lesley B. Cormack, 'Maps as Educational Tools in the Renaissance', in *HC3*, I, 622–36.

[54] Thomas Elyot, *The Boke Named the Gouernor* (London, 1531), f. 37*r-v*. See also Peter Barber, 'Mapmaking in England, ca. 1470–1650', in *HC3*, II, 1589–669, at 1598–9.

[55] Dee, *Geometrie*, preface, sig. A4*r*; cited in full in Tolias, 'Maps in Renaissance Libraries', at 638.

names of almost all regions, tribes, towns, rivers and mountains added, more suitable for the study of antiquity and for the reading of historical works than those published up to now'.[56] Sir Walter Ralegh's preparatory materials for his gargantuan *History of the World* included a notebook in which he sketched copiously annotated maps.[57]

The capacity of maps to aid comparative analysis was one of the reasons why studying them was widely held to be important for the education of children and statesmen. The scholar Constantijn Huygens, secretary to the statholder of the Dutch Republic, believed that maps would help his sons Christiaan and Constantijn, aged ten and eleven, future poet and natural philosopher respectively, to understand geography. The elder Huygens noted in 1638 that 'to encourage them even more, I had the four parts of the world by Willem Blaeu mounted in my entrance hall, where they often played, in order to provide them with a fixed image of the state of the world and its divisions'.[58] A study of Antwerp art inventories from the first half of the seventeenth century revealed that some 175 out of 1,570 recorded maps were displayed on walls.[59] Since the map trade was centred in Amsterdam in this period, the figures there might well be higher. Such maps were the speciality of Dutch publishers, and their finely engraved and richly illustrated world maps entered collections throughout Europe.

Maps also helped policy-makers to conceptualize the challenges of the New World. The Anglican minister, Oxford scholar and apologist for English imperial expansion Richard Hakluyt the Younger used maps for rhetorical and practical purposes. Hakluyt recorded that a version of Sebastian Cabot's world map 'is to be seene in her Majesties privee gallerie

[56] Schilder, *MCN*, II, 99: 'Hispaniarum nova descriptio, hactenus editis castigatior, et plurimis locis auctior, et additis ubique fere regionum, populorum, urbium, fluviorum et montium priscis nominibus, ad antiquitatis studium, et lectionum historiarum multo accomodatior'.

[57] BL-Mss, Add. MS. 57555. Sir Walter Ralegh's notebook. For mapmaking and note-taking by Ortelius and by Ralegh, see Popper, *Ralegh's History of the World*, chap. 3.

[58] Arthur Eyffinger, *Huygens Herdacht. Catalogus bij de tentoonstelling in de Koninklijke Bibliotheek ter gelegenheid van de 300ste sterfdag van Constantijn Huygens* (The Hague: De Bibliotheek, 1987), 126: 'Om haer meer ende meer daerin te stijven dede ick in mijn voorhuys, daer sij veeltijds speelden, ophangen de 4 deelen vande Wereld van Willem Blaeuw, daerbij sij een' vaste gestaltenisse van 'swerelds maecksel ende verdeelinghe in den sinn kregen'. The translation is from *MCN*, V, 101–2. These maps may well have been Blaeu's 1608 wall maps, or, more likely, the most recent reissues by Henricus Hondius; See *MCN*, V, 102, for the latter identification; the states of Blaeu's wall maps are listed at 77–89.

[59] *MCN*, VI, 44; for examples, see 45–6. For extracts which provide specific information about a map, see ibid., appendix, 50–4. The data came from the first five volumes of Erik Duverger, *Antwerpse kunstinventarissen uit de zeventiende eeuw* (Brussels: AWLSK, 1984–); many more have since been published.

at Westminster, and in many other ancient merchants houses'. He related how the Florentine explorer Giovanni da Verrazzano gave Henry VIII an 'old excellent mappe' which was presently in the study of John Locke, and noted that Elizabeth I's private gallery contained a globe that might also have belonged to Verrazzano. Verrazzano had presented the isthmus between the Atlantic and the Pacific in northeastern North America as extremely narrow, a perspective that spurred English colonization attempts in the far north of the Americas. Such maps and globes were important tools with which Elizabeth I and her advisors made choices about English overseas expansion.[60] While England was not a key mapmaking centre in the sixteenth and early seventeenth centuries, the English court attracted a number of overseas cartographers in search of royal patronage, including Sebastian Cabot, Jean Rotz and Diogo Homem.[61]

Scholars, merchants and leisured readers consulted maps alongside travel and geographical writing in order to contextualize information that was geographically specific, such as the locations of historical events or particular peoples. The Oxford scholar and clergyman Robert Burton wrote about maps in the same breath, as it were, as travel writing when he asserted that:

> To some kind of men it is an extraordinary delight to study, to looke vpon a geographicall mappe, and to behold, as it were, all the remote provinces, townes, citties of the world, and never to goe forth of the limits of his study.... What greater pleasure can there be then to view those elaborate maps of Ortelius, Mercator, Hondius, &c. To peruse those bookes of citties, put out by Braunus, and Hogenbergius. To reade those exquisite descriptions of Maginus, Munster, Merula, Boterus, Leander Albertus, Camden, Leo Afer, Adricomius, &c. Those famous expeditions of Christoph. Columbus, Americus Vesputius, Marcus Polus the Venetian, Lod. Vertomannus, Alosius Cadamustus, &c. Those acurat diaries of Portingalls, Hollanders, of Bartison, Oliuer à Nort, &c Hacluits *Voiages*, P. Martyr, Benzo, Lerius, Linchcostens relations .... to ... other remote places of the world ... those parts of America set out and curiously cut in pictures by Fratres à Bry.[62]

Burton provides here a litany of geographical genres: maps and atlases; the city-view compendia of the likes of Braun and Hogenberg; cosmographies

[60] For these examples, see Wallis, 'The Royal Map Collections of England', 463–4.

[61] For Cabot, see Sandman and Ash, 'Trading Expertise'; for Rotz, see *Boke of Idrography*, ed. Wallis.

[62] Robert Burton, *The Anatomy of Melancholy* (Oxford, 1621), 351–2.

and geographies that summarized the world in textual form; travellers' accounts and illustrated travel compendia. Some travel books and maps were printed to be consulted together. Matthias Ringmann and Martin Waldseemüller's *Cosmographiae introductio* or *Introduction to Cosmography* of 1507 refers frequently to the map that it accompanied.[63] When mapmakers chose to illustrate one type of people over another in a given area, they informed readers' views about which societies were most important.[64] In this way, maps inflected the reading of travel and geographical writing.

The scholarly regard for the synthetic gaze of the large format, small-scale map also informed the tastes of aristocrats educated by these scholars. The turn of the sixteenth century saw attempts among scholars and wealthy burghers to effect cultural shifts in the self-image of ruling aristocracies.[65] These efforts encouraged such kings as François I and Henri II of France to cultivate humanistic learning. One of the ways in which such monarchs demonstrated their erudition was by commissioning or purchasing the latest works of geography. In the long sixteenth century, the rapid remodelling of the shape of the earth's landmasses and the nature of its peoples made illustrated maps a way of demonstrating one's engagement with this expansion of knowledge. The Valencian palace of the duke of Calabria contained the type of study in which a noble might apply Renaissance scholarly ideals: 'next to a gallery of paintings of his ancestors, were gathered scientific instruments such as a world globe, two iron spheres of yellow and green, various navigation charts and plans of artillery equipment'.[66] By the mid-sixteenth century, maps were frequently seen at court at Dresden, Munich and Wolfenbüttel.[67]

The surviving painted map rooms at Italian courts demonstrate the cultural and political importance of maps in courtly settings. Wealthy patrons devoted significant time, money and space in their palaces in order

63 Matthias Ringmann and Martin Waldseemüller, *Cosmographie introductio quibusdam geometriae [ac] astronomiae principiis ad eam rem necesariis* (St. Dié, 1507).

64 For map-use among scholars, see, e.g., Catherine Delano Smith, 'Map Ownership in Sixteenth-Century Cambridge: The Evidence of Probate Inventories', *IM*, 47, (1995), 67–86, at 75–7.

65 See, e.g., Michael Wintroub, *A Savage Mirror: Power, Identity and Knowledge in Early Modern France* (Stanford, CA: Stanford University Press, 2006).

66 J. M. Morán and F. Checa, *El Coleccionismo en España: De la cámara de maravillas a la galería de pinturas* (Madrid: Cátedra, 1985), 45, my translation.

67 Meurer, 'Cartography in the German Lands', 1242. For maps made for royal patrons, see Helen Wallis, 'Sixteenth-Century Maritime Manuscript Atlases for Special Presentation', in *Images of the World: The Atlas through History*, ed. John A. Wolter and Ronald E. Grim (Washington, DC: Library of Congress, 1997), 3–29.

to assemble distinctive, graphic ways of envisioning the world and its treasures, and to place themselves symbolically at the centre of it all. Numerous painted map cycles were commissioned for magnificent public rooms in the *palazzi* of the Italian states.[68] These cycles illuminate the ways in which maps functioned as organizational and reference tools that could also make claims about control over land, peoples and precious goods mnemonic. A striking example is the painted map programme of the Medici Guardaroba in the Palazzo Vecchio of Florence. Here, fifty-three maps of regions across the world were painted onto enormous cupboards that ran in a double row around the length of the Guardaroba; behind each map, items from that part of the world were stored. The viewer standing in the centre of the room enjoyed the illusion of reaching from the centre of the earth to any part of it, and drawing out local artefacts and natural wonders.[69]

An early sixteenth-century treatise on the office of cardinal, Paolo Cortesi's *De cardinalatu* (1510), included an extended section on the design of a cardinal's palace.[70] The treatise offered an iconographic strategy for numerous design features of painted map cycles. Cortesi observes that 'the more subtle a mathematical concept a painting displays, the more learned the picture will appear', and that the representation of complicated machines 'permits more subtle reasoning [by the viewer]'. The attention paid to delineating coastlines and scientific instruments on a large map intended for display would have provided a rhetoric of expertise for the map as a whole. On the subject of illuminating distant parts of the world, Cortesi pronounces that nothing delighted a scholar more than 'a painted picture of the world' or a description of those parts which had come to light during recent voyages. The scholar's appetite for wonders was considerable:

> And the same holds true for paintings done from life which show the different characteristics of various creatures. The rarer the creature shown in the painting, the more the zeal for novelty should be praised. And in this genre we recommend the depiction of riddles and fables.

[68] For book-length treatments of Italian map cycles, see Milanesi, *Marvel of Maps*; Rosen, *Mapping of Power*.

[69] The iconographic programme was only partially completed. For the Guardaroba project, see Rosen, *Mapping of Power*, esp. chaps. 3–4.

[70] Discussed in ibid., 61–2. The text is transcribed, translated and discussed in Kathleen Weil-Garris and John d'Amico, 'The Renaissance Cardinal's Ideal Palace: A Chapter from Cortesi's *De cardinalatu*', *Memoirs of the American Academy in Rome*, 35 (1980), 45–123.

> Their interpretation sharpens the intelligence and [inspection of] their learned representation fosters the cultivation of the mind.[71]

Here, Cortesi recommends that a patron select for illustration the unusual elements of newly explored regions, since parsing the difference between surprising creatures 'done from life' and fables sharpened the viewer's critical faculties and, no doubt, stimulated learned conversation among patrons and guests.[72] This passion for displaying novelties in order to contemplate them was one that was also fed by Renaissance illustrated maps.

Conclusions

By the end of the sixteenth century, illustrated cartography was one of the scholarly achievements that emblematized European intellectual achievement and artisanship. Explorers from the Low Countries carried maps and prints as trading goods, as in the case of Willem Barentz's expedition in search of a northeast passage to Asia in 1596. The expedition was forced to leave them behind at their shelter in Nova Zemyla, off the coast of northwest Russia. When the shelter was rediscovered in 1871, it contained a fragment of Jodocus Hondius the Elder's 1590 map of England, the earliest Dutch map with decorative borders.[73] Similarly, Richard Hakluyt suggested that travellers to China should display a map of England, and offer as gifts Abraham Ortelius's atlas along with costume books, herbals and bestiaries.[74]

In Portugal, Seville and Normandy, manuscript map traditions flourished in the sixteenth century, although the Wars of Religion disrupted the Norman tradition in the second half of the century. Highly decorated maps

[71] For transcription and translation, see Weil-Garris and D'Amico, 'The Renaissance Cardinal's Ideal Palace', 95–6: 'Eademque est zographiae describendae ratio qua diversorum exprimitur animantium natura notatior, in qua eo est commenti sedulitas laudanda magis quo minus nota animantium genera exprimi pingendo solent. Eodemque modo in hoc genere aenigmatum apologorumque descriptio probatur qua ingenium interpretando acuitur fitque mens litterata descriptione eruditior.'

[72] For a longer discussion of Cortesi's instructions concerning painted maps, see Rosen, *Mapping of Power*, 62–3.

[73] *MCN*, VI, 36.

[74] Richard Hakluyt, *The Principal Navigations, Voyages and Discoveries of the English Nation*, 8 vols., (Glasgow: Maclehose, 1903–5), III, 272, cited in Mary C. Fuller, *Voyages in Print: English Travel to America, 1576–1624* (Cambridge: Cambridge University Press, 1995), at 6.

were usually made for royalty, officials and wealthy clients. In Portugal and Seville, the makers were often official mapmakers. Their maps could be used to make territorial claims, and were occasionally used in treaty negotiations or given as diplomatic gifts. Around the Lower Rhine and in the Low Countries, most maps were printed by commercial rather than official state mapmakers. These cartographers had less contact with explorers and navigators than their Iberian and Norman counterparts. Their printed maps were owned by merchants, townspeople and scholars as well as by rulers and aristocrats, and allowed viewers to gain a broad overview of the contents and geographical divisions of the world.

Illustrated world maps were generally made by a group of artisans including cartographers, illuminators and scribes for manuscript maps, and designers (of illustrations), engravers or etchers, calligraphers, and printers or publishers for printed ones. In both manuscript and printed map workshops, these artisans often worked with university-trained cosmographers or mathematicians. When maps were made for specific commissions, the clients also influenced their contents. While this means that the choice and execution of images cannot usually be assigned to particular individuals, it is likely that named mapmakers on manuscript maps and publishers on printed maps wielded much influence. By focusing on the maps themselves as artefacts that constructed particular geographic and ethnographic views, we can explore the emergence and significance of their iconography. When I refer to 'the mapmaker' in this book, I mean the person or persons named on the map, who can generally be assumed to have approved its various features, or any unnamed person who fulfilled this function. Where it is possible, I distinguish between the publisher, the illustrator and the cartographer.

Not only did the contents of maps come from a wide range of international sources, both recent and ancient, but so too did the scholars and artisans who put them together. For the successful management and claiming of empire, both theoretical and practical knowledge needed to come together. The activities of these workshops were transnational, and may fruitfully be analysed together. Moreover, manuscript and printed map traditions have distinct but interrelated histories. These workshops were settings in which epistemological authority was constructed by virtue of a synthesis of multiple kinds of expertise and experience: travellers' empirical observations, cartographers, humanist scholars, mathematicians, illuminators, designers, calligraphers and engravers, to name a few.

Map users thought about maps in informational and pedagogical terms; therefore, if printed maps were to sell well, their content needed to adhere to contemporary conventions of reliability and authority. What we see in Renaissance cartography is a widespread rhetoric about how mapmakers derived the geographical and ethnological content from the most recent sources, acquired using the most careful observations, and synthesized via methodical comparison to old and new sources. This rhetoric is most visible in the titles of maps, where such terms as 'accuratissima' ('most accurate') and 'novissima' ('newest') are abundant. Representing new peoples became an essential part of this engagement with the new and the formulation of newness to serve particular purposes.

Given the artisanal contexts and audiences outlined above, what kinds of questions can we ask productively about the ethnographic material on Renaissance maps? Period readings of the cultural work done by these images allow us to trace the chains of influence and the choices taken by those artisans who participated in producing particular works and the messages that their intended viewers are likely to have taken away. Cartographic methods emerged out of, and in dialogue with, scholarly and artisanal relationships, imperial and commercial goals, and common philosophical concerns. The methods and reasoning behind images of Amerindians on maps, then, are points of departure for new perspectives on the impact of the New World on the Old; on the way spatial thinking was inflected by the panoptical gaze of the map of a continent or of the entire world; and on the discursive and reading practices of the Renaissance and the ways in which readers responded to gridded maps.

3 | Spit-roasts, barbecues and the invention of the Brazilian cannibal

Cannibalism appeared on the first map of the Americas to illustrate the region's peoples, and was the most frequent motif for Brazil on maps well into the seventeenth century.[1] Yet travel accounts about Brazil and the Caribbean Islands, from their earliest appearance, offered ample discussions of peaceful activities. Most mapmakers in the first half of the sixteenth century chose to represent in this region cannibal activities that might discourage long-distance trade, itself a popular iconographical theme on late medieval maps and a financial spur for things geographical in the Renaissance. Given the appearance of both peaceful and man-eating peoples in the earliest sources, how and why did cannibalism become the signature motif, on maps, for the inhabitants of northeastern South America, appearing frequently on maps produced for audiences in Portugal, the German lands, Spain and the Low Countries?

The earliest cannibal iconography on maps, drawing on coastal and insular accounts from the Columbian and Vespuccian voyages that described Arawak-speaking Taíno and Carib peoples, constructed a memorable but hypothetical people for the Brazilian interior. These maps pre-dated, by almost half a century, writings by Hans Staden, André Thevet and Jean de Léry that described cannibalism among some of the numerous Tupi (Tupi-Guaraní speaking) and other tribes who inhabited coastal areas of northeast Brazil. These travel accounts are widely cited for their influence on visual culture, mapping and ethnographic writing, and on European constructions of the Brazilians as eaters of human flesh.[2] Until the 1590s, however, the vibrant illustrations in the accounts of

[1] My sample of illustrated maps was drawn from over 2,000 maps of the Americas, world maps and atlases c.1500–1650 consulted. Out of some 110 cartographic works illustrating Amerindians c.1500–1625, some sixty-five depict cannibalism in northeastern South America, in the region that would come be known as Brazil. The Brazilian cannibal motif continued in subsequent decades.

[2] See, e.g., Eve M. Duffy and Alida C. Metcalf, *The Return of Hans Staden: A Go-between in the Atlantic World* (Baltimore, MD: Johns Hopkins University Press, 2011); Alida C. Metcalf, *Go-Betweens and the Colonization of Brazil, 1500–1600* (Austin, TX: University of Texas Press, 2005); Frank Lestringant, *Cannibals: The Discovery and Representation of the Cannibal from Columbus to Jules Verne*, trans. Rosemary Morris (Cambridge: Polity Press, 1997).

Staden, Thevet and Léry had little direct influence on maps, which, nonetheless, continued to depict cannibalism in Brazil by drawing on sources about the Caribbean islands and the coast of northern South America.

This chapter illuminates the processes by which European mapmakers across different centres of production carefully positioned images and descriptions of a man-eating people in a region they named Brazil. In so doing, these mapmakers collectively constructed a coherent imagined community; their maps constitute the foundational works in the European invention of the Brazilian as cannibal.[3] I argue that neither the fact that the region's peoples were emblematized by cannibal savagery, nor the precise practices associated with them, nor their location, was inevitable given the source material in circulation. The use of images of cannibalism to emblematize northeastern South America, far from being inherent or self-evident, was constructed and maintained.[4]

Despite mapmakers' careful consultation of various sources and their desire to offer information that their audiences would consider to be accurate and authoritative, the process of translating ethnography from the genre of travel account to that of map led to the geographical translation of the cannibals and an expansion of their terrain in European eyes. The ways in which ethnographic map imagery was commonly read in the sixteenth century – as emblematic of what all the inhabitants of a region had in common – meant that mapmakers effectively associated all of Brazil's inhabitants with a practice that, in the eyes of colonial administrators of the Iberian empires, constituted a justification for their enslavement.[5]

One might wonder whether scenes of cannibalism on maps can be brought to bear on the thorny problem of the reality of cannibal peoples.[6]

[3] For the concept of 'imagined communities' in the context of the rise of nationalism, see Anderson, *Imagined Communities.*

[4] A similar point in relation to displayed peoples in nineteenth-century exhibitions appears in Sadiah Qureshi, *Peoples on Parade: Exhibitions, Empire, and Anthropology in Nineteenth-Century Britain* (Chicago, IL and London: Chicago University Press, 2011), 4.

[5] For indigenous slavery in the Spanish empire, see Van Deusen, *Global Indios.* For Brazil, see Hal Lanfgur and Maria Leônia Chaves de Resende, 'Indian Autonomy and Slavery in the Forests and Towns of Colonial Minas Gerais', in *Native Brazil: Beyond the Convert and the Cannibal, 1500–1889*, ed. Hal Langfur (Albuquerque, NM: University of New Mexico Press, 2014), 132–65; Stuart B. Schwartz, 'Indian Labor and New World Plantations: European Demands and Indigenous Responses in Northeastern Brazil', *American Historical Review*, 83:1 (1978), 73–9.

[6] Indeed, this problem has been termed 'the original anthropological question'; see Neil L. Whitehead, 'Guayana as Anthropological Imaginary: Elements of a History', in *Anthropologies of Guayana: Cultural Spaces in Northeastern Amazonia*, eds. Neil L. Whitehead and Stephanie W. Alemán (Tucson, AZ: University of Arizona Press, 2009), 1–20, at 8.

Recent research in forensic archaeology, ethnohistory, anthropology and other fields has revealed evidence that clearly corroborates certain accounts of indigenous anthropophagy among some tribes.[7] Illustrated maps of the world or of the continents, however, rarely provide independent evidence of anthropophagy because few mapmakers had travelled to the areas they mapped. The illustrations on this type of map were largely based on the writings and testimony of others, and thus their portrayals of cannibalism do not constitute independent evidence of the practice.[8]

The focus in this chapter is on how mapmakers interpreted their sources, why they composed images in particular ways, and how the iconography of Brazilian cannibalism was likely to have been read in the contexts of Renaissance knowledge-making and colonial expansion. Questions explored here include: how representative of these sources was the emphasis placed on cannibalism on maps? What light can we shed on Renaissance mapmakers as makers of knowledge about human variety? And what do these findings tell us about how early modern science was a visual pursuit that was both shaped by and constitutive of colonialism?

'Brazil' in this book includes, but also exceeds, the boundaries of modern Brazil. The term covers the Amazonian basin and the northern and eastern coasts of South America between the Amazon and Rio de la Plata estuaries. The term was first used in early sixteenth-century Portuguese sources. I use the term 'Brazilian' *sous rature* to refer to the region's peoples as a whole, since what is under study are the processes by which emblematic characterizations of the region's inhabitants emerged on maps and subsumed various peoples with semisedentary and non-sedentary lifestyles.

[7] See, e.g., Hans Staden, . . . *True History: An Account of Cannibal Captivity in Brazil*, ed. and trans. Neil L. Whitehead and Michael Harbsmeier (Durham, NC: University of North Carolina Press, 2008), XLIII–XLIV; Neil L. Whitehead, 'Carib Cannibalism: The Historical Evidence', *Journal de la société des Americanistes de Paris*, LXX (1984), 53–74; Donald W. Forsyth, 'Three Cheers for Hans Staden: The Case for Brazilian Cannibalism', *Ethnohistory*, 32:1 (1985), 17–36. Three problems continue to fan the flames of the argument about the reality of cannibalism in the colonial world. First, few scholars are fully conversant with the wide range of research tools from the sciences, social sciences and the humanities that have been brought to bear on the problem. Second, accounts about cannibalism survive for numerous settings and periods, from New Guinea and New Mexico to southern France, adding further challenges to the comparison of evidence. Third, the post-colonial turn in recent scholarship has made it difficult for scholars to ascribe practices that deeply offend current sensibilities to colonial settings when much of the evidence was gathered in colonial, imperial or other invasive contexts. For an overview of approaches, see *Cannibalism and the Colonial World*, ed. Francis Barker et al. (Cambridge: Cambridge University Press, 1998).

[8] One of the few exceptions is Jean Rotz's 1542 manuscript atlas, which is discussed in Chapter 4.

To Carib or not to Carib? Language games and imagined communities

The ethnic distinction made in travel accounts between peaceful Arawaks and warlike Caribs was partly one of geographic locale and ritual practices, but it elided a large number of native tribal identities while constructing an artificial binary that served to legitimize the enslavement of native persons. 'Carib' became a colonial construct from the earliest encounters – an ethnic group defined by the practice of cannibalism.[9] Beginning in 1503, Spanish royal edicts and laws denoted groups that practised cannibalism or resisted evangelization as Carib (*caribe*) and defined them as 'indigenous insurgents', and those who accepted Christianity as Arawak (*aruaca*) or *guatiao* (*taíno*).[10] 'Caribs' and 'Arawaks' were two groups with different political relationships to the Spanish, but it was a colonial construct that this was a fixed ethnic binary.

Indigenous ethnic and political groups did not remain the same over time and, by the early sixteenth century, European attempts at conquest and the consequent famine and disease had transformed native allegiances and prompted migrations among survivors in the circum-Caribbean region.[11] Native groups made choices about whether to self-identify as *caribe* or *aruaca*. Some capitalized on the Spanish construction of the *caribe* as cannibal by directing the Spanish in search of slaves and booty at their enemies.[12] Into the nineteenth century, indigenous, Afro-Brazilian and Luso-Brazilian groups accused one another of cannibalism in order to consolidate their own territories.[13] The Englishman Lawrence Keymis, who travelled in Amazonia in the late sixteenth century, recounted that the Moruga people accused the 'Arwaccas' ('Arawaks') of abducting

[9] Neil L. Whitehead, 'The Crises and Transformations of Invaded Societies: The Caribbean (1491–1580)', in *Cambridge History of the Native Peoples of the Americas*, ed. Frank Salomon and Stuart B. Schwartz (Cambridge: Cambridge University Press, 1999), 864–903, at 867, 870; Neil L. Whitehead, *Of Cannibals and Kings: Primal Anthropology in the Americas* (University Park, PA: Pennsylvania State University Press, 2011), 4–5.

[10] Whitehead, *Primal Anthropology*, 6–12 and Document 4; Whitehead, 'Guayana as Anthropological Imaginary', 7–9. For the 1503 edict, see Michael Palencia-Roth, 'The Cannibal Law of 1503', in Early Images of the Americas: Transfer and Invention, ed. Jerry M. Williams and Robert E. Lewis (Tucson and London: University of Arizona Press, 1993), 21–64.

[11] Whitehead, *Primal Anthropology*, 6.

[12] Ibid., 11–12; Whitehead, 'Invaded Societies: The Caribbean', 871.

[13] Hal Langfur, *The Forbidden Lands: Colonial Identity, Frontier Violence, and the Persistence of Brazil's Eastern Indians, 1750–1830* (Stanford, CA: Stanford University Press, 2006), 28–9, 53, 182–3, 194, 198, 243–5, 259–60, 273, 276.

their wives, a practice that Spanish voyages to the Caribbean islands had identified with the Carib.[14] There were soon 'Black Caribs' – escaped African slaves who joined indigenous groups – and white cannibals – Norman sailors who had gone native among the Brazilian Tupi and participated in their rituals.[15] European notions of these peoples came from these complex interactions on the ground, mediated through Spanish colonial writing that had its own purposes.

Similarly, Portuguese colonists oversimplified ethnic and political allegiances in northeastern Brazil, dividing the peoples into supposedly nomadic, truculent Tapuia *vs.* village-based, tractable Tupi-Guaraní. The Portuguese used the term 'Tapuia' to signify those who resisted colonization. In fact, 'Tupi' covered a number of Tupi-Guaraní groups with shared linguistic and cultural origins who engaged one another in constant warfare, and the Tupi used the term 'Tapuia' to signify those who spoke Arawak, Carib and other languages.[16] While this chapter focuses on the invention of Carib culture on maps, the following will examine the case for Tupi culture.

In practice, peoples from the greater circum-Caribbean region encompassing the Antilles Islands and northern South America belonged to some forty language families. Many belong to one of three main language groups: Tupi-Guaraní, Arawak and Macro-Gê.[17] But ethnic groups, be they tribes, nations or peoples, far from being eternal, are constantly in a state of change, are continually re-defined, and are constructed differently by members and outsiders. Colonial Brazil was a setting of widespread 'ethnogenesis', or the emergence and categorization of 'new peoples'.[18]

Portuguese constructives

the invention of Carib culture on maps in the focus of this chapter

[14] Lawrence Keymis, *A Relation of the Second Voyage to Guiana* (London, 1596), sig.C.2.*v*.

[15] Neil L. Whitehead, 'Black Read as Red: Ethnic Transgression and Hybridity in Northeastern South America and the Caribbean', in *Beyond Black and Red: African-Native Relations in Colonial Latin America*, ed. Matthew Restall (Albuquerque, NM: University of New Mexico Press, 2005), 223–43, at 229–30.

[16] Hal Langfur, 'Introduction: Recovering Brazil's Indigenous Pasts', in *Native Brazil: Beyond the Convert and the Cannibal, 1500–1900*, ed. Hal Langfur (Albuquerque, NM: University of New Mexico Press, 2014), 1–28, at 7–16.

[17] John Monteiro, 'The Crises and Transformations of Invaded Societies: Coastal Brazil in the Sixteenth Century', in *Cambridge History of the Native Peoples of the Americas*, ed. Frank Salomon and Stuart B. Schwartz (Cambridge: Cambridge University Press, 1999), 3 vols., III:i, 973–1023, at 976–7. For an introduction to the peoples of Brazil and their main language families, see also John Hemming, 'The Indians of Brazil in 1500', in *The Cambridge History of Latin America*, ed. Leslie Bethell, 11 vols. (Cambridge: Cambridge University Press, 1984–2008), I, 119–43.

[18] See Schwartz, Stuart B. and Frank Salomon, 'New Peoples and New Kinds of People: Adaptation, Readjustment, and Ethnogenesis in South American Indigenous Societies (Colonial

Where interaction with particular peoples is under discussion, I use specific terminology. Travellers and geographers themselves had difficulty distinguishing between local populations with different languages, territories, practices and cultures, and with historical changes to these societies.[19] When referring to particular source texts and maps, I deploy their own terminology while attempting to identify the people to whom they refer.

Columbus's *Diario*

Columbus's journal from his first voyage in search of the Indies (1492–3) contains the earliest appearance of the neologism 'cannibal' in any European language.[20] 'Carib' was an indigenous term that was later adopted into European lexicons. The linguistic invention of the terms 'cannibal' and 'cannibalism' characterized the Caribs by their man-eating proclivities.[21] Columbus's journal survives in the form of a lengthy summary, known as the *Diario*, transcribed by the Dominican friar Bartolomé de las Casas.[22] Las Casas copied verbatim tracts of particular interest to him and those he deemed worthy of quotation.[23] The *Diario* is thus an intertextual work, recording Columbus's words through Las Casas's responses to them.[24]

Eaters of human flesh appear in the earliest reference to New World monsters, on 4 November 1492. Columbus, on the island of Cuba, was in conversation with members of the Taíno people. He 'understood that, far from there, there were one-eyed people and others with dogs' muzzles who ate human beings; upon seizing a person, they cut his throat and drank his blood and cut off his genitals'.[25] Columbus reports their existence on the

Period)', in *Cambridge History of the Native Peoples of the Americas*, ed. Frank Salomon and Stuart B. Schwartz (Cambridge: Cambridge University Press, 1999), 443–501.

19 Monteiro, Crises and Transformations'.

20 Margarita Zamora, *Reading Columbus* (Berkeley, CA: University of California Press, 1993), 7.

21 Hulme, *Colonial Encounters*, 15.

22 David Henige, *In Search of Columbus: The Sources for the First Voyage* (Tucson, AZ: University of Arizona Press, 1991), 22.

23 *RC vi, SE*, 3–4, 17; David Abulafia, *The Discovery of Mankind: Atlantic Encounters in the Age of Columbus* (New Haven, CT and London: Yale University Press, 2008), 110: Las Casas also included material from the *Diario* in one of his histories of the Indies, but this contained more of Las Casas's own interventions.

24 An important analysis in this vein is Zamora, *Reading Columbus*, 43–51, esp. 49.

25 *RC vi, SE*, DB48.8 (includes an English translation to which I have at times made minor changes): 'Entendió . . . que lexos de allí avía hombres de un ojo, y otros con hoçicos de perros que comían los hombres, y que en tomando uno lo degollavan y le bevían la sangre, y le cortavan su natura'.

basis of indigenous testimony, but one cannot help wondering how much of the Indians' speech he could have understood after a few weeks in the region.[26] His interpreter spoke Hebrew, Aramaic and some Arabic – languages Columbus expected to hear when he reached Asia.[27] Even the interpreter was absent at this point, having been sent on a reconnaissance mission on 2 November.

The man-eater's next appearance, on 23 November, introduces the word cannibal, or rather 'canibales', to the European *episteme*. Still on Cuba, Columbus hears from the Taíno that on the island called Bohío were 'people … who had one eye in the middle of their foreheads and others whom they called "canibales", of whom they showed themselves to have a great fear'.[28] The two types of people collapse into one on 26 November:

> All the people whom he has found up to today, he says, have the greatest fear of those from Caniba, or Canima, and they say that the latter live on this island of Bohío … and he believes that those people go out to carry the former off to their own lands and homes, as they are great cowards and know nothing about weapons.… They said that the people here had only one eye each and dogs' faces, but the admiral believed that they were lying, and felt that the people who used to capture them must belong to the Great Khan's dominion.[29]

These 'Caniba' were the Island Caribs or Karipuna, denoted as man-eaters by the Taíno. Both groups of Arawak-speaking peoples, they had gradually migrated from the eastern coast of South America to the island chains of the Greater and Lesser Antilles.[30] Columbus seems reluctant to accept that he has stumbled into the territory of marauding, one-eyed, dog-headed man-eaters, despite the presence of *cyclopes*, *cynocephali* and *anthropophagi* in medieval travel and encyclopedic works relating to the Eastern part of the world. He had hoped to carry the word of Christianity

26 For Columbus's (mis)understanding of situations, see, e.g., Peter Mason, *Deconstructing America: Representations of the Other* (London and New York, NY: Routledge, 1990), 101.

27 Hulme, *Colonial Encounters*, 20.

28 *RC vi, SE*, DB59.4: 'gente que tenía un ojo en la frente, y otros que se llamavan caníbales, a quien mostravan tener gran miedo'.

29 Ibid., DB62.11–62.13: 'Toda la gente que hasta oy a hallado diz que tiene grandíssimo temor de los de Caniba o Canima, y dizen que biven en esta ysla de Bohío … y cree que van a tomar a aquéllos a sus tierras y casas, como sean muy cobardes y no saber de armas.… dezían que no tenían sino un ojo y la cara de perro; y creýa el Almirante que mentían, y sentía el Almirante que devían de ser del señorío del Gran Can que los captibavan'. The use of the third person is the result of Las Casas's transcription.

30 Abulafia, *Discovery of Mankind*, 115; Whitehead, 'Invaded Societies: The Caribbean'.

to the Great Khan of Cathay on behalf of the Catholic Monarchs, Ferdinand and Isabella; what he most wished to see were signs of Eastern civilization, not savagery.[31] The ensuing supposition that the Indians must be lying, however, is at odds with his interpretation of their term 'Caniba' as a reference to 'subjects of the Great Khan' – the Eastern potentate he had promised to reach – rather than to monsters with canine faces.[32] Unable, perhaps, to avoid the possibility of having misunderstood the Indians, Columbus turns uncertainty to his own advantage, attaching selected sounds from their speech to his desired outcome.

The linguistic triangle of 'canibales', man-eating *cynocephali* and the Great Khan, out of which the word cannibal would evolve, eventually displacing and redefining the older anthropophage, is clear.[33] Over the next few weeks, Columbus continued to record his disbelief in man-eaters and dismissed the testimony of people who lived in fear of the Bohío islanders.[34] When he failed to find the kingdom of the Great Khan, he resurrected the fearsome *Caniba*, now recording claims about their man-eating tendencies with more conviction.[35] On 26 December, he even promised some villagers who described how the Caribs had abducted their people that 'the monarchs of Castile would command that the Caribs be destroyed' – a reversal of his position exactly a month earlier, when he had been convinced that 'they were lying'.[36]

Columbus's *Diario* provides two insights for contextualizing cannibal imagery and texts on maps: first, the neologism 'canibal' was originally a term for the Carib, an ethnic group; their name soon became synonymous with the practice of eating human flesh, a process that re-defined the Carib by a single characteristic. Second, the *Diario*'s monstrous discourse introduced a classical ethnological framework into an empirical account of the Americas. The use of 'canibal' to refer to a single people in the Antilles would not be preserved on maps, where the ethnography of the Caribs would, as it were, overwhelm that of the Taíno and other groups.

[31] For the *Diario*'s interlocking discourses of civilization and savagery, see Hulme, *Colonial Encounters*, 20–34.

[32] For Columbus's aims and geographical expectations, see, e.g. Abulafia, *Discovery of Mankind*, 24–30.

[33] For a masterful account of how the word 'Carib' would come to mean 'anthropophage', see Hulme, *Colonial Encounters*, 16–22, 39–43. See also Lestringant, *Cannibals*, 15–19.

[34] See entries for 5, 11 and 17 December. [35] 13 January.

[36] *RC vi, SE*, DB, 91.25: 'los reyes de Castilla mandarían destruyr a los caribes'.

Columbian and Vespuccian voyages in print

Travel writing from the voyages of Columbus and Vespucci is typically characterized as sensational, full of cannibals, promiscuous sexual behaviour and the absence of morals. In fact, peaceful visions of the inhabitants of the circum-Caribbean basin receive more column-inches in these works; references to violent activities are buried in the larger narrative. This is also the case in the early Portuguese travel writing about Brazil, notably the account of the first known landfall, penned by Pedro Vaz de Caminha.[37] Accounts from the Columbian voyages of the late fifteenth century describe encounters with an Arawak-speaking people, the Taíno, who inhabited the Antilles island chain in the Caribbean. These people were apparently simple, beautiful and timid; they had no concept of money, providing valuable commodities in exchange for beads. Two letters ascribed to Columbus, apparently written on the return voyage, announced the results of his first expedition and described the inhabitants of the Antilles.[38] One letter, sent to Luis de Santángel, *Escribano de Ración* or keeper of the royal privy purse, received a contemporary printing. Santángel had assisted in procuring funds for the first voyage.[39] The letter appeared in twelve editions in 1493 alone in Spanish, Latin, Catalan and Italian, and was printed widely across Europe thereafter.[40]

In *Letter to Santángel*, Columbus presents New World anthropophagy and monstrosity as unusual occurrences: 'I have so far found no monstrous people, as many expected'; the inhabitants are in fact very beautiful and not 'black as in Guinea'; the sun's rays are not as intense as they are in Guinea.[41]

[37] Discussed in Chapter 4, near n. 66.

[38] In works generally ascribed to Columbus, the mediatory effects of printers, copyists and abstractors are impossible to separate fully from their purported author. One may go so far as to consider, with Margarita Zamora, that 'the very signature "Columbus" must be seen as an aggregate, a corporate author as it were' (Zamora, *Reading Columbus*, 7). Of course, all printed travel accounts were the result of similar mediations.

[39] Christopher Columbus, *Letters from America: Columbus's First Accounts of the 1492 Voyage*, ed. and trans. B. W. Ife (London: King's College, London, 1992), 7; Zamora, *Reading Columbus*, 5.

[40] Christopher Columbus, *Epistola … de su gran descubrimiento …* (Barcelona, 1493). For other editions, see *EA*, I, 1–2. Zamora, *Reading Columbus*, 5: The Latin editions are mis-addressed to Rafaél (rather than Gàbriel) Sánchez, the treasurer for the kingdom of Aragon. Ibid., 9–10: Columbus probably wrote two letters to the Catholic monarchs, dated 14 Feb and 4 March 1493. No version of the first survives; the second, containing many of the same passages and sprinkled with messianic statements, was probably suppressed. For text and translation, see ibid., Appendix.

[41] Columbus, *Letters from America*, 58–61: 'fasta aqui no he hallado ombres monstrudos como muchas pensauan'; 'negros como en Guinea'.

Readers familiar with the works of Aristotle and the Hippocratic corpus would have been predisposed to thinking of these islands as attractive locales for finding such civil societies as the empire of the Great Khan that Columbus wished to reach. The Taíno described to their interlocutors a warlike, Arawak-speaking people they called the Carib, said to dwell in the coastal region of northeast South America and on nearby islands rather than deep in the interior where mapmakers' illustrations would place them:[42]

> ...I have found no monstrous men nor heard of any, except on one island ... which is inhabited by people who are held in all the islands to be very ferocious and who eat human flesh. These people have many canoes in which they range around all the islands of India robbing and stealing whenever they can.[43]

Here, Columbus uses a broad definition of *monstrudos* encompassing physical and behavioural aberrations. Thus he introduced the Antillian anthropophages to European audiences within the conceptual framework of Plinian monstrosity.[44]

The *Letter* presents marauding anthropophages as an exception rather than the norm in the Antilles islands. The naked people of Hispaniola lacked iron, steel and weapons, and were 'amazingly timid faced with marvels' ('*muy temerosos a marauilla*'):

> ...they are so lacking in guile and so generous with what they have that no one would believe it unless they saw it.... I forbade the men to give them such worthless things as pieces of broken crockery and pieces of broken glass and the ends of laces.... There was a sailor who had a piece of gold weighing two and a half *castellanos* in exchange for a lace....[45]

42 It is important to note, however, that the linguistic relatedness of groups changes over time, and that it is not necessarily linked to shared culture or kinship. In Amazonia, socio-ethnic groups did not fissure across monolingual lines. See especially Neil L. Whitehead, 'Arawak Linguistic and Cultural Identity through Time: Contact, Colonialism, and Creolization', in *Comparative Arawakan Histories: Rethinking Language Family and Culture Area in Amazonia*, ed. Jonathan D. Hill and Fernando Santos-Granero (Urbana, IL and Chicago, IL: University of Illinois Press, 2002), 51–73, at 51–4.

43 Columbus, *Letters from America*, 58–61 (I have made minor changes to the translation): 'monstruos no he hallado ni noticia saluo de una ysla ... que es poblada de una iente que tienen en todas las yslas por muy ferozes, los qualles comen carne umana. Estos tienen muchas canoas con las quales corren todas las yslas de India, y roban y toman quanto pueden'.

44 For the writings of Galen, Aristotle and Pliny on human difference, see Chapter 1.

45 Columbus, *Letters from America*, 50–3: 'ellos son tanto sin engaño y tan liberales de lo que tienen que no lo creeria sino el que lo viese.... Yo defendi que no se les diesen cosas tan siuiles como pedazos de escudillas rotas y pedazos de vidrio roto y cabos de agugetas ... que se acerto hauer un marinero por una agugeta de oro de peso de dos castellano y medio'.

3.1 Christopher Columbus, *De insulis inventis* (Basle, 1493), title-page, detail. Beinecke Rare Book and Manuscript Library, Yale University, Taylor 32.

Timid and generous, willing to exchange treasure for trinkets, and lacking technological apparatus that would allow them to resist effectively should they ever become truculent, the Taíno in this letter were everything a trader could wish for, and a stark contrast to the bloodthirsty Caribs said to prey upon them. This notion of pliable peoples is as much a construction that served mercantile sponsorship as the idea about warlike cannibals was in the service of slavery.

The illustration in the 1493 Basle edition of the *Letter*, which derives from woodcuts in Mediterranean travel accounts, emblematizes this view of peaceful inhabitants (Fig. 3.1).[46] The stock iconographical elements present a timorous, graceful people fleeing from the Hispaniola coast at the sight of a European ship. One islander and a figure in a rowing boat extend their arms to each other, perhaps offering gifts or trading objects. These figures represent people off the coast of Asia, in characteristic boats and hats – Columbus, of course, wished to reach (and believed he had

[46] Christopher Columbus, *Epistola de insulis nuper inventis* (Basle, 1493), title-page. Susi Colin, *Das Bild des Indianers*, 183, B1; *NRC-XI*, 294. For descriptions of illustrations from other Columbian texts, see Colin, *Das Bild des Indianers*, B2-B5; Santiago Sebastián, *Iconografía del indio americano, siglos XVI-XVII* (Madrid: Ediciones Tuero, 1992), 25–30.

reached) the outer reaches of the empire of the Great Khan of Cathay, a place rich in tradeable goods.[47] Early sixteenth-century mapmakers who drew on letters from the Columbian corpus thus had access to a visual representation of simple inhabitants with an idyllic way of life, and of pliable trading partners.

Columbus's second voyage (1493), announced by a pamphlet known as the Scillacio-Coma letter, also described two contrasting peoples. The letter, written by the Barcelona physician Guillermo Coma based on received news, was translated into Latin by the scholar Nicolò Scillacio and subsequently printed.[48] It outlined the Caribs' bloodthirsty practice of feeding on their Taíno neighbours, information that the crew gleaned from their peaceful indigenous interlocutors:

> The islands are submissive to the Cannibals. That ferocious and untamed people feeds on human flesh, so that I might accurately call them anthropophages. They continuously wage war on the gentle and frightened Indians in order to get hold of their flesh – these are the prey, they are the hunters. They ferociously ravage, plunder and roam in search of the Indians: they devour the unwarlike ones, abstain from their own, spare the cannibals.[49]

In its first appearance in print here, the term 'cannibal' identifies a particular people whom the expedition did not encounter first-hand, rather than the entirety of the Antillian island population.[50] No less a personage than the captain of the expedition, Pedro Margarit, saw scenes to corroborate this:

> Pedro Margarit, a very reliable Spaniard . . . says that he saw there with his own eyes several Indians skewered on spits to be roasted over burning coals for the indulgence of gluttony, while many bodies, from which the

[47] Colin, *Das Bild des Indianers*, 185, B.6: The figures also illustrated the Italian edition of 1493 and reappeared, reversed, in the first edition of Vespucci's letter to Piero Soderini.

[48] Nicolò Scillacio, *De insulis meridiani atque Indici maris . . . nuper inventis* (Pavia, 1494), preface: Scillacio was doctor of arts and medicine and professor of philosophy at Pavia. For a discussion of Coma's probable authorship, see Juan Gil and Consuelo Varela, eds., *Cartas de particulares a Colón y relaciones coetáneas* (Madrid: Alianza, 1984), 177–8. Coma is unlikely to have participated in the expedition, but probably heard of it (perhaps from Pedro Margarit, who is mentioned in the letter, or his circle) on the return of the first ship; see Rubiés, 'Travel Writing and Humanistic Culture', 157–8.

[49] *RC xii, AC*, 6.2.8 (includes translation, which I have amended slightly): 'Insulae Canabillis [sic] parent: gens illa effera et indomita carnibus vescitur humanis, quos anthropophagos iure nuncupaverim. Adversus Indos molles scilicet et pavidos bella gerunt assidue ad usum carnium: ea captura, ille venatus; populantur, depredantur, crassantur truculentius Indos, devorant imbelles, a suis abstinent, parcunt Canaballis'.

[50] For timidity, see also ibid., 6.2.14.

> heads and extremities had been torn off, lay around in heaps. The Cannibals themselves do not deny this, but openly confirm that they eat other people.[51]

Elsewhere, however, Coma wrote about the peaceful Taíno, their impressive woodworking skills and their generosity.[52]

The events of Columbus's voyages were also recorded by the courtier and humanist chronicler Pietro Martire d'Anghiera, or Peter Martyr. Peter was personally acquainted with Columbus: he had been present at court when Columbus returned from his first voyage and he had taken pains to interview as many members of the expedition as possible.[53] Peter disseminated this testimony via Latin letters to his correspondents; versions of his letters, some edited by his correspondents, some by Peter Martyr himself, and some by subsequent compilers, were printed in the early decades of the sixteenth century.

A vivid description of cannibals, which appeared across the earliest three printed editions of Peter's letters in print with minor variations, would be taken up by influential German mapmakers. Angelo Trevisano, one of Peter's correspondents and secretary to the Venetian ambassador to Spain, sent Italian translations of Peter's letters to Venice where they were published anonymously in a travel compendium entitled *Libretto de tutta la nauigatione* (1504).[54] The geographer Fracanzano da Montalboddo incorporated the book into his *Paesi novamente retrovati* of 1507.[55] Peter Martyr himself began printing his travel material in 1511 and 1516, as the *Oceani decas* or *Ocean Decades*,[56] and also in various letters in his *Opus epistolarum* of 1530.[57]

[51] Ibid., 6.2.10: 'Vidisse hic se oculis testatur Petrus Margarita optimae fidei Hispanus, . . . Indos plures verubus affixos ad luxum gulae assari super ardentibus prunis, cum multa cadavera iacerent acervatim, quibus capita exempta extremaque corporis evulsa: quin illud Canaballi non diffitentur, palam hominibus vesci se affirmant.'

[52] Ibid., 6.2.9 and 6.2.19, respectively.

[53] *RC v, PM*, 6; John Boyd Thacher, *Christopher Columbus: His Life, His Work, His Remains, as revealed by Original Printed and Manuscript Records*, 3 vols. (New York, NY: Knickerbocker Press, 1903), I, 39–40.

[54] Angelo Trevisano, *Libretto de tutta la navigatione de re de Spagna de le isole et terreni nuouamente trouati* ... (1504). See also idem, *Libretto de tutta la nauigatione de re de spagna de le isole et terreni nouamente trouati: A Facsimile*, intro. by Lawrence C. Wroth (Paris, 1929).

[55] Fracanzano da Montalboddo, *Paesi novamente retrovati & novo mondo da Alberico Vesputio Florentino intitulato* (Vicenza, 1507). *EA*, I, 10–18, *s.v.*: Six editions of the latter had appeared by 1513 in Italian, Latin and German, printed at Vicenza, Milan and Nuremberg, respectively; four French printings were made in Paris in 1515.

[56] *EA*, I, *s.v.* Editions up to 1628 are described in *BA*, I, nos 1547–1564 and 45010–45013.

[57] *RC v, PM*, xi.

In terms of column inches, cannibalism is again the exception rather than the rule in these texts which describe how expedition members encountered the Taíno people whom the accounts unanimously describe as peaceful, even timid, and easy to trade with. The sailors did not meet the ruthless Caribs, but merely reported what the Taíno related about them. We cannot be sure how well – or how little – the Europeans understood Taíno language and gesture. Nevertheless, for the readers of these accounts, these new islands contained both fearsome anthropophages and beautiful, peaceful people.

The second set of narratives that included descriptions of Amerindians as anthropophages followed Vespucci's voyages.[58] In the period to 1530, narratives about Vespucci's travels were disseminated more widely than those about Columbus's voyages (some 60 editions and issues to Columbus's 22), with more than half the works appearing in vernaculars.[59] Two accounts often attributed to Vespucci were printed in a variety of formats. Scholars argue over their composite authorship and whether Vespucci made four voyages (as he claims) or two (for which documentary evidence survives). Since these texts were first disseminated as Vespucci's accounts, and since maps refer to Vespucci by name, I shall refer to these texts as Vespucci's letters.[60] These pamphlets contain information about Tupi peoples who lived on the coast of the northwestern South American mainland and its interior, and Carib peoples who dwelled primarily on the coast. While both groups practised cannibalism, and while the differences between them were not sharp or fixed over time, sixteenth-century travel writers described a variety of ritual practices, distinguishing several treatments of human body parts and mortuary practices while subsuming others under the loose rubric of man-eating. The accounts also documented various other aspects of their lives.[61]

Vespucci's first letter, which he wrote in Italian to his employer Lorenzo di Pierfrancesco de' Medici, documents a voyage in 1499 to the South American coast near the Amazon estuary. Vespucci describes an unnamed

[58] For a Vespucci biography, see Felipe Fernández-Armesto, *Amerigo: The Man Who Gave His Name to America* (London: Weidenfeld & Nicolson, 2006); for bibliography and sources, see *NRC-V*.

[59] Rudolf Hirsch, 'Printed Reports on the Early Discoveries and Their Reception', in Fredi Chiappelli et al., eds., *First Images of America: The Impact of the New World on the Old*, 2 vols. (Berkeley, CA and London: University of California Press, 1976), II, 537-[59], at 540 and Appendix 1.

[60] For authorship issues, see Fernández-Armesto, *Amerigo*, 2–3, 114–135; Abulafia, *Discovery of Mankind*, 244.

[61] Whitehead, 'Invaded Societies: The Caribbean'.

people who resemble the Tupi-Guaraní tribes of northeast Brazil. He mentions that they set stones and bones into holes in their faces, a practice that later travellers ascribed to the Tupinambá.[62] The letter was translated into Latin and printed at Paris in 1503;[63] subsequent editions (entitled *Mundus Novus*) were numerous.[64] Vespucci's second account was addressed to Piero Soderini, head of the Florentine Republic and former pupil of Vespucci's uncle, and printed at Florence in 1505–6.[65] The letter outlined four voyages, although Vespucci probably made only two and borrowed material from the Columbian corpus. Vespucci presented a range of indigenous behaviours including cannibalism, nakedness, naivety in trading and the lack of trappings of European society.

Illustrations in these accounts contain similar themes to those in the Columbian texts. A woodcut in the 1505 Leipzig edition of the *Mundus Novus* depicts the inhabitants as nearly naked in feather costumes and bearing bows, arrows and clubs.[66] The 1505 Strasbourg edition contains two simple woodcuts on the title-page. One shows naked inhabitants; the other, European ships approaching land.[67] A German broadsheet, probably printed at Augsburg by Johann Froschauer in 1505,[68] drew on this letter for its caption (Fig. 3.2).[69] It describes the Amerindians' costumes, their habit of eating and smoking human body parts, and their sexual promiscuity:

> This picture shows us the people and island that were discovered by the Christian king of Portugal or by his subjects. The people are thus naked, handsome, brown; their heads, necks, arms, private parts [and the] feet of

[62] Staden, *True History*, ed. Whitehead.

[63] Amerigo Vespucci, *Albericus Vesputius Laurentio Petri Francisci de Medicis salutem plurimam dicit* (Paris, 1503); *EA*, I, no. 503/9; Amerigo Vespucci, *Letters from a New World: Amerigo Vespucci's Discovery of America*, ed. and with intro. by Luciano Formisano (New York, NY: Marsilio Pub, 1992), xix: an earlier version was written in Portuguese to King Manuel of Portugal; no copy survives.

[64] *EA*, I, nos 505/11–15, 505/17–24. Fifteen issues appeared in 1505 alone, in cities including Augsburg, Antwerp, Basle, Nuremberg, Strasbourg and Venice.

[65] Amerigo Vespucci, *Lettera . . . delle isole nuouamente trovate* (Florence, 1505). Vespucci, *Letters*, xxii; *EA*, I, no. 505/16.

[66] Illustrated in, e.g., Abulafia, *Discovery of Mankind*, fig. 21; Colin, *Das Bild des Indianers*, fig. 7.

[67] Amerigo Vespucci, *De ora antarctica per regem Portugallie pridem inventa* (Strasbourg, 1505).

[68] *Dise figur anzaigt uns das volck und insel die gefunden ist durch den cristenlichen künig zu Portigal oder von seinen underthonen* (s.l., [1503]). This has been considered as the earliest South American image in print; see, e.g., Rudolf Schuller, 'The Oldest Known Illustration of the South American Indians', *Journal de la Société des Americanistes de Paris*, N. S., 16 (1924), 111–18; William C. Sturtevant, 'First Visual Images', 420. For descriptions of this and other woodcuts from Vespucci editions, see Sebastián, *Iconografía*, 32–43.

[69] Established in Schuller, 'Oldest Known Illustration', at 115–7.

3.2 *Dise figur anzaigt uns das volck und insel die gefunden ist* ([Augsburg?], [c.1503]), woodcut, attributed to Johann Froschauer.
Bayerische Staatsbibliothek München, Einbl. V,2.

men and women are lightly covered with feathers. The men also have many precious stones in their faces and chests. Nor does anyone possess anything, but all things are in common. And the men have as wives those who please them, be they mothers, sisters, or friends, among whom they make no distinction. They also fight with each other and eat each other, even the slain, and hang the same flesh in smoke. They live to be a hundred and fifty years old and have no government.[70]

[70] 'Dise figur anzaigt vns das volck vnd insel die gefunden ist durch den cristenlichen künig zu Portigal oder von seinen vnderthonen. Die leüt sind also nacket, hübsch, braun wolgestalt von leib. ir heübter halsz. arm. scham. füsz frawen vnd mann ain wenig mit federn bedeckt. Auch haben die mann in iren angesichten vnd brust vid edel gestain. Es hat auch nyemantz nichts sunder sind alle ding gemain. Vnnd die mann habendt weyber welche in gefallen. es sey mutter, schwester oder freündt. Darjnn haben sy kain vnderschaid. Sy streyten auch mit ainander. Sy essen auch ainander selbs die erschlagen werden. vnd hencken das selbig fleisch in den rauch. Sy werden alt hundert vnd fünfftzig iar. Vnd haben kain regiment.' For a larger illustration, see Max Justo Guedes and Gerald Lombardi, *Portugal-Brazil: The Age of Atlantic Discoveries*

In the caption of this print, in contrast to the captions on early maps, cannibalism appears almost as an afterthought, interspersed within a litany of attractive qualities.[71] Indeed, the inhabitants' longevity may have suggested to readers that they lived in proximity to the Fountain of Youth, mentioned in the *Romance of Alexander* and the *Book of John Mandeville*.[72] The viewer's attention is more evenly divided between cannibalism and other activities. A nursing mother accompanied by three children share the lower foreground with three male warriors. Above their heads and to the right are motifs of cannibalism: four figures handle, eat or observe the eating of human limbs; a human head and limbs hang prominently from a beam. The European ships in the background remind the viewer that this information came from recent voyages.

Three woodcuts adorn the 1509 edition of Vespucci's letter to Soderini.[73] This edition was printed by Johann Grüninger of Strasbourg, who would soon print several influential maps depicting cannibals in Brazil. One woodcut shows anthropophages chopping limbs on a table, a nursing mother and other figures (Fig. 3.3).[74] Another details the

(New York: Brazilian Cultural Foundation, 1990), no. 93. I have also consulted the transcription in Jan van Doesborgh, *De novo mondo. Antwerp, Jan van Doesborch [about 1520]. A Facsimile of a Unique Broadsheet*, ed. and trans. Maria Elizabeth Kronenberg (The Hague: Martinus Nijhoff, 1927), at 20. The translation is from Schuller, 'Oldest Known Illustration', 111; I have made minor amendments.

71 The broadsheet seems to have inspired a woodcut by the Flemish printer Jan van Doesborch or Doesborgh that appeared in his *Of the Newe Landes and of ye People founde by the Messengers of the kynge of Portyngale named Emanuel* ... ([Antwerp], c.1520), title-page and sig. [A.ii.r], For comparisons of editions, see *De novo mondo*, ed. Kronenberg, 1–5; Robert Proctor, *Jan van Doesborgh, Printer at Antwerp: An Essay in Bibliography* (London: Bibliographical Society, 1894), 32–3. Several elements are common to both the *Carta Marina* and the Doesborgh scenes: the body parts hanging from above, the nursing woman and the man with a bow. Van Doesborgh's woodcuts are dated to c.1511–23. Van Doesborgh, *De novo mondo*, ed. Kronenberg, 9, hesitantly suggests 1520; Sturtevant, 'First Visual Images', 446, n. 13 gives a broader range.

72 See Jorge Magasich-Airola and Jean-Marc de Beer, *America Magica: When Renaissance Europe Thought It Had Conquered Paradise*, trans. Monica Sander (London: Anthem Press, 2000), 44–51.

73 Amerigo Vespucci, *Diss büchlin saget wie die zwen durchlüchtigsten herren ... haben ... funden vil insulen vnnd ein Nüwe welt von wilden nackenden Leuten vormals vnbekant* (Strasbourg, 1509). Its publisher, Johann Grüninger, also issued maps illustrated with cannibals, as we shall see. For a description of the illustrations, see Colin, 'Wild Man and the Indian', 17–18. *EA*, no. 509/11: This was a German translation of a Latin version that had been published with Martin Waldseemüller's *Cosmographiae introductio*. For Waldseemüller and his works, see later.

74 Vespucci, *Diss büchlin*, sig. B.i.*v*.

3.3 Amerigo Vespucci, *Diss büchlin sagt ...* (Strasbourg, 1509), sig. B.i.*v*.
The Huntington Library, San Marino, California, 18657.

3.4 Amerigo Vespucci, *Diss büchlin sagt...*(Strasbourg, 1509), sig. E.iiii.*v*.
The Huntington Library, San Marino, California, 18657.

moment when a woman raises a jawbone to bring down a European sailor, who is later cooked and eaten (Fig. 3.4).[75] A figure who might have been interpreted as a troglodyte appears in the background. A third

[75] Ibid., sig. E.iiii.*v*.

image shows Europeans in the Caribbean, one of whom appears to be greeting some indigenous women.[76]

As a whole, the Columbian and Vespuccian sources provided a range of characterizations of the Tupi, Carib and Taíno peoples. Despite describing cannibalism, they also offered reasonable grounds for concluding that at least some of these peoples were far from depraved. Their lack of clothing and other trappings of 'civilized' life, together with the extreme western (and, by extension, far eastern) geographical location of the Caribbean, could well have suggested to viewers that these peoples inhabited the Terrestrial Paradise.

Emblematizing Circum-Caribbean peoples: two cartographic approaches

By contrast to travel accounts and their illustrations, which created the binary of peaceful Taíno and voracious Carib, on map imagery, the Taíno motifs are almost completely absent until the late sixteenth century; the man-eating Carib dominated the earliest representations.[77] This selection of anthropophagous images over those of trade or idyllic life occurred on maps produced in the German lands, Portugal, Spain and the Low Countries.[78] Some mapmakers produced manuscript maps for individual patrons; others produced printed maps to be sold on the open market. Despite these differences in audiences, key motifs of Carib anthropophagy – the spit-roast, the cooking-pot and the limbs hanging from trees – appeared across mapmaking centres. The cannibal butchering-table, a scene reminiscent of medieval iconographic traditions of host desecration and Far Eastern cannibalism but absent from the New World sources, and yet placed in Brazil by the Strasbourg workshop of Johann Grüninger, also travelled across multiple centres of map production.[79] Cannibals on maps were a community invented by a transregional

[76] Ibid., sig. D.iiii.*r*.

[77] An important exception here is the representation of the Tupi on maps produced in Normandy, the subject of Chapter 4.

[78] These examples are analysed in Davies, 'Amerindians on European Maps', chapters 4 and 5.

[79] For an example of a butchering-table associated with the Far East, see Paris, Bibliothèque Nationale de France, Bibliothèque de l'Arsenal, 'Devisement dou monde' 16th century, Mss. Fr. 5219, 119*v*. This is a late example of an illuminated manuscript of Marco Polo's account of the east.

group of mapmakers who, nevertheless, depended on travellers' accounts for content and authority.

The earliest surviving map to illustrate an Amerindian, the manuscript map known as the Kunstmann II map, was probably the work of a Portuguese or Italian mapmaker working in Portugal c.1502–6.[80] The map's New World vignette is the earliest known image of the spit-roasting of human flesh in the Americas, an iconic motif that would later appear across print culture, manuscript images and the decorative arts.[81] The mapmaker or illuminator clearly devised the image by reading travel accounts, but the scene is independent of illustrations in surviving broadsheets and in printed accounts of New World travels that pre-date it. The mapmaker engaged selectively and creatively with multiple sources about this region but, contrary to the conventional narrative of the mapmaker as derivative copier of illustrations devised by others, made up his own.

Although the mapmaker drew on the most recent cartographic information from the Vespuccian voyages, the map's only image for the New World derives from the experiences detailed in the Columbian accounts. The largest illumination on the map is a vignette in Brazil showing a kneeling figure roasting a person whole on a spit (Fig. 3.5). The position of the victim's hands suggests that they have been tied together, and that the arms have been trussed up to the side of the body. These details point to the Scillacio-Coma letter relating to Columbus's second voyage, where we learn that Pedro Margarit saw 'several Indians skewered on spits'.[82] By contrast, Vespucci's description of anthropophagous cookery specifies that bodies were jointed before they were

[80] Munich, Bayerische Staatsbibliothek, Cod. icon. 133. Ivan Kupcík, . . . *Munich Portolan Charts: 'Kunstmann I - XIII' and Ten Further Portolan Charts* (Munich and Berlin: Deutcher Kunstverlag, 2000), 6: Friedrich Kunstmann (1817–1887) was a Munich clergyman who produced a facsimile atlas of thirteen portolan charts numbered 'Kunstmann I' to 'Kunstmann XIII': *Atlas zur Entdeckungsgeschichte Amerikas. Aus Handschriften der K. Hof- und Staats-Bibliothek, der K. Universitaet und des Hauptconservatoriums der K. B. Armee*, ed. Friedrich Kunstmann et al. (Munich, 1859); for the Kunstmann II map, see Blatt II. Kupcík, *Portolan Charts*, 28–31: The map does not show Madagascar; hence, it predates either the discovery of the island in 1506, or widespread knowledge of it. The Brazilian coastline is derived from Vespucci's 1501–2 voyage, which gives the map a *terminus post quem* of 1502. There is no direct evidence of the map's date, creator or intended audience, but the geographical elements, some of which date from Vespucci's voyages, give us the date-range for its production.

[81] For examples across visual culture, see Honour, *New Golden Land*; Karl-Heinz Kohl, ed., *Mythen der Neuen Welt, zur Entdeckungsgeschichte Lateinamerikas* (Berlin: Frölich & Kaufmann, 1982).

[82] See near n. 43.

3.5 Kunstmann II map, c.1506, detail from Brazil.
Bayerische Staatsbibliothek München, Cod. icon. 133.

cooked.[83] The map's inscriptions also offer information drawn from the Columbian voyages. A caption near the Caribbean islands informs the reader that they are called 'Antilia', and that 'all these islands and lands were discovered by a Genoese by the name of Columbus'.[84] Many elements from the nearby captions also appear in the Scillacio-Coma letter: anthropophagy; snakes; parrots; numerous references to gold; cinnamon; and scattered, lawless peoples.[85] A few appear in Columbus's *Letter to Santángel* as well: gold, cinammon and anthropophages.[86]

This image, iconic to the modern eye, was not one that emerged straightforwardly or unconsciously from the sources. Indeed, the map-maker may not have had an illustration of cannibal spit-roasting to hand. The only print showing anthropophagy that might have been in circulation before it was completed in 1505–6 is Froschauer's c.1506 woodcut (Fig. 3.2). This print may not have reached the Kunstman map's illuminator; and, even if it did reach him, it does not contain spit-roasting iconography.

The process of devising a geographically specific vignette, together with the convention of placing images of people who lived in a particular region within that region on the map, led to an image of Antillian and coastal anthropophagy becoming the emblematic scene for Brazil. The inhabitants of the Brazilian interior – a region extrapolated from Vespucci's excursions along the coastline, the extent of which was unknown – were thus emblematized by a practice that had apparently been witnessed by native peoples encountered in the Antilles Islands. Nevertheless, it was precisely this practice of comparing multiple travellers' accounts and synthesizing selected material into a visual form that made maps authoritative reference sources.

It was not inevitable that these workshop practices would lead to the region of Brazil being associated primarily with anthropophagy. The motif

[83] Here I disagree with scholars who have suggested that the image derives from the capture, execution and consumption of a sailor on Vespucci's third voyage to the New World, c.1501–2 (see, for example, *BAV*, V, 251; Susi Colin, 'Woodcutters and Cannibals: Brazilian Indians as seen on Early Maps', in *AEM*, 175–81, at 176; Sebastián, *Iconografía*, 30–1). The Kunstmann II vignette does not match Vespucci's version of the roasting process: 'where the women themselves were already hacking our young man up into pieces, and, at a great fire they had built, were roasting him before our eyes, showing us many pieces and then eating them' (Vespucci, *Letters*, 89; *NRC-V*, I, 370–1: 'ubi mulieres ipsae erant, quae iuvenem nostrum, quem trucidaverant (nobis videntibus) in frusta secabant, necnon frusta ipsa nobis ostentantes, ad ingentem quem succenderant ignem torrebant, et deinde posthaec manducabant'.).

[84] 'Omnes istae insulae ac terrae inventae fuerunt ab uno Genuensi nomine Columbo'.

[85] *RC xii*, *AC*, 6.2.8–6.2.25. [86] Columbus, *Letters from America*, 50–63.

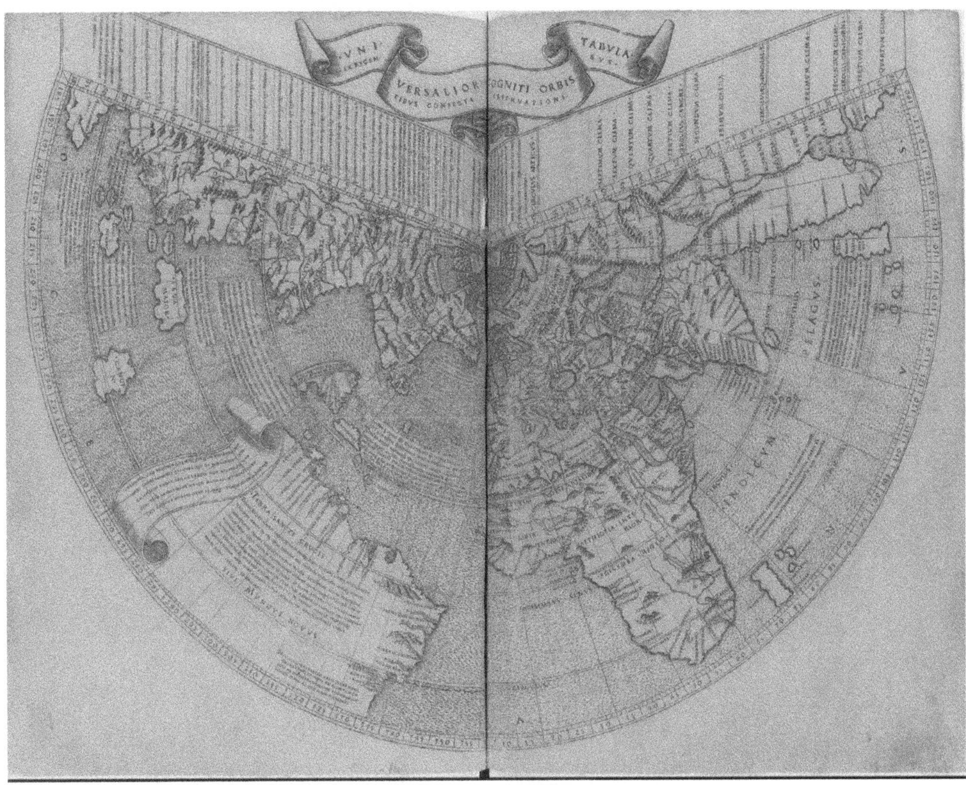

3.6 Johannes Ruysch, *Universalior cogniti orbis tabula ex recentibus confecta observationi* (Rome, 1507). Courtesy of the John Carter Brown Library at Brown University, JCB Z P975 1507 / 2-SIZE (copy 1).

is not the central focus on the 1507 world map by Johannes Ruysch, the earliest printed world map to include commentary on the Americas, which appeared in the 1508 Rome edition and in late issues of the 1507 edition of Ptolemy's *Geographia*.[87] The map extends from the North Pole to some 38 degrees below the equator, and divides the world below the Arctic Circle (*circulus arcticus*) into seven climatic zones north of the equator and four zones south of the equator (Fig. 3.6). The map's southern edge is just south of the tip of Africa, and passes though a large landmass to the west entitled 'Terra sancte crucis sive Mundus novus' (Land of the Holy Cross or New World). The lower reaches of 'Mundus novus' remain unknown, falling outside the map. They lie to the southeast of the east Asian islands that include Java major and Java minor.

[87] Johannes Ruysch, *Universalior cogniti orbis tabula ex recentibus confecta observationi* (Rome, 1507).

Since the map encompassed the entire known world on a space of approximately 45 cm by 60 cm, we must assume that Ruysch thought carefully about what information to include on it. For the extensive text captions, the most prominent of which appear in the New World, Ruysch could have drawn on the edition of Vespucci's *Mundus Novus* that Matthias Ringmann had published to accompany Martin Waldseemüller's 1507 world map.[88] The central caption summarizes many of the key elements of Vespucci's ethnography of the northeast coast of what is now Brazil: warfare, the lack of leaders and religion, feather headdresses, *anthropophagi*, herbal cures and longevity. It offers brief notes on the region's natural history and commodities. While Vespucci had only traversed the coastal areas, the caption appears in the centre of the landmass. For a Renaissance viewer, the caption would have signified activities across this landmass. The map's fairly general approach to summarizing the region is in keeping with late medieval decisions about what to include on maps. Ruysch's map and the Kunstmann II map, appearing within five years of one another, illuminate how different visions of Brazil's peoples could be devised from the same sources.

Mapping cannibals

The earliest printed map to illustrate New World anthropophages, Martin Waldseemüller's world map of 1516 known as the *Carta Marina* (Fig. 3.7), helped to circulate the spit-roasting image that had appeared in the tradition of Portuguese manuscript cartography. The map's vignette of cannibalism in the Brazilian interior – taken from printed descriptions about the Caribbean islands, and appearing decades before European printed travel accounts about Brazil itself – spread to maps across multiple centres of production and to imagery on prints (Fig. 3.8).[89] The Latin

[88] Martin Waldseemüller and Matthias Ringmann, *Cosmographie introductio quibusdam geometriae [ac] astronomiae principiis ad eam rem necessariis* (St. Dié, 1507). For the map's publishing history, see John W. Hessler, *The Naming of America: Martin Waldseemüller's 1507 World Map and the 'Cosmographiae introductio'* (London: GILES, 2008). For a recent overview, see Hessler and Van Duzer, *Seeing the World Anew.*

[89] While Vespucci had travelled along part of the Brazilian coast, and Waldseemüller drew on Vespucci, it was his information about the Carib peoples of the Caribbean islands and part of the mainland coast, rather than his discussions of the Tupi peoples of the South American mainland, that Waldseemüller used.

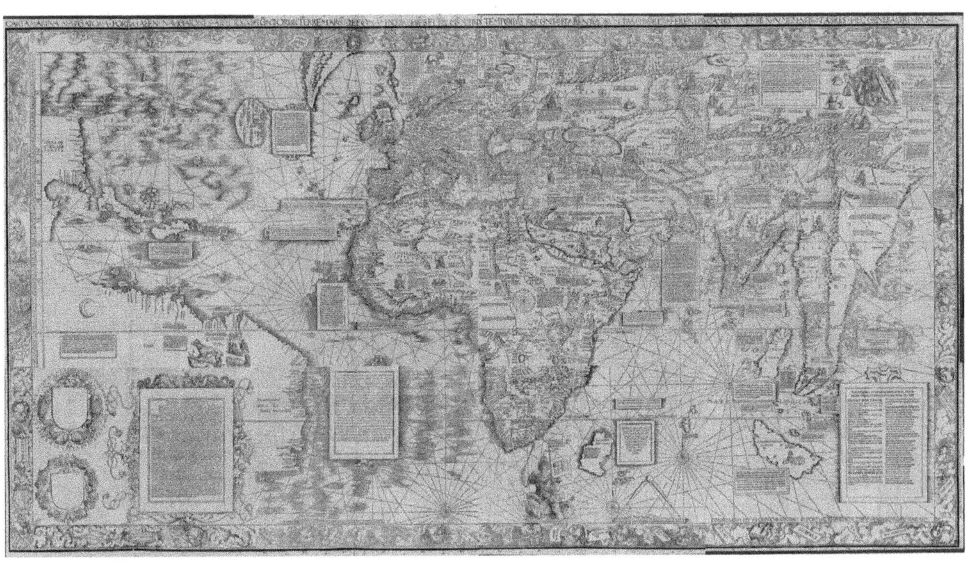

3.7 Martin Waldseemüller, *Carta Marina* ([Strasbourg?], 1516).
Image courtesy of the Jay I. Kislak Foundation and the Library of Congress.

3.8 Martin Waldseemüller, *Carta Marina* ([Strasbourg?], 1516), detail from Brazil.
Image courtesy of the Jay I. Kislak Foundation and the Library of Congress.

map's initial print run may have been around 1,000.[90] The *Carta Marina* was a publishing success: in the 1520s and 1530s, German editions followed, with Lorenz Fries producing these three-quarter sized editions, shortening some of the legends as he rendered them in the vernacular.[91]

Waldseemüller was part of a group of humanists, known as the Gymnasium Vosagense, based in St Dié, on the western foothills of the Vosges mountains.[92] The Gymnasium, despite its inland location far from the Atlantic ports, had privileged access to some of the latest travellers' information. The group worked under the patronage of René II, Duke of Lorraine, under whose auspices his chaplain and secretary Gaultier Lud established a scholarly printing press. The duke also procured, from his contacts in Lisbon, manuscripts relating to the discoveries in the western ocean. These included a French translation of the letter Vespucci had sent to Soderini (here addressed to René II) and a number of maps.[93]

The *Carta Marina*'s man-eating vignette (Fig. 3.8) is compositionally similar to the scene on Johann Froschauer's broadsheet (Fig. 3.2).[94] On the latter, the cannibalism is muted by the broader scenes of social interaction. While human body parts hang from the rafters of a wooden

[90] Martin Waldseemüller, *Carta Marina* ([Strasbourg?], 1516). The sole surviving copy is in the Jay I. Kislak Collection in the Library of Congress, Washington, DC. The *Carta Marina* comprises twelve woodcuts printed on separate sheets, each 45.5 x 62 cm. Only a single copy, a proof state, is known today. For facsimiles, see Hessler and Van Duzer, *Seeing the World Anew*; Fischer and Wieser, *Oldest Map*.

[91] Hildegard Binder Johnson, *Carta Marina: World Geography in Strassburg, 1525* (Minneapolis, MN: University of Minnesota Press, 1963).

[92] For overviews of the Gymnasium, see Albert Ronsin, 'L'Amérique du Gymnase vosgien de Saint-Dié-des-Vosges', in *La France-Amérique (XVIe-XVIIIe siècles)*, ed. Frank Lestringant (Paris, 1998), 37–64; Seymour I. Schwartz, *Putting 'America' on the Map: The Story of the Most Important Graphic Document in the History of the United States* (Amherst, NY: Prometheus, 2007), 34–49. For further bibliography, see Hiatt, *Terra Incognita*, 218, n. 6.

[93] Ronsin, 'L'Amérique', 38–9.

[94] The vignette also shares features with a woodcut of uncertain date by the Flemish printer Jan van Doesborgh, *Of the Newe Landes*, (title-page and sig. [A.ii.*r*]) and idem, *De novo mondo*. Common to the Doesborgh and Waldseemüller images are the body parts hanging from above, the nursing woman and the man with a bow. Van Doesborgh's woodcuts are dated to c.1511–23. The *Carta Marina* could have been one of its sources, rather than vice versa. Alternatively, both may have drawn independently on the Froschauer woodcut. In any case, there are no surviving printed precedents for the *Carta Marina*'s spit-roast and hunter and neither printed nor manuscript examples of the hunter draped with a body predate the map. *De novo mondo*, 9, hesitantly suggests 1520 for the date of the Doesborgh woodcut; Sturtevant, 'First Visual Images', 446, n. 13 gives a broader range. for a bibliographical overview, see *De novo mondo*, 1–5; Proctor, *Doesborgh, Printer at Antwerp:*, 32–3. See also n. 64.

structure and a fire beneath serves to smoke them,[95] the broadsheet does not revolve around its discreet scene of spit-roasting. The nursing figure and man carrying a bow in the foreground of the print form, by contrast, a cannibalistic composition on the map: the seated woman gnaws a human limb; the nearby man carries one of his victims. The jewels in faces mentioned in Vespucci and in Froschauer's caption, and illustrated on the broadsheet, do not appear.

As with the 1506 Kunstman II map, the *Carta Marina* illustrates cannibalism within the northeast portion of Brazil (Fig. 3.8). The scene shows the return of a hunter with his victim, the spit-roasting of the carcass in jointed portions and the eating of flesh. The limbs on a tree suggest a further stage – hanging the meat in order to tenderize it and to keep it out of the reach of animals. Some of these details had been described in Peter Martyr's *Oceani decas*:

> Entering the houses they discovered they had ... human flesh in their kitchens, some boiled along with flesh from parrots and ducks, some fixed on skewers ready to be roasted.... They also found the head of a recently killed youth hanging from a beam, still dripping with blood.[96]

This incident took place on Guadeloupe during Columbus's second voyage, and the interpretation in the *Oceani decas* may have inspired the spit-roasting and meat-eating elements.[97] By re-imagining the scene out-of-doors, the artist kept the design simple and gave prominence to the cooking stages.

A menacing inscription identifies this region as 'the land of the cannibals; those who live here are anthropophages'.[98] A lengthier caption informs us that:

> Here is the most cruel nation of anthropophages (whom people call cannibals) which invades the neighbouring islands. They capture people of both sexes by fearful pursuit. They are accustomed to castrating male prisoners just as we do with rams, capons and bulls so that they become fatter for slaying. The old men, however, they directly consign to

95 Established in Schuller, 'Oldest Known Illustration', at 115–7.

96 *RC v, PM*, 1.2.4: 'Domos ingressi habere ... in eorum coquinis elixas cum psittacis et anserinis carnibus carnes humanas, et fixas verubus alias assandas comperere.... Invenere etiam caput nuper occissi iuvenis trabi appensum, sanguine adhuc madidum.'

97 This information also appears in the manuscript letter of Dr Chanca. Peter Martyr either had access to a copy, or heard Chanca's evidence in person. For the letter, see Columbus, *Four Voyages of Columbus*, at 20–73.

98 'Terra cannibalorum qui hanc habitant Anthropophagi sunt'.

> slaughter. They devour the intestines, together with the outer limbs, as a fresh delicacy. The flanks and other parts of the body they preserve in salt. They sustain the female prisoners for the purpose of breeding as we keep hens for eggs, but the old women they set to toil and servitude.[99]

The information paraphrases a passage from one of the versions of Peter Martyr's writings about the Columbian voyages to the Caribbean islands, rather than any journey into the continental interior. The caption most closely resembles a passage in the first edition of Peter's *Oceani decas*.[100]

Three practical factors may have prompted Waldseemüller's placement of cannibals in Brazil. The first was the iconography of the Portuguese manuscript charts which, as another caption informs the reader, formed some of his sources. The *Carta Marina*'s cartography resembles that of 'King Hamy' type maps,[101] of which the Kunstmann II map is an example (Fig. 3.5). No other surviving Portuguese map before 1558 includes similar illustrations, so it is impossible to be sure how representative the Kunstmann II map is of the iconography of any maps that Waldseemüller or his printer Johann Grüninger had to hand.[102] Diogo Homem's 1558 atlas known as the Queen Mary Atlas shows the limbs in trees and spit-roasts, and describes the people of Brazil as *Canibales* who eat human flesh (Fig. 3.9).[103] The Waldseemüller iconographic tradition was an extended synthesis of anthropophagous elements in printed texts about the Caribbean and in the Portuguese manuscript map tradition.

Second, Waldseemüller may have drawn here on Vespucci's *Mundus novus*. The *Mundus Novus* noted the presence, in coastal northern Brazil (a landmass whose full extent was as yet unknown), of 'human flesh salted and suspended from beams throughout the houses, as we hang up bacon

[99] 'Genus que hic antrophagorum [sic] crudelissimum (quos Canibales vocant) insulas vicinas invadit dira persecutione capiunt homines utriusque sexus. Masculos captivos decastrare solent tanquam nos arietes capones bovesque ut crassiores mactationi evadant. Senes autem mox occisioni tradunt et intestina cum exterioribus membris recenti sapore manducant. Latera et alie quidem partes corporis sale conservant. Mulieres captivas sustinent ratione partus sicuti galline apud nos propter ova. Sed vetulas ad labores et ministeria constituunt.'

[100] I deduced this after comparing the map's caption to Trevisano, *Libretto*; Montalboddo, *Paesi*, 1507; idem, *Paesi novamente retrovati* (Milan, 1508); idem, *Newe vnbekanthe Landte* ... (Nuremberg, 1508); idem, *Itinerarium Portugallensium* ... (Milan, 1508), and the 1511 and 1516 editions of the *Oceani decas*.

[101] Johnson, 'German Cosmographers', 27; Hans Wolff, 'The Munich Portolan Charts: Past and Present', in *AEM*, 127–44, at 134.

[102] Maps containing the term 'cannibal' include the Juan de la Cosa map (1500) and the Zorzi map (1500), and the Ruysch map (Rome, 1507).

[103] BL-Mss, Add. MS. 5415.a., f. 23*v*. For a facsimile and discussion, see *The Queen Mary Atlas* ed. Peter Barber (London: Folio Society, 2005) and the accompanying commentary volume.

3.9 Diogo Homem, 'Queen Mary Atlas', 1558, detail from Brazil.

and pork at home'.[104] While the *Carta Marina*'s caption was clearly derived from a Columbian text, as I shall demonstrate later, the vignette of hanging limbs was perhaps inspired by this passage from Vespucci's *Mundus Novus*.

The third factor, one that certainly informed the positioning of many map images, is the challenge posed by scale and composition. The cannibal image would have been almost invisible had it been placed in the tiny Caribbean islands; and mapmakers did not place people associated with particular regions in the ocean, but within the lands they inhabited.[105] The practical considerations of representing nature in a finite space inflected not just mapmaking, of course, but all branches of natural inquiry. Tall plants, for example, might be bent, chopped or sliced to fit on a page while providing sufficient detail of their most important parts.[106] Given the additional spur of Vespucci's references to anthropophages along the Brazilian coast, the placement within a large but indeterminate landmass – which might turn out to be an enormous island – of an amalgamation of Columbian and Vespuccian information about anthropophages was a reasonable decision.[107]

The decision to use ethnographic information from Columbus's rather than Vespucci's voyages for the South American interior was deliberate. This perhaps reflects the change in Waldseemüller's perception, in the period 1507–16, of the relative achievements of Columbus and of Vespucci, the man whose name – Amerigo – Waldseemüller had given to America on his 1507 world map.[108] An earlier stage in this change of heart is visible in the 1513 edition of Ptolemy to which Waldseemüller

[104] *NRC-V*, I, 311: 'per domos humanam carnem salsamet contignationibus suspensam, uti apud nos moris est lardum suspendere et carnem suinam'; Vespucci, *Letters*, 50.

[105] This is the case for all the maps I have examined; I have not found any exceptions elsewhere, apart from classicized scenes portraying figures such as Poseidon, rather than inhabitants of lands nearby, and ethnographic imagery placed in frames outside the map border or in distinct insets. In the late sixteenth century, when Dutch mapmakers began to place peoples in rows and columns on the edges of their maps, they created clearly defined spaces for them. A few unillustrated maps predating Waldseemüller briefly mention 'cannibals' as inhabitants of the Antillean islands. These include the Juan de la Cosa map (1500) and the Zorzi map (1500), and the Ruysch map (Rome, 1507).

[106] Bleichmar, *Visible Empire*, 104.

[107] For the notion of Brazil as another island, see Lestringant, *Cannibals*, 42. There was – and is – no ontological reason to justify why some landmasses are deemed to be islands while others are continents. See Martin W. Lewis and Kären E. Wigen, *The Myth of Continents: A Critique of Metageography* (Berkeley, CA and London: University of California Press, 1997).

[108] For his subsequent rejection of Vespucci, see Johnson, 'German Cosmographers', 32–3. This map does not illustrate Amerindians.

contributed; here, South America was named 'Terra Incognita' rather than 'America'. A nearby caption observed that 'this land with neighbouring islands was discovered by the Genoese Columbus by order of the Castilian King'.[109] In 1516, on the *Carta Marina*, Waldseemüller continued to associate the largest new landmass in the west with Columbus rather than with Vespucci: he drew on the insular Caribbean ethnography of the Columbus letters, pushing it into the Brazilian interior. Thus, the term 'cannibal', originating from the name of the Carib tribes of coastal Brazil and the Antilles, came to be associated with all the inhabitants of Brazil. While the sources do not state who devised each of the map's elements, there is an editorial consistency across the representation of cannibalism on this map.

The immediate priority for German mapmakers was to sell maps to viewers who wished to contemplate the world as a whole. While this goal differed from the needs of the colonial administrators who invoked native cannibalism to justify conquest and the enslavement of Caribs, German maps drew on and helped to circulate the iconographic strategies of Portuguese manuscript charts drawn up for imperially minded audiences.[110] The placement of the map vignette and caption in the South American interior suggested that cannibalism was practised on the enormous landmass, not on some small speck-like islands. While the widespread identification of Brazil with cannibalism in the European imagination in the second half of the sixteenth century is well known, Waldseemüller's map was the reason why, by the 1510s, the region of Brazil was already attracting cannibals from elsewhere.

The French Calvinist Jean de Léry was one traveller who paid great attention to the positioning and details of the imagery on maps. Léry was a member of the 1555–60 expedition to set up the first French colony in Brazil. The naval officer Nicolas Durand de Villegagnon had secured sponsorship from both Catholic and Huguenot patrons, but it appears that, during the expedition, Villegagnon had three Huguenots killed. The rest began to fear for their lives, left the French compound and lived amicably with the Tupinambá, a people of southeastern Brazil, while

[109] Ptolemy, . . . *Geographiae opus* (Strasbourg, 1513), 'Terrae Novae' map: 'Hic terra cum adjacentibus insulis inventa est per Columbum Januensem ex mandato Regis Castelle'.

[110] While it is possible that these mapmakers also saw Spanish manuscript maps depicting cannibals in northern South America, there is no evidence for such maps. Very few illustrated Spanish world maps survive from the sixteenth century.

waiting for the next ship that could take them home.[111] The expedition was a failure; the Portuguese defeated the colony in 1560.[112]

Twenty years later, Léry published his *Histoire d'un voyage faict en la terre du Bresil* (1578).[113] Here, Léry described the barbecue or *boucan*, a cooking arrangement that was apparently unknown in Europe, paying attention to the iconographic details:

> I shall here refute the error of those who, as one case see in their maps of the world, have represented and painted for us the savages of the land of Brazil. . .roasting human flesh on a spit, as we cook mutton joints and other meat; furthermore, they have also falsely shown them cutting it with great iron knives on benches, and hanging the meat up for display, as our beef butchers do over here. Since these things are no truer than the tales of Rabelais about Panurge escaping from the spit larded and half-cooked, it is easy to see that those who make such maps are ignorant, and have never had knowledge of the things they set forth.[114]

Léry evidently expected to see in Brazil on maps precisely located vignettes that articulated the Tupi practices that he had witnessed. His diatribe against all the 'wrong' motifs on maps – motifs he implies are tropes invented by the imagination – is a roll call of the iconography on early sixteenth-century German printed maps.

This passage underlines several fundamental points in my argument. First, into the 1570s, mapmakers based depictions of cannibalism mainly on information about people whom contemporary travel accounts denoted

[111] Jean de Léry, *History of a Voyage to the Land of Brazil, Otherwise Called America*, trans. Janet Whatley (Berkeley, CA: University of California Press, 1990), xvi–xx. For a discussion of the expedition, see Frank Lestringant, *Le Huguenot et le sauvage: L'Amérique et la controverse coloniale, en France, au temps des guerres de religion (1555–1589)*, 3ème éd. revue et augmentée (Geneva: Droz, 2004).

[112] Léry, *Voyage*, ed. Whatley, xix–xxi.

[113] Jean de Léry, *Histoire d'un voyage fait en la terre du Bresil* (La Rochelle, 1578). The *Histoire* was printed in some fourteen editions in the sixteenth century, including in a Dutch translation printed by Cornelis Claesz. A slightly extended version was printed in Geneva in 1580.

[114] Jean de Léry, *Histoire d'un voyage fait en la terre du Brésil [1580]*, ed. Jean-Claude Morisot (Geneva, 1975), 219 (chap. XV): 'ie refuteray ici l'erreur de ceux qui comme on peut voir par leurs cartes vniuerselles, nous ont non seulement representé & peint les sauuages de la terre du Bresil. . .rostissans la chair des hommes embrochee comme nous faisons les membres de moutons & autres viandes: mais aussi ont feint qu'auec de grands couperets de fer ils les coupoyent sur des bancs, & en pendoyent & mettoyent les pieces en monstre, comme font les bouchers la chair de boeuf par-deça. Tellement que ces choses n'estans non plus vrayes que le conte de Rabelais touchant Panurge, qui eschappa de la broche tout lardé & à demi cuit, il est aisé à iuger que ceux qui font telles cartes sont ignorans, lesquels n'ont iamais eu cognoissance des choses qu'ils mettent en auant'; idem, *Voyage*, ed. Whatley, 126–7. I have made minor amendments to the translation.

as Caribs, rather than as Tupinambá. Second, it was difficult for mapmakers to ascertain the geographical extent of the use of the spit-arrangement in the Americas. Third, the placement of Carib iconography within Brazil led a contemporary reader to infer that cannibalism was practised across the whole region – a characterization with serious ramifications for the region's inhabitants. Fourth, the customs and appearance of Brazilian cannibals on maps were a construction by armchair – or, in this case, workshop – ethnographers.

Léry added that when the colonists cooked a guinea hen on a spit, 'they laughed at us, and seeing the meat continually turned, refused to believe that it could cook, until experience showed them so'.[115] This extraordinary statement – an eyewitness observation in service of a counterfactual argument to damn further the map illustrators – is a rare viewer's response to ethnographic material on maps. The Carib scenes that mapmakers used did not reflect Tupinambá customs and thus, for Léry, with the placement of scenes of anthropophagy inside Brazil on maps, the Caribs had been deployed erroneously to emblematize all the region's peoples.[116]

Early sixteenth-century maps were foundational visual works in the invention of the Brazilian as cannibal. This motif, selected from a wider range of possibilities in the original travel accounts, became part of a broader discourse conceptualizing Brazil's inhabitants in word and image in ways that legitimized native slavery. As early as 1503, under pressure from merchants and administrators in Santo Domingo, Queen Isabella of Castile issued a decree whereby the *indios caribes* 'from the Caribbean islands and Cartagena' could be enslaved if they resisted evangelization. While legislation in 1570 outlawed indigenous slavery in Portuguese Brazil, the law contained a similar loophole that permitted the enslavement of prisoners taken in a just war. In both cases, allegations of cannibalism were considered legitimation for just war. Cannibals were sufficiently inhuman not to be covered by natural law. Gradually, ethnic terms such as *caribe*

[115] Léry, *Histoire*, ed. Morisot, 220 (chap. XV): 'eux se rians & moquans de nous ne voulurent iamais croire, les voyans ainsi incessament remuer qu'elles peussent cuire, iusques à ce que l'experience leur monstra du contraire'; idem, *Voyage*, ed. Whatley, 127.

[116] No spits appear in the illustrations of accounts about the Tupi peoples that preceded Léry's, either; the accounts of Hans Staden and André Thevet both depict the *boucan*. See Staden, *Warhaftige Historia*, part 1, Kaps XX, XXXIX, XLI–XLIII; part 2, Kap. XXVIII; André Thevet, *Les Singularitez de la France Antarctique* (Paris, 1557), chap. XL. For a classic study of the iconography of cannibal cookery in the editions of Staden's and Léry's accounts in the De Bry collection of voyages, see Bernadette Bucher, *Icon and Conquest: A Structural Analysis of the Illustrations of de Bry's Great Voyages*, trans. Basia Miller Gulati (Chicago, IL and London: University of Chicago Press, 1981), chaps. 5 and 6.

and Chichimeca were re-defined in colonial Spanish and Portuguese America to mean peoples who were innately given to inhuman, irrational behaviour.[117]

While the map imagery of Brazilian cannibals pre-dated the gradual implementation of forced indigenous labour, the motifs continued into the mid-seventeenth century on Dutch maps, particularly those printed in Amsterdam. That this should be the case even on works printed by map publishers who also published polemical literature against Spanish colonial practices, and through the period when the Dutch were in conflict with Portugal for the colonial possession of Brazil, highlights the disjunction between the overt stance of sympathy taken by, for example, the map publisher Cornelis Claesz and his publishing decisions as a whole.

West is east

The conceptual proximity of the Far East and the New World on the Ruysch world map of 1507 (Fig. 3.6) offers another point of departure for analyzing cannibal iconography on the Waldseemüller *Carta Marina*. While the connection between America and east Asia is difficult to see on maps that place them on opposite sides of a sheet – particularly for modern eyes used to the enormous expanse of the Pacific Ocean – the Ruysch map makes the extrapolation of anthropophages from Java and from the Caribbean Islands to the large island – *Mundus novus* – in between highly reasonable. Viewers could thus have seen the *Carta Marina*'s cannibal vignette as confirming expectations about the distant east and – by extension – about the lands found by sailing to the far west. Anthropophages had long been associated with the Far East. Marco Polo's *Divisament du monde* and the *Book of John Mandeville* place man-eaters in Java; the region is populated with man-eaters on Waldseemüller's *Carta Marina*.

In the *Uslegung der mercarthen*, an illustrated geographical glossary printed to accompany Lorenz Fries's 1525 German translation of Waldseemüller's map, Fries distinguishes between the 'Canibalien' in chapter 60 of the *Uslegung* and the inhabitants of 'Prasilia' in chapter 82 (who are, albeit, shown wearing what appear to be necklaces of human teeth). The book contains an image of dog-headed cannibals managing a cannibal

[117] Van Deusen, *Global Indios*, 3–4.

butcher's shop at the head of the 'Canibalien' chapter and as the title-page image.[118] The distinction anticipates one that would appear in later eyewitness accounts. Thevet, for example, would draw one between 'good' and 'bad' anthropophages: The Tupi, in Thevet's view, merely consumed the flesh of prisoners of war and their offspring; the Cannibals, by contrast, indiscriminately ate human flesh as civil people ate mutton.[119] This distinction between Brazilians and 'Canibalien' is not preserved on Fries's German language world map, which the *Uslegung* accompanied; here, there are anthropophages in Brazil, and the Caribbean islands are unillustrated. Perhaps the exigencies of squeezing images into spaces came into play here.

These images would also have resonated with German mercantile interests in long-distance trading voyages. Many German investors helped to sponsor Iberian eastward and westward voyages.[120] Scenes of anthropophagy, far from raising fears for the safety of their investments, might well have helped to bridge conceptually the unknown distance between those lands reached by sailing west from the Spice Islands of the east. Cartographical knowledge in this era of oceanic exploration comprised not merely where things were in relation to a coordinate system, but also the routes via which they were reached.

The German investors' market might even have inflected the shape of South America – labelled 'Terra Nova' on the Carta Marina. The westward voyages were undertaken in search of eastern islands. By 1516, it was clear that numerous islands had been found by sailing west. By presenting Terra Nova as a separate landmass from Asia, Waldseemüller also denoted it as an island – albeit an enormous one – although he had no way of knowing whether or not Terra Nova was attached to Asia in the east. As he puts it in the *Cosmographiae introductio*, 'the earth is now known to be divided into four parts. The first three of these are connected and are continents, but the fourth part is an island because it has been found to be completely surrounded on all of its sides by sea'.[121] The point about this

[118] Lorenz Fries, *Carta Marina* (Strasbourg, 1525); Lorenz Fries, *Uslegung der mercarthen, oder Carta Marina ...* (Strasbourg, 1525). For an overview, see Johnson, *Carta Marina*.

[119] Whitehead, 'Black Read as Red', 227–8; Lestringant, *Cannibals*, 44–8.

[120] Johnson, *German Discovery of the World*.

[121] Some map scholars have taken this statement to be evidence of secret knowledge about the existence of the Pacific Ocean. There is, however, a simpler, more compelling reason. Some aspects of the claim are clearly false – not only was South America not separate from the land in the north, but the whole American landmass was potentially connected to Asia in the far north; not until 1728 was the narrow waterway between Siberia and Alaska found, and hence the separation between Asia and the Americas. Thus we have no reason to believe that

new island was not its separation from east Asia, but its *similarity* to it as part of a longer island chain associated with spices and anthropophages. In a cultural landscape in which islands were associated with prized commodities, the notion of an enormous island hugging the equator and spreading southwards could well have excited mercantile buyers of the map.[122] In this way, the selection of anthropophages to emblematize Brazil fitted the expectations of merchants desirous of profitable westward voyages to the Far East.

If associating the distant west with the lucrative lands of the distant east was financially attractive, one might ask to what extent the western hemisphere on Waldseemüller's *Carta Marina* of 1516 was merely a reflection of earlier illustrated cartography of Asia. In fact, the types of information that Grüninger's workshop added to the map varied across the parts of the world; the geographical specificity of the iconography rose sharply for the lands in the far west, even though the number of illustrations diminished. Late medieval *mappaemundi* had been less specific with the placement of illustrations insofar as Asia and Africa tended to be illuminated with numerous scenes, without a clear sense of distinct places with different peoples.[123] Similarly, on the *Carta Marina*, Europe was densely covered with place names with the occasional coat of arms, mountain range or river. The ethnography of Africa and Asia on the *Carta Marina* continued the iconographic conventions of medieval illuminated maps:[124] numerous images of kings, often jostling for space, are interspersed with small, occasional depictions of monstrous peoples. On many sixteenth-century world maps, the region of the Americas is replete in blank spaces, all the better to distinguish its constituent regions from one another – precisely denoted by empty areas between them. The makers of the *Carta Marina* and contemporary maps, while clearly informed by classical and medieval

Waldseemüller's supposition that the land in the west was an island was anything other than a guess, albeit one that fits the later discovery of the Pacific. For this, see also Davies, 'America and Amerindians', 359.

122 Ibid. See also Ricardo Padrón, '"The Indies of the West": Or the Tale of how an Imaginary Geography Circumnavigated the Globe', in *Western Visions of the Far East in a Transpacific Age* (Aldershot, Hants, Burlington, VT: Ashgate, 2012), 19–42, at 23–6.

123 Two examples are the thirteenth-century Ebstorf and Hereford maps.

124 See, for example, the Psalter Map (c.1265), the Hereford Map (c.1300), the Fra Mauro Map (c.1459), the Catalan Atlas (c.1375) and the Ebstorf Map (thirteenth century). For the monstrous peoples of the northern climes on this map, see Chet Van Duzer, 'A Northern Refuge of the Monstrous Races: Asia on Waldseemüller's 1516 Carta Marina', *Imago Mundi*, 62:2 (2010), 221–31.

traditions, did not duplicate the cookie-cutter monarchs or the full range of Old World monsters indiscriminately across the American landmasses.

The significance, for the Americas, of the precise placement of ethnographic data is again made clear in an edition of Ptolemy's *Geographia* begun by Waldseemüller, completed by the physician and mapmaker Lorenz Fries and printed by Johann Grüninger in 1522. In Brazil, near a cannibal vignette closely modelled on the *Carta Marina*, is a caption: 'Antropophagi hic sunt' (here there are anthropophages), signalling to viewers that this very spot was where the activity took place. As Christian Jacob put it in his reflection on the 'hic sunt…' construct on illustrated maps, 'the image produces meaning by its very localization'.[125] In essence, location, direction and route, however imperfectly known, were the organizing principles for structuring knowledge – ethnographic or otherwise – in cartographic form in the Renaissance. Mapmakers were not prepared, by and large, to add to the Americas information that had not come from westward voyages.

The travels of the German Brazilian cannibal

The *Carta Marina* and its later editions informed influential makers of printed maps, cosmographies and geographies including Sebastian Münster, Peter Apian, Oronce Fine, Joachim Vadian and Abraham Ortelius.[126] A new motif – the cannibal hut – emerged when a map illustrator consulted a travel edition with the *Carta Marina*'s iconography in his mind's eye. The world map, the work of humanist geographer Sebastian Münster, first appeared in a 1532 compendium of travel accounts and geography that included extracts on cannibals derived from the *Libretto* or the *Paesi*.[127] Its illustrations have been attributed to Hans Holbein the Younger.[128] The bottom-left corner of the map contains new and old motifs of anthropophagy, creatively combined to offer a diorama of daily cannibal life (Fig. 3.10).[129]

125 Ptolemy, … *Opus geographia* (Strasbourg, 1522), map 28; Jacob, *Sovereign Map*, 171.

126 Fischer and Wieser, *Oldest Map*, 40.

127 Johann Huttich, *Novus orbis regionum ac insularum veteribus incognitarum, una cum tabula cosmographica, et aliquot aliis consimilis argumenti libellis* …, preface, Simon Grynaeus (Basle and Paris, 1532). For contents and editions, see *BA*, IX, nos 34100–34107.

128 Dackerman, *Prints*, 246, item 84. Holbein had produced illustrations for another mathematical work of Münster's, also printed in Basel by Henricus Petrus, in 1544; see ibid., 246, item 58. The map also appeared in the Basle editions of 1537 and 1555. For Münster's writing on America, see Davies, 'America and Amerindians'.

129 Sebastian Münster, *Typus cosmographicus universalis* (Basle, 1532).

3.10 Sebastian Münster, *Typus cosmographicus universalis* in Johann Huttich, ed., *Geographica universalis* (Basle, 1532). Beinecke Rare Book and Manuscript Library, Yale University, 1986 +106.

All the elements of Léry's complaint appear here. The American vignette contains the butchering-table and joints roasting on a spit, which were both becoming customary. A man leads a horse to which a trussed figure has been tied. The hand protruding from a cooking pot reflects printed descriptions; Peter Martyr had mentioned human body parts boiled with animals.[130]

The hair-raising image of a head and limbs hanging from a hut does not appear in any known illustrations that pre-date it. It (or its lost source) amalgamated two motifs from Vespuccian sources: huts and body parts hanging from roofs. The description of the cannibals' houses as wooden huts had appeared in both Columbian and Vespuccian texts, but neither mentioned body parts hanging outside them. In the Soderini letter we merely learn that: 'Their dwellings are firmly constructed in the shape of a bell from large trees fastened together, and are covered with palm leaves, which offer most ample protection against the winds and storms.'[131] In the Scillacio-Coma letter from Columbus's second voyage, the huts are pleasing objects of marvel:

> The elegance of the magnificent houses, built with thicker reeds and resembling canopies, instantly turned the faces of our men in wonder. The ingeniously worked wood aroused delight; the perfectly handled timbers, covetousness.[132]

Far from necessarily eliciting disgust or horror, this extract shows how huts could stimulate feelings of admiration. By embellishing the cannibals' pyramid-shaped houses with the hanging body parts described elsewhere, the map illustration turned a marvellous object demonstrating artisanal skill into one highlighting violence.[133]

130 The printed sources include the *Libretto* and *Paesi* (chap. xcii) and the 1511 and 1516 editions of Peter Martyr.

131 Martin Waldseemüller, *The Cosmographiae introductio [1507] in Facsimile*, ed. Charles George Herbermann, intro. Joseph Fischer and Franz von Wieser (Freeport, NY: Books for Libraries Press, 1969 [first published in 1907]), LIII–LIV and 97; Waldseemüller and Ringmann, *Cosmographie introductio*, sig. c.i.*r*-*v*: 'illorum domus campanarum instar constructae sunt firmiter ex magnis arboribus solidatae palmarum foliis desuper contectae et adversus ventos et tempestates tutissime . . . esse'. I have amended the translation slightly.

132 *RC xii*, 6.2.9: 'Domus magnificae arundinibus textae crassioribus, conopea imitatae, quarum elegantia nostrorum ora verterunt protinus in admirationem; ligna affabre extructa voluptatem, tigna examussim elaborata cupidinem auxere'. Huts also appear in Peter Martyr's text: *RC v*, *PM*, 1.2.3; and hanging limbs, in ibid., 1.2.4.

133 The hut reappeared in a simpler form – minus some of the dismembered limbs and the person peeking out of the entrance – in Münster's 1540 map of America, *Novae insulae, XVII nova tabula* in idem, *Geographia universalis, vetus et nova, complectens Claudii Ptolemaei Alexandrini enarrationis libros VIII* (Basle, 1540). The map was reprinted in multiple editions of Münster's *Cosmographia universalis* from 1544.

The motifs developed in the Rhenish lands soon spread to other regions of production. A number of motifs that appeared on Waldseemüller's 1516 *Carta Marina* resurface on later Portuguese manuscript maps.[134] It is impossible to be certain whether the manuscript illuminators had seen the *Carta Marina*, which may have been produced in 1,000 copies, and was succeeded by later editions. The similarities could equally be the consequence of Waldseemüller's own dependence on Iberian manuscript cartography. Portuguese manuscript maps contain several motifs in the region of Brazil that are characteristic of early sixteenth-century travellers' descriptions of Carib, rather than Tupi, peoples. Key among these was the roasting-spit that, as we shall see in Chapter 4, the Tupi peoples who Léry encountered did not use. Since Portuguese traders in Brazil had had dealings (peaceful and otherwise), with the local Tupi tribes, the Carib cast of Brazilian ethnography on maps suggests that these traders' accounts, none of which are known to have been printed in this period, had only a limited effect on wider perceptions of the peoples of Brazil, even in Portugal.

Mapmakers in the Low Countries began producing maps illustrated with the world's peoples in the mid-sixteenth century. Their main source of cartographic information was Spain; the few Spanish printed maps had been produced at Antwerp, a city with a highly developed printing tradition in the sixteenth century. For iconographic material, however, these mapmakers drew on German illustrations, a practice that helped to cement Waldseemüller's mainland cannibal practices within the map traditions of the Low Countries and, through their circulation in Spain, England and elsewhere, to inflect viewers' opinions about the inhabitants of the New World.[135]

Conclusion

Mapmakers managed alterity through dietary difference, a tradition of ethnography with an ancient lineage. Despite this, the choice of Waldseemüller or his printer Grüninger to place cannibals – and only cannibals – in Brazil constituted a departure from the medieval conventions for illustrating the inhabitants of the southern and western extremes of the world, from the vantage-point of Europe. While surviving world maps from the

[134] For examples, see Davies, 'Amerindians on European Maps', chap. 4.

[135] Numerous examples are discussed in Davies, 'Amerindians on European Maps', chapters 4 and 5.

thirteenth century placed *anthropophagi* in Africa and Asia, they also included a host of other extraordinary figures that had appeared in Pliny, such as the long-eared *Panotti* and one-legged *Sciapodes*. Similarly, a wide range of monstrous peoples appears in the easternmost regions of Asia, and in Africa, on sixteenth-century maps.[136]

This type of imagery might appear at first sight to be highly sensationalized, devised from the medieval monster tradition by a printer with his eye on sales figures. Waldseemüller's *Carta Marina*, however, is so richly covered in Latin inscriptions that identify its monstrous peoples that we must assume that he, or other humanists, were involved in choosing the material and devising the illuminations. The details of the iconography of Brazilian cannibalism can be traced beyond Grüninger's workshop to contemporary travellers' accounts. Indeed, even the monsters in the Old World on the *Carta Marina* had been described by earlier travellers, or by authors who had spoken to eyewitnesses.[137] For scholar-geographers, ethnographic marvels from eyewitness sources were credible.

Nevertheless, there was no reason why German humanists should necessarily have emphasized monstrosity over peaceful activities. The Venetian Fra Mauro map (c.1459) was based heavily on Marco Polo's *Divisament dou monde*, and yet it concentrates on information of relevance to merchants, particularly the locations of spices.[138] Just as Fra Mauro was working in Venice at a time when the city's sons were actively engaged in trade with the east, Waldseemüller and other German cartographers and printers could have chosen to emphasize the trading possibilities of this new world, with a German mercantile audience in mind.[139] German mapmakers might have begun a tradition of illustrating commodities such as gold, pearls and brazilwood in map interiors.

Equally, the Americas could have been epitomized by images of the Terrestrial Paradise. By the fifteenth century, both southern Africa and Asia were associated with Paradise. While these may seem to be mutually

[136] See, for example, the Rylands and Desceliers 1550 manuscript maps, studied in Chapter 4.

[137] See Johnson, 'Buying Stories', for the ways in which German publishers and cosmographers paid attention to particular details in travel writing, and valued eyewitness authority in ancient texts, and judged new authorities against them.

[138] Angelo Cattaneo, *Fra Mauro's Mappa Mundi* (Turnhout: Brepols, 2011), 205–11. For the map's inscriptions, see Piero Falchetta, *Fra Mauro's World Map: With a Commentary and Translations of the Inscriptions* (Turnhout: Brepols, 2006).

[139] For German mercantile interests overseas, particularly the spice trade, see Johnson, *German Discovery*, 92–103 and chap. 4 in the same work.

contradictory locations, in fact, there had long been an association between the two regions, as well as a cross-fertilization of what was to be expected in each.[140] Travellers to the Caribbean and the South American mainland had suggested that Paradise was nearby; the nudity of the local inhabitants was thought by some to corroborate this.

Stephanie Leitch's thoughtful monograph on early sixteenth-century ethnographic images in German print culture emphasizes the roles played by humanist scholarship and by exotic artefacts and specimens made available by local merchants. Leitch focused on two artists, Hans Burgkmair and Jörg Breu, and prints they made in c.1508 and 1515, respectively. In this study of mapping others in largely the metaphorical sense,[141] Leitch asserts that: 'Humanist mediation kept these artists' representations free from both the discourse of monstrous races that historically characterized travel accounts, as well as from the propagandistic and colonial taint that would mark images of these same subjects in the wake of conquest.'[142] The engagement of Rhenish mapmakers with the Americas reveals a contrasting facet of German print culture. In 1516, the Grüninger workshop created an iconic Amerindian image on the *Carta Marina* that reinforced rather than exploded the discourse of monstrous peoples. Despite Waldseemüller's humanist training, the makers of this map also placed a number of monstrous peoples around the northern, southern and eastern edges of the Old World. These included the chopper-happy anthropophage in Java and the Parossites in Tartaria who subsisted on an ethereal diet of the vapours of cooked meat.[143] Since Latin texts about these beings appear on the map, we must assume that an educated

[140] Scafi, *Mapping Paradise*, 218.

[141] Leitch, *Mapping Ethnography*. Few of the prints discussed are also maps. The important exception is the map in the 1492 *Nuremberg Chronicle*, which Leitch discusses in chap. 2. Leitch also argues that Hans Burgkmair's famous multi-block ethnographic woodcut (1508) is a map (76–7). I take a different view: while the woodcuts do arrange the peoples of Africa and Asia in the order in which the merchant Balthasar Springer encountered them on his voyage to East Asia, this is not sufficient reason to call Burgkmair's ethnographic frieze a map. The only space that is represented visually is the space within each vignette. While the sailing-route from Europe to East Asia was two-dimensional, the woodcuts have been designed as a one-dimensional frieze, not as a map of the sailing-route. One might consider the frieze as a visual itinerary, however, but it is no closer to a portolan *chart* or an itinerary map than it is to a portolan (a book of written sailing-directions).

[142] Leitch, *Mapping Ethnography*, 3.

[143] For Waldseemüller's sources for the monsters of northern Europe and Asia, see Van Duzer, 'Northern Refuge': this shows that the main sources were ultimately John of Plano Carpini's travel narratives, as abstracted in the *Speculum historiale* of Vincent de Beauvais, and a cosmographical treatise, Pierre d'Ailly's *Imago Mundi*. In both cases, it is very likely that most of the ethnographic illustrations on Waldseemüller's map were original compositions.

individual was involved in devising the violent ethnographic content that Waldseemüller's successor, Fries, would reinforce.

Sebastian Münster, another humanist working in the 1530s–1550s, continued this tradition; his 1532 world map emblematized the inhabitants of America through every anthropophagous trope available: butchering tables; amputated limbs jostling uneasily with shrunken heads hanging from rafters, like so many sides of ham (or perhaps *Würste*); and cannibal cooking-pots (which do represent Tupi practice) from which dismembered hands protrude in a forlorn but ultimately futile fashion. By 1550 and the publication of the most comprehensive edition of Münster's *Cosmographia* in his own lifetime, a range of printed texts described other Amerindian peoples, notably the inhabitants of the Inca and Mexica regions. All the same, the cannibals are the only Amerindian people that Münster chose to discuss at length in the *Cosmographia*. Münster lists many of his sources in a catalogue of authors that appears among the work's prefatory materials. Among these are Columbus, Vespucci and Lorenz Fries. The cannibals' monstrous behaviour echoed that of Andaman islanders and other anthropophages who were splattered across the sensational pages of medieval sources from the *Wonders of the East* to the *Book of John Mandeville*.[144]

Waldseemüller's decision to link information about the anthropophagy of the Caribbean with Brazil constructed a particular notion of Brazilian activities in the European imagination. While a Portuguese manuscript map might have inspired the image, the *Carta Marina* disseminated it in print. Western European printed and manuscript map traditions were intricately entangled; elements of the *Carta Marina*'s iconography – relating to the New and Old Worlds – also appeared in French manuscript maps and shaped subsequent Portuguese manuscript maps.[145]

Renaissance German mapmakers made choices for the details, composition and location of ethnographic material on maps; map viewers paid attention to these choices. There was reasonable cause in the available sources for the invention of Waldseemüller's Amerindian anthropophages, if not for Münster's continuing deployment of them at the expense of every other Amerindian people. In addition, anthropophages had long been associated with the spice-rich islands of the Moluccas. For both Portuguese manuscript maps commissioned to celebrate Portuguese navigational achievements, and for German maps drawing on those maps and printed

[144] Anthropophages appear on on the edges of the habitable world on medieval maps such as the Hereford map; see Mittman, *Maps and Monsters*, 40, 57–8.

[145] See Chapter 4.

texts, choosing the cannibal motif for Brazil connected the lands found by sailing west to the riches of the Far East. Finally, dietary practices had commonly helped to delineate different peoples in the Old World on maps. Since there was almost no evidence in the travel accounts of physical abnormalities among the Amerindians, the most fundamental way in which these peoples could be distinguished from Europeans was through the representation of their anthropophagy.

The circulation of these maps and of geographical works informed by them formed part of the intellectual landscape in which native peoples were being coerced or enslaved into working in gold and silver mines in the Caribbean islands, Mexico, Brazil, Peru and the northern Andes. Indigenous persons and transported Africans developed Afro-indigenous populations and cultures over time in these mining regions, as well as mulatto (Afro-European) and mestizo (indigenous-European) groups.[146] Individuals identified as Carib cannibals were the only peoples of the Caribbean islands and nearby mainland regions who could legally be enslaved, although many persons were enslaved through the loopholes in the terminology.[147] Mapmakers chose cannibalism for epistemological reasons, but their choices created the kind of Indian who chimed with colonial linguistic invention. German maps, however, went a step further than the binary of 'peaceful' and 'warlike' Indians, and implied instead that all of the peoples of Brazil were cannibals and thus lawfully enslavable.

[146] For *mestisaje* or cultural intermixing in mining communities, see Kris Lane, 'Africans and Natives in the Mines of Spanish America', in *Beyond Black and Red: African-Native Relations in Colonial Latin America*, ed. Matthew Restall (Albuquerque, NM: University of New Mexico Press, 2005), 159–84; for the same in Brazil, see Stuart B. Schwartz and Hal Langfur, 'Tapahuns, Negros da Terra, and Curibocas: Common Cause and Confrontation between Blacks and Natives in Colonial Brazil', in *Beyond Black and Red: African-Native Relations in Colonial Latin America*, ed. Matthew Restall (Albuquerque, NM: University of New Mexico Press, 2005), 81–114.

[147] See Van Deusen, *Global Indios*.

4 Trade, empires and propaganda

Brazilians on French maps in the age of François I and Henri II

To European readers of contemporary travel writing in the first half of the sixteenth century, the region they had come to know as Brazil was a land of ferocious cannibals. As we saw in Chapter 3, early German printed travel editions, geographical works and maps were instrumental in circulating graphic vignettes of cannibals dismembering their victims, hanging limbs from rooftops and roasting body parts on spits. The motif of the Brazilian cannibal was the earliest for a New World people to appear on maps and the most prevalent, appearing on works produced in Portugal, Spain, the German lands and the Low Countries. In the light of such evidence, a complaint made in the 1530s by the Norman poet and navigator Pierre Crignon may seem surprising:

> If the king would but loosen the bridle on French merchants, in less than four or five years they would win for him the friendships and ensure the obedience of the Brazilian natives without other arms than persuasion and good conduct.[1]

Crignon was frustrated by the policies of François I of France limiting French access to Brazil, a region claimed by the Portuguese crown. To Crignon, were François to permit the French – in particular, Norman sailors – to travel to Brazil, they would be able to trade successfully with the indigenous Tupinambá tribes.

What was the basis for Crignon's assertion? It is unlikely that his complaint was merely an empty promise – he had already been to Brazil, and would presumably not have wished to send his countrymen to cannibal cooking-pots for want of proper preparation and caution. Nor was he alone in his opinion. Crignon's view of the Tupinambá as amenable trading partners is echoed across Norman visual culture, from stained-glass windows to pieces of sculpture and, in particular, on illuminated

[1] See A. Anthiaume, *Cartes marines, constructions navales, voyages de découverte chez les normands, 1500–1650*, 2 vols. (Paris: Ernest Dumont, 1916), II, 194: 'Si le Roi . . . voulait lâcher la bride aux négociants français, en moins de quatre ou cinq ans ceux-ci lui auraient conquis l'amitié et assuré l'obéissance des indigènes brésiliens, sans autres arms que la persuasion et les bon procédés'.

Norman manuscript maps. The peaceful iconography on Norman maps contrasts sharply with other European cartographic traditions. It also differed from the illustrated maps circulating in sixteenth-century France more generally, many of which originated outside France. As the Huguenot traveller Jean de Léry had noted, mapmakers 'in their maps of the world, have not only represented and painted the savages of the land of Brazil roasting human flesh on a spit, as we cook mutton joints and other meat . . . but also cutting it with great iron knives on benches, and hanging the meat up for display, as our beef butchers do over here'.[2]

The differences between Brazilians as represented in Norman nautical circles (i.e., among mapmakers and travellers) and as depicted in other traditions prompt questions about the construction, circulation and interpretation of knowledge about distant regions. Although it has been rightly suggested that these illustrations reflected French trading experiences,[3] they have not been analysed alongside contemporary textual descriptions. Several questions remain to be answered. What relationships existed between Norman cartographic imagery and travel writing? To what extent was map imagery based on widely circulating printed sources of the type consulted by Portuguese, German and Dutch mapmakers? In what ways were their unusually peaceful depictions of Brazilians informed by local economic and political agendas, rather than by perceived realities? How did these ornate and expensive artefacts, often given as gifts, function within the culture of gift exchange? This chapter addresses these questions and seeks to rethink the methodology for approaching the iconography of maps in relation to the interplay between cultural encounters, trade and Atlantic empires.

Seven surviving Norman maps and atlases depicting the inhabitants of Brazil predate the first French attempt to set up a colony in Brazil in 1555–6. They also predate the influential illustrated narratives by Hans Staden, André Thevet and Jean de Léry. The three works offering the most extensive treatments of Brazilian ethnography form the focus here: the Rotz Atlas (1542), the Vallard Atlas (1547) and the Desceliers planisphere or world map (1550).[4] These works, analysed comparatively alongside travel writing and the Norman political and economic milieu, allow us to reconstruct what their Brazilian imagery would have signified to contemporary viewers.

[2] See Chapter 3, near n. 114. [3] Colin, *Das Bild des Indianers*, 133–50.

[4] BL-Mss, Royal MS. 20.E.IX, Rotz Atlas; HL, HM 29, Vallard Atlas; BL-Mss, Add. MS 24095.

Normandy and Brazil

In the first half of the sixteenth century, Normandy was a centre of long-distance trade. The prosperous port city of Dieppe, where the majority of Norman mapmakers were based, had the largest share of maritime commerce in Normandy, perhaps in all of France.[5] Transoceanic traders required ships and navigational aids including maps, fuelling further local enterprise. For Norman ports, long-distance trade was a 'key industry' in the Braudellian sense: the health of a number of activities, from cloth-making to cartography, spice trading to shipbuilding depended on the continuation of direct trade with Brazil and the East Indies.[6]

Brazil was of particular economic importance, supplying such commodities as brazilwood, cotton, pearls, parrots and monkeys. A red pigment extracted from brazilwood was used by cloth- and tapestry-makers in Normandy and Flanders. It was cheaper than the pigment that was shipped from the Far East via a much longer journey, but had similar properties.[7] In the second half of 1529 alone, two hundred tonnes of dyewood were unloaded at Honfleur.[8]

The patterns of sponsorship of French trade differed from the state-sponsored paradigm that operated in Spain and Portugal. The Treaty of Tordesillas (1494) signed by the Iberian kingdoms, and based on papal bulls, divided the world between them.[9] On this basis, these nations attempted to monopolize trade and settlement in those parts of the Americas, Africa and Asia reached by oceanic voyages. At first, the French did not object, but in 1536 François I sent an envoy to Pope Clement VII asking for an arbitration. Clement decreed that Pope Alexander VI's earlier bull applied only to the known lands and not to those discovered later by other nations. This freed French explorers to claim parts of America, albeit

[5] H. Pigeonneau, *Histoire du commerce de la France*, 2 vols. (Paris; Léopold Cerf, 1885–89), II, 136–7.

[6] See Fernand Braudel, *Civilisation and Capitalism, 15th-18th Century*, 3 vols., trans. Siân Reynolds (London: Fontana, 1985), II, 311–4.

[7] Olive Patricia Dickason, 'The Brazilian Connection: A Look at the Origin of French Techniques for Trading with Amerindians', *Revue française d'histoire d'outre-mer*, LXXI (1984), 129–46, at 129–31. For the trade before the discovery of America, see Jean-Marc Montaigne, *Le Trafiq du brésil: navigateurs normands, bois-rouge et cannibales pendant la renaissance* (Rouen: ASI Communication, 2000), 38.

[8] Michel Mollat du Jourdin, 'Premières relations entre la France et le Brésil: des Verrazani à Villegaignon', *Cahiers de l'Institut des hautes études de l'Amérique latine*, 6 (1964), 59–74, at 66.

[9] *RC x, LD*, 12.

without Iberian approval.[10] Nevertheless, during much of this period, voyages leaving Norman and Breton ports had little royal support.[11]

Continuous diplomatic pressure on the French Crown from the Iberian monarchs meant that the impetus behind French exploration and maritime politics came not from the court in Paris, but from private sponsors – merchant ship-owners and outfitters known as *armateurs*.[12] Early forays in Brazil and Guinea convinced them that trade rather than colonial establishment was the most profitable enterprise for their agents.[13] Thus French voyages had different objectives from Iberian ones, favouring quick profits over long-term colonization. Among the ship-owning dynasties, the Ango family was probably the most active in Dieppe. Jean Ango the Younger, the family's best-known scion, financed numerous expeditions to the Americas and the Far East.[14] He was appointed lieutenant to the Admiral of France in 1536.[15]

The king's good will was of paramount importance to Norman *armateurs*. From the point of view of their Portuguese rivals, Norman merchants could not lawfully trade in Brazil. The Portuguese crown did not approve of what it perceived as interlopers in its territory. It attempted to restrict French incursions into Brazil through a combination of diplomatic activities, sanctioning attacks on Norman trading ships and bribing French officials and even *armateurs*. Portuguese forces and French privateers frequently engaged each other in battle, both at sea and in Brazil. Reparations for subsequent losses formed part of the benefits each side sought through diplomatic channels.[16] François I was also pressured by the *armateurs* themselves, who desired unimpeded trading opportunities.

[10] R. J. Knecht, *The Rise and Fall of Renaissance France, 1483–1610* (London: Fontana, 1996), 290–1.

[11] Gayle Brunelle, 'The Images of Empire: Francis I and His Cartographers', in *Princes and Princely Culture, 1450–1650*, ed. Martin Gosman et al., 2 vols. (Leiden and Boston, MA: Brill, 2003–5), I, 81–102, 83–4. The exceptions were the 1524 voyage of Giovanni da Verrazzano, Jacques Cartier's three voyages to northeast America (1534–38) and the Coligny expedition to Brazil (1555–6). Dozens of ships sailed every year solely for private trade.

[12] Charles André Julien, *Les Débuts de l'expansion et de la colonisation françaises (XVe-XVIe siècles)* (Paris: Presses universitaires de France, 1947), 73–6.

[13] L. Vitet, *Histoire des anciennes villes de France. Première série. Haute-Normandie. Dieppe*, 2 vols. (Paris: Alexandre Mesnier, 1833), II, 147.

[14] See Eugène Guénin, *Ango et ses pilotes d'après des documents inédits* (Paris: Imprimerie Nationale, 1901). For an overview of French trade in exotic commodities, see Michel Mollat du Jourdin, *Le Commerce maritime normand à la fin du Moyen Âge* (Paris: Plon, 1952), 249–67.

[15] Charles de La Roncière, *Histoire de la marine française*, 6 vols. (Paris: Plon, 1899–1932), III, 244.

[16] Regina Tomlinson, *The Struggle for Brazil: Portugal and 'The French Interlopers' (1500–1550)* (New York, NY: Las Americas Publishing, 1970), 60–72.

The king needed their financial support in his intermittent war against the Emperor Charles V.[17] The *armateurs* knew that this gave them bargaining power – as did the riches they obtained through trade and piracy. Jean Ango, for instance, presented those who helped him with gifts from these enterprises. In 1529, he presented François's admiral Philippe Chabot with 'a magnificent diamond' in exchange for a letter of marque[18] allowing him to collect compensation (by force) for his losses to the Portuguese fleet.[19] When the Portuguese heard of this, they in turn bribed Chabot to curtail French expeditions, presenting him with 25,000 écus, a tapestry worth 10,000 écus and 16,000 francs.[20] Henri II, on his ascent to the throne, was equally fickle, issuing letters of marque and withdrawing them whenever he wished to switch allegiances.[21] In 1549, Henri granted the city of Rouen a monopoly of 208 commodities, limiting the right to import brazilwood to that city and to Marseille.[22] This spelled the ruin of many Dieppois merchants; Jean Ango died penniless.[23] The economic lives of the *armateurs* who had invested heavily in ships and equipment, of the purveyors of *nauticalia*, and of the pilots, cartographers and sailors of Normandy swung regularly from boom to bust. The Normans' Brazilian project was a lucrative but vulnerable one, a private enterprise, but one dependent on state approval.

The iconography of Brazil on Norman maps needs to be analysed in the context of the vital part played by the brazilwood trade in the French economy and in the Atlantic political sphere, particularly in the maritime world of Dieppe's mapmakers. A planisphere by Pierre Desceliers in 1550 contains the arms of Henri II, of Anne de Montmorency, constable of France, and of Claude d'Annebaut, Admiral of France (Fig. 4.1). Their presence suggests that the map may have been a political gift to the king from Montmorency and Annebaut.[24] Norman activities in Brazil were dependent on the goodwill of all three offices. Annebaut's predecessor,

[17] Wintroub, *Savage Mirror*, 24–33.

[18] This was a licence allowing the bearer to capture an enemy's merchant vessels.

[19] Tomlinson, *Struggle*, 64–5.

[20] Ibid., 66; Charles André Julien, *Les Voyages de découverte et les premiers établissements (XVe-XVIe siècles)* (Paris: Gerard Monfort, 1948), 107.

[21] Tomlinson, *Struggle*, 72.

[22] Dickason, 'Brazilian Connection', 134.

[23] Paul Gaffarel, *Histoire du Brésil français au seizième siècle* (Paris: Maisonneuve, 1878), 110–11.

[24] Sarah Toulouse, 'L'art de naviguer: hydrographie et cartographie marine en Normandie, 1500–1650', 2 vols., thèse doctorat, École Nationale des Chartes, Université de Paris, 1994, I, 37. For a sumptuous facsimile of the map, with transcriptions and translations of the legends and descriptive commentary on the map's sources, see Chet Van Duzer, *The World for a King: Pierre Desceliers' Map of 1550* (London: The British Library, 2015).

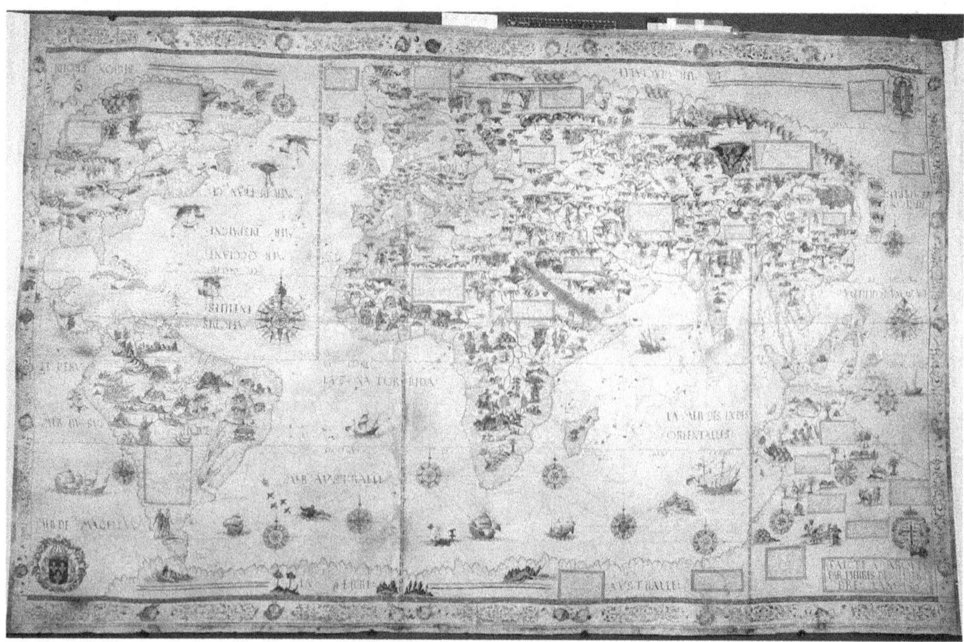

4.1 Pierre Desceliers, 'Mappemonde', 1550.

Philippe Chabot, had loomed large in the minds of the members of the French expedition that made landfall in Brazil in 1504. When the crew erected a cross there, they inscribed it with the names of the pope, the king, 'Monseigneur l'Amiral de France', their captain and each crewmember.[25] The navigator Pierre Crignon dedicated his *Perle de cosmographie* to Chabot in 1534.[26] Montmorency was a close advisor to and favourite of Henri. It was Montmorency's cousin, Admiral Gaspar de Coligny, who sent a colonizing mission to Brazil in 1555.[27]

Henri's arms also appear on two other Norman works. The anonymous and undated manuscript known as the Hague Atlas bears three coats of arms: the royal arms of France; the arms of Henri II while he was the Dauphin or heir apparent to the throne; and a partly covered escutcheon, possibly of the queen, with a crown discernible at one end. Each map also

[25] *Le Voyage de Gonneville (1503–1505) & la découverte de la Normandie par les Indiens du Brésil*, étude & commentaire de Leyla Perrone-Moisés (Paris, 1995), 24.

[26] Rotz, *Boke of Idrography*, 6–7.

[27] For the cultural and religious contexts of French encounters with Brazil, see Lestringant, *Le Huguenot et le sauvage*, chap. 2.

carries Henri's symbol, a fleur-de-lys, pointing north, and a crescent moon – the symbol of Diane de Poitiers – in the south. Since Diane officially became *la dame du Dauphin* in 1540, the atlas must have been produced no earlier; the geographical features suggest a date of c.1545.[28] The anonymous Harleian planisphere appears to have been given the arms of the Dauphin Henri in the first instance. These were later changed to the arms of the king, suggesting that the map was completed around the time of Henri's accession to the throne.[29]

Norman maps participated in the economies of gifts and artworks. Natalie Zemon Davis's study of modes of gift giving has revealed their wide-ranging use in the building of bonds between individuals and communities in sixteenth-century France.[30] More generally, Marcel Mauss, in his ground-breaking study of gifts in traditional societies, showed how gifts place obligations of reciprocity on the recipient; thus, far from being free, gifts form part of a cyclical system of exchange of things as symbols of honour and regard.[31] Both Davis and Mauss note how gifts can go wrong: gifts to sixteenth-century French officials were sometimes denounced as bribes; among Native American tribes of the Pacific Northwest, the escalation of competitive gift exchange could lead to violence.[32] What, then, was the significance of giving an expensive, highly illustrated map as a gift to Henri II? And how might the depiction of Brazilians on such a map have been informed by this gift-giving context?

Large, illuminated manuscript maps and atlases that were given as gifts embodied artefactual, intellectual and political value. As expensive, decorative objects made by skilled artisans, they were status symbols that signalled the education and taste of those who commissioned and owned them. Their rarity and value indicated the high regard held by the donor for the receiver. Maps were also intrinsically intellectual artefacts. They gave Renaissance viewers a synthesized overview of a fast-changing world-picture, incorporating new information about numerous parts of the world.

28 For the dating, see Helen Wallis, 'Sixteenth-Century Maritime Manuscript Atlases for Special Presentation', in *Images of the World: The Atlas through History*, ed. John A. Walter and Ronald E. Grim (Washington, DC: Library of Congress, 1997), 3–29, at 19–20. Henri was the Dauphin between 1536 and 1547.

29 BL-Mss, MS. Add. 5413. For a facsimile, see C. H. Coote, *Autotype Facsimiles of Three Mappemondes: 1: The Harleian, or anonymous, Mappemonde, c.1536* ([Aberdeen: privately printed], 1898).

30 Davis, *Gift*, 154–9.

31 Marcel Mauss *The Gift: The Form and Reason for Exchange in Archaic Societies*, trans. W. D. Halls (London: Routledge, 2002 [first published: 1950]), 6–9.

32 Davis, *Gift*, 145–8. Mauss, *Gift*, 51–4.

The political implications of the shape of the world meant that this picture was contested rather than fixed. Territorial claims made by a map's contents could hint to a recipient the ways in which the donor could give them control over desirable regions. Norman illuminated maps did not merely provide knowledge and political spin; the knowledge they provided about Brazil itself represented another gift-in-process: French access to dyewood, and to an empire of trade if not of territory.

Norman maps constituted both intellectual and political capital. In this sense, they were what Mario Biagioli, writing about Galileo's telescopes, has termed 'instruments of credit': both physical apparatus and 'techniques [Galileo] used to maximize the credit he could receive from readers, students, employers, and patrons'.[33] Norman maps accrued credit as obligation, representing the gifts given to France by the Norman *armateurs*. What the maps' emphasis on the dyewood trade presented to Henri II was the promise of continued commercial riches. It is significant that the three maps and atlases that bear his coat of arms date between 1545 and 1550, the years immediately before and after his accession to the throne. Such gifts were a means of building a personal connection between a client and a new royal patron. The image of Brazil as a fertile and peaceful territory where French traders and Brazilians cooperated to collect dyewood, despite the presence of cannibals, was a strategic construction, a selective crafting of information based on experience. Such scenes presented the Norman Brazil trade as a source of valuable income – one that François I had already drawn upon when the need had arisen, notably to finance his wars against Charles V. Implicitly, the *armateurs* were donors to the king, not diplomatic embarrassments who complicated his dealings with Portugal and Spain. Maps exhibited the skills of their makers and also created links of obligation between recipients, makers and donors. Just as Galileo construed Jupiter's moons as the 'Medicean Stars' in order to build a connection with his desired patron, the presentation of Brazil on Norman maps highlighted a web of royal obligations to the Norman maritime world. Both the Medicean stars and the inhabitants of Brazil were, to use Biagioli's terms, 'not discoveries in the modern sense of the term', but rather constructed objects 'that, while displaying some of the features of our notion of scientific discovery, also participated in the economies of artworks and monuments'.[34]

[33] Mario Biagioli, *Galileo's Instruments of Credit: Telescopes, Images, Secrecy* (Chicago, IL and London: University of Chicago Press, 2006), 1–2.

[34] Ibid., 3.

A pageant organized for Henri II's royal entry into Rouen on 29 September 1550 indicates how important it was for Norman port cities to establish a royal connection. One tableau in the pageant presented a Brazilian village scene. Fifty Brazilians from Bahía came to Rouen, allegedly of their own free will, to participate in the celebration (Fig. 4.2).[35] They were joined by 250 naked French sailors who were acquainted with Brazil, their bodies painted black and red. Both the Amerindians and their French emulators enacted Tupinambá village life along the banks of the Seine, their activities mirroring those in contemporary travel texts and maps. The Tupinambá chopped, carried and bartered wood in exchange for metal implements such as chisels, hatchets and fishhooks. That the very trees were painted red illuminates the strong association between dyewood and Brazil which the organizers expected in the minds of the spectators, particularly Henri II. Other participants lay in hammocks or stalked birds and animals with bows and arrows. The climax was a mock battle between the Tupinambá and the Tabajara (enemies of the Tupinambá who had good relations with the Portuguese), ending with the defeat of the Tabajara and the incineration of the Portuguese fortress.[36] At the same time, a Portuguese corsair attacked a French ship anchored on the Seine near the Brazilian village. The portrayal of the Portuguese as the aggressors was of course partisan, since French ships also raided the Iberian fleets. A contemporary manuscript indicates boats near the island on the Seine that represented Brazil; the oarsmen bear shields emblazoned with the arms of France and of the admiral, Claude d'Annebaut.[37] All of these scenes would have been familiar tropes to viewers already acquainted with Norman manuscript maps, including Henri II. When Henri was Dauphin, he was already in possession of the Hague Atlas and the Harleian map, both of which depicted woodcutters in Brazil, as we shall see.

[35] The engraving is from a contemporary account, *C'est la déduction du sumptueux ordre, plaisantz spectacles et magnifiques théatres, dressés et exhibés par les citoiens de Rouen* ... (Rouen, 1551), sig. K.2*v*-K3*r*. For an analytical description, see Wintroub, *Savage Mirror*, chap. 1. For an edition, see *L'entrée de Henri II à Rouen, 1550*, introduction by Margaret McGowan (Amsterdam: Theatrum Orbis Terrarum, 1973). A manuscript of watercolour illuminations of the event is housed in the Bibliothèque Municipale de Rouen, MS.Y.28; for an edition of the manuscript, see *L'entrée de Henri II roi de France à Rouen*, ed. S. De Merval (Rouen: Société des Bibliophiles Normands, 1868). For other contemporary accounts, see Michael Wintroub, 'Civilizing the Savage and Making a King: the Royal Entry Festival of Henri II (Rouen, 1550)', *Sixteenth Century Journal*, 29 (1998), 465–94, n. 4; for possible meanings and purposes of the Brazilian tableau, and for further literature describing the entry, see Wintroub, *Savage Mirror*, 35–42 and Jean-Marie Massa, 'Le mond luso-brésilien dans la joyeuse entrée de Rouen', in *Les Fêtes de la Renaissance*, études réunies et présentées par J. Jacquot and L. Konigson (Paris: Éditions du CNRS, 1975), 105–16.

[36] Julien, *Colonisation*, 183–4.

[37] *L'entrée*, ed. Merval, 15 and plate 9.

4.2 Brazilian tableau at the entry of Henri II into Rouen, 1550 in *C'est la déduction du sumptueux ordre* . . . (Rouen, 1551), sig. [K.ii.*v*-iii*r*], engraving. Houghton Library, Harvard University, Typ 515.51.272.

The Rouen entry graphically demonstrated the riches of Brazil: animals, parrots and other birds with fantastic plumage, monkeys with fine pelts, edible, pharmacological and other plants, and, of course, dyewood. Many of the birds and animals had been loaned from the collections of the local *bourgeoisie*, another indication of the cultural impact of Brazil on Rouen. Some of the organizers were either participants in overseas trade or relatives of those who were.[38] Although descriptions of the entry show that it featured many of the elements found on maps that predate it, it is compositionally distinct from them; and they, in turn, are distinct from one another. The Brazilian *mis-en-scène* may have been staged in appreciation of Henri's decision, the previous year, to grant Rouen trading privileges. The event was probably intended to further advance the concerns of Rouen's mercantile community. Henri would later rescind the existing edict outlawing French voyages to Portuguese possessions.[39] In addition, the royal entry could well have played a part in convincing Henri to send a colonization party to Brazil – Villegagnon's expedition of 1555–6.[40]

Both the iconography of Norman maps and that of the Rouen entry are examples of gifts that offered their donors the potential to subvert, to an extent, the patronage relationship to their own ends. Michael Wintroub has shown the way in which the Rouen entry, in common with other royal entries, tried to subtly dictate the terms of the city's relationship with the new king, and to offer a moral mirror, in the form of a series of tableaux, of the kind of king they wished him to be.[41] Gifts were persuasive artefacts; their content needs to be interpreted in relation to the agendas of their donors. One might go so far as to suggest that the Norman Brazil enterprise prompted much wider cycles of gift exchange, of which illuminated maps formed a part. The *armateurs* gave France Brazil and helped to pay for its wars against Spain. Indeed, Ango was partially ruined by his contributions to François I's war effort.[42] Norman maps were gifts that drew attention to the *armateurs*' gift, and encouraged reciprocal gifts in return in the form of letters of marque to the *armateurs*. These letters allowed the *armateurs* to continue trading in Brazil and to board Portuguese ships, thus facilitating future gifts to the French king. The Portuguese did not stand passively by, but offered their own political gifts through diplomatic channels, as well as outright bribes. The Norman Brazil project

[38] Wintroub, *Savage Mirror*, 84.

[39] Frederic Baumgartner, *Henry II: King of France, 1547–1559* (Durham, NC and London: Duke University Press, 1988), 136.

[40] Hamy, 'Bas-relief', 5.

[41] Wintroub, *Savage Mirror*, 8, 40–62.

[42] Guénin, *Ango*, 163.

had a peculiar dependency on fickle royal views concerning its value. The *armateurs* were in direct competition with the Portuguese crown for the favour of the French kings. The legality of their actions at a particular time depended not only on their own relationship with the king, but also with his wider political needs. For example, at times when he was not at war with Spain, he did not need the money the *armateurs* could provide for outfitting his army. The French king thus partook of two different gift-giving/diplomatic circles around which the onus of obligation passed from group to group in a 'pass-the-port' fashion. The desirability for the king of one bottle of port over the other determined the speed at which he reciprocated the gifts made to him. Ultimately, Norman gift giving was only partially successful.

The woodcutters of Brazil on French manuscript maps

The Norman school of cartography flourished between the 1540s and 1580s, with the majority of surviving illustrated works dating between 1540 and 1550. Over 250 Norman maps survive in the form of atlases, planispheres (single-sheet world maps) and maps within manuscript cosmographies and portolans (books of sailing directions). They comprise a total of thirty-seven discrete works or collections[43] of which twelve contain ethnographic images.

In order to ascertain the impact of economic and political concerns on the Brazilian images of Norman maps, we must first establish how the images compare to the iconography of other maps that were available to Norman mapmakers, and the extent to which the iconography was derived from contemporary travel writing on Brazil. Little documentary evidence sheds light on the Norman map illuminators' identities; the illuminations on some examples are considered to be in the style of the Norman school, added by French miniature painters.[44] Some Norman cartographers came from Dieppe; indeed, Norman mapping of this period has historically been known as the 'Dieppe School' of cartography.[45] These maps are manuscript

[43] For a listing of works known to date, see Toulouse, 'Marine Cartography', Appendix 1.

[44] See, e.g., Marcel Destombes and D. Gernez, 'Un Atlas nautique du XVIème siècle à la Bibliothèque Royale de la Haye (Pays-bas)', *Congresso Internacional de História dos Descobrimentos: Actas*, II (1961), 151–61, at 151; *PMC*, V, 132–3; Toulouse, 'L'art de naviguer', II, 400–403.

[45] This terminology is problematic. Some works are by cartographers known to have worked elsewhere in Normandy. Others are anonymous but have been assigned to the same tradition

rather than printed works, and relied heavily on Portuguese charts for their topographic features.[46] The cartography of the works known as the Rotz, Hague and Vallard atlases was probably based directly on Portuguese examples.[47] The French obtained Portuguese maps through purchase and via capture; French pirates blockaded routes to Iberian ports on occasion, boarding and raiding ships.[48] In addition, some Portuguese mapmakers settled in Normandy.[49] The cartographers of the Hague and Vallard atlases may themselves have been Portuguese.[50]

The relationship between the ethnographic illustrations in the Portuguese and Norman traditions, however, is far less clear. Eight surviving Portuguese manuscript maps and atlases place cannibalism or woodcutting in Brazil.[51] Of these, four examples illustrated Brazil exclusively with cannibalism. These include the Kunstmann II map (c.1502–6), the earliest map depicting inhabitants of the Americas (Fig. 3.5)[52], and three atlases by Diogo Homem. Homem's 1558 atlas contains a lone woodcutter in a thicket, but the central image shows the body parts hanging from trees and the spit-roasting limbs that were associated with the region of Brazil (Fig. 3.9).[53] The nearby caption informs us that 'cannibals eat human flesh and fight with poisoned arrows'.[54] A fifth example is arguably the 1529 Weimar planisphere, the work of Diogo Ribeiro who was based at this time at Seville, at the Casa de la Contratación. This notes that the people of Brazil ate their enemies' flesh, but also that they would transport brazilwood to European ships for trifles.[55] The sixth, the 1519 Miller Atlas, describes the Brazilians on a text cartouche as human flesh-eating savages.

on stylistic grounds. Furthermore, the production of the maps took place within a broader context of commerce and exploration – maps, mapmakers, merchants and money circulated through towns such as Rouen, Honfleur and Le Havre as well Dieppe. Therefore, although Dieppe was the centre of this tradition, 'Norman school' is preferred here, as it is in Sarah Toulouse, 'Marine Cartography and Navigation in Renaissance France', in *HC3*, II, 1550–68.

46 Toulouse, 'Marine Cartography', 1555.

47 For the carto-bibliographical aspects, see *PMC*, V, 132–40.

48 Jean Rotz, *The Maps and Text of the Boke of Idrography presented by Jean Rotz to Henry VIII now in The British Library*, ed. Helen Wallis (Oxford: Roxburghe Club, 1981), 40.

49 See Luís de Matos, *Les Portugais en France au XVIe siècle. Études et documents* (Coimbra: Por ordem da Universidade, 1952), 15–18.

50 *PMC*, V, 133.

51 For large-scale reproductions and carto-bibliographical overviews, see *PMC*.

52 Munich, Bayerische Staatsbibliothek, Abteilung für Handschriften und Alte Drucke, Cod. icon. 133. See discussion in Chapter 3.

53 BL-Mss, Add.MS 5415.a., f. 23*v*. See also Chapter 3, near n. 104. The other two examples are Homem's atlases of 1564 and 1568.

54 'Canibales carnibus [h]umanis vescuntur ac venenatis sagit[t]is proeliantur.'

55 For discussion and facsimiles, see *PMC*, I, 87–106 and plates 38–41.

The illustrations focus on depicting them chopping wood, but a small fire in the northeast corner seems to show cannibal cookery (Fig. 4.3).[56] The seventh work, Pero Fernandes's c.1545 map, depicts a woodcutter in northern South America.[57] The eighth, a map of the Atlantic drawn by Sebastião Lopes in 1558, depicts one figure in Brazil, peacefully chopping wood.[58]

The iconography on the small number of existing Portuguese maps is divided between woodcutting and cannibal motifs, with cannibalism being marginally dominant. By contrast, Norman examples show wood-cutting and Norman-Tupi trade much more frequently: out of twelve sixteenth-century works depicting Amerindians, only three include depictions of cannibals in Brazil, and none of these illustrates cannibals exclusively, or more prominently, than woodcutting. A Norman manuscript mapmaking manual recommended that a master map be created via the following steps: rhumb lines, latitude scale, distance scale, the topographical information and the wind-roses. This design could then be traced onto other maps using carbon paper.[59] The illustrations, however, were not to be copied from a master map: 'the rest of the ornamentation is at the discretion of the chartmaker'.[60] Such practices explain why Norman and Portuguese cartography are more similar than their iconography.

It is worth considering the extent to which the figures above may simply be the consequence of the chance survival of particular manuscripts. Maps used at sea rarely survive. A comparatively larger proportion of illustrated maps, housed in libraries and rich estates, remain. Portuguese works sent as gifts to dignitaries outside Portugal survived the Lisbon earthquake of 1755. Many Norman charts and the Dieppe archives were destroyed in the English bombardment of the town in 1694, although these are unlikely to have been those made for royal patrons.[61] Thus while surviving charts are not representative of the range of maps produced, they are more representative of the illustrated works.

[56] BNF-Cartes (Bibliothèque Nationale de France, Département des Cartes et plans), Rés. Ge. DD. 683 and Rés. Ge.AA 640.

[57] Vienna, Österreichische Nationalbibliothek, Kartensammlung, FKB 272–11.

[58] BL-Mss, Add MS 27303.

[59] BNF-Mss, MS. fr. 19112, Guillaume Le Vasseur, 'Traicté de la geodrographie ou art de naviguer', 1608, ff. 85–6. For this and other examples, see Toulouse, 'Marine Cartography', 1557–9; Toulouse, 'L'art de naviguer', II, 377–87. Carbon-based lines on extant maps show that actual practice coincided with this; see ibid., 381; Tony Campbell, 'Egerton MS 1513: A Remarkable Display of Cartographical Invention', *IM*, 48 (1996), 93–102, at 95.

[60] BNF-Mss, MS. fr. 19112, f. 86: 'le reste de l'ornement demeure a la discretion de celui qui faict la charte'.

[61] Rotz, *Boke*, 38.

4.3 Miller Atlas, 1519, detail from Brazil.
Bibliothèque nationale de France, Département des Cartes et plans, Rés. Ge DD 683.

While the precise proportions of surviving works with different iconographies is to some extent dependent on chance, it is important to note that the Portuguese works as a whole do not show the same range of peaceful scenes that appears on Norman works. Instead, they show a broader range of cannibal scenes. Most significantly, despite the presence on Portuguese maps of some scenes containing woodcutters, there are no scenes of Europeans trading with Tupi peoples, a motif that does appear on Norman maps. The best example is the Miller Atlas (1519), which depicts woodcutting activities more clearly than any other Portuguese example (Fig. 4.3). The Tupi shown here chop and carry logs, but do not transport it to the coast; nor are any Europeans shown interacting with them. The imagery is undercut somewhat by the only caption that describes these people; it detailed their cannibalistic activities.

We must, therefore, look elsewhere for clues to the sources of inspiration for the Norman trading illustrations. Ethnographic representations on these maps drew on a wide range of contemporary and medieval sources and traditions. The lack of captions and text on Norman maps means that in order to understand what the Brazilian illustrations might have meant to their viewers, we must establish what sources of information were available to map illustrators and map readers, and how these sources characterized the inhabitants of Brazil.

Most sixteenth-century cartographers, artists and map illuminators did not see with their own eyes the regions they depicted. Nevertheless, it is possible that some sketches drawn from life, or made by eyewitnesses at a later date, informed the iconography of Brazil on Norman maps. In 1564, the Dieppois Huguenot artist Jacques Le Moyne de Morgues joined an outgoing French expedition to Florida. The objective of the expedition, led by René de Laudonnière, was to establish a Huguenot settlement; Le Moyne was appointed as writer and illustrator.[62] While the pre-1555 Norman-Brazil voyages had not been trying to establish settlements,[63] Dieppe's importance as a centre of illuminated manuscript maps might have encouraged seamen on voyages to Brazil to provide information to mapmakers about the appearance of the inhabitants as well as its topography.[64] Le Moyne, born around 1533, was probably too young to have been one of them. Just two of his original watercolours of human figures survive; printed and manuscript derivatives give us a sense of the many lost examples. All of these indicate that his distinctive style was significantly different to that of images on the surviving Norman maps and atlases.[65] By the 1580s, he had fled to England to escape the French Wars of Religion.[66]

The Rotz Atlas of 1542, a set of twelve sea-charts, is the earliest surviving work definitively known to have originated in Normandy.[67] Its maker, Jean Rotz, was a Dieppois sea captain and hydrographer (a maker of marine charts) with Scottish ancestry. In 1539, he had visited Guinea and Brazil.[68] Rotz's atlas was at least partly based on his own experience. He claims that it was drawn 'as precisely and truly as was possible for me to

[62] Paul Hulton, *The Work of Jacques Le Moyne de Morgues: A Huguenot Artist in France, Florida and England* 2 vols. (London: British Museum, 1977), I, 3–4.

[63] There are very few surviving Norman maps depicting Amerindians after 1555. Léry, *History of a Voyage*, ed. Whatley, xix–xxi: the first French expedition to set up a colony in Brazil set out in 1555, but soon failed, falling to the Portuguese in 1560.

[64] Wallis suggests that the Dieppe voyages had painters on board; see *Rotz Atlas*, 44–5.

[65] For reproductions of all these illustrations, see Hulton, *Le Moyne*, II.

[66] Ibid., I, 4.

[67] BL-Mss, Royal MS. 20.E.IX.

[68] Rotz, *Boke of Idrography*, 3, 6–7, 17. Rotz's father, David Ross, had moved to Dieppe and married a Frenchwoman.

do, drawing as much on my own experience as on the certain experience of my friends and fellow navigators'.[69]

By far the most richly illustrated map in the atlas is the double-page sheet devoted to coastal Brazil (Fig. 4.4). It details a range of Tupi activities: along the lower edge of the map are scenes of battles between Indian groups, ceremonial dancing and a vignette of a man tied to a collection of stakes who is about to be struck with a club. The palisade in the centre of the map surrounds hammocks warmed from below by fires. Similar images appeared later in printed travel accounts, notably those of the German gunner Hans Staden and the French friar André Thevet, and in sixteenth-century Jesuit accounts.[70] Rotz's imagery is not exclusively peaceful, however. The centre of the map's right-hand edge reveals a seated figure cooking a human leg on a barbecue, while a dismembered body lies on the ground to the right of the palisade. As we saw in Chapter 3, vignettes of cannibals cooking their victims had had a wide circulation in printed and manuscript images since at least 1505.[71]

What is unusual about Rotz's map of Brazil when compared to maps from other centres of production is its predominant imagery of peaceful exchange between Europeans – presumably Norman sailors – and Brazilians. We see the Tupinambá cutting trees with metal hatchets, and removing the bark with a tool resembling a metal cutlass.[72] The Tupinambá also trade the wood for items that resemble mirrors or hatchets, suggesting to the viewer that they had obtained metal tools from traders. They also transport the wood to the coast, and help the traders to load them onto a boat.

This iconography of trade on the Rotz atlas parallels accounts from two voyages, one Portuguese, the other French, that remained unpublished in the sixteenth century.

[69] BL-Mss, Royal MS. 20.E.IX, fol. 2*v*: 'au plus certain et vrai quil ma este possible de faire tant par mon experience propre que par la certaine experience de mes amis et compagnons navigateurs'; Rotz, *Boke of Idrography*, 80.

[70] Staden, *Warhaftige Historia*, chaps XXVIII–XXXIV. For Jesuits in Brazil, see, e.g., Alida C. Metcalf, 'The Society of Jesus and the First Aldeias of Brazil', in Hal Langfur, ed., *Native Brazil: Beyond the Convert and the Cannibal, 1500–1900* (Albuquerque, NM: University of New Mexico Press, 2014), 29–61.

[71] See also William C. Sturtevant, 'First Visual Images of Native America', in *FIA*, I, 417–54, esp. 420.

[72] For this identification, see Wallis, *Boke of Idrography*, 72. The woodcutting motif also appears on three of the four illustrated Norman works that post-date the French attempt to set up a colony in Brazil in 1555–6. These are BNF-Cartes, S. H. Archives, no. 6 (Pierre de Vaulx, Atlantic map, 1613); BNF-Cartes Rés. Ge D 13871 and Rés. Ge C 5007 (Jacques de Vau de Claye's Brazil and Rio de Janeiro maps); CV-ADG, D.2.z.14 (Le Testu's *Cosmographie*).

4.4 Rotz Atlas, 1542, ff. 27*v*–28*r*, detail from South America.

In 1500, a Portuguese fleet sailing west under the command of Pedro Àlvares Cabral reached a land he named *Ilha da Vera Cruz*, part of a region that would soon be known as Brazil. A letter detailing the discovery was sent by the fleet's appointed writer, the knight Pedro Vaz de Caminha, to

King Manuel of Portugal.[73] Vaz writes approvingly of the innocence (*inocência*) of the indigenous people, who go about entirely naked in an Edenic fashion. Cabral's fleet traded with the Tupinikin – one of the Tupi peoples – on several occasions, giving them caps, hats, bells and what Vaz describes as 'other trifles of little value which they were carrying'.[74] In return, the Portuguese received feather headdresses and a mantle, bows and parrots.[75] Since the Tupinikin would part with items valued by a civilized society in exchange for mere 'trifles' (*cousinhas*), they were, to Portuguese eyes, as ignorant of economics as they were of modesty and shame. The unevenness in the balance of trade was remarked upon in numerous early accounts of Atlantic voyages, and must have been encouraging to the Norman *armateurs*. The loading of boats that Rotz illustrated is described in Vaz's account: the men 'mingled so much with us that some of them helped us to load wood and put it in the boats, and they vied with us and derived much pleasure therefrom'.[76]

The promising trading potential of the Tupinambá is also noted in the first French account of Brazil. This appeared in the deposition taken after the expedition led by Binot Paulmier de Gonneville; the expedition reached Brazil in 1504. We learn that 'the Indians, being a simple people, ask only to lead a happy life free of hard work'.[77] Although there is no mention of brazilwood, the Tupinambá traded many items of immense value to the

73 Pedro Álvares Cabral and Pedro Vaz de Caminha, *The Voyage of Pedro Álvares Cabral to Brazil and India*, ed. and trans. William Brooks Greenlee (London: Printed for The Hakluyt Society, 1938), 3. Langfur, 'Recovering Brazil's Indigenous Pasts', 24, n. 1: recent scholarship suggests that the expedition set out intending to reach South America rather than, as Vaz de Caminha claims in his letter, India; the expedition may have had information from a reconnaissance mission led by Duarte Pacheco Pereira in 1498. See Bailey W. Diffie and George D. Winius, *Foundations of the Portuguese Empire, 1415–1580* (Minneapolis, MN: University of Minnesota Press, 1977), 450–2; Jorge Couto, *A construção do Brasil: Amerindios, portugueses e africanos, do início do povoamento a finais de quinhentos*, 2nd ed. (Lisbon: Cosmos, 1997), esp. 149–60; Disney, *Portugal and the Portuguese Empire*, 204–5.

74 José Manuel Garcia, *O descobrimento do Brasil nos textos de 1500 a 1571* (Lisbon: Calouste Gulbenkian Foundation, 2000), 29: 'outras cousinhas de pouco valor que levavam'. For a contextual discussion of Vaz de Caminha's views on the Tupinikin and their anthropophagy, see Disney, *Portugal and the Portuguese Empire*, 207–10.

75 Garcia, *Descobrimento do Brasil*, 28–29. Despite their best efforts, though, they were unable to procure any gold. Towards the end of the letter Vaz reluctantly admits that 'up to now we are unable to learn whether there is gold or silver, or anything of metal or iron; nor have we seen any'; ibid., 34: 'até agora, não pudemos saber que haja ouro, nem prata, nem nenhuma cousa de metal, nem de ferro; nem lho vimos'.

76 Ibid., 30: 'misturaram-se todos tanto connosco que nos ajudavam deles a acarretar lenha e meter nos batéis e lutavam com os nossos e tomavam muito prazer'.

77 *Voyage de Gonneville*, 20: 'étant les Indiens gens simples, ne demandant qu'à mener joyeuse vie sans grand travail'.

sailors far from home – such as food – in return for what the Europeans considered to be trifles, like the mirror being traded for wood in the centre left of the Rotz map of Brazil; 'the said goods amassed close to 100 quintals [5000kg], which would have fetched a good price in France'.[78]

Vespucci's *Letter to Soderini* noted similar opportunities.[79] Vespucci presented a range of indigenous behaviours, including nakedness, the lack of trappings of European society, and naivety in trading. As a merchant, Vespucci paid particular attention to potential commodities. He observed what the Amerindians themselves valued, commodities that were deemed useful in Europe, and moments of gift exchange. The Tupinambá 'are liberal in giving, and rarely deny you anything'.[80] Vespucci writes how 'we bought from them around 150 pearls, for a single bell, along with a bit of gold, which we added as a gift to them'.[81] A similar encounter took place later: 'We acquired 119 marks of pearls for no more than forty ducats, because what we gave them was nothing other than bells, mirrors and glass beads and brass leaves; one of them traded all the pearls he had for one bell.'[82] The numerous editions and translations of letters attributed to Vespucci had little impact on Norman iconography, however. These letters and their illustrations highlighted cannibal practices, but none showed woodcutters. As we shall see later in this chapter, the mapmaker Pierre Desceliers borrowed from Vespucci's writing while consciously omitting a passage on cannibalism.

Rotz's image of Brazil, while reflecting the gamut of activities that had also been described in published and unpublished sources, placed relatively little emphasis on cannibalism. The bright crimson tunics of the French traders and the reddish logs carried by the Tupinambá draw the viewer's attention away from the more unsavoury aspects of Tupi life. To the right of the wood-transportation scene is a group of Tupinambá who appear to be marching alongside French traders bearing muskets. The image, far

78 Ibid., 23: 'desdites denrées en fut bien amassé près de cent quintaux, qui en France auraient valu bon prix'.

79 Vespucci, *Letters from a New World*, ed. Formisano, xxii. The first edition was Amerigo Vespucci, *Lettera ... delle isole nuouamente trovate* (Florence, 1505).

80 *NRC-V*, I, 334: 'In dando sic naturaliter liberalissimi sunt ut nihil, quod ab eis expetatur, abnegent'; Vespucci, *Letters*, 65.

81 *AV-C*, I, 357: 'ab eis interim 150 uniones unica nola emimus, cum auro modico, quod eis ex gratia contulimus'; *AV-F*, 80.

82 *AV-C*, I, 363: '119 unionum marchas precio (ut estimabamus) 40 non superante ducatos ab eis comparavimus. Nam nolas, specularia cristallinosque nonnullos necnon laevissima electri folia quaedam eis tantum propterea tradidimus. Nempe quotquot quilibet eorum obtineret uniones, eos pro sola nola donabat'; *AV-F*, 84.

from suggesting that Rotz's comrades were in danger of being eaten by these cannibals, might well have indicated that the Tupinambá were on such good terms with them that they practised joint military manouevres. Indeed, alliances between the Tupinambá tribes and the Normans greatly facilitated Norman incursions into areas that were claimed by the Portuguese.

The unusual richness of the illustrations may be explained by Rotz's aspirations to royal patronage. Rotz recounts how he had initially set out to present his atlas to François I of France, but decided towards the end of the work to dedicate it instead to Henry VIII of England.[83] The lavish illustrations of Brazil – the most detailed in the entire atlas – reveal Rotz attempting to convince a royal patron that he was particularly knowledgeable about the New World.[84] The atlas, then, was an intellectual gift that held the possibility of further reward: first-hand experience from a Norman sailor. Rotz hoped that his expertise would prompt Henry to offer him a post and to sponsor his own voyages. Around 1531 a Brazilian king had been brought to Henry's court, and the English had begun to trade in Brazil.[85] Unfortunately for Rotz, while his overtures led to his appointment as royal hydrographer in 1542, Henry's interest in voyages to the Americas proved to be transient. Rotz returned to France in 1547.[86]

The concentration on trade is even greater on the Brazil sheets of the Vallard Atlas (1547).[87] Two its fifteen maps cover northeastern South America and show Europeans, presumably Frenchmen, trading with Brazilians for dyewood.[88] A double-page map shows the eastern seaboard from Brazil to the Straits of Magellan (Fig. 4.5). In addition to generically peaceful scenes of Amerindians with bows and arrows, and also with logs (presumably dyewood), there is a detailed scene of European-Tupinambá trade in the foreground. At the centre, a trader provides some women with a mirror in exchange for a parrot, and perhaps also a monkey.

[83] BL-Mss, Royal MS. 20.E.IX., f. 2*r*. For François's use of cartographical knowledge as royal propaganda and Rotz's experience at his court, see Brunelle, 'The Images of Empire', 95–100.

[84] Wallis, *Boke of Idrography*, 38.

[85] Alden T. Vaughan, *Transatlantic Encounters: American Indians in Britain, 1500–1776* (New York, NY: Cambridge University Press, 2006), 11.

[86] Wallis, *Boke of Idrography*, 9–12.

[87] HL, HM 29. The atlas is so named because of an annotation on the first page: 'Nicolas Vallard de Dieppe / 1547'. Vallard is believed to have been its author or an early owner (Anthiaume, *Cartes marines*, I, 93–4: surviving records in Dieppe contain a mention of a family called Vallart or Vallard.).

[88] HL, MS. HM 29, map 12.

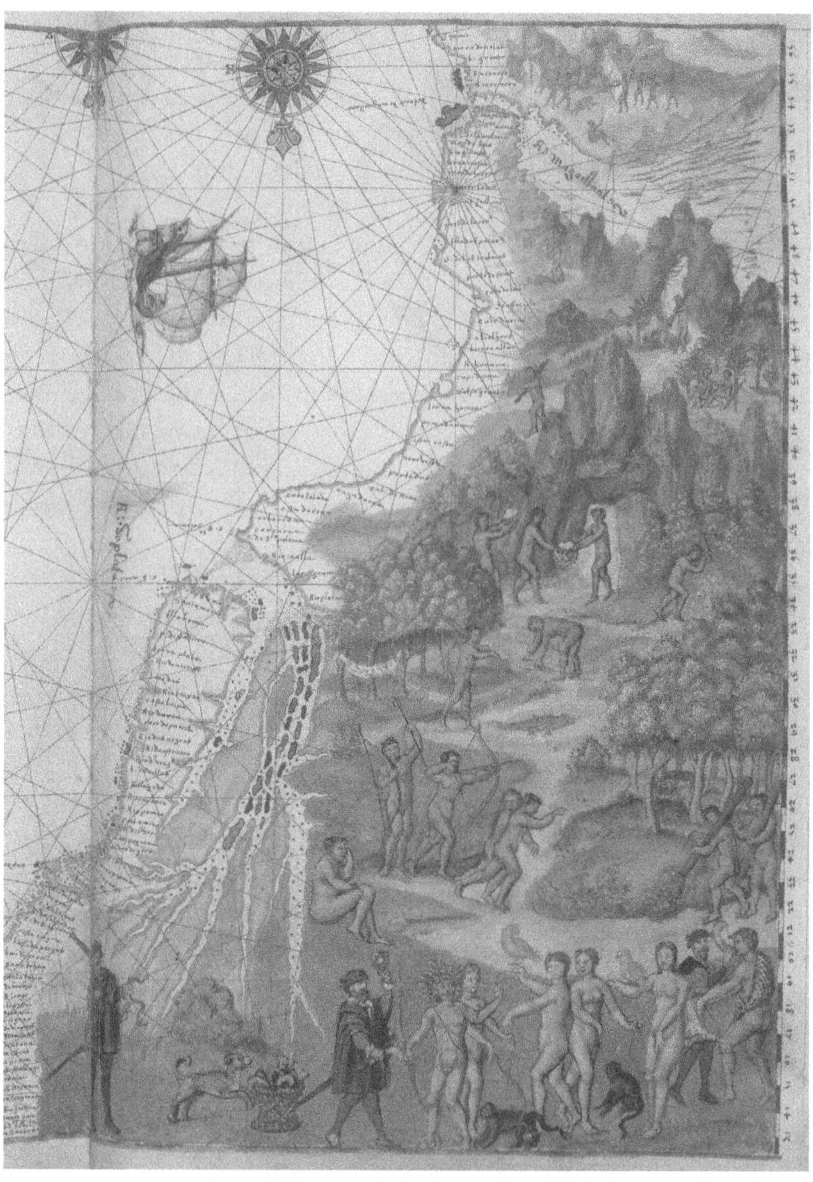

4.5 Vallard Atlas, 1547, map 12, detail from eastern South America. The Huntington Library, San Marino, CA, HM 29.

An image of the Brazilian as woodcutter, and a reference to women trading with visitors, later appeared in François Deserps's costume book of 1562. Under the portrait of a Brazilian woman is the verse, 'the women there are dressed just as / this picture shows and represents. / There, monkeys, and parrots also, / they put up for sale to strangers'

4.6 François Deserps, *Receuil de la diuersité des habits* (Paris, 1562), unpaginated, image of a Brazilian woman. Houghton Library, Harvard University, Typ 515.64.734.

(Fig. 4.6).[89] The Brazilian man is characterized by trade rather than dress – 'he applies himself to the natural work of / cutting down Brazil trees in order to trade them' (Fig. 4.7).[90] The genre of the costume book usually focused on civil images of (mostly) Europeans rather than on savage peoples. This does not, however, mean that Deserps must have manufactured peaceful rather than cannibalistic images of Brazil's inhabitants simply to fit them into his costume book. Although we cannot be sure that Deserps had not seen the Vallard Atlas, it is much more likely that the Tupinambá illustrations in these two works were independent,

[89] François Deserps, *Recueil de la diuersité des habits qui sont de present en usaige tant es pays d'Europe, Asie, Affrique et Illes sauvages, le tout fait apres le naturel* (Paris, 1562), reproduced in facsimile as *A Collection of the Various Styles of Clothing which are Presently Worn in Countries of Europe, Asia, Africa, and the Savage Islands, All Realistically Depicted* . . ., ed. Sara Shannon (Minneapolis, MN: James Ford Bell Library, 2001), at 138: 'Les femmes là sont vestues ainsi, / Que ce pourtrait le monster [sic] et represente, / Là les Guenons, et perroquets aussi, / Aux estrangers elles mettent en vente.' For an overview of contemporary costume books, see Rublack, *Dressing Up*.

[90] Deserps, *Recueil de la diuersité*, 'Leur naturel exercise s'aplique / Coupper bresil pour en faire trafique.'

Le Bresilien.
L'homme du lieu auquel le Bresil croist.
Est tel qu'icy, à l'œil il apparoist,
Leur naturel exercice s'applique
Coupper Bresil, pour en faire trafique,

4.7 François Deserps, *Receuil de la diuersité des habits* (Paris, 1562), unpaginated, image of a Brazilian man. Houghton Library, Harvard University, Typ 515.64.734.

based on Norman trading experiences in Brazil.[91] The sylvan setting of Deserps's man and woman of Brazil suggests another strand of influence. Outdoor life was often associated with the wild men of folklore, people who lived in forests or caves, without the trappings of civilized life.[92]

On the Vallard Atlas, the scene of monkey- and parrot-trading is flanked by images showing the goods that were exchanged for them. To the left is a basket of what appear to be hatchets. On the right, another figure in European dress offers a curved knife or hatchet to a Tupi. The artist seems to be aware of Norman practices of trading of glass and ironmongery. The Gonneville expedition report had noted that the sailors did indeed trade 'combs, knives, hatchets, mirrors, glass beads and such trinkets'.[93] While we cannot say that these motifs came from a particular text or traveller, the evidence is indicative of the close attention that was paid here to travellers' testimony.

[91] In addition, Deserps could of course have consulted the illustrated narratives by Staden and Thevet for details of Tupi costume and armaments.

[92] For the iconography of the wild man, see Chapters 1 and 3.

[93] *Voyage de Gonneville*, 23: 'peignes, couteaux, haches, miroirs, rassades et telles babioles'.

Although there are no surviving descriptions of the Tupinambá-Norman brazilwood trade that predate any of the maps examined here, later accounts offer corroborating evidence for many elements of the cartographic vignettes. André Thevet discussed the brazilwood trade in two of his books.[94] In his *Singularitez* (1557) we learn that 'when the Christians ... go there to obtain brazilwood, the savages of the country cut it down and chop it up themselves, and they carry it three or four leagues in a single journey up to the ships; I leave you to imagine the effort needed, and this for the desire to acquire some meagre clothes of poor linen or a shirt'.[95] The amount of French labour saved by the Tupinambá added to the profitability of exchanging prized brazilwood for items that were inexpensive in Europe. In his *Cosmographie universelle* (1575), Thevet illustrated the Brazilians chopping trees and noted that the quality of the brazilwood was so good that one could obtain two tinctures out of it.[96] His description of the willingness of the Brazilians to carry logs for Europeans parallels the vignettes that had appeared on many earlier Norman works, including the Rotz and Vallard atlases.[97]

Further corroboration appears in Jean de Léry's *Histoire*, first printed in 1578. Léry apparently penned his first draft in brazilwood ink.[98] Léry, like Thevet, stressed the importance of indigenous labour in a country that lacked beasts of burden: 'if the foreigners . . . were not helped by the savages, they could not load even a medium-sized ship in a year'.[99] In return for simple clothing and tools,

> the savages not only cut, saw, split, quarter and round off the brazilwood, with the hatchets, wedges and iron tools given to them by the French and

94 This and other references to dyewood are noted in Marchant, *Barter*, 41–2. For Thevet's time in Brazil, see Frank Lestringant, *André Thevet: cosmographe des derniers Valois* (Geneva: Droz, 1991), 89–100.

95 Thevet, *Singularitez*, ff. 116–7: 'Quand les chréstiens ... vont par-delà pour charger du brésil, les sauvages du pays le coupent et dépècent eux-mêmes, et aucunes fois le portent de trois ou quatre lieues jusques aux navires; je vous laisse à penser à quelle pein, et ce pour appétit de gagner quelque pauvre accoutrement de méchante doublure ou quelque chemise.'

96 André Thevet, *La Cosmographie universelle* (Paris, 1575), tome IV, liure XXI, chap. XVII, f. 950*v*.

97 Further examples showing Brazilian wood-cutters are: The Hague, Koninklijke Bibliotheek, Hague (Vallière) Atlas, c.1545, MS 129 A 24; Manchester, John Rylands Library, Special Collections, Rylands (Henri II) planisphere, 1546, French MS 1*; BL-Mss, Harleian (Dauphin) chart, c.1547, Add. MS. 5413; and the Desceliers 1553 planisphere (destroyed), known through a facsimile, E. Oberhummer, *Die Weltkarte des Pierre Desceliers von 1553* (Vienna, 1924).

98 Léry, *Histoire*, preface, sig. [A.j.*r*.].

99 Ibid., 174 (chap. XIII): 'n'estoit que les estrangers que voyagent par-dela sont aidez des sauuages, ils ne sçauroyent charger vn moyen nauire en vn an'. Here and elsewhere, translations are from Léry, *History of a Voyage*, trans. Whatley.

> by others . . . but also carry it on their bare shoulders, often from a league or two away, over mountains and difficult places, clear down to the seashore . . . where the sailors receive it.[100]

This exchange of ironmongery for Brazilian goods corroborates Norman map vignettes showing Tupinambá willingness to prepare and carry logs. Tupinambá generosity did not simply spare French labour; it also reduced their need for fixed bases in Brazil. The uneasy and often hostile relations between French traders and the Portuguese Crown meant that the French did not establish settlements or factories in Brazil for processing or collecting logs. Their first attempt at running a factory was put paid to by the Portuguese.[101] In case the reader is left with the sense that the Tupinambá are being exploited, Léry hastens to explain that before the Tupinambá were presented with European tools, they did not have the means to fell a tree other than by setting fire to the base.

A visual parallel of the cartographic iconography appears on two oak panels that comprise the only surviving portion of the façade of the Hôtel du Brésil. This building stood at 17 rue Malpalu in Rouen and accommodated such visiting Brazilians as those who participated in the royal entry celebrations of 1550.[102] The panels, of a total length of nearly four metres, depict Brazilians aiding the dyewood trade. On the longer piece, the right-hand portion shows a partly cut forest in which they fell more trees. Another figure uses an implement to remove the bark from a tree. Of two men carrying tree-trunks, one leads a boy carrying a bird (a parrot, perhaps), with a monkey at his feet. Also noteworthy are the parrots balancing on several tree-trunks. On the second panel, logs are collected and presented to two sailors loading a boat; a two-masted ship is anchored nearby.[103] None of these compositions is identical to a map image, but the content is certainly similar to the range of imagery found on the Rotz and Vallard atlases.

There were, then, general correspondences between images in Norman cartography, visual culture and printed and manuscript sources on Brazil,

[100] Léry, *Histoire*, 174 (chap. XIII): 'Les sauuages . . .non seulement auec les coignees, coings de fer, & autres ferremens que les François & autres donnent, coupent, scient, fendent, mettent par quartiers & arrondissent ce bois de Brésil, mais aussi le portent sur leurs espaules toutes nues, voire le plus souuent d'vne ou deux lieues loin, par des montagnes & lieux assez fascheux iusques sur le bord de la mer . . . où les mariniers le reçoyuent'.

[101] Tomlinson, *Struggle*, 67–8.

[102] E.-T. Hamy, 'Le Bas-relief de l'Hôtel du Brésil au Musée Départmental d'Antiquités de Rouen', *Journal de la Société des Américanistes de Paris*, Nouvelle série (1907), 1–6, at 5; Ferdinand Denis, *Une Fête Brésilienne célébrée à Rouen en 1550* (Paris: J. Techener, 1850), 25.

[103] Dickason, 'Brazilian Connection', 135.

but no clinching evidence of direct links to texts. It seems legitimate to infer that mapmakers were relying, at least partly, on oral and informal methods to gather information. In one case, however, we can be sure about a Norman mapmaker's direct reliance on – and selective borrowing from – a printed source containing detailed descriptions of anthropophagous practices.

Pierre Desceliers' 1550 planisphere illustrates neither the dyewood trade nor cannibalism, although Vespucci's writings were clearly one of his sources. Desceliers was a priest, a cartographer and a teacher of mathematics and navigation whose students included *armateurs*, sea captains and apprentice-pilots, including Jean Ango. Many of his former pupils entered the employ of the elder Ango (Jean's father), with whom Desceliers collaborated on occasion.[104] The map contains a lengthy caption that fills northern and central South America (Fig. 4.1):

> The men and women are of medium build. The men are naked and red-skinned, with large faces.... Their weapons are bows, arrows and clubs which they know how to use well.... They recognize no leaders, being men without order living freely.... They sleep in cotton beds hung from trees. Their language differs every hundred leagues. They have clean bodies because they wash frequently, living without law or marriage. Their houses are large – capable of accommodating 600 people – and covered with palm leaves. Every seven or eight years they move because and in fear of illness.... Their riches are birds' feathers and green and white stones.[105]

The map's layout is similar to that of world maps that the German cartographer and scholar Lorenz Fries devised as German translations of Martin Waldseemüller's 1516 world map.[106] Nevertheless, Desceliers's inscription has no parallel in Fries's maps, which depicted cannibals in Brazil and described them in an accompanying booklet.[107] Instead, the

[104] Gaffarel, *Jean Ango*, 5–6.

[105] BL-Mss, Add. MS. 24065: 'Les hommes et femmes sont de moyen stature. hommes nuds de couler rousge, larges faces. Leurs armes sont arcz, flesches, massues desquoy ilz scauient bien vser.... Ilz n'ont capitaines, hommes sans ordre vivantz en liberté. Ilz dorment en lictz de coton pendus aux arbres. Leur language diffère de cent lieues en cent lieues. Ilz sont netz de corps car ilz se lauent souuent, viuent sans loy, sans mariage. Leurs maisons sont grandes, Ly peult demoures 600 persones, couvertes de feuilles de palmes. De 7 ou 8 ans ilz changent de lieux pour cause et crainte des malladies.... Leur richesses sont plumes de d'oyseulx, pierres vertes et blanches.'

[106] For Waldseemüller, see Chapter 3.

[107] Noted in Jean Michel Massing, 'La Mappemonde de Pierre Desceliers de 1550', in *Henri II et les arts*, ed. Hervé Oursel and Julia Fritsch (Paris: École du Louvre, 2003), 231–48, at 235. Since Waldseemüller is known to have used Portuguese maps, it has also been argued that the

above quotation closely matches information published in Vespucci's *Letter to Soderini*. The letter is worth quoting at length and comparing to Desceliers's inscription:

> They are of medium stature and very well proportioned. The colour of their skin inclines to red, like the skin of a lion, and I believe that if they went around covered with clothes, they would be white like us. . .. Their arms are bows and arrows, which they knew how to make very accurately. . .. They have no war-leaders and no commanders, and they march (since everyone is a lord of himself) preserving no order. . .. They sleep in certain large nets made of cotton, and suspended in the air. . .. They are very clean and neat in their bodies, because they very frequently wash themselves. . .. They observe neither law nor legal contract in their marriages. . .. Their homes are constructed in the shape of bells, but strongly built of very large trees and covered with palm leaves, secure from tempests and winds. In some places they were so large that we found 600 people in a single house. . .. They move their homes or dwellings every seven or eight years, and when questioned as to the reason for this, they gave a reply concerning nature, saying they did this at times of the intense heat of the sun on account of which, because of the length of time they lived in the houses, the air became infected and corrupt, which caused various illnesses in their bodies. . .. Their wealth consists of the feathers of birds of many colours, or in the fashion of beads which we call 'paternosters' in the common tongue; they make plates or counters from the fins of fishes, or from white or green stones, and for ornament they hang these from their cheeks, lips and ears; and they also regard other similar worthless and trifling things for riches, which we considered entirely paltry. . ..[108]

correspondence between his map and the Norman ones is likely to be the result of the latter's reliance on similar Portuguese sources rather than on one of the Waldseemüller or Fries maps. The large number of cartouches with text on the Desceliers 1550 map, however, brings it much closer visually to the Waldseemüller/Fries maps than to any Portuguese one other than the Miller Atlas, the only textually rich Portuguese example. Moreover, Portuguese cartography used fewer illustrations (again, the Miller Atlas is the only existing counter-example) and did not place cannibals in the East Indies (see facsimiles in *PMC*).

108 *AV-C*, II, 328–34: 'Hii mediocris existentes staturae multum bene proporcionati sunt, quorum caro ad rubedinem (veluti leonum pili [sic]) vergit; qui si vestimentis operti mearent, albi credo tamquam nos extarent. . .. Arma eorum arcus sunt et sagittae, quas multum subtiliter fabricare norunt. . .. Nulla belli capita nullosve praefectos habent, quinimmo (cum eorum quilibet ex se dominus extet) nullo servato ordine meant. . .. In retiaculis quibusdam magnis ex bombice factis et in aere suspensis dormitant. . .. Corpore valde mundi sunt et expoliti, ex eo quod seipsos frequentissime lavant. . .. Nullam legem, nullum legitimum thori foedus in suis connubiis observant. . .. illorum domus campanarum instar constructae sunt firmiter ex magnis arboribus solidatae, palmarum foliis desuper contectae et adversus ventos et tempestates tutissimae, nonnullisque in locis tam magnae ut in illarum unica sexcentas esse

Desceliers has summarized Vespucci's description of several pages, selecting particular traits and habits: skin colour, weapons, lack of leaders, hammocks, houses, wealth and ornaments. He presents the information in the same order as Vespucci, which clearly signals his dependence on the passage. He has changed its tone – we move from a first-person narrative to an impersonal report. For instance, in the description of the evacuation and transplantation of villages in Vespucci's letter it is clear that the explorers themselves obtained the information. Desceliers summed this up as: 'Every seven or eight years they move because and in fear of illness'. His account is detached, almost omniscient, with no indication of a mediator, or any sense that an interpretation of the Amerindians and their customs is what is presented. Desceliers refers only to some of the riches mentioned by Vespucci, trimming the passage for clarity. This direct quotation contrasts with the more fluid relationship between most images on Norman maps and printed travel accounts.

Particularly interesting is the omission of any mention on Desceliers' map of Brazilian cannibalism. By contrast, Vespucci's text then provides lurid details of the Amerindians' consumption of human flesh. Desceliers and other Norman mapmakers may have made little of cannibalism since the threat was smaller for the French than for other Europeans. Hans Staden's *Warhaftige Historia* (1557) described how he had been held captive for nine months by the Tupinambá. On several occasions, he narrowly escaped being killed and eaten by assuring the Tupinambá that he was French, as the two peoples were on good terms. Other Europeans had evidently tried this before; Staden says of the Tupinambá king, 'he had already helped to catch and eat five Portuguese who had all said that they were French but had lied'.[109] In the early seventeenth century, the English traveller Anthony Knivet recounted a similar story.[110]

personas invenerimus. . ..Octennio quolibet aut septennio suas sedes habitationesve transferunt; qui eius rei causam interrogati, naturale responsum dederunt, dicentes quod phoebi vehementis aestus occasione hoc facerent, ob id quod ex illorum longiore in eodem residentia aer infectus corruptusque redderetur, quae res in eorum corporibus varias causaret aegritudines. . .. Eorum divitiae sunt variorum colorum avium plumae aut in modum lapillorum illorum quos vulgariter pater noster vocitamus, laminae sive calculi quos ex piscium ossibus lapillisve viridibus aut candidis faciunt; et hos ornatus gratia sibi ad genas, labia vel aures suspendunt; alia quoque simila futilia et levia pro divitiis habent, quae nos omnino parvi pendebamus'; Vespucci, *Letters*, 61–5.

109 Staden, *Warhaftige Historia und Beschreibung eyner Landschafft der Wilden, Nacketen, Grimmigen Menschfresser Leuthen, in der Newenwelt America gelegen* . . .(Marburg, 1557), chap. XXVIII: 'Er hette schon funff Portugaleser helffen fangen und essen die alle gesagt hetten sie weren frantzosen und hettens doch gelogen'.

110 This was first printed in 1625 by Samuel Purchas; see his *Hakluytus Posthumus: Purchas his Pilgrimes*, 20 vols. (Glasgow: Maclehose, 1905–7), XVI, 222–3.

While Norman mapmakers were clearly choosing to emphasize trade and peaceful inhabitants over cannibalism, this does not constitute a fictionalization of the situation in Brazil. As Staden's and Knivet's accounts show, French relations with the Tupinambá do seem to have been good. A sixteenth-century manuscript navigation manual provides further evidence of the cordial relationship between the Tupinambá and Norman navigators. Prepared by the Rouennais Jean Cordier, it includes a Tupinambá-French glossary. Eighty-five terms and phrases are translated. The majority deal with everyday life: greetings, members of the family, words denoting hunger or thirst, objects and clothing, distance and weather.[111] Norman interpreters were important mediators between the French and the Tupinambá. Sometimes these intermediaries overstepped their instructions, and went native, even participating in cannibal feasts. They became culturally Tupi, even taking local wives. One of them, Goset, mentioned by Lery, was made a chief, and gave his name to the tribe that had adopted him.[112] While the Normans may not have been in danger of being eaten, they were well aware of cannibal practices. Since they too were implicated, however, they would have been keen to underplay these practices.

Norman ethnographic iconography beyond Brazil

We can gain further insights into how Norman mapmakers used ethnographic sources and imagery, and the significance of their iconographic strategies for Brazil, by looking at how they illustrated other parts of the world. Illustrated Norman manuscript atlases and maps were effectively a combination of two medieval cartographic traditions. One was the encyclopedic world map: the general conventions for the iconography included representing enthroned kings, cities and peoples (often monstrous) in distant parts of the world. The tradition drew on classical and medieval source texts.[113] The other was the portolan chart tradition: the coastlines contained detailed information of use to sailors, but the interiors were relatively empty.[114] During the sixteenth century, Norman

111 BNF-Mss, MS fr. 24269, 'S'ensuyt le langaige du Brésil et du françoys', fos. 53*r*.-54*r*. Discussed with extracts in Mollat du Jourdin, 'Premières relations', 72.

112 Gaffarel, *Ango*, 29–30; Léry, *Histoire*, ed. Morisot, 220 (chap. XV).

113 An important exception is the Fra Mauro Map at the Biblioteca Nazionale Marciana (c.1450). This contains almost no illustrations of people, but does illustrate cities and draw on a range of classical authorities and medieval travel texts; See Cattaneo, *Fra Mauro's Mappa Mundi*, chap. 5.

114 For these traditions and their hybrids, see Barber, *Queen Mary Atlas*, 3–12.

mapmakers began introducing new images of rulers, cities and inhabitants based on contemporary sources.

The imagery on Norman maps in North America, Asia and Africa further demonstrates the mapmakers' interest in French exploratory voyages. In North America on the Vallard Atlas, and on the Desceliers 1550, Rylands and Harleian world maps, the illustrations document Jacques Cartier's expeditions to Newfoundland and Canada.[115] The Vallard images probably represent Cartier's third voyage, commanded by Jean-François de la Roque, sieur de Roberval, which included male and female colonists.[116] On the Rylands map, in what is now Canada, the enthroned chief of Saguenay is flanked by attendants. To the left is a large army and a single European figure, the French captain 'Mons. de Roberual', faces them. On the Harleian map, the chief of Saguenay sits on a box-shaped throne holding a spear in place of a sceptre. This imagery drew on information from the Cartier voyages that had yet to appear in print. At the same time, the decision to use enthroned leaders to represent their peoples was a tradition that went back to medieval *mappaemundi*. The imagery in Canada indicates a closer engagement between tradition and new information than appeared in Brazil on Norman maps, where the information was predominantly based on new compositions as well as new material.

Norman map illuminators did rely upon printed images on occasion. The imagery developed for Sumatra shows how Norman mapmakers were drawn to illustrate the region because of recent French voyages, but drew on earlier printed sources to execute their scenes. A royal procession in Sumatra appears on the Vallard (Fig. 4.8) and Rotz atlases. These and several other nearby vignettes were probably inspired by the expedition of Jean and Raoul Parmentier, who sailed from Dieppe around southern Africa to Sumatra in 1529. This voyage carried a 'peintre' who may have produced illustrations that had currency in cartographic circles.[117] The imagery on the maps indicates that the Rotz and the Vallard artist, or the artists who provided them with sketches drawn from life, were also familiar with a version of Hans Burgkmair's 1508 multi-block woodcut frieze of the inhabitants of Africa and Asia; a cruder version of Burgkmair's woodcuts,

[115] RGS, mr 6.G.10 (0), 13–15; W. F. Ganong, *Crucial Maps in the Early Cartography and Place-Nomenclature of the Atlantic Coast of Canada* (Toronto: University of Toronto Press, 1964), 237–54: numerous place names and much of the topography matches the voyages' records and itineraries.

[116] RGS, mr 6.G.10 (0), 15. Ganong, *Crucial Maps*, 237, 247: the main figures on the Harleian map and Vallard Atlas may represent Cartier himself.

[117] Rotz, *Boke of Idrography*, 43, 68–70; 44–5: 'peintre' could refer to a cartographer or an artist.

4.8 Vallard Atlas, 1547, map 2, Terra Java, detail of procession.
The Huntington Library, San Marino, CA, HM 29.

by Wolf Traut, appeared in print alongside Springer's account in 1509 (Fig. 4.9).[118] Burgkmair devised the frieze, probably in collaboration with the humanist Konrad Peutinger, from a printed report by the Tirolese merchant Balthasar Springer. Springer had accompanied Francisco Almeida's 1505–6 mission to India; this had established the first Portuguese viceroyalty there.[119] The Wolf Traut woodcuts included a scene of procession in which the subjects of the 'king of Cochin' carry him on a litter, shade him with a parasol, and announce his progress with their horns and tambourines.[120] Thus we know that information from German printed works was circulating in Norman mapmaking circles and being drawn on for iconographic material.

And yet, all the elements on the Burgkmair woodcut do not appear on the Rotz or Vallard sheets. Both lack figures playing long, horn-shaped musical instruments - instead, they wield spears. On the Rotz sheet, some figures are carrying horns and the central one rides a horse; on the Vallard sheet (Fig. 4.8), two figures hold ring-shaped objects, perhaps tambourines. Thus, even if Burgkmair's woodcut or a later version was known to the artists, neither reproduced it precisely.

Those parts of the world that had not been visited by French navigators contain proportionally fewer depictions based on specific events or expeditions. Africa, Asia and most of Europe are largely characterized by rulers as well as by monstrous peoples. On the Rotz Atlas, Parmentier's voyage is also recorded in Madagascar, which contains an image of an incident in which three French sailors were killed in July 1529.[121] The atlas contains no other distinctive ethnographic imagery in Africa. In both Asia and Africa, it was French overseas activities that Rotz most wished to emphasize. In so doing, he highlighted the expertise he was offering to the English crown.

The Rylands map depicts an array of humanoid beings in Asia: long-eared and long-lipped folk, 'pigmeons', a centaur and *blemmyae* (Fig. 4.10). These monstrous peoples were the traditional inhabitants of the distant east and south in classical and medieval writings such as Pliny the Elder's *Historia naturalis* and the medieval *Marvels of the East* manuscripts. On the 1546 Rylands map, they jostle uneasily against the fully dressed kings of

[118] Balthasar Springer, *Die Merfart und erfarung nüwer Schiffung* (s.l., 1509).

[119] For Burgkmair, Peutinger and this frieze, see Leitch, *Mapping Ethnography*, 64–74.

[120] The figure being carried is the size of a child. This and other scenes resembling those on Burgkmair's woodcuts also appeared on a piece of sculpture in Dieppe.

[121] Jean Parmentier and Raoul Parmentier, *Voyage à Sumatra en 1529. Journal de bord* (Clermont-Ferrand: Paleo, 2001), 25–6.

4.9 Balthasar Springer, *Die Merfart und erfarung nüwer schiffung* (s.l., 1509), woodcut by Wolf Traut after Hans Burgkmair, of a procession of the king of Cochin.
Bayerische Staatsbibliothek München, Rar. 470.

4.10 Pierre Desceliers, 'Mappemonde', c.1546, detail from Asia.
Copyright of the University of Manchester, French MS 1*.

ancient civilizations. 'Le grand cam' or Great Khan of 'Kathay' receives an audience at his tent; nearby, a shaggy, dog-headed monarch and his equally hirsute subjects mirror the scene, implicitly muddling the boundary between human and animal.[122] Two naked people chop up a third figure on a large block, echoing a scene in Java on the Vallard Atlas, and on Desceliers's later maps. In Africa, monstrous peoples include a *blemmya* on the Rylands map and the Desceliers 1550 map; the latter also contains a figure with many arms, and two with disc-lips.[123] This wondrous

[122] For the juxtaposition of Eastern monsters and monarchs, see Chapter 3, near n. 97.

[123] For a discussion of monarchs and monsters, see Massing, 'Image of Africa', 58–61.

ethnography was not an imaginary one but one derived from a long transmission of information in travellers' accounts about real people and cultural groups with distinctive practices – such as the stretching of ear lobes – or unusual inherited anatomical variations.[124]

Motifs of monsters and monarchs had frequently appeared on late medieval world maps such as the Catalan Atlas.[125] Leaders were used to represent their kingdoms: distinctions between them were suggested by their costume, their thrones and, occasionally, by their subjects. Not all maps that depicted leaders represented them with the same level of distinguishing characteristics; in the Portuguese map tradition, for example, the images veer towards the generic. On the Norman maps, the historically specific images in Africa and Asia are limited Madagascar and Sumatra, the regions of French activity.

Norman illustrations across the Americas are usually site-specific. They are largely unaccompanied by explanatory captions, unlike those on many maps from Iberia, Germany and the Low Countries. The motifs Norman mapmakers used for Mexico, Patagonia and Peru had been described in widely circulated travel accounts.[126] The maps sometimes characterized central America using an image of Tenochtitlán, the capital city of the Mexica.[127] Hernan Cortés's expedition to Mexico in 1519 had revealed it to European eyes for the first time when he reported the capture of the city in his third letter to Charles V. This letter was printed in Spanish in 1523; a Latin edition of the text with a map of the city appeared at Nuremberg the next year. Between 1524 and 1547, five further editions of the map were printed at Venice.[128]

On the Vallard Atlas, Tenochtitlán comprises a central city on an island in the middle of the lake (Fig. 4.11). Seven bridges radiate out to the mainland, each terminating at another city or fort. On the source map printed at Nuremberg, the city has six bridges, and looks distinctly

[124] For modern medical evidence of hereditary anatomical variations in regions where medieval maps show monstrous peoples, see Friedman, *Monstrous Races*, 24.

[125] For monarchs and a few references to monsters, see the Catalan Atlas (BNF-Mss, MS Espagnol 30), discussed in Jean Michel Massing, 'Observations and Beliefs: The World of the *Catalan Atlas*', in *Circa 1492*, 27–33; see also idem, 'Catalan Atlas', in *Circa 1492*, 120–1 (includes map illustrations); and NL, Greenlee MS 26, f. 16*v*, depicts Prester John.

[126] See Chapters 5 and 7.

[127] This iconography and the associated travel writing is analysed in Chapter 7.

[128] For Cortés's letter, see *EA*, I, no. 522/5. For the map's likely sources and dates of editions, see Barbara E. Mundy, 'Mapping the Aztec Capital: the 1524 Nuremberg Map of Tenochtitlán, its sources and meanings', *IM*, 50 (1998), 11–33. The iconography of Tenochtitlán is discussed in Chapter 7.

4.11 Vallard Atlas, 1547, map 10, detail of Tenochtitlán.
The Huntington Library, San Marino, CA, HM 29.

different from the outlying forts or towers. No captions or prefatory text details the atlas's sources. While the Vallard mapmaker may have taken the image of Tenochtitlán from the illustration to Cortés's letter, he could also simply have copied it from an earlier map, as it appears on a number of Portuguese examples.[129]

Tenochtitlán's conquest by Spanish conquistadors was clearly not a French or a Portuguese triumph. Nevertheless, its inclusion would have had some relevance to Norman prowess. In 1523, Cortés had sent three ships laden with booty from the palace of the Inca Guatimozin (also known as Cuauhtémoc) to Charles V of Spain. In addition to the jewellery, ivories, inlaid masks, gold vessels and other *objets d'art*, a number of jaguars were added to the cargo. When the ships arrived in the Azores, they encountered a Norman blockade under the captaincy of Jean Fleury, equipped partly by Jean Ango. After a bloody battle, two of the three ships surrendered their cargo to Fleury's forces.[130] A stained glass window from c.1523–28 in the church at Villequier in Normandy records the names of sailors who paid for it, and depicts a treasure ship in naval combat. France may not have conquered Mexico, but, on this occasion, it certainly conquered its treasures.[131] Windows at Neuville-lès-Dieppe and Vatteville also celebrate Norman maritime activities with depictions of ships.[132]

[129] See, e.g., BL-Mss, MS Add. 21592, f.16*r*.

[130] Roncière, *Histoire de la marine française*, III, 249–50.

[131] Ibid., III, 250–1.

[132] Michel Mollat du Jourdin and Jacques Habert, *Giovanni et Girolamo Verrazano, navigateurs de François 1er: dossiers de voyages* (Paris: Imprimerie Nationale, 1982), 43, 75.

Examining the ethnographic iconography in regions beyond Brazil shows how Norman mapmakers amalgamated a range of sources: classical and medieval iconography from the medieval world map tradition; new printed images such as those by Hans Burgkmair and the map of Tenochtitlán; and oral testimony about recent French expeditions such as that of the Parmentier brothers to southeast Asia. Brazil received more detailed illustration than any other region, and contained images on a much larger number of Norman works. The subject matter for Brazil, however, almost completely devoid of stock images, shows that mapmakers did not deem existing models to be suitable, and chose instead to develop their own iconographic programmes.

Interpreting the imagery

How might viewers of these maps interpreted have the customs and appearance of these peoples? Contemporary conceptions of peoples who possessed neither the trappings nor the vices of civilization as similar to wild men thus might well have prompted viewers to perceive these peoples in a positive light. While the peoples in Brazil on Norman maps had neither curly hair, nor body-hair (which they plucked out), nor animal-skin costumes, their near-nudity, open-air lifestyle and frequent association with tree trunks offered parallels with the folkloric wild man.[133]

The 1550 Rouen entry pageant for Henri II is an especially pertinent context. The pageant placed the Tupinambá in a broader scheme that characterized them as heroic warriors. As one chronicler of the pageant put it, in skill and bravery, they surpassed even the Trojans, who were thought to be the ancestors of the French.[134] The Brazilian scene was immediately preceded by one of Hercules – associated with skill, strength and bravery – battling a Hydra. These values were core to the ancient French nobility. Henri II was known for his own martial prowess, deeply suited to the French ideal of the warrior king. At the same time, the image of Hercules as a wild barbarian was being transformed in humanist literature into a personification of humanist values.[135] The writings of later

[133] Stephens, *Giants*, 59.

[134] *C'est la deduction*, sig. K.iii.*v*, noted in Wintroub, *Savage Mirror*, 40 and 61, near n. 81.

[135] The purpose of the entry as a whole seems to have been to encourage Henri to marry his martial skills with those of humanist learning; see Wintroub, *Savage Mirror*, 47–9 and 58–62 for a compelling argument. Around 1495–1500, a broadsheet portrayed the Holy Roman Emperor Maximilian I as *Hercules Germanicus*; for Maximilian as Hercules, see Silver, *Marketing Maximilian*, 23–4. For the broader context of the heroic wild man in Renaissance Germany, see Chapter 1, near n. 67.

French travellers to Brazil offer evidence of a conceptual connection between Hercules and Brazilians. Marc Lescarbot, the early seventeenth-century explorer, author and lawyer, compared Brazilians to images of Hercules; André Thevet added an engraving of the Tupinambá leader Quoniambec to his *Portraits et vies des hommes illustres* (1584), and described him as a New World Hercules.[136]

Brazilian representations on Norman maps are a complex blend of reality and selective advertising. They show how even maps with political agendas were not necessarily devoid of accurate information. The Norman experience of Brazil was different from that of other European groups, partly because the French monarchs frequently changed their minds over whether or not to outlaw their subjects' activities in Brazil, a situation that prompted Jean Rotz to offer his expertise to Henry VIII of England instead. While Portuguese merchants were also engaged in the brazilwood trade, their crown did not need to be convinced of the importance of supporting their activities. Their maps contain cannibal, woodcutter and more general ethnographic scenes, but the cannibal motifs are more prevalent.

These maps prompt us to question the approach by which the non-cartographic contents of maps are automatically reduced to either decoration, invention or propaganda in both traditional interpretations of cartography and the revisionist approach of J. B. Harley and later scholars.[137] It is clear that mapmakers did not necessarily prefer sensational or violent images to peaceful ones for the sake of selling more maps. It is also clear that ethnographic spin was not necessarily negative, and that sympathetic relations between Europeans and others in the field, as it were, could be interpreted back in Europe in a similar light. Norman mapmakers were well aware of the cannibal practices of the Tupi people, even representing it on some of their maps, but cannibalism was never presented as the most important aspect of Tupi life, or of European encounters with the Tupi. By making arguments based on contextualized period readings and a range of textual, visual and artefactual evidence, we see a much wider body of the cultural work done by Renaissance maps.

[136] Wintroub, *Savage Mirror*, 62; André Thevet, *Les Vrais Portraits et vies des hommes illustres* (Paris, 1584), f. 661*v*.

[137] See especially. J. B. Harley, 'Maps, Knowledge and Power', in *The Iconography of Landscape: Essays on the Symbolic Representation, Design and Use of Past Environments*, ed. Denis Cosgrove and Stephen Daniels (Cambridge: Cambridge University Press, 1988), 277–312, and J. B. Harley, 'Deconstructing the Map', *Cartographica*, 26 (1989), 1–19. Other treatments of maps as propaganda and tools of political control include Buisseret, *Monarchs, Ministers and Maps*; for maps as artefacts that glorified their owners, see, e.g., Fiorani, *Marvel of Maps*.

5 | Monstrous ontology and environmental thinking

Patagonia's giants

In 2003, on the island of Flores, Indonesia, paleoanthropologists excavated fossilized bones from a species of *hominin*[1] averaging just 1.06 m (3½ feet) in height. *Homo floresiensis*, as members of this species would soon be called, had become extinct only 17,000 years ago, their presence overlapping with that of *Homo sapiens*. Scientific controversy ensued over their taxonomy: were they a late-surviving species of *hominin*, another species of Great Ape or a few diseased individuals? Such interpretative disputes are frequent in palaeoanthropology.[2] One physical anthropologist, reflecting on this and other palaeoanthropological discoveries including that of *H. neanderthalensis*, observed that what debates surrounding these findings 'have in common is a fossil discovery that is fundamentally inconsistent with prevailing notions about the course of human evolution'.[3] In each case, there were three competing interpretations: the specimens were either diseased but human individuals, or a hitherto unknown (non-human) animal species, or evidence of the need for a paradigm shift in human evolutionary history.[4] Within a few years of the identification of *H. floresiensis*, the consensus that this species was a *hominin* necessitated that scientists revise the genealogy of *H. sapiens*.

The classificatory possibilities raised in these debates parallel Renaissance questions about whether the Patagonian 'giants' encountered by European travellers on the southeast coast of South America were a monstrous people, a few defective individuals, or merely some very tall but perfectly normal human individuals. The Tehuelche people in what is now southeast Argentina were distinctly taller than most Renaissance Europeans, and, in particular, taller than the undernourished poor who made

[1] In current scientific literature, 'hominin' refers to modern humans, extinct human species and their immediate ancestors.

[2] For an introduction to defining humans, see Felipe Fernández-Armesto, *So You Think You're Human?* (Oxford: Oxford University Press, 2004).

[3] Leslie C. Aiello, 'Five Years of Homo floresiensis', *American Journal of Physical Anthropology*, 142 (2010), 167–79, 142.

[4] Ibid.

up the rank and file of ships' crews.[5] As late as the early twentieth century, scholars considered inquiry into whether these people were giants to be a serious object of philosophical and natural philosophical investigation.

Mapmakers reading the earliest European travel accounts about Patagonia had to contend with the giant at the nexus of three conceptual challenges. First, there was the problem of ontology: were monsters, or some monsters, also people and therefore capable of reason and salvation, and were giants that sort of people? Since monsters hid their intermediate causes, giants would share the same distinctive characteristic (great height) regardless of whether they were descendants of ancient gods, or monstrous due to the effects of their physical environment. How, then, could one determine the appropriate interpretative tradition for understanding why Patagonia contained giants? Second, there were questions concerning probability and knowledge. Some sailors claimed to have seen giants, but how many giants needed to be seen before one could consider the gigantism of Patagonia's people to be an essential, rather than occasional, characteristic? Finally, since the first travel accounts that described giants contained no illustrations, there was the ever-present problem of visual epistemology: how does one render an illustration of something one has never seen, on the basis of a brief written description? How can one extrapolate from texts to draw what they do not describe?

Accounts of the Patagonians elucidate part of the history of attempts to map the distribution, variety and limits of the human and the order of living beings. Just as new fossil evidence regularly re-shapes notions of human and animal evolution and the classification of species, Renaissance Europeans' encounters with hitherto unknown peoples and animals and their attempts to understand them re-shaped the concept of the human, the genealogy of humanity, and the boundaries between human, monster and animal. In this chapter, I argue that European writers and mapmakers mapped the Patagonians in terms of the ontology of the human and the monstrous and, in so doing, redrew the boundaries between humans and

[5] Alejandra Pero, 'The Tehuelche of Patagonia as Chronicled by Travelers and Explorers in the Nineteenth Century', in *Archaeological and Anthropological Perspectives on the Native Peoples of Pampa, Patagonia, and Tierra del Fuego to the Nineteenth Century*, ed. Claudia Briones and José Luis Lanata (Westport, CT and London: Bergin & Garvey, 2002), 103–19, at 104: Tehuelche men appear to have averaged almost six feet in height, whereas Spanish sailors would have been closer to five feet and 3 inches tall. For an eighteenth-century defence of the existence of giants in Patagonia, see Gabriel François Coyer, *Letter to Dr Maty . . . containing an abstract of the relations of travellers of different nations, concerning the Patagonians* (London, 1767). 'Duviols, 'Patagonian "Giants"', n. 12.

the monstrous peoples described by classical authors. Since environments were believed to shape bodies and temperaments, Patagonia's giants raised the possibility that the region deformed humans, and might even affect European settlers.

Giants in European interpretative traditions

In the Renaissance, the term 'giant' embodied a panoply of symbolic and moralistic connotations, signifying several ontological possibilities. Giants appeared in two strands of the classical tradition. One, that of the Titanomachy or Gigantomachy, had roots in Greek origin myths.[6] In *Theogony*, or *Origin of the Gods*, written by the poet Hesiod in the eighth century BCE, Gaia, the Earth, bore, without coupling, such offspring as Ouranos (Sky). Gaia subsequently mated with Ouranos to produce twelve Titans, three Cyclopes and three Hecatonceires (huge creatures with 100 hands and 50 heads apiece). Members of each generation of Gaia's Titanic children mated with her to produce offspring who attempted to kill their own fathers, children or cousins. One of these, Zeus, overthrew the Titans altogether, and ushered in an age of greater civility. In a variant cosmology, Gaia's progeny were monsters known as Gigantes, marked by great size, legs ending in snakes' tails, and the behavioural monstrosity of brutishness. These Giants also fought Zeus and the gods of Olympus using boulders and uprooted trees, whereas their vanquishers used the bows and arrows and swords of a more civilized society.[7] The Gigantomachy tradition set up a binary opposition between giants and humans while provoking the anxious conclusion that humans were descended from giants and were, from the giants' point of view, dangerous and savage.

A second classical tradition in which giants appeared was that of monstrous peoples inhabiting distant and different environments, exemplified by the *Historia naturalis* of Pliny the Elder. This tradition was taken up in the Middle Ages in the *Romance of Alexander*, in the *Book of John Mandeville* and in the *Divisament dou monde* of Marco Polo. More broadly, in the traditions of humoralism that informed elite and popular notions of medicine, minds and bodies were thought to be shaped by their environment.

[6] Stephens, *Giants*, 60–1; Bartra, *Wild Men*, 26–8.

[7] My overview of the Greek origin myths is informed by a longer treatment in D. Felton, 'Rejecting and Embracing the Monstrous in Ancient Greece and Rome', *ARC-MM*, 103–31, at 106–11.

Movement to new places could trigger physical and mental changes to people and their offspring.[8]

At the time of the Magellan circumnavigation in the 1520s, Patagonia was the southernmost edge of the earth to be visited by Europeans. Its giants thus bore two hallmarks of a Plinian monstrous people: they all shared an unusual inherited characteristic, and they lived far from Europe. For Renaissance readers of Pliny, these features suggested that Patagonia's giants were not isolated, accidental, monstrous births but rather the object of a wide-ranging force that had rendered them monstrous. The question of whether they were, nonetheless, rational and capable of salvation remained. Since the boundary between human and monster was itself uncertain, such a community could potentially pollute the lineage of 'normal' humans.

The Biblical tradition has a long history of vague and contradictory writing about giants and gigantic peoples whose location, appearance, height, relationship to humanity and moral significance are never fully explained.[9] Readers could, for example, think about giants as a monstrous people who had originally been human but had been transformed through degeneration, probably as a divine punishment for the sins of their ancestors. Such predecessors included Adam's fratricidal son Cain and Ham (who ridiculed his father Noah when he saw him naked and inebriated).[10] In the *Book of Genesis*, antediluvian humans were gigantic in stature, and those descended from Cain were corrupt in behaviour.[11] In a passage that received much commentary in the Middle Ages, 'sons of God' were said to have taken 'daughters of men' (usually read as Cain's unholy kin) as their wives; their children were giants, 'the mighty men of old'. Their subsequent wickedness made God wish he had never brought man into being, and prompted him to expunge them all from earth save Noah and his kin.[12] The ensuing Flood was said to have covered the highest mountaintops in order to kill all living things except those on Noah's ark.

While the Biblical Flood – which, according to *Genesis* VII:20, exceeded mountaintops by fifteen cubits (over twenty feet) – was supposed to have rid the earth of human life save Noah's family, some theologians posited that the postdiluvian giants of the Hebrew Bible must have survived the flood. Any being tall enough to stand on the tallest mountain and raise a

[8] For Pliny and for humoral theory, see Chapter 1 of this book. [9] See, e.g., Cohen, *On Giants*.

[10] See Chapter 1. For related medieval explanations for degeneration, see Livingstone, *Adam's Ancestors*, 13–14.

[11] *Genesis* VI:4. [12] Cohen, 'Monster Culture', 15.

5.1 Martin Schongauer, *Shield with Stag Held by Wild Man* (Germany, c.1480–90), engraving.
The Metropolitan Museum of Art, Harris Brisbane Dick Fund, 1928, www.metmuseum.org, 28.26.7.

single nostril out of the water could, in theory, have survived; and the giant King Og of Bashan was purported to have ridden on top of the ark.[13]

More generally, vague but highly variegated giants appear frequently in religious and epic works from the ancient Near East, from the *Epic of Gilgamesh* to the apocryphal gospels. In the folkloric traditions of the late antique and medieval Latin West, the wild man or woman was often also a giant (Fig. 5.1). In the late Middle Ages and the Renaissance, the giant wild man received both negative and positive glosses.[14] Classical, Christian and folkloric traditions, then, offered a multitude of giants to whom the Patagonians could be compared. Patagonia demanded that geographers engage with a storm of monster-inducing climatic and theological discourses.

Patagonians as a monstrous people: Antonio Pigafetta's account

The earliest printed accounts describing the inhabitants of Patagonia reflect the multifarious ontology of giants in the Renaissance. Descriptions of the inhabitants of a land called Patagonia first appeared in European

[13] Cohen, *Of Giants*, 20.

[14] Stephens, *Giants*, 59–60; ibid., 356, n. 2; Bernheimer, *Wild Men*, 23–33, 42–8, 84–93, illns 15 and 20. For the motifs of wildness, see Chapter 1.

writing after the circumnavigatory expedition led by Ferdinand Magellan and Juan Sebastián Elcano, which set sail in October 1519.[15] Eighteen men, out of 270 who set sail in three ships, returned to Spain three years later.[16] The journal of Antonio Pigafetta, a knight and supernumerary on the Magellan voyage, was the earliest by a European traveller to Patagonia. It was first printed in French at Paris[17]; Italian translations appeared in Venice (1536 and 1550) and English translations in London (1555, reprinted in 1577).[18]

Pigafetta described the appearance of the Tehuelche people whom the expedition's members encountered at what is now Puerto San Julián,[19] along the southeast coast of South America:

> they saw a man as large as a giant in the port, dancing and singing … and putting dust on his head. … And he was so tall that they did not even reach his waist. And he was well proportioned, having a large face, encircled with yellow paint, and also around his eyes and two hearts painted on his two cheeks, his hair dyed white, and clothed in animal skins, skillfully sewn together. … The feet of the giant were wrapped in the said skin, like shoes, and he had a short, stout bow in his hand. The thick string was made from the gut of the said animal, and he had a bundle of very long cane arrows, feathered like ours. …[20]

15 The expedition had sailed from Seville. Magellan was killed in the Philippines; Elcano led the expedition home. Duvernay-Bolens, *Géants patagons*, 41: an exception is a textual reference on Waldseemüller's 1516 map to the isle of giants off the Brazilian coast, following Vespucci, and predating the Magellan circumnavigation.

16 One ship, the *Santo Antonio*, had deserted in the Straits of Magellan and returned to Spain the previous year; the other, the *Trinidad*, remained at Tidore for repair.

17 Antonio Pigafetta, *Le Voyage et navigation faict par les Espaignolz es isles de Mollucques* (Paris, c.1525).

18 Antonio Pigafetta, *The First Voyage Around the World, 1519–1522: An Account of Magellan's Expedition*, ed. Theodor J. Cachey Jr. (Toronto, ON: University of Toronto Press, 2007), xlvii–xlviii. For extant manuscripts, see ibid., xlvi. For other expedition records, see ibid., l–li; Pigafetta, *Magellan's Voyage*, ed. Skelton, 2–5; idem, *First Voyage*, ed. Cachey, l-li.

19 Pigafetta, *Magellan's Voyage*, ed. Skelton, 153, nn. 12–13.

20 For a facsimile and translation of the first printed edition, see Antonio Pigafetta, *The Voyage of Magellan: The Journal of Antonio Pigafetta … from the edition in the William L. Clements Library, University of Michigan, Ann Arbor*, trans. Paula Spurlin Paige (Englewood Cliffs, NJ: Prentice-Hall, 1969), 11–12 (chap. X): '. . .veirent vng homme de stature de geant estant au port dansant, chantant … et mettant pouldre sur sa teste. … Et cestuy estoit tant grand que ne luy venoient point a la ceinture. Et estoit bien dispose ayant la face grande et paincte entour de iaulne, et autour des yeulx deux cueurs painctz es deux ioues, les cheueulx tainctz de blanc, vestu de peaulx de beste cousues subtilement ensemble. … Les piedz du geant estoient enueloppez de la dicte peau en facon de souliers, & vng arc gros & court en la main. La corde grosse faicte des boyaux de ladicte beste & vne trousse de fleches moult longues de canne, empennees comme les nostres'. The editions by Skelton and Cachey cited earlier are of manuscript versions of the text.

This passage reveals both the multiplicity of interpretative frameworks through which a European observer could apprehend a tall person and how an initial evaluation might change on further reflection. Pigafetta first describes the figure the expedition observed as a man – albeit a tall one – rather than a giant. His good proportions also signal that we are not to consider him an aberration. He exhibits signs of civility – the skins 'skillfully sewn' into clothing, and the recognizable use of skins 'like shoes' and arrows 'feathered like ours'.[21] Midway through this description the person moves from having the height of a giant to actually being a 'geant'. By the next chapter of the narrative, we see the side-head 'Aultre geant' (another giant) at the beginning of the section. Given the rich cultural valency of the term 'giant' in this period, this was a significant shift. A Renaissance reader might well have wondered whether this was a monstrous individual, a representative of a Plinian monstrous people, or a wild man, rather than an ordinary human.

Other elements indicate that the move from 'like a giant' to 'giant' was not a mere slip of Pigafetta's quill, but that the possibility that these beings had a liminal ontological status might well have been crossing Pigafetta's mind. The naming of the Patagonians is an apt example. Pigafetta relates that Magellan 'called these people Patagonians',[22] and that this region was called 'Pathagonia'.[23] While sixteenth-century writers proposed several possible etymologies for the term, the fact that Pigafetta did not explain it suggests that he judged that his audience was already familiar with it.[24] The term probably originates in the popular Spanish chivalric romance *Primaleón*, first printed at Salamanca in 1512, and soon widely translated.[25] The romance described an island inhabited by wild men dressed in skins and a certain 'Patagón', a large creature born of an animal, the most monstrous being on earth.[26] Born of sodomy, sporting a dog's head

[21] Amerigo Vespucci had briefly mentioned the presence of exceptionally tall people along the southeast coast of South America, further north of the region where the Magellan expedition made its landfall: Auguste Guinnard, *Trois Ans chez les patagons: Le récit de captivité d'Auguste Guinnard (1856–1859)*, introduction & dossier historique de Jean-Paul Duviols (Paris: Chandeigne, 2009), 15.

[22] Pigafetta, *Voyage of Magellan*, ed. Paige, 18 (chap. XIII): 'Le capitaine apelle ce peuple Pathagoni.'

[23] Ibid., 18 (chap. XIV).

[24] For this point, see Duvernay-Bolens, *Géants patagons*, 11.

[25] *Libro segundo de Palmerin que trata los grandes fechos de Primaleón* (Salamanca, 1512), chap. CXXXIII. Its author is unknown.

[26] For possible etymologies, see Duviols, 'Patagonian "Giants"', 129–30; Duvernay-Bolens, *Géants patagons*, 11–12; Auguste Guinnard, *Trois Ans chez les patagons: Le récit de captivité d'Auguste Guinnard (1856–1859)*, introduction & dossier historique de Jean-Paul Duviols (Paris, 2009), 15–16.

and the feet of a stag, the giant subsequently polluted human lineage. Pigafetta's *Voyage*, written in an Italian courtly tradition of Renaissance travel writing,[27] would have appealed to many of the same readers as works like *Primaleón*. We cannot be certain what Pigafetta thought of the Patagonians' place in the order of nature – he does not tell us this explicitly – but his naming of the Patagonians could well have raised the possibility of their monstrous hybridity in the minds of his readers.

Although Pigafetta does not define the Tehuelche as monsters, his account might well have led learned viewers to a euhemeristic interpretation of *Primaleón* in which the Patagonian giants illuminated the sort of historical giants whose deeds had inspired chivalric romances. We see just such a leap when, almost a century later, the Spanish chronicler and poet Bartolomé Leonardo de Argensola applied circular logic to connect the Tehuelche to the giants of romances. In his history of the Moluccas, Argensola noted that, given the cowardly behaviour of the Patagonian giants met by members of Pedro Sarmiento de Gambóa's 1578–9 expedition, which made landfall in Patagonia, 'the cowardice that authors of the fabulous books commonly called chivalric romances attribute to their giants does not seem inappropriate'.[28]

Amadis of Gaul was another romance that may have led courtly audiences to similar interpretations of the Patagonians. Probably written in Spanish in the first half of the fourteenth century, it was printed at Saragossa in 1508 and widely translated and reprinted in the sixteenth and early seventeenth centuries.[29] Here, too, the giant is monstrous in the sense of being an uncommon creature, potentially a human–animal hybrid. Amadis's challenges include battling Ardan Canileo the Feared, a creature who

> was ugly and very disfigured and coarse, the like of which was never seen.... he was of the blood of giants, for there are more there than in other places, and he was not enormously large of body, but was taller than other men who were not giants. He had heavy limbs and broad shoulders and a thick neck, and a heavy, well-proportioned chest, and hands and legs to correspond. He had a large, flat-nosed, dog-like face,

[27] See Pigafetta, ed. Cachey, xii–xv.

[28] Bartolomé Leonardo de Argensola, *Conqvista de las islas Malvcas* (Madrid, 1609), lib. III, 126: 'no parece impropria la cobardia que aplican à sus Gigantes los escritores de los libros fabulosos, que llaman vulgarmente de Cauallerias'. For a similar point, see María Rosa Lida de Malkiel, 'Para la toponimia argentina: Patagonia', *Hispanic Review*, XX (1952), 321–3, at 323.

[29] Garci Rodríguez de Montalvo, *Amadis of Gaul*, trans. Edwin B. Place and Herbert C. Behm, 2 vols. (Lexington, KY: University of Kentucky Press, 1974), I, 9. For editions, see I, xiii–xlvii.

> and because of this resemblance they called him Canileo (Dog-lion). His nose was flat and wide and was all red and covered with thick black spots, with which his face and hands and neck were sprinkled, and he had a fierce expression resembling that of a lion. He had thick twisted lips, and curly hair and a beard that he could scarcely comb.[30]

Canileo, then, is very much the giant as an abject monster, whose tainted blood was a genealogical and geographical marker. Aesthetically repulsive beyond common experience, his giant blood might have come from the giants of the Old Testament, beings who were not only gigantic in stature but, in the case of Cain's descendants, were also lustful, violent and savage.[31] Given Canileo's other attributes, readers might even have wondered whether Canileo's gigantic ancestors had mated not only with other people, but also with animals.[32] Viewed through these traditions, Canileo's physique was not a pleasurable wonder but a monstrance of corruption and animality lodged in the lineage of humanity.

The man-giant Canileo's hair, resisting attempts to tame it, functions as a metonym for the uncivilizable monster. His flat nose, 'twisted lips, and frizzy hair' might also have suggested to Renaissance readers that he descended from black Africans. The sixteenth-century French jurist Jean Bodin observed that 'in Ethiopia, where, we have said, the race of men is very keen and lustful, no one varies markedly from the uniform type. They are all small, curly-haired, black, flat-nosed, blubber-lipped, and bald, with white teeth and black eyes.'[33] The English sailor George Best similarly

30 Garci Rodríguez de Montalvo, *Amadís de Gaula*, anotación de Juan Bautista Avalle-Arce (Madrid: Pozuelo Espasa Calpe, 2008), Libro II, cap. VXI (454): 'era feo y muy desemejado y esquivo que se nunca vio.. . . era de sangre de gigantes, que allí los ay más que en otras partes, y no era descomunalmente grande de cuerpo, pero era más alto que otro hombre que gigante no fuesse. Avía sus miembros gruessos, y las espaldas anchas y el pescueço gruesso, y los pechos gruessos y cuadrados, y las manos y piernas a razòn de lo otro. El rosto avía grande y romo de la fechura de can, y por esta semejança le llamavan Canileo. Las narizes avía romas y anchas, y era todo brasilado, y cubierto de pintas negras espessas, de la cuales era sembrado el rosto y las manos y pescueço, y avía brava catadura así como semejança de león. Los beços avía gruessos y retornados, y los cabellos crispos que apenas los podía penar, y las barvas otrosí'; the translation, with minor amendments, is from *Amadis of Gaul*, trans. Place and Behm, I, 612–3 (Book II, chap. LXI).

31 *Genesis* 6:4.

32 For an example of this type of fear, see the anecdote about Samuel Pepys in Chapter 1.

33 Jean Bodin, *Methods for the Easy Comprehension of History*, trans. Beatrice Reynolds (New York, NY: Columbia University Press, 1945), chap. V, 143; Jean Bodin, *Methodus ad facilem historiarum cognitionem [1566]* (Aalen: Scientia, 1967), 144: 'in Aethiopia, ubi hominum genus acutissimum et salacissimum esse diximus, nemo tam sui similis est, quam omnes omnium. Sunt autem parvi, crispi, atri, simi, labeones, glabri, albissimis dentibus, nigris oculis'. See, more generally, K. J. Lowe, 'The Stereotyping of Black Africans in Renaissance Europe', in *Black*

wrote about the Ethiopians' 'hair like wooll curled short'. There were thousands of black African slaves in Renaissance Spain, a presence that Spanish literature and painting reflected.[34]

By evoking both prevailing stereotypes of the black African and the sins of the antediluvian men whom God had wished to exterminate, the monstrously tall Canileo also embodied moral transgression. For courtly readers, then, a strong textual tradition existed for seeing Pigafetta's account of New World giants as signifying the descendants of those who were either sinful or were not fully capable and – in both cases – could pollute the rest of humanity with their monstrosity. If beings resembling Canileo were ever found, they would have raised several questions: how many such creatures existed, and by what means could one identify them? What of the distinctiveness of humanity: could anyone be sure that he was descended solely from Adam's seed, and not also from the seed of giants or animals? Canileo 'was taller than other men who were not giants', but he was not enormous: was this a sign that he was part human? Where, then, was the line between tall humans and such beastly individuals as Canileo? Courtly map viewers familiar with such tales might well have seen in the Patagonians real-world equivalents of Canileo.

The nomenclature on maps for the giants of South America shows the prevailing influence of Pigafetta's account in cartographic circles across Iberia, Normandy, the German lands and the Low Countries.[35] The earliest surviving maps to refer to peoples in southern South America connected them to the monsters of chivalric romance by associating them with the term 'Patagonia'. These were the manuscript world maps by the Portuguese-born Diogo Ribeiro, *cosmógrafo mayor* at the Casa de la Contratación in Seville. Ribeiro had made navigational instruments and charts for Magellan's circumnavigatory fleet, and had translated Portuguese travel manuscripts into Spanish.[36] The appearance of the term 'Patagonia' on Ribeiro's works seven years after the return of the expedition's survivors indicates a line of transmission from Pigafetta to Ribeiro. Although we cannot know for certain whether Ribeiro spoke to Pigafetta

Africans in Renaissance Europe, ed. K. J. Lowe and T. F. Earle (Cambridge: Cambridge University Press, 2005), 17–47.

[34] See Jeremy Lawrance, 'Black Africans in Renaissance Spanish Literature', in *Black Africans in Renaissance Europe*, ed. K. J. Lowe and T. F. Earle (Cambridge: Cambridge University Press, 2005), 70–93.

[35] For further examples, see Davies, 'Amerindians on European Maps', chap. 7.

[36] *PMC*, II, 89. These manuscripts include Munich, Bayerische Staatsbibliothek, Abteilung für Handschriften und Alte Drucke, Diego Ribero [Diogo Ribeiro], Cod. Hisp. 12, 'Libro de la navegacion de la India de Portugal', 1524.

or saw a version of his account, all ships from the Indies were required to dock at Seville, and their crews had to be de-briefed at the Casa.[37] Returning pilots were expected to provide geographical and navigational information to the Casa's cosmographers;[38] Ribeiro's informants were probably participants of the voyage. Indeed, information from the Magellan-Elcano expedition would thus have circulated in nautical circles before both the presentation of Pigafetta's account to Holy Roman Emperor Charles V and the work's printed publication. A caption in Patagonia on Ribeiro's 1529 world map known as the Weimar planisphere relates how Magellan discovered the region on his way to the Moluccas, and that 'those who live in this land ... are men of great stature, almost giants'.[39] Since these maps also denote this region as 'Tiera de Patagones' these beings were perhaps to be read as abnormal creatures, in the manner of the giant Patagón, monsters whose physical or mental aberrations made their relationship to humanity uncertain. If the Patagonians were not rational humans, the Spanish could more easily justify conquest and domination.[40]

The Casa did not merely produce maps intended to record and facilitate navigation (and indeed, maps were not the primary navigational aid at the time), but also produced display maps to make strategic and imperial claims. Ribeiro's large, illustrated maps were intended for royalty, sometimes functioning as diplomatic gifts.[41] The maps' intended audience was certainly to be found in courtly circles where members read *Primaleón*. To such readers, the giants in Pigafetta's account were fundamentally different from humans and yet raised questions about the extent to which they had polluted, and could continue to pollute, human lineage.

Patagonians as monstrous errors: Maximilianus Transylvanus's account

The giants spotted by the Magellan-Elcano expedition did not, however, have to be read as a fault-line in the bedrock of human genealogy. The

[37] See Chapter 2, near n. 4. [38] Sandman, 'Mirroring the World', 88.

[39] Cortesão, *Cartografia*, 156: 'Los que abitan esta tierra ... son hombres de grandes cuerpos casi gigantes'. The map is preserved in the Landesbibliothek, Weimar. A similar inscription appears on his map known as the Wolfenbüttel map (1533): Wolfenbüttel, Herzog August Bibliothek, Cod. Guelf. 104 A and B Aug. fol. This place name also appears on Ribeiro's 1529 Vatican planisphere, Biblioteca Apostolica Vaticana, MS Borgiano III.

[40] See Chapters 3 and 7. [41] See Chapter 2.

Renaissance cultural imaginary also left room for the possibility that each giant was an individual monstrous accident, of the sort found in Europe. This interpretation emerged from the Aristotelian tradition of natural history, and was the view espoused in a letter by Maximilianus Transylvanus, secretary to Charles V, and a pupil of the humanist Peter Martyr.[42] Maximilianus and Peter Martyr had been present at the Spanish court at Valladolid when the surviving members of the circumnavigatory expedition were interviewed.[43] The scholars had heard the depositions of Pigafetta and Sebastián Elcano, and Peter set Maximilianus the letter to write as a Latin exercise.[44] Maximilianus's letter, which he addressed to his father the Cardinal-Archbishop of Salzburg, is dated 22 October 1522, the month in which the *Victoria*, alone of the five ships that had commenced the circumnavigation, returned to Spain. The proud father had the letter printed in 1523 and 1524, at Rome and Cologne,[45] as *De Moluccis insulis*.[46] The letter was translated into Italian at Venice in 1536,[47] and reprinted in various travel compendia.[48]

The expedition's first encounter was intended to be understood as one with regular people rather than with monstrous ones: Maximilianus describes the indigenous people as men, women, or children, who lived in a cottage containing two rooms. The Tehuelche provided 'barbarous entertainment' for the Spaniards. The Spaniards attempted to coerce the Tehuelche men to bring their families and board their ships. The men then retreated into a room and reappeared in battle-dress:

> [they appeared] covered with these fearful skins from the sole of the foot to the very top of their heads, with their face dyed with various colours,

[42] The first edition was Maximilianus Transylvanus, *De Moluccis insulis* . . . (Cologne, 1523). Subsequent references are to this edition.

[43] Pigafetta, *Magellan's Voyage*, ed. Skelton, 5.

[44] Pigafetta, *Voyage of Magellan*, ed. Paige, XI.

[45] Ibid., XI; idem, *Magellan's Voyage*, ed. Skelton, 4. Magellan was, of course, trying to reach the Moluccas Islands by sailing west from Spain rather than east.

[46] The first edition was Maximilianus Transylvanus, *De Moluccis insulis* . . . (Cologne, 1523). Subsequent references are to this edition.

[47] *EA*, I, 423, *s.v.*

[48] Pigafetta, *Magellan's Voyage*, ed. Skelton, 4; Pigafetta, *First Voyage* ed. Cachey, li-lii. *EA*, nos 542/3 and 542/4: the account appeared in Johannes Boemus, *Omnium gentium mores, leges et ritus* (Antwerp and Venice, 1542). An abstract of the voyage appeared in Pietro Martire d'Anghiera, *De orbe novo* . . . *decades octo* (Alcalá de Henares, 1530), decas V, lib. VII. For references to Patagonians in Maximilianus's and later texts, see Frank Lestringant, 'La Flèche du patagon ou la preuve des lointains: sur un chapitre d'André Thevet', in Jean Céard and Jean-Claude Margolin, eds., *Voyager à la Renaissance* (Paris: Maisonneuve et Larose, 1987), 468–96, at 493–6.

> with bows and arrows. Thus adorned in this terrible and astounding fashion and of a far greater stature than before, they appear for battle.[49]

Maximilianus sketches the Tehuelche as tall but savvy dressers who used animal-skins to project a more fearsome image of themselves. Nevertheless, from this point, he refers to them as *Gigantes*, and even as 'enormous giants' (*egregii tamen Gigantes*).[50]

Despite the tantalizing nomenclature Maximilianus does not appear to have intended for his father (the addressee of his letter) to interpret the Tehuelche as a monstrous people of the sort to be expected, after Pliny, at the harsh southern latitudes of the Straits of Magellan. He does not use the terms 'Patagonian' or 'Patagonia'. Although Magellan did not survive the trip, Pigafetta did, returning to Valladolid – where Maximilanus would interview survivors of the expedition – and presenting a manuscript of his account to Charles V.[51] It is difficult to be sure whether Maximilianus also spoke with Pigafetta, whom he does not name in the letter, or whether he had access to this manuscript. Maximilianus begins his letter by stating how he had taken great care to obtain an account of the facts from both the commanding officer (Elcano) and his sailors.[52] Maximilianus does not seem to have come across Pigafetta's use of the term 'Patagon', and asserts that the sailors 'appeared in their narrative, not merely to have abstained from fabulous statements, but also to contradict and refute those made by ancient authors'.[53] His scepticism of the concept of monstrous peoples is clear:

> For who ever believed that the Monosceli, the Sciapodes, the Scyrites, the Spithamaei, the Pygmies or other of this kind were rather monsters than

49 Maximilianus Transylvanus, *Moluccis insulis*, sig. A.V.*r-v*.: 'aliis quibusdam horribilibus pellibus, a planta pedis ad summum verticem tecti, facie variis coloribus infecta, arcubus et sagittis ad praelium terribili et stupendo hoc accincti ornatu, et longe maioris quam antea staturae in aciem prodeunt'; idem, *First Voyage*, ed. Quirino, 115. Photographs of the Techuelche peoples taken in the late nineteenth and twentieth centuries illuminate these full-length skin costumes. See, e.g., Alfredo Prieto, 'Patagonian Painted Cloaks: An Ancient Puzzle', in *Patagonia: Natural History, Prehistory and Ethnography at the Uttermost End of the Earth*, ed. Colin McEwan et al. (Princeton, NJ: Princeton University Press, 1997), 173–85.

50 Maximilianus Transylvanus, *Moluccis insulis*, sig. A.V.*v*.

51 Pigafetta, *Voyage of Magellan*, ed. Paige, chap. CXIV. Ibid., XII: the whereabouts of this copy are not known.

52 Pigafetta, *First Voyage*, ed. Cachey, lii: Maxmilianus, the husband of the niece of Cristóbal de Haro, one of the backers of the expedition, 'may have had stronger than scholarly curiosity about the voyage'.

53 Maximilianus Transylvanus, *Moluccis insulis*, sig. B.i.*v*.: 'non modo nihil fabulosi afferre, sed fabulosa omnia alia a veteribus authoribus prodita, refellere et reprobare, narratione sua viderentur'; idem, *First Voyage*, ed. Quirino, 111.

> men? Yet, although the Castilians in their voyages westwards, and the Portuguese sailing eastwards, have sought out, discovered and surveyed so many places even beyond the Tropic of Capricorn . . . without anything certain being able to be heard about monstrous men of this kind; and therefore all such accounts ought to be regarded as fabulous, and as old wives' tales handed down in some way or other without any firm source.[54]

Implicit here is the dilemma of how to know when a series of observations (many tall individuals in Patagonia) added up to a general law (the Patagonians giants are a monstrous people). Maximilian grappled with the challenge of making knowledge about something that could not be proved absolutely, but could only be known as a probability.

In a classic article, Steven Shapin argued that the changing nature of the way the physical sciences were practised in seventeenth-century England heralded a shift from thinking about physical knowledge as something that had to be proved absolutely to something that was posited via revisable hypotheses. This shift, argued Shapin, broke down 'the radical distinction between "knowledge" and "opinion"'.[55] Barbara Shapiro argued that changes to the practice of natural philosophy in seventeenth-century England were part of a broader shift across religious, legal, historical and other knowledge-making settings in which probabilistic knowledge gained authority despite its definition as that which could not be demonstrated to be always and absolutely true 'knowledge'.[56] The case of the Patagonian giant would become an issue about the credibility of witnesses whose testimony could not offer certain knowledge that the southern tip of Patagonia caused humans to become giants. Apart from the fact that there was no agreement about a giant's minimum height, there were several ethnic groups in the region, with different characteristics. Such problems of probability and multiple witnesses had long resided at the core of

[54] Maximilianus Transylvanus, *Moluccis insulis*, sig. B.i.*v*-B.ii.*r*: 'Nam quis Monoscelos, seu Sciopodas, Scyritas, Spitamaeos, Pygmaeos et multa huiusmodi monstra potius, quam homines esse crediderit, quum et a Castellanis in Occidentem per meridiem, et a Portugallensibus in Orientem velificantibus, tot loca ultra Tropicum Capricorni quaesita, inventa, lustrata fuerint . . . neque tamen unquam de huiusmodi Monstrosis hominibus certi quicquam audiri potuit, credi debet ea omnia fabulosa, et mendacia esse anilia, nullo certo authore per manus quodammodo tradita'; idem, *First Voyage*, ed. Quirino, 111.

[55] Steven Shapin, 'Pump and Circumstance: Robert Boyle's Literary Technology', *Social Studies of Science* 14 (1984), 481–520, at 482.

[56] Barbara J. Shapiro, *Probability and Certainty in Seventeenth-Century England: A Study of the Relationships between Natural Science, Religion, History, Law and Literature* (Princeton, NJ: Princeton University Press, 1983).

knowledge about distant places, and prompted the drive to encyclopedic reportage of sometimes contradictory evidence, leaving readers to make up their own minds. Contrary to Shapiro's and Shapin's view that belief probabilistic knowledge was a seventeenth-century development, in the history of making knowledge about the natural history of distant places, there was no radical distinction between knowledge and opinion, either before or during the early modern period. What is more, synthesizers who had not witnessed phenomena with their own eyes had long been essential in a context in which no single individual or group had collected all the empirical evidence.

For Maximilanus, not only were South America's 'gigantes' human beings rather than monsters, but there were no monstrous peoples in the East Indies, either. He narrates that on the island of Gilona (Gilolo, in the Moluccas), the expedition-members saw some men with such long ears that they reached down to their shoulders.[57] These indigenous informants told the Magellan-Elcano crew that 'in a nearby island there were men who had such long and wide ears that one ear could, when they liked, cover the whole of their heads. But as our men [the Europeans] were in search not of monsters but of spices, they did not trouble themselves about such rubbish, but sailed direct for the Moluccas'.[58] Once again we are assured of the sober and reliable character of Maximilianus's witnesses who are correctly able to see indigenous testimony about so-called monsters for the 'rubbish' that it was. It is impossible to separate Maximilianus's sceptical response from the words of his interlocutors – was he putting words in their mouths? – but, taken together with the absence of the term 'Patagon' from his account, Maximilianus clearly gave short shrift to information that supported the existence of monstrous peoples rather than monstrous individuals. Such oral testimony as Maximilianus received about them was, for him, false rather than potentially capable of re-shaping his notion of the human. While Maximilian saw the value of seeking out oral testimony about distant lands, he had no compunction about discounting those elements that he knew *a priori* to be false.

57 Maximilianus Transylvanus, *Moluccis insulis*, sig. B.iv.*v*. These beings appear in, for example, writings by Pliny, Solinus and Pomponius Mela.

58 Maximilian and Pigafetta, *First Voyage*, ed. Quirino, 126; Maximilianus Transylvanus, *Moluccis insulis*, sig. B. iv.*v*.: 'haud longe distare aliam insulam, ubi homines essent non solum pendulis, sed adeo latis amplisque auriculis, ut cum ex usu esset, altera earum universum caput contegeret. Nostri aut que non monstra, sed aromata quererent omissis nugis recta ad Moluccas tendunt'.

Mapping Patagonians, making meaning

The giants on maps constitute the earliest known visual images of the inhabitants of the southernmost tip of the Americas, predating illustrations in travel accounts, encyclopedias and prints. From the mid-sixteenth century, giants began appearing on manuscript maps produced in Seville, Portugal and Normandy, and on printed maps from the workshops of Antwerp, Amsterdam and the German lands. While we cannot know for certain whether any of these map illuminators had access to images on sources other than maps, the wealth of the surviving printed and manuscript maps with such images decades before the earliest survival in other media suggests that many mapmakers drew giants *ab initio* or armed only with earlier map illustrations. The variety of the images and the ways in which they became more specific over time suggest that artists actively reflected on the nature of the giants and on ways of representing it. By excavating the ways in which these artists assembled these giants – their costumes, weapons and other features – one can better understand the analytical processes by which they extrapolated from paltry details in order to produce knowledge.

When mapmakers devised visual codes for the giants' physical attributes and placed them within the space of southern South America on maps, they narrowed the range of possibilities for the giants' origin, character and relationship to Europeans in the eyes of their readers. Since the placing of a single giant within a landmass on a map was read as signifying what all people in the region shared, map imagery implicitly established Patagonia's giants as a monstrous people rather than as monstrous individuals. By inflecting the ontology of Patagonians in the minds of other artists, artisans and scholars, these images shaped other media and helped to make the ontology of Patagonian gigantism a topic of scholarly debate into the eighteenth century and beyond.[59]

Mapmakers' representations of giants, which drew primarily on Pigafetta's account,[60] effectively offered their viewers solutions to three problems: how to construct a visual representation of these beings from a written description; which interpretative traditions offered the best

[59] For the later debates, see Duvernay-Bolens, *Géants patagons*, chap. 2.

[60] The exception appeared around the turn of the seventeenth century, when a few Dutch and German mapmakers experimented with a new motif and inscription, of a Patagonian giant who used arrows to induce vomiting. This material was drawn from Maximilanus; it does not appear in Pigafetta's text. See Davies, 'Amerindians on European Maps', chap. 7.

explanation for giants; and whether or not gigantism was a universal trait in Patagonia. The first problem, that of giving a written description a visual form, is one that mapmakers are conventionally believed to mangle by either seeing source texts through their preconceptions or copying existing illustrations with no regard for their relevance. While Pigafetta's descriptions of the giants' clothing and weaponry are sparse, representations of giants on maps reveal how illustrators extrapolated imaginatively but carefully to provide their viewers with a visual feast. These decisions were important because clothing and weaponry helped map viewers to identify the type of giant depicted.[61] In Biblical iconography, particular weapons indicated levels of civility; in medieval iconographical traditions, giant wild men carried staffs and shields.[62] In late medieval visual culture, the motif of the wild man also functioned as a heraldic device; wild men bore shields depicting coats of arms (Fig. 5.1). The iconographic variations across the maps are unlikely to have been the result of carelessness.[63] Large, illuminated manuscript and printed maps were expensive merchandise; no workshop could afford to be careless in their execution.

Map illuminators attempted to represent testimony about Patagonia's people in the light of existing knowledge about distant environments and their peoples. The earliest iconographic example is a world map made in 1544 by Sebastian Cabot, pilot-major at the Casa de la Contratación or House of Trade in Seville. A figure in Patagonia wears a long, brightly coloured robe (Fig. 5.2). The map inscription, however, describes giants wearing animal skins as described by Pigafetta and Maximilianus. This discrepancy suggests that the text and the image are the work of different artisans – a common practice.[64]

The giant does not hold a bow and arrow, as Pigafetta described, but a staff and shield. This decision may have been inspired by Vespucci's account of his second voyage to the eastern seaboard of South America some way north of southern Patagonia; Vespucci had related how '[these giants] were armed with immense bows and arrows, and with great stakes or staffs the size of long poles', but he did not mention

[61] D. Felton, 'Rejecting and Embracing the Monstrous in Ancient Greece and Rome', in *ARC-MM*, 103–131, at 119.

[62] Chapter 2, near n. 53. See, e.g., BNF-Mss, MS fr. 2810, f. 216*r*, an early-fifteenth century manuscript containing the *Book of John Mandeville*, which illustrates anthropophagous giants alongside a giant holding a staff.

[63] For discussion of a larger number of examples, see Davies, 'Representations of Amerindians', chap. 7.

[64] The map was drawn in Seville but printed at Nuremberg.

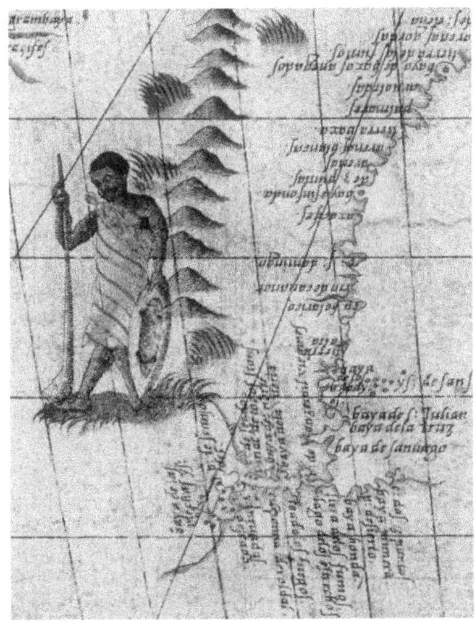

5.2 Sebastian Cabot, world map (Nuremberg, 1544), detail of giant.
Bibliothèque nationale de France, Département des Cartes et plans, Rés GE AA 582.

shields.[65] This was not the only iconographic extrapolation available to the artist, who could equally have chosen to depict the giant as a folkloric wild man and equipped him accordingly with a staff. Nevertheless, this is not a completely conventional wild man; the giant wears a proper cloth costume rather than skins. His shield is no longer heraldic; rather, it is part of the giant's weaponry. This subtle transformation shows the artist imaginatively reconstructing a plausible indigenous practice by synthesizing a slim text by an eyewitness and judicious selections from the iconography of the wild man. The consequent mash-up is a plausible explanation of recent observations and traditions concerning giants. The resulting manifestation of visual euhemerism validated new and old ideas about giants.

The robed giant on Cabot's map most likely inspired the giant figure in the 1551 world map by Sancho Gutiérrez, a fellow chart-maker for the Casa since 1539. The Gutiérrez map's artist saw fit to re-think the giant in the light of multiple sources (Fig. 5.3).[66] The giant on this map is gracefully

[65] Waldseemüller, *Cosmographiae introductio*, 129 and LXXXIII: 'Hii et enim ingentes arcus et sagittas necnon et sudes perticasve magnas instar clavarum ferebant'.

[66] Sancho Gutiérrez, world map, 1551, Kartensammlung, K I 99.416, Österreichische Nationalbibliothek, Vienna. For bibliography and the geography of America on the Gutiérrez map, see Harry Kelsey, 'American Discoveries noted on the Planisphere of Sancho Gutiérrez', in *Early Images of the Americas: Transfer and Invention*, ed. Jerry M. Williams and Robert E. Lewis (Tucson, AZ and London: University of Arizona Press, 1993), 247–61. It is not unlikely

5.3 Sancho Gutiérrez, world map, 1551, detail of giant.
Österreichische Nationalbibliothek, Wien, Kartensammlung, K I 99.416.

proportioned and wears a costume reminiscent of a Roman toga. The club, shield and beard suggest an Old Testament prophet. By dressing these figures in robes rather than in the skins described by Pigafetta, the artists of the Cabot and the Gutiérrez map hinted that these people could weave cloth and thus had some level of ingenuity. These wild men, then, had the potential for civic improvement.

The second problem with which mapmakers engaged was that of the nature and extent of gigantism in Patagonia. Was the condition confined to a few individuals, or was it an essential quality passed down from parents to children? The first image of a female giant appeared alongside one of a male on the 1550 manuscript planisphere made in Normandy by Pierre Desceliers (Fig. 5.4). By illustrating male and female examples, Desceliers' image suggested that these 'giants found by the Spanish' might breed to produce more giants.[67] Early modern viewers perceived mapmakers' choices for illustrative ethnographic details as revealing what people in a given region had in common.[68] Hence, viewers could well have understood

that Gutiérrez knew Cabot's map, and might even have worked on it. The two maps are similar in terms of geographical, textual and iconographical content, and may have been drawn up from the same master map. For a comparative analysis, see Harry Kelsey, 'The Planispheres of Sebastian Cabot and Sancho Gutiérrez', *Terrae Incognitae*, XIX (1987), 41–61.

[67] BL-MSS, MS. Add. 24065: 'geantz trouves par les espagnolz'.

[68] See, e.g., Chapters 2 and 3.

5.4 Pierre Desceliers, 'Mappemonde', 1550, detail of Patagonian giants.
© British Library Board, Add. MS. 24065.

the caption and figures on Desceliers' map as indicating a form of gigantism that was inherited and that appeared in such works as Pliny's *Historia naturalis*.[69] If this were the case, then new questions about whether the environment of Patagonia deformed people would arise.

In the last quarter of the sixteenth century, printers in the Low Countries began to corner the market in printed maps rich in ethnographic illustrations. One such map, Gerard de Jode's map of South America (1576), transmitted an explicit, influential message concerning the heritability of Patagonian gigantism by including child giants (Fig. 5.5).[70] The standing figures have the large heads and stocky proportions of children when compared to the reclining giantess. Again, this inherited aberration appearing on a map would have indicated to contemporary viewers that the Patagonians were a monstrous people rather than individual monstrous births. The caption, which frequently re-appeared on later maps,[71]

69 For monsters and the maternal imagination and for explanations for causes of monstrosity more broadly, see Chapter 1.

70 Gerard de Jode, *[South America]* (Antwerp, 1576). One incomplete copy survives in the Library of Congress, Washington, DC, where it is currently catalogued as a map of western South America by Gerard Mercator. For the attribution to De Jode, see Burden, *Mapping*, I, no. 47.

71 On some maps, cartographers combined Plancius's figures with this caption. These maps include: Arnold Florentin van Langren's map of South America, which appeared in Jan van Huygen van Linschoten, *Itinerario. Voyage ofte Schipvaert* (Amsterdam and The Hague, 1596); the 1595 manuscript map probably made by Evert Gijsbertz, illustrated in Zandvliet, *Mapping for Money*, 70; Levinus Hulsius's map of Patagonia (see note below).

Hic habitant Gygantes dicti Patagones pedum
longitudine. 9. vel. 10. aut plus eo pinguntque
facies suas varys coloribus ex diuersis herbis
expressis.

5.5 Gerard de Jode, map of America (Antwerp, 1576), detail.
Courtesy of the Library of Congress, Geography and Map Division, G5200 1569 .M2 Vault.

notes that the 'giants called Patagones' are 'nine or ten feet or more in height', and that 'they paint their faces in various colours extracted from a variety of plants'.[72] The height gives readers a comparator to their own, but also to the giants in *Genesis*, and to the theoretical fifteen-foot minimum for a giant capable of surviving the Flood by standing on the highest mountain. Patagonia's giants were evidently too short to have done this. De Jode presumably inferred the nature of the face paint, something that the travel texts do not mention, from the fact that many European pigments were vegetable based. His extrapolation complicated the story: these beings, though monstrous, had crafts.

Gerard de Jode suspected that his decision to present the Patagonians as giants would, like the theory that the earth had been populated by giants in the past, receive a mixed response. On the commentary for a map of America that appeared in his atlas of 1578, he declared, perhaps defensively, that 'I would not call them giants undeservedly, since scarcely any of

72 '...Gygantes dicti Patagones. Pedum longitudine 9 vel 10 aut plus eo pinguntque facies suas variis coloribus ex diversis herbis expressis.' De Jode's giants range from 2.7 to 3 m in height.

5.6 Aldrovandi, *Monstrorum historia* (Bologna, 1642), 35, detail.
Reproduced by kind permission of the Syndics of Cambridge University Library, M.13.43.

the Portuguese reached their waist-band'.[73] While we cannot be certain that De Jode also meant that these beings were ontologically different from humans, the caption, echoing Pigafetta's observation that the Magellan expedition's sailors did not even reach the waist of the first giant they encountered, suggests an unbridgeable gap – reflected visually by the waist-band – between Europeans and Patagonians.

Despite De Jode's cautiousness, the naturalist Ulisse Aldrovandi included these giants in his *Monstrorum historia*.[74] Aldrovandi's entry on giants (in Patagonia and beyond) cites Pliny alongside a raft of sixteenth-century explorers and writers including Pigafetta and Maximilianus. The volume contains an illustration of the 'giants of America' (Fig. 5.6) that is clearly derived from Gerard De Jode's map; the text described the giants in

[73] Gerard de Jode, *Speculum*, preceding plate II: 'Gigantes non iniuria dixerim, cum Lusitanorum vix aliquis eos aequarit, qua medii cinguntur.' Giants are not illustrated here. De Jode's son Cornelis re-used this text in a later edition (Cornelis de Jode, *Speculum*, f. 3; map on facing page). The map of America in this edition included depictions of giants; these were identified by the giant inscription from Gerard de Jode's 1576 map.

[74] Aldrovandi, *Monstrorum historia*, 34.

very similar language. Aldrovandi cited 'the map of America by Cornelius Judeus' as his source:

> Here we present images of giants nine or ten feet tall, living in a certain region of America which is called Patagonia, and they paint their faces with various colours extracted from certain plants: for they are drawn in this way in the map of America by Cornelius Judaeus [de Jode].[75]

Gerard de Jode's 1576 map (Fig. 5.5) was re-issued by his son Cornelis around 1595. No copy of the re-issue is known.[76] Aldrovandi evidently consulted Cornelis's 1595 re-issue, borrowing not only the image, but also the text, a case of ethnographic information travelling from map to book. Aldrovandi's choice of image effectively addresses the complaints of sceptics like Maximilianus: Patagonia's giants were a monstrous people, not individual aberrations.

A sustained critique of those who manifested monstrosity appeared in John Bulwer's *Anthropometamorphosis, or Man Transform'd.* First published in 1650, with expanded editions in 1653 and 1654, the book railed against the self-made monsters of contemporary fashion and cosmetic practices. While most of the types of monstrosity Bulwer catalogued were the result of practices that had to be carried out on single bodies – tattooing, head-binding and so on – Bulwer also included one inherited change: the blackness of the African. Bulwer writes that people who are black had once transformed themselves willfully in this way, implying that inherited monstrosities might have once been chosen monstrosities.[77] A people who deviated from the 'natural' state of humanity might even have had ancestors who had sinned in the manner of Ham. Viewers of Patagonian giants might similarly have wondered whether their height was a sign of a willfully chosen error.

Early modern writers who analysed what Andrew S. Curran has termed 'the anatomy of blackness' viewed maps and geographies with the diagrammatic significance of latitudinal lines in mind. One of the English polymath Thomas Browne's arguments against the notion that the sun had caused the blackness of Africans was that 'it hath been doubted by severall

[75] Ibid., 34: 'Hic damus icones Gigantum novem vel decem pedum, habitantium in quadam regione Americae, qui Patagones nuncupantur, et variis coloribus ex herbis quibusdam expressis facies suas pingunt: sic enim in tabula Americae a Cornelio Iudaeo delineantur.'

[76] Burden, *Mapping*, no. 47; no example survives.

[77] John Bulwer, *Anthropometamorphosis: Man Transform'd; or, the Artificial Changeling.* 1650).

moderne writers, particularly by [the mapmaker] Ortelius'.[78] Browne contends that if the sun were the cause, then other peoples who inhabited the same latitudes as black Africans 'should also partake of the same hue and complexion, which notwithstanding they do not'.[79] He further observes that:

> [T]his defect is more remarkable in America, which although subjected unto both the Tropicks, yet are not the Inhabitants black betweene, or neere, or under either, neither to the southward in Brasilia, Chili, or Peru, nor yet to the northward in Hispaniola, Castilia, del Oro, or Nicaraguava; and although in many parts thereof it be confessed there bee at present swarmes of Negroes serving under the Spaniard, yet were they all transported from Africa, since the discovery of Columbus, and are not indigenous or proper natives of America.[80]

This example is one of several points in the text that show how Browne thought carefully about the relationship between the peoples and geography of America, and consulted (or wished his readers to believe that he had consulted) maps that showed the relation of each of America's regions to the lines demarcating the tropics. The apparent failure of humoral theory to explain the fixity of black skin would offer pro-slavery authors a place from which to argue by analogy that other aspects of humans, and in particular their mental capacities, were fixed in the blood.

Environmental interpretations of monstrous peoples

The third intellectual arena in which images of Patagonian giants on maps participated was the question of the proper interpretative tradition through which to make sense of these giants. While placing giants within a particular area on a map implied that gigantism was an inherited characteristic shared by all Patagonians, there were still multiple possible reasons for it. Indeed, the very reading of Patagonians as giants challenged existing authorities for, from the perspective of geographical symmetry, Patagonia should not have spawned giants. The Tehuelche lived around the latitude of 49 degrees south, roughly the same distance from the equator as Paris and Nuremberg. Despite this, Patagonia's location gave commentators a way to think about them as monsters, and to subvert the Ptolemaic coordinate system's relationship with climate.

[78] Thomas Browne, *Pseudodoxia Epidemica: or, Enquiries into very many Received Tenets, and commonly presumed Truths* (London, 1646), 323.
[79] Ibid., 324–5. [80] Ibid., 325.

The reason for this asymmetric treatment of northern and southern latitudes may lie in the classical geographical tradition in which the latitudes of Greece and Rome were the base co-ordinates from which normativity in human difference was measured. By this reckoning, the South Pole was further away than the North Pole, and monsters could be expected at 49 degrees south even if they did not appear at the same latitude north of the Equator. Monstrous peoples in the north in, for example, Olaus Magnus's account of northern Europe, were further north from the equator than Patagonia was south of the Equator.[81]

André Thevet, Royal Cosmographer to Charles IX of France, chaplain to Catherine de' Medici and chaplain on the first French expedition to set up a colony in Brazil, speculated on the ontological boundary – or lack thereof – between the 'Geans' whom he denotes in passing as 'monstres' and the 'Canibales'.[82] In his *Cosmographie universelle* (1575) he writes:

> Of others they say that they are descended from the Cannibals, who are a tall people, not that they approach the proportion and breadth of those here, but being in the Austral land, they took in the air of that place and, by consequence, their children became larger than their ancestors. You also see, that men are much taller in cold regions than in hot or temperate ones, although hot countries nurture wiser and more discerning men.[83]

What Thevet illuminates here is a spatial approach to human difference that tied it to the airs, waters and places of classical humoral theory. His surmise that giants are merely cannibals who found their way to a latitude that changed their descendants might have made his readers wonder what impact this place might have on European bodies. For colonial administrators and medical practitioners who sought to understand and control the impact of the environment of Asia, Africa the Americas on travellers and colonists, such extrapolations did not bode well.[84]

81 Olaus Magnus, *Historia de gentibus septentrionalibus* (Rome, 1555).

82 For Thevet's writing on Patagonian medical practices and on comedic aspects of the Patagonians' height, see Frank Lestringant, 'Les Patagons de la carte (1520–1620)', in *Patagonie: images du bout du monde*, ed. Christine Maine (Paris/Arles 2012), 12–27, at 18–19.

83 Thevet, *Cosmographie*, tome IV, liure XXI, chap. I, 905*v*: D'autres disent, qu'ils sont descenduz des Canibales, lesquels sont gens de haulte stature, non qu'ils approchent de la proportion & corpulence de ceux cy, mais estans en la terre Australe, ils ont reçeu l'air du païs: & par consequent leurs enfans sont deuenuz plus grands que ceux desquels ils ont prins origine. Aussi voyez vous, que és regions froides les hommes y sont beaucoup plus grands qu'és chaudes & temperees, & au contraire les païs chaulds nourrissent les hommes plus subtils & ingenieux'.

84 For literature, see Chapter 1, near n. 10.

Thevet described how a Patagonian giant captured by the Spanish died when the ship transporting him made landfall on the island of Arguin, off the west coast of Africa.[85] Thevet, who claims to have encountered this crew on their arrival, surmised that the giant died either because he did not receive food that suited him, or because the difference in the air was harmful to him. Thevet added that he spoke with a sailor who showed him a coffin containing the enormous bones of the said giant, and comes to the opinion that men of such monstrous height ('si monstreuse grandeur') could not be found in Europe ('nostre climat'), discounting recent findings of bones in Paris as those of a young whale rather than of a man. He concludes that it is cold regions that nurture taller, larger and more savage men, because the hearty climate sustains them.[86]

This conviction that cold climates engender larger people than temperate ones is a recurring point in the *Cosmographie.* Thevet takes issue, for example, with the notion that the people of Mexico are giants, a claim he attributes to Girolamo Cardano.[87] Sixteenth-century chronicles had noted that Tenochtitlán, the capital of the Mexica empire, was at both high altitude and temperate latitude.[88] Thevet argues that these people were not as tall as the Germans, and other people in the vicinity were so short that there were no peoples in Europe who did not surpass them in height. His evidence is that neither the region's air temperature, nor location, nor food could cause 'this monstrosity of the body in these people', for it lay halfway between the hot and the cold, and could not nourish giants in the manner of the region south of Rio de la Plata.[89]

The maps that Thevet consulted inflected his thinking on the relationship between environment and human physique. As a cosmographer, mapmaker and traveller, Thevet was immersed in contemporary cartography. At various points in the *Cosmographie*, he points out where his opinions differ from existing maps, chronicles and cosmographies.[90]

85 The island contained a Portuguese slave-trading post at the time.

86 Ibid., II, f.907*v*.

87 *André Thevet's North America: A Sixteenth-Century View*, ed., trans., notes and intro., Roger Schlesinger and Arthur P. Stabler (Kingston and Montreal: McGill-Queen's University Press, 1986), 189, n. 58: there is no trace of this assertion in Cardano's *oeuvre*.

88 See Chapter 7 in this book.

89 Thevet, *Cosmographie*, tome IV, liure XXII, chap. XV, 990*r*.: 'ceste monstruosité de corps en ce people'.

90 See, e.g., his disapproval of Münster and of maps of Africa in ibid., tome I, liure I, chap. VII, 16*v*.–17*v*., and of Pliny, Johannes Boemus and François de Belleforest on idolatry in the Canary Islands in ibid., tome I, liure III, chap. IX, 82*r*.

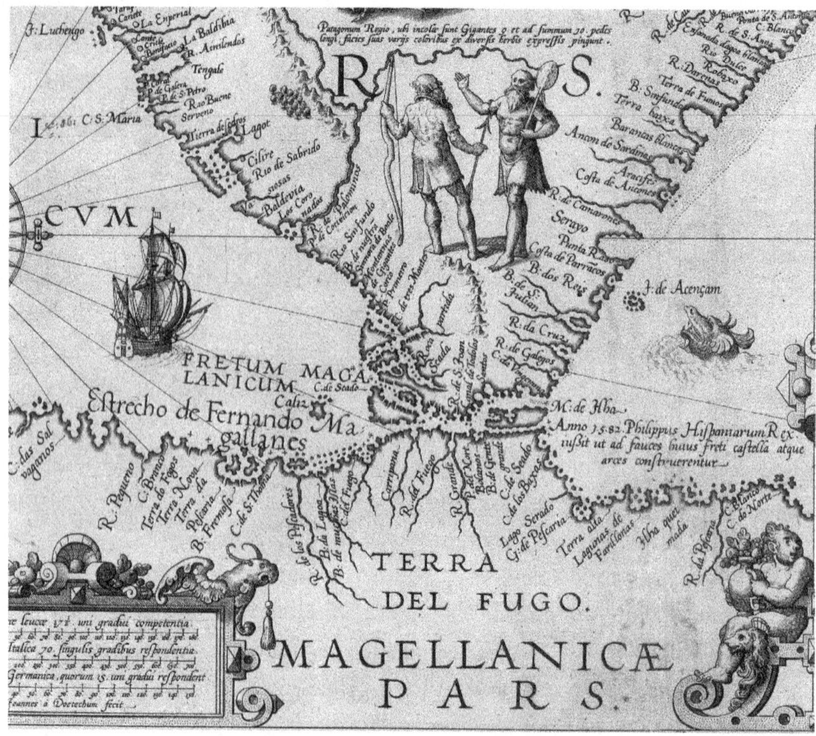

5.7 Petrus Plancius, map of southern South America (Amsterdam, c.1592–4), detail. Courtesy of the John Carter Brown Library at Brown University, Cabinet Gg59 PIP.

Patagonia abutted *Terra incognita*, a theoretical southern land that had traditionally been associated with excess and monstrosity.[91] Where the Americas ended and this monstrous land began was open to conjecture. On the Flemish cartographer Petrus Plancius's c.1592–4 map of southern South America, Peruviana, of which Patagonia is a part, ends in small southern islands that blend into those of 'Terra del Fugo', a part of 'Magellanicae pars' – the unknown southern land on this map (Fig. 5.7). Tierra del Fuego could just as reasonably have been deemed to be part of the landmass to the north – as it would become on later maps – as to the hypothetical southern landmass. On Plancius's map, Patagonia is 'Terra del Fugo', a choice that reveals the interpretative fault-line between the evolving concept of Patagonia and the ancient concept of the Antipodes.

Ancient ideas about how the antipodean climate was likely to engender monsters could be used to explain the Patagonians'

[91] See Hiatt, *Terra Incognita* for a study of geographical thinking on the region.

gigantism.[92] The sixteenth-century French jurist and philosopher Jean Bodin asserted that 'the further men move from the equator, the larger they grow, as in the land of the Patagonians, who are called giants', showing his allegiance to the notion of a tribe of giants of the Plinian variety, deformed by their environment.[93] A seventeenth-century geographer, Cornelis Wytfliet, made a related, climatological, point by asserting that it was the cold and the humidity of Patagonia that had caused its inhabitants to become tall and pale.[94]

The climate of antipodean lands did not merely affect bodies, but also temperaments. To ascribe gigantism to a people was to introduce the possibility that they were also mentally monstrous. Such is the implication in the Norman cartographer Guillaume Le Testu's manuscript atlas, *Cosmographie universelle* (1555–6).[95] On the text page facing a map of southern South America, we learn that 'around the region of the kingdom of giants are men ten to twelve cubits in height, who only speak in whistles', a conversational trait that has no connection to existing sources about the region.[96] Pigafetta had merely observed that 'they pronounce all their words gutturally'.[97] Le Testu, by casting these people as even less capable of regular speech than was the case in his sources, characterized inhabitants of latitudinal extremes as lacking elements of civilized society. His charge of the incomprehensibility of the Patagonians is an extrapolation from classical humoral theory and from Pliny's *Historia naturalis*.

From at least the mid sixteenth century, mapmakers in the Low Countries operated in a milieu in which Spain's relationship to its colonies had local resonances.[98] On Petrus Plancius's map of South America (c.1592–4), the giants' short, European-style, collared tunics and well-trimmed beards and moustaches are clearly visible (Fig. 5.7).[99] The map

92 See, e.g., Wey Gómez, *The Tropics of Empire*, 50, 84–9, 218–21. For conceptions of the Antipodes, see also Hiatt, *Terra Incognita*.

93 Bodin, *Methods*, chap. V, 93.

94 Cornelius Wytfliet, *Histoire vniverselle des Indes Occidentales et Orientales, et de la conversion des Indiens* (Douai, 1611), 66.

95 CV-ADG, D.2.z.14, f. 43*v*.

96 Ibid., f. 44*r*: 'Envyron le royaulme de guiganton [sic] sont hommes ayans dix et douxe couldees de haulteur, et ne parle que par sifler'. For references to giants on maps, see also Anthiaume, *Cartes marines*, 231–4.

97 Pigafetta, *Voyage of Magellan*, chap. XVIII: 'pronuncent tous leurs motz en la gorge.'

98 See especially Schmidt, *Innocence Abroad*.

99 Petrus Plancius, *Haec pars Peruvianae, regiones Chicam & Chilem complectitur, & Regionum Patagonum* (Amsterdam, 1592–4). Another example is Josua van den Ende, *Nova et exacta terrarum orbis tabula geographica ac hydrographica* (Amsterdam, 1604), printed by Willem Blaeu.

derives from one that had been printed in 1562 at Antwerp but, true to the pattern seen in earlier depictions of giants on maps, the giants' costume, physique and weaponry have been re-imagined.[100] While the club might suggest that these figures were wild men or savage Amerindians, the well-fitting tunics that show off the wearers' musculature and easy postures suggest well-to-do burghers meeting mid-stroll. Perhaps the map's engraver, Van Doetecum, wished to show off his skill for future commissions, and the somewhat hybrid image of these giants is the result.[101]

But it is also possible that, in late-sixteenth century Amsterdam, this map-printing workshop was making an oblique point about Dutch political struggles against Spanish rule. Two of the ten printers of Dutch translations of Bartolomé de las Casas' *Brevíssima relación*, a catalogue of Spanish misdeeds arranged by region in the order in which they were perpetrated, also printed maps. One of these map printers, Cornelis Claesz, produced eight editions of the text in various forms: prose with learned quotations; engravings with captions, and verse.[102] Claesz produced a pamphlet that combined De Bry's engravings with Dutch translations to the extensive accompanying captions.[103] The pamphlet's title-page informs the viewer that 'the furious frenzy perpetrated by the Spaniards in the West Indies is here illustrated',[104] 'from which everybody can see what kind of people the Spaniards are, and about which one can read more in the Mirror of Spanish Tyranny'.[105]

[100] Diego Gutiérrez, *Americae sive quartae orbis partis nova et exactissima descriptio* (Antwerp, 1562). The map was engraved and presumably illustrated by the Flemish engraver and printmaker Hieronymus Cock.

[101] These figures also appear in Bertius, *Tabularum libri quatuor*, 367, where the giant on the right has been given a shield.

[102] Schmidt, *Innocence Abroad*, 169.

[103] Bartolomé de Las Casas, *Narratio regionum indicarum per Hispanos quosdam devastatarum verissima* (Frankfurt am Main, 1598). For the illustrations, see Tom Conley, 'De Bry's Las Casas', in *Amerindian Images and the Legacy of Columbus*, ed. René Jara and Nicholas Spadaccini (Minneapolis, MN and London: University of Minnesota Press, 1992), 103–31, at 107–26.

[104] Bartolomé de Las Casas, *Den Spieghel vande Spaensche Tyrannie beeldelijcken afgemaelt* (Amsterdam, 1609), f. 1r: '[Af-beeldinghe vande Spaensche Tyrannije]. De woedende rasernije der Spaengiaerden der West-Indien bedreuen wordet hier af ghebeeldet'; Schmidt, *Innocence Abroad*, 169; for a brief discussion of the Dutch editions, see 169–70: Dutch prose translations followed Las Casas's text 'relatively faithfully'.

[105] Las Casas, *Den Spieghel*, f. XVII: 'Waer upt elck can sien wat de Spaengiaerden voor gasten zijn; waer van men breeder can lesen inden Spieghel vande Spaensche Tyrannye.' Although this text was a digest of Las Casas's tract, full translations of the *Brevissima relacion* were also called the 'Mirror of Spanish Tyranny' in several languages.

Las Casas had set the Amerindians up in opposition to the conquistadors in terms of civility and barbarism, inverting the usual Aristotelian argument. The Indians possessed 'towns, provinces and kingdoms'[106] – indicators of European-style government and communal living. The conquistadors, by contrast, had 'degenerated from being men'.[107] Not only had they destroyed the Amerindians' civil structures, claimed Las Casas, but in so doing they had themselves lost their humanity. The indigenous peoples were 'gentle, peace-loving, humble and docile',[108] the victims of men who were 'iniquitous, tyrannical, condemned by any natural, canon and civil law, and are deemed wicked and detestable'.[109]

These views resonated with the Dutch, who saw in the Amerindians kindred spirits suffering Spanish tyranny. Two French translations, including the first, were published at Antwerp and Amsterdam, respectively.[110] The preface to the earliest indicates the interest of readers and commentators in Spanish rule of the Indies and in its ramifications for the Low Countries.[111] As Benjamin Schmidt has argued, the reception and representation of America in the Low Countries were intricately interwoven with the Dutch relationship with the Habsburg Empire, and particularly with Spain. Whereas the conquistadors' activities had been received as heroic exploits before the start of the Dutch Revolt in the 1560s, the Spanish were increasingly seen as tyrants in their practices in the Low Countries and in the Americas. Dutch writing about Amerindians as peoples who had experienced similarly unjust domination emerged not

[106] Las Casas, *Brevissima relacion*, 3: 'pueblos, provincias y reinos'; idem, *A Short Account of Destruction of the Indies*, ed. and trans. Nigel Griffin (London, 1991), 31. I have made small alterations to the translation.

[107] Idem, *Brevissima relacion*, 3: 'degenerar del ser hombres'; idem, *Destruction of the Indies*, 31.

[108] Idem, *Brevissima relacion*, 6: 'pacíficas, humildes y mansas'; idem, *Destruction of the Indies*, 32.

[109] Idem, *Brevissima relacion*, 6: 'son inicuas, tiránicas, y por toda ley natural, divina y human, condenadas, detestadas e malditas, deliberé'; Idem, *Destruction of the Indies*, 32. The notion that a heathen people could be noble also had a number of antecedents: the wild man in medieval thought; 'savage' peoples in the *Book of John Mandeville*; the Nestorian Prester John who was reputedly a better Christian than the Pope; and Saladin, the Muslim sultan of Egypt and Syria who purportedly had values that were closer to Christian ones than those of any king in Europe.

[110] Hanke and Giménez Fernández, *Bartolomé de las Casas*, nos 476 and 516: Las Casas, *Tyrannies et cruautez des espagnols, perpetrées és Indes Occidentales* (Antwerp, 1579); idem, *Le Miroir de la tyrannie espagnole perpetrée aux Indes Occidentales* (Amsterdam, 1620). Some editions produced in England, France and Germany also made reference to the work's relevance for Dutch readers.

[111] Las Casas, *Tyrannies*. The first edition printed in the Low Countries appeared in Dutch in 1578.

because of new information about these peoples, but because of the United Provinces' changed relationship to Spain.[112] The importance of Las Casas to Dutch readers (indicated by the number of editions produced) suggests that this view of Amerindians as possessing rather than lacking indicators of civility informed many Dutch viewers of Amerindians on maps. In this context, the depiction of the inhabitants of Patagonia as similar in some respects to Dutch burghers might well have been a veiled critique of Spanish atrocities against a civil people.

At the heart of debates about the Patagonian giant was the Augustinian problem of monstrous peoples: life *had* been found beyond the *oikoumene*, and even beyond the torrid zone, but that still left unanswered the question of what manner of life it was. If the giants proved to be monsters, there would still be no consensus on whether or not they were descended from Adam. Debates over the nature of Patagonian giants were thus disputes between different ontologies for monsters and – more broadly – between differing epistemological frameworks for understanding nature's wonders.

What was at stake? Since wild people were believed to inhabit regions unsuitable for civilized humans,[113] the portrayal of the Patagonians as wild threw into doubt the habitability of Patagonia for European colonists. The number of giants that needed to be spotted before they could be seen as a general law of Patagonian natural history, however, rather than as accidents, was far from clear. Another resonance was the notion of monstrosity as a sign of the error of a human parent, often of the mother whose imagination was thought to have the power to transform the 'natural' shape of a person. Such a monster could also point to the person – or creature – who was its father, or, to the creature in the maternal imagination at the time of conception.[114] If the giants were the result of the straying of the maternal imagination their height was not a pleasurable wonder but a monstrance of bad behaviour. In this context, the inherited gigantism observed in the Patagonians was not merely a natural wonder, but potentially a sign of a willfully chosen, moral error.

What happened when the locale of a people whose practices were distant from Europeans when compared against Aristotle's theory of civility and barbarism was juxtaposed on top of the geographical positioning of monstrous peoples in Pliny? And how could one sew together Biblical theories

[112] Schmidt, *Innocence Abroad*, xxv. [113] Husband, *Wild Man*, 2–3.

[114] Ibid., 54. For monsters and the maternal imagination, see Marie-Hélène Huet, *Monstrous Imagination* (Cambridge, MA: Harvard University Press, 1993); Wiesner-Hanks, *Hairy Girls*, 131–8.

of generation and those from classical antiquity? Here, Pigafetta and Maximilanus headed in different interpretative directions. Pigafetta's account could have been read as implying that Patagonia's giants were evidence of the dangers of exploration and colonization. By reaching the eastern edges of the earth, the Magellan expedition had crossed the boundary between human and Biblical time, and between the purity of Noah's descendants and the corruption of the antediluvian Giants of the Old Testament.

While Pigafetta's giants thus harboured the possibility of polluting human genealogy, Maximilianus considered the giants to be merely individual accidents of nature. What we see in this period are several broad types of monster: the metaphorical monster, monstrous by means of deviant behaviour; the physical, empirically observable monster that is one of nature's mistakes; and – this one was contested – the tribe of physical monsters who gave birth to others in their own image, and who would not (by implication) be monstrous to one another, a notion explicitly espoused in the *Book of John Mandeville*. Maximilianus's anxieties were twofold: first, he was unconvinced that sufficient empirical evidence existed to prove the reality of a monstrous people rather than some chance monstrous individuals perceived by some travellers. This highlights the difficulty of deciding when there was enough evidence to prove something in nature. Second, such commentators showed great emotional resistance to 'difficult middles'.[115]

The structure of maps illustrated with giants had implications for Renaissance understandings of their origins, characters and humanity (or lack thereof). Viewers of these maps were versed in the particular visual codes within which map illustrators devised images of giants. Once mapmakers began producing world maps that fused Ptolemy's co-ordinate system to the portolan chart and *mappamundi* traditions, descriptions and illustrations of what inhabited different parts of the world took on a more precise geographical structure. As new information about the lands west of the Atlantic appeared, it was located (insofar as mapmakers could do so) in a specific place. These maps made comparative arguments about human diversity that were considerably more geographically specific that those of medieval *mappaemundi*. They did not suggest that there was any particular danger of interbreeding in Patagonia, but did suggest that the local climate could engender monsters. By bringing *terra incognita*, an unknown but anticipated antipodean land, to the edges of Patagonia and

[115] Jeffrey Jerome Cohen, *Hybridity, Identity and Monstrosity in Medieval Britain: On Difficult Middles* (New York, NY: Palgrave Macmillan, 2006).

creating the concept of Magellanica, mapmakers subverted the relationship between humoral theory and the gridded latitude system. In so doing, they introduced giants to a temperate zone.

Giants on Renaissance maps blurred the boundary between civilized humans, wild persons who could be civilized through instruction, and monstrous peoples. They suggest that mapmakers' interests in representing giants went far beyond reflecting the contents of travel accounts. While the ethnographic information in travel writing on Patagonia was occasional, dispersed, and structurally subsumed within a chronological narrative about the experiences of the traveller, on a map it took centre stage as the primary information provided about the region after its topographical outlines were established. The importance that mapmakers placed on supplying the newest information about human variety prompted them to engage in the complex process of constructing visual records for inhabitants they had not witnessed themselves. The visual code of the map argued for the mapmakers' authority as synthesizers with the necessary perspective to compare and evaluate observations made in the field, incorporate them into the web of existing knowledge, and disseminate it in the most useful format.

Writers and geographers who reflected on the significance of the Patagonians' size and location considered the implications for knowledge about how tropical climates worked and for settler colonialism. How familiar might map viewers have been with learned discourses on the concept of the human, on the relationship between humans and monstrous peoples or individuals, and on the perception of savage or wild peoples as inhabiting an Edenic position in human hierarchy, rather than an almost bestial one? One source of indirect evidence is contemporary drama, a genre which we might anachronistically term early modern television.[116] Monsters in Renaissance drama and in chivalric romances indicate that ideas about the relationship between humans and monsters reached beyond geographers, mapmakers and scholars.

It is possible to discern thought experiments on monstrous ontology and the possibility of human–monster miscegenation in such plays as Shakespeare's *Othello* and *The Tempest*. By 1611, when Shakespeare's *The Tempest* was first performed, the playwright could expect at least some of his audience to be familiar with all of these themes. Caliban is an

[116] The historiography on drama as a site of mediated cultural encounter is extensive. Key works include *'The Tempest' and its Travels*, ed. Peter Hulme and William H. Sherman (London: Reaktion, 2000); Floyd-Wilson, *English Ethnicity and Race*.

anagram of can[n]ibal; we are told incessantly that he is a 'monster' formed by the union of a witch and the devil; Caliban's mother Sycorax worshipped a god called Setebos, the god of the Patagonians in Pigafetta's account; Caliban vents at being denied the island his mother left to him but Prospero, the human master of the island does not recognize Caliban's claim of possession; Caliban's words barely register as human speech to the ears of the shipwrecked sailors; Prospero fears – and Caliban boasts – that Caliban and Miranda might engender a tribe of monsters; Caliban's 'hagseed' is resistant to all climates.[117]

Just as, in the eighteenth century, the genealogy of the black African powered debates about polygenesis, the Patagonian giant was the pivot around which sixteenth-century debates about the ontology of the human turned. Scholarly commentators who were sceptical of testimony about giants were not questioning the presence of very tall people or other physically unusual individuals. Rather, they were questioning what kind of being – or monster – they were and, by implication, whether Patagonia's environment possessed degenerative powers.

Renaissance giants were far from evidence of publishers playing fast and loose with the truth in order to appeal to their markets' most frivolous needs, or signs of the gullibility and general critical limitations of Renaissance minds. Natural philosophical inquiries into the issue of the giant-human-dwarf-pygmy continuum are part of what we might call the *longue durée* history of the question of what it means to be human.[118]

As Felipe Fernández-Armesto put it, writing about the present age, '[b]eing human has never felt so beastly'.[119] Genetics, paleoanthropology and other sciences make it difficult to sustain the concept of species as an essential rather than merely classificatory category. We wonder about the possibility of a post-human future in which technology has altered *H. sapiens* beyond recognition.[120] Our monsters are corporations that are legally recognized as people; humans with synthetic anatomies and pathogens are created in laboratories.[121] Deep-sea trawlers encounter giant squid, which no longer count as monsters since 'monster' is widely

117 This material will be discussed in an article on Shakespeare's monsters and the problem of miscegenation.

118 For eighteenth-century debates about black skin, see Curran, *Anatomy of Blackness*. For the possibility of *longue durée* intellectual history, see David Armitage, 'What's the Big Idea? Intellectual History and the Longue Durée', *History of European Ideas*, 38:4 (2012), 593–607.

119 Fernández-Armesto, *So You Think You're Human?*, 5.

120 For post-human futures, see ibid., chap. 5.

121 Jeffrey Andrew Weinstock, 'Vision, Horror, and Contemporary Culture', in *ARC-MM*, 273–87.

accepted to mean imaginary being rather than incomprehensible category-breaker. The SETI programme attempts to make contact with extra-terrestrials by means of their best guesses at what might constitute universal language; animal rights activists fight for the rights and welfare of animals; and the NIH Human Microbiome Project studies microbial communities that inhabit different areas of the human body, and the ways in which they affect health and behaviour.[122] Thus we might usefully reflect on recent debates over the social, ontological and moral dimensions of category-challenging findings and practices within a longer chronology of attempts to come to terms with the concept of the human, the nature of its boundaries, and the implications of understanding 'human' as a fluid, subjective category that is inseparable from its environment.

[122] For this project, see www.hmpdacc.org, last accessed 28/07/2015.

6 The epistemology of wonder

Amazons, headless men and mapping Guiana

In 1594, the English mathematician Thomas Blundeville published an essay entitled 'A Plaine and Full Description of Petrus Plancius his vniuersall map…' in his *Exercises*, a popular work on cosmography and navigation. The essay described a map by the Flemish mapmaker Plancius, on which cannibals and giants appear in the New World.[1] Blundeville evaluated these beings in the context of other ethnological wonders thus:

> they are meere lies that are woont to be told of the pigmeans, in that they should bee but a foote and a halfe high, and like wise that which hath bene spoken of people, that should haue their heads, their noses, their mouthes, and their eies in their breastes, or of those that are headed lyke a dog, or of those that haue but one eie, and that in their forehead, or of those that haue but one foote and that so great, as that it covereth and shadoweth all their bodie, or of those that haue greate eares hanging downe to the ground. All these are meere lyes, invented by vain men to bring fooles into admiration, for monsters are as well borne in Europe, as in other partes of the world.[2]

Blundeville's list of unlikely beings echoes the catalogue of monstrous peoples in Pliny's *Historia naturalis* and in medieval iconographic traditions. Blundeville contends that, if monstrous beings do exist in distant places, they are not 'a nation of people' with a monstrous trait – as Sir Walter Ralegh would soon term a headless people said to live in Guiana – but rather individual instances of monsters of the sort found in Europe. For Blundeville, as for Maximilianus Transylvanus whose scepticism we encountered in Chapter 5, the explanations traditionally offered for domestic monsters were sufficient to explain even frequent instances of distant monsters. Blundeville does not doubt the existence of monsters – breakers of existing categories – *per se* any more than Maximilianus did. His complaint is instead that mapmakers were presenting monsters in distant places as widespread, ontologically distinct types or what we would call species.

[1] Thomas Blundeville, *Exercises* (London, 1594). This went through many editions; the map described was Plancius's 1592 world map.

[2] Ibid., 262.

And yet, it was precisely this ontological slippage from isolated monstrous births to monstrous peoples that the visual language of maps facilitated. Renaissance map viewers read the distinctive characteristics of individual figures on maps as a summary of what people in a region had in common, and of how they differed from other peoples; Jean de Léry's complaint that mapmakers depicted people in the Brazilian interior cooking humans on spits rather than on barbecues, discussed in Chapter 3 of the present book, is a vivid example. Nevertheless, the question of whether monsters could exist outside the medical context of the individual monstrous birth continued to be debated. Blundeville's reservations point to the uneasy boundary between conceptions of monsters in Europe and monsters abroad.

Of all the New World peoples on early modern maps, perhaps none had as mixed a reception as the inhabitants of Guiana. In 1596, *The Discoverie of the Large, Rich, and Bewtiful Empyre of Guiana*, the travel narrative of the English courtier and corsair Sir Walter Ralegh, appeared in print. For the next two decades, Guianian headless men and, to a lesser extent, Amazons inspired illustrations and captions on Dutch maps, and in the travel editions of the Frankfurt printer Theodor de Bry and the Nuremberg printer Levinus Hulsius.[3] Since Ralegh, mapmakers and printers all wished to sustain their credibility and authority, why include such beings? What kinds of textual and visual rhetoric might give viewers greater confidence in their makers' methods?

The transmission of Ralegh's ethnography has much to tell us about the epistemology of the wondrous. In this chapter, I contrast the ways in which Ralegh described and authenticated Amazons and headless men with the ways in which Dutch and German mapmakers and printers did the same on the maps and imagery they composed in response to Ralegh's unillustrated text. Despite their differences, they all shared the desire for persuasiveness. Guiana's wonders were intrinsically credible for viewers who expected wondrous natural phenomena in the equatorial east, and they may at first have made these maps more rather than less credible. Particular sorts of textual and visual rhetoric gave viewers confidence in the methodology of these works.

[3] The Hulsius and De Bry publishing houses produced complementary travel editions, with Hulsius printing small, abridged quartos, each with less accomplished, predominantly fewer, illustrations than the corresponding De Bry edition. Except in rare occasions, the De Bry edition of a travel account preceded the Hulsius edition. For the relationship between the two firms and their editions, see Van Groesen, *Representations of the Overseas World*, 346–52.

Approaching wondrous ethnography in Ralegh's *Discoverie*

Selling colonial ventures in late-sixteenth century England was far from simple. While the sun never set on the Spanish empire, the English Crown, court and merchant investors remained largely unconvinced that the capital required to finance such voyages – often in the face of open disapproval and hostility from Spain – was likely to turn into a profitable investment.[4] When Sir Walter Ralegh decided to risk his person on a journey in search of Guiana, he hoped to find an empire rich with gold mines that was rumoured to exist in the upland areas of the upper Amazon and northern South America, east of Peru – known for its gold, of course. Such a find, hoped Ralegh, would facilitate his return to court and the favour of his queen, Elizabeth I, whom he had offended in 1592 by marrying her lady-in-waiting, Elizabeth Throckmorton, without the Queen's permission. The Queen had sent both Ralegh and Elizabeth to the Tower for several months; Ralegh was banned from appearing at court, and from performing his duties as Captain of the Queen's Guard, for five years.[5] In 1595, Walter Ralegh travelled to Guiana; the courtier Sir Robert Cecil, the younger son of William Cecil, the Lord Burghley (one of Elizabeth's chief advisors for much of her reign), sponsored the expedition, which the Court had refused to support.[6]

Ralegh sent the original manuscript of his *Discoverie of Guiana* to Cecil and circulated it at court in an attempt to raise sponsorship for a second expedition in search of gold.[7] This failed: Ralegh had brought back very little gold, and it was rumoured that this ore was not gold at all. In an attempt to interest potential backers outside court in a second voyage, Ralegh had his account printed in London in March 1596.[8] This appeared

[4] Walter Ralegh, *The Discoverie of the Large, Rich, and Bewtifvl Empyre of Guiana* (London, 1596); see *Sir Walter Ralegh's Discoverie of Guiana*, ed. Joyce Lorimer (Ashgate, 2006), xviii. Page references are to the first edition (also given in square brackets by Lorimer). The literature on the sixteenth-century beginnings of the English empire is copious. See, for example, Kim Sloan et al., *A New World: England's First View of America* (London: British Museum, 2007); David Harris Sacks, 'Discourses of Western Planting: Richard Hakluyt and the Making of the Atlantic World', in *The Atlantic World and Virginia, 1550–1624*, ed. Peter C. Mancall (Chapel Hill, NC: University of North Carolina Press, 2007), 410–53. On the challenges of seeking sponsorship, see Fuller, *Voyages*, 11–14.

[5] Ralegh, *Discoverie*, ed. Lorimer, xxii.

[6] Ibid., xxiii; Anna R. Beer, *Sir Walter Ralegh and His Readers in the Seventeenth Century* (Basingstoke: Macmillan, 1997), 3.

[7] Ibid., 9. This is London, Lambeth Palace, MS 250, Sir Walter Ralegh, 'Sir Wallter Ralleghes Dyscourse: of his first voyadg to Guiana', 1595 (hereafter L-LP, MS 250).

[8] For the printing history, see Ralegh, *Discoverie*, ed. Lorimer, lxxvi-lxxxii.

in a climate of scepticism about his claim to have found Guiana at all. Ralegh was not writing for a living here so much as writing for his life.[9] What, then, are we to make of his decision to describe Amazons and *Ewaipanoma* when his very life depended on his credibility?

The work of Lorraine Daston and Katharine Park on monstrous births and other wonders and by John Friedman on medieval ideas about monstrous peoples offer valuable approaches which can be applied to the epistemology of wonder in Ralegh's *Discoverie*. Neil L. Whitehead analysed Ralegh's text alongside archaeological and ethnohistorical evidence. Surprisingly, these works and recent literature in the history of science, medieval studies and ethnohistory remain largely untapped by scholarship on monstrous peoples in Renaissance travel writing and cartography. Scholars have traditionally critiqued Ralegh's words on Guiana's inhabitants as the stuff of metaphor, generic convention and imagination.[10] I take a different approach by asking questions about what work Ralegh's claims performed, analyzing them in relation to the type of truth he set out to provide.[11] I unpack Ralegh's ethnography in the context of his desire to find backers for another prospecting expedition and to recover the good favour of his queen.

All of Ralegh's rhetorical efforts were aimed at bolstering what Lorraine Daston and Katharine Park have called the extrinsic credibility of a phenomenon.[12] Ralegh's descriptions of Amazons, and, particularly, headless men, neither of which he claims to have seen with his own eyes, offered readers a variety of corroborating sources. Ralegh does not give his reader explicit clues as to whose testimony is most reliable, but the sheer number of people who believe in these headless beings was, for him, compelling evidence for their existence. What Ralegh does not do is to engage with whether headless beings were *intrinsically* credible: in other words, Ralegh saw no need to show how these beings were possible in nature, as we shall see.

Ralegh could well have heard stories of Amazons and headless *Ewaipanoma* from his local informants. Whitehead analysed Ralegh's account

[9] For this point, see Philip Edwards, *Last Voyages: Cavendish, Hudson, Ralegh: The Original Narratives*, introduced and edited by Philip Edwards (Oxford: Clarendon Press, Oxford and New York, NY: Oxford University Press), 5, cited in Ralegh, *Discoverie*, ed. Lorimer, 5.

[10] For such approaches, see Campbell, *Witness and the Other World*, chap. 6; Braham, 'Monstrous Caribbean'.

[11] For a similar approach, see, Julia Schleck, *Telling True Tales of Islamic Lands: Forms of Mediation in English Travel Writing, 1575–1630* (Selinsgrove, PA: Susquehanna University Press, 2011), 18.

[12] Daston and Park, *Wonders*.

extensively alongside ethnohistorical, archaeological, oral historical and anthropological sources and historiography. Whitehead's anthropological re-thinking of the *Discoverie* opened the field of vision for considering the parts played by indigenous peoples in the shaping of Ralegh's thinking and actions, and the historical consequences of these interactions, providing critical tools with which to analysed the wonders in Ralegh's *Discoverie*, rather than to exoticize them. Whitehead argued that it is possible to glimpse native practices and real historical interactions and geographies in Ralegh's text. These descriptions, when compared to those by later recorders and even, at times, to contemporary native practices, are in many cases reflective of the nature of indigenous societies.[13] Indigenous myths, for example, relate the presence of women who lived without men (an anxiety caused, perhaps, by the prevalence of Amazonian societies in which women were preeminent), and of distant tribes with shoulders almost as high as their heads.[14] Similarly, Edmundo Magaña's study of perceptions of distant others among the tribes of northern and north-eastern South America revealed that many of these tribes categorized outsiders by physical and behavioral aberrations.[15] We cannot assume from the rarity (not even impossibility!) of matrilineanal societies or the implausibility of literally headless men that Ralegh manufactured such accounts from thin air for the purposes of entertaining his audience – an audience that, moreover, he was seeking to impress with his reliability.

It was not inevitable that Ralegh would choose to repeat accounts of headless folk and of women who lived without men. Ralegh openly cast the social, political and economic elements of indigenous Guianian societies in ways that encouraged colonial activity and might bolster his own position at court. We need, therefore, to explain why Ralegh, faced with his indigenous interlocutors' accounts of monstrous peoples, would insert them into a work intended to raise confidence in the gold mines he had failed to locate.

Ralegh's claim – and, presumably, belief – that Guiana contained rich veins of gold was reasonable given prevailing geo-humoral expectations.

[13] Ralegh, *Discoverie*, ed. Whitehead, 26, chap. 2; Neil L. Whitehead, 'The Historical Anthropology of text: The Interpretation of Ralegh's *Discoverie of Guiana*', *Current Anthropology*, 36 (1995), 53–74, esp. 54–6.

[14] Whitehead, 'Guiana as Anthropological Imaginary', 5; Ralegh, *Discoverie*, ed. Whitehead, 91–7.

[15] See Edmundo Magaña, 'Note on Ethnoanthropological Notions of the Guiana Indians', *Anthropologica*, XXIV (1982), 215–33; idem, 'Hombres salvajes y razas monstruosas de los Indios Kaliña de Surinam', *Journal of Latin American Lore*, 8 (1982), 63–114; and also idem, ed., *Les monstres dans l'imaginaire des Indiens d'Amérique latine* (Paris, 1988).

According to traditions of climatic theory, since gold had been found in the hot, equatorial regions of West Africa, it could equally be expected to be abundant in Guiana.[16] Both regions fell into the 'torrid zone' delineated by authors of classical antiquity as an environment that gave rise to monstrous peoples.[17] Sixteenth-century editions of Ptolemy's *Geography* were one visual source that made tropical monstrosity visible, sometimes placing one-eyed beings with faces in their chests in Africa. On the 1513 Strasbourg edition of Ptolemy's *Geographia*, for example, such a figure appears in West Africa, in the region of Guinea.[18] Given Ralegh's experiences on the ground and what prevailing geographical authorities had written about the tropics, it was reasonable for Ralegh and his readers to surmise that *Guiana* should also contain gold and monstrous beings.

El Dorado in the European imaginary was a bricolage of multifarious indigenous beliefs and gold-working practices for which abundant historical and archaeological evidence survives.[19] Ralegh's *El Dorado* referred to a city made of gold, ruled by one *El Dorado* or the Golden One who, anointed annually with gold dust, paddled to the centre of an enormous lake where he would make votive offerings of gold figures. The Muisca peoples of the highlands of present-day Colombia did have ancient gold-working traditions and numerous rituals in which gold featured prominently. Indigenous leaders exchanged golden gifts.[20] Golden votive objects called *tunjos* have been found in the lake of Guatavita, on the edge of present-day Bogotá. A *tunjo* found in Lake Siecha, another sacred lake for the Muisca, even represents *El Dorado* the man, and retinue, traversing a lake.[21] The material evidence, then, indicates how Ralegh's writing about *El Dorado* had a basis in encounters on the ground, through which native peoples shaped European ideas about Guiana's gold.

16 For associations between equatorial regions, heat and gold, see, e.g., Wey Gómez, *Tropics of Empire*.

17 See Chapter 1.

18 Claudius Ptolemy, *Claudii Ptolomaei Geographicae enarrationis libri octo* (Strasbourg, 1525), map entitled 'Tabula moderna primae. Partis Aphrica, et tabula secunde partis Aphricae'.

19 A number of examples are held by the Museo del Oro, Bogotá and the British Museum; see Elisenda Vila Llonch, *Beyond El Dorado: Power and Gold in Ancient Colombia* (London: British Museum, 2013).

20 Whitehead, 'Guayana as Anthropological Imaginary', 4–5.

21 Ralegh, *Discoverie*, ed. Whitehead, 72.

Ethnographic witnessing in Ralegh's *Discoverie*

The authority of the early modern eyewitness, like that of the natural philosopher, was socially negotiated. Travellers deployed various strategies in their attempts to imbue their accounts with credibility. These included emphasizing the physical, mental and moral trials and tribulations that the traveller had faced; underlining the fact that he (as it so often was) had witnessed directly that of which he spoke; and articulating the common cultural, religious and social values shared by the traveller and his perceived audience.[22] Ralegh's writing on marvellous peoples and goldmines was not, however, about what he had witnessed himself, but about what those whom he had spoken with had witnessed. Ralegh's problem, then, was how to translate their knowledge and eyewitness authority to himself, and his credibility – carefully constructed through the rhetoric of his own journey and loyalty to his queen – to them.

Ralegh places multiple witnesses on the stand to give first-hand evidence about headless men, Amazons and gold. He then offers us a range of reasons why the reader should consider each testimony reliable, thus negotiating, for his witnesses, authority in the eyes of his readers. We learn about Guiana's Amazons thus:

> I made inquirie amongst the most ancient and best traueled of the Orenoqueponi, and I had knowledge of all the riuers between Orenoque and Amazones, and was very desirous to vnderstand the truth of those warlike women, bicause of some it is beleeued, of others not.[23]

In his readers' first encounter with the wondrous peoples of Guiana, Ralegh emphasizes his critical acumen: those whom he questioned were 'the most ancient and best traueled'. Since, however, the claims of such people cannot be tested by others, they are, in fact, able to fabricate safely[24] – indeed, Ralegh himself has the same licence.

Nevertheless, Ralegh places the responsibility for veracity on others: he will merely 'set downe what hath been deliuered me for truth of those women'.[25] He starts by stating that 'the memories of the like women are very ancient as well in Africa as in Asia.... in many histories they are verified to haue been, and in diuers ages and provinces'.[26] His New

[22] See, e.g., Pagden, *European*; Frisch, *Invention of the Eyewitness*, chap. 2; Greenblatt, *Marvelous Possessions*; Campbell, *Witness and the Other World*, 230.

[23] Ralegh, *Discoverie*, 23.

[24] For this common proverb, see Lestringant, 'Flèche', 467.

[25] Ralegh, *Discoverie*, 23.

[26] Ibid.

World 'Amazones' also behave like their classical counterparts: 'But they . . . do accompanie with men but once in a yeere, and for the time of one moneth, which I gather by their relation to be in Aprill'; sons conceived this way are returned to the fathers, whereas daughters are kept.[27] An important difference between them and the Amazons of antiquity is that the Guianians do not cut off one breast. Despite having unnatural behaviour, and therefore monstrous practices, these people did not, at least, deform their bodies on purpose.

Ralegh's testimony on the headless *Ewaipanoma* is in fact hearsay from indigenous informants:

> [They] are a nation of people, whose heades appeare not aboue their shoulders, which though it may be thought a meere fable, yet for mine owne parte I am resolued it is true, because euery child in the prouinces of *Arromaia* and *Canuri* affirme the same: they are called *Ewaipanoma:* they are reported to haue their eyes in their shoulders, and their mouths in the middle of their breasts, and that a long train of haire groweth backward betwen their shoulders.[28]

These interlocutors were problematic on several fronts. First, they were not European, and hence did not share the same ethical status, broadly conceived, as Ralegh's readers in England. Their level of civility, brand of religion (or idolatry), mental capacities and socio-political credentials are uncertain.[29] Ralegh's concern that his description of *Ewaipanoma* would be dismissed as 'meere fable' echoes Blundeville's recent dismissal of similar claims as 'meere lies'.

Secondly, children were commonly seen as relatively unreliable witnesses.[30] Ralegh attempts to deal with this problem rhetorically. He offers an argument based on the number rather than nature of witnesses: headless men were so familiar in these parts that 'every child' knew of their existence. He then mentions that he had 'brought with mee into England' one of these very children, the son of Topiawari, king of Arromaia, thus introducing the (unlikely) possibility of his readers seeing him for themselves. Since Topiawari's son is of noble blood, this would also have elevated his testimony in the eyes of English gentlemanly readers, despite

[27] Ibid., 23–4. [28] Ralegh, *Discoverie*, 69–70.

[29] For ethical connections between witnesses and their audiences, see Frisch, *Invention of the Eyewitness*, chap. 2. For the lower status of second-hand testimony, see Shapiro, *Culture of Fact*, 15–16, 71. For a comparative analysis of indigenous ethnographic testimony recorded by various travellers to Guiana, see Ralegh, *Discoverie*, ed. Whitehead, 91–101.

[30] Shapiro, *Culture of Fact*, 16, 42.

his non-English, non-European ancestry.[31] Ralegh suggests that he was himself initially sceptical of this youth's stories (implicitly, as Ralegh's own readers might be), but that the youth was able to substantiate his claims: 'when I seemed to doubt of it, hee tolde me that it was no wonder among them, but that the headless people were as great a nation, and as common, as any other in all the prouinces . . . and if I had but spoken one word of it while I was there, I might haue brought one of them with me to put the matter out of doubt'.[32]

Ralegh supported the indigenous children's testimony by stressing that independent sources concurred with it. He reminds his readers that headless men also appeared in the *Book of John Mandeville*, a work with which 'so many people' agreed[33]:

> Such a nation was written of by *Maundevile*, whose reportes were held for fables many yeares, and yet since the East *Indies* were discovered, wee finde his relations true of such thinges as heeretofore were held incredible: whether it be true or no the matter is not great, neither can there be any profit in the imagination, for mine owne part I saw them not, but I am resolved that so many people did not all combine, or forethinke to make the report.[34]

Mandeville's account had described a people on the Andaman Islands in the Indian Ocean as 'ugly folk without heads, who have eyes in each shoulder; their mouths are round, like a horseshoe, in the middle of their chest. In yet another part there are headless men whose eyes and mouths are on their backs'.[35] Not only does Ralegh use Mandeville to authenticate his indigenous Guianian informants, but, in a cycle of testimonials, travellers to the East Indies authenticate Mandeville's premise that wondrous beings exist in the eastern/western reaches of the world. The sheer number of people who attested to the existence of such beings reduced the likelihood that they did not exist even if one of the sources – such as the *Book of Mandeville* – turned out to be a fabrication. Ralegh uses the *Book* cautiously to triangulate the nature of the beings he had not seen. At the same time, he distances himself from the work, most likely in order to preserve his argument even in

[31] For the relatively high regard in which English travellers held Amerindian leaders, see Kupperman, *Indians and English*, 92–6.

[32] Ralegh, *Discoverie*, 70.

[33] Thevet also used a range of witnesses, sources and rhetorical strategies to bolster his account of the Patagonian giants; see Lestringant, 'Flèche', 469–77. For multiple witnesses, see Shapiro, *Culture of Fact*, 18, 124.

[34] Ralegh, *Discoverie*, 70. [35] Mandeville, *Book*, 137.

the eyes of those who had reservations about it.[36] In addition to concerns about the truthfulness of the account, others regarding textual corruption had been voiced. The Anglican clergyman and travel editor Richard Hakluyt, for example, included Mandeville in the 1589 edition of his *Principal Navigations* in Latin only, whereas the rest of the work included English translations of all texts in other languages. Hakluyt appended a Latin 'admonition to the reader' to the text and, in the 1598 edition, excised Mandeville altogether. The problem with Mandeville in Hakluyt's (and later in Samuel Purchas's) eyes was primarily the textual corruption of centuries of transmission.[37]

Ralegh points out that recent travels to the Far East seemed to substantiate many things from Mandeville that were 'held incredible'. Although the texture of his defensive analogy may suggest a litany of excuses for what Ralegh has not seen himself, within the genre of travel writing – defined broadly to include maps – this passage is an example of a reader conceding that while someone else may find this anecdote difficult to swallow, he believes there are sufficient grounds for doing so. There was, in other words, a difference between that which was impossible and that which merely appeared to be so. The Venetian geographer Giovanni Battista Ramusio, who argued that Portuguese voyages to the east had corroborated Marco Polo's account of the same region, voiced a similar opinion on almost incredible information in Polo.[38]

The final authority that Ralegh presents for Guiana's headless people is a Spanish traveller:

> I spake with . . . a man of great trauell, and after he knew that I had ben in *Guiana*, and so farre directlie west as *Caroli*, the first question he asked me was whether I had seene anie of the *Ewaipanoma*, which are those without heades: who being esteemed a most honest man of his word . . . told me that he had seen manie of them: I may not name him because it may be for his disadvantage. . . .[39]

Ralegh acknowledges here the difficulty that his readers would have in believing in headless people, but also asserts that such claims were not likely to do their reporters any favours. In this context, implies Ralegh, it was the Spaniard's honesty that compelled him to admit what he had seen. By analogy, Ralegh's admission of belief in *Ewaipanoma* attests to his own

[36] For Mandeville's ethical stance and its shifting fortunes during the early modern period, see Frisch, *Invention of the Eyewitness*, 53.

[37] See, e.g., Fuller, *Voyages in Print*, 175–7.

[38] Davies, 'The Wondrous East', 224–6.

[39] Ralegh, *Discoverie*, 71.

trustworthiness: he could expect no personal benefit by claiming to have seen such beings, and yet did so because he believed in their existence.[40]

Ralegh adds that this Spaniard was known to two Flemish merchants in London, 'who also heard what he auowed to be true of those people'. Just as Topiawari's son in England bolstered the children's testimony, these merchants corroborated the account of a distant (and foreign) witness. The multiplication of second-hand evidence may have helped Ralegh's credibility.[41] By aligning both his opinion on *Ewaipanoma* – gleaned from multiple witnesses – and his reluctance to report them with his Spanish interlocutor's choices, Ralegh also aligns himself elliptically with that nation of *doradistas* whom the English held, at once, in admiration and enmity.

Spaniards had been making incursions into Amazonia since the early decades of the sixteenth century, and consequently had been interacting with the region's peoples in ways that far exceeded Ralegh's relatively brief visit. Independent evidence survives to show that indigenous interlocutors had described the *Ewaipanoma* to Spanish travellers. Spanish letters captured at sea by Captain George Popham, which reached Elizabeth's Privy Council two months after Ralegh's return, mentioned men whose shoulders rose higher than their heads. These letters were printed and bound at the end of Ralegh's *Discoverie*.[42]

Ralegh's overall strategy of mining extant authorities on the phenomena his interlocutors described, using one to corroborate the other, mirrored the approach of early modern scholars attempting to evaluate historical testimony when the purported events could (obviously) not be re-witnessed firsthand.[43] As Mary Fuller has shown, Ralegh used similar reports of near misses, riddled with subjunctives, to explain why he had failed to return to England laden with gold.[44] While one might therefore see this simply as a rhetorical strategy intended to convince an audience of something that an author does not himself believe, the reasonableness of Ralegh's accounts of wondrous peoples and gold-working is borne out by independent evidence about his experience, from folktales to archaeological remains.

40 For the relationship between personal gain and a witness's reliability, see Shapin, *Social History*, 83, 93.

41 Ralegh, *Discoverie*, 71.

42 Ralegh, *Discoverie*, ed. Lorimer, xxv; for the Popham letter, see Ralegh, *Discoverie*, 109.

43 See, for example, Popper, 'An Ocean of Lies'.

44 See Fuller, *Voyages in Print*, 65–71; Mary Fuller, 'Ralegh's Fugitive Gold: Reference and Deference in *The Discoverie of Guiana*', in *New World Encounters*, ed. Stephen Greenblatt (Berkeley, CA: University of California Press, 1993), 218–40.

What both sets of claims illuminate is the importance of process in building a justification of travellers' claims.

The changes between a fair manuscript draft of the *Discoverie* and the first printed edition offer another point of entry for understanding epistemologies of the wondrous. The manuscript, now housed in Lambeth Palace Library in London and known as Lambeth Palace MS 250, had been sent to Sir Robert Cecil, Ralegh's chief patron, and the Lord High Admiral Charles Lord Howard. It is annotated in a hand that has been identified as Cecil's. It was evidently returned to Ralegh, who revised the *Discoverie* text for publication in line with these annotations. We may be reasonably certain that Cecil wished to bolster Ralegh's reputation at this stage; Cecil invested in the follow-up expedition headed by Lawrence Keymis that set out in 1596, the year in which Ralegh's *Historie* was first printed, so he was at least committed to the exploration of Guiana.[45] Some annotations indicate Cecil's attempt to absorb salient information scattered throughout the manuscript. Other notes reveal his interest in environmental and political factors that might facilitate a successful expedition, such as indigenous allies. A number of Cecil's revisions served to bolster trust in the viability of the enterprise.[46] In many places, Cecil marked up passages that Ralegh then removed from the printed version. These included references to spleen stones, the bacchanalian distractions of Guiana for drunkards, womanizers and tobacco-smokers, and a mysterious beast called *Jawari*.

Lorimer observed that Cecil 'read the manuscript with a critical eye, acutely conscious of which arguments might sell with the Queen and Privy Council and which would most certainly not'.[47] And yet, the passages about the existence, appearance and customs of the Amazons and the *Ewaipanoma* remained almost completely unchanged. This restraint is rather surprising given the sceptical, cutthroat world in which Ralegh was trying to sell dreams about gold-rich Guiana. And yet, evidently neither Ralegh nor Cecil feared that including monstrous peoples in a promotional narrative would jeopardize the willingness of potential donors.[48] Monstrous peoples were not, in themselves, incredible, even though other wondrous phenomena, such as spleen stones, that were excised might well have been removed for fear that they would reduce Ralegh's credibility.

45 Ralegh, ed. Lorimer, *Discoverie*, xxxi.
46 These changes are discussed in ibid., lxxiv–lxxvi.
47 Ibid., xxxiv.
48 My overview of the manuscript in this paragraph draws on Ralegh, *Discoverie*, xxi–xxxiii.

The *Ewaipanoma* also appear in the account of the sailor Lawrence Keymis, who had undertaken a subsequent voyage to Guiana on Ralegh's behalf. Here, they are substantiated in many of the same ways as they are in Ralegh's text.[49] Keymis's relation was printed in the same year as Ralegh's *Discoverie*, and was consulted by Jodocus Hondius the Elder, on whose map the earliest known image of an *Ewaipanoma* appears; Hondius cites Keymis on the map. Keymis's account is a forest of place names and convoluted directions tracing his itinerary. Readers must unwind their own Ariadne's thread in order to follow the testimonial trail by which Keymis learned of these extraordinary people.

Keymis relates that, in the region of the River Raleana (the Orinoco River), he spent an entire night in 'long discourse' with the chief of the Moruga Indians. The chief confirmed their mutual friendship through ceremonies such as spitting in his right hand. The strangeness of this detail was an oblique reassurance to Keymis's readers both that he had really travelled (and therefore seen something unusual) and that his informant had reason to answer his queries to the best of his knowledge (since Keymis and his informant had entered into a mutual bond). This chief informed Keymis:

> That of all others the Charibes that dwell high vp in the Orenoque, know most of the inland, and of those nations, & that speak no other language, then such as Iohn your Interpreter doth well vnderstand. He [the Moruga chief] certified me of the headlesse men, and that their mouthes in their breasts are exceeding wide . . . and the Guianians call them Ewaipanomos. What I haue heard of a sorte of people more monstrous, I omit to mention, because it is no matter of difficultie to get one of them, and the report otherwise will appear fabulous.[50]

In this dense passage, five types of witness – Caribes, the interpreter John, the Moruga chief, the Guianians and Keymis himself – perform a complicated dance that reinforces one another's testimony. The Caribs are the most knowledgeable about Guiana's peoples, and Keymis's interpreter is well acquainted with the Carib language, so we may be assured that what Keymis relates to us about these peoples is trustworthy. Both the Moruga chief and the (unspecified) Guianians know the wondrous *Ewaipanoma*, and corroborate one another's stories. Keymis, by alluding to a people who are allegedly even more monstrous than the *Ewaipanoma* and the Amazons, peoples he will not commit to print, fashions himself as a critical

[49] Lawrence Keymis, *Second Voyage to Guiana.* [50] Ibid., sig. C.3*r*-*v*.

sifter of information, reluctantly setting down reliable evidence about monstrous peoples even though he was uncertain that it would convince his readers.

Although Keymis announces that he will not repeat testimony about an even more incredible people than the *Ewaipanoma*, the side-head to this passage reveals what it was that he heard. The inscription announces that: 'They haue eminent heads like dogs, & liue all day time in the sea. They speake the Charibes language'.[51] Perhaps Keymis's manuscript, when supplied to the printer, included this information under erasure, and the printer decided to print it. The information was evidently visible under the excision. The Moruga chief may well have been describing a manatee, an animal with these characteristics that inhabits the rivers of Amazonia.

In his *An Impartial Description of Surinam upon the Continent of Guiana in America* (London, 1667), George Warren deploys the same rhetorical strategy of intimating that wonders even greater than the ones he reports are being withheld. In the chapter, 'Of things there Venomous and Hurtful', we are told that

> of snakes,'tis certain there has been some kill'd neer thirty foot long, and of a greatness proportionable to their length: I know some people are so foolishly incredulous in things of this nature, that they will believe nothing which cannot be visibly demonstrated within the limits of their own thresholds; therefore, for fear of being thought to use the authority of a traveller, I dare not repeat how huge a morsel one of them will swallow at a time: but far less danger resides in one of those huge creatures, then their presence may seem to threaten; for they are not at all venomous, and especially when full, very un-weildy.[52]

The snake in question was no figment of imagination but rather one of the large, non-venomous snakes native to Amazonia such as a species of anaconda. Warren turns the tables on the long-standing armchair explorer's gripe that travellers can lie with impunity and, like so many Mandevilles, spin tall tales that their listeners cannot refute. While the notion that those who don't trust the word of others are 'foolishly incredulous' might strike one as oxymoronic, Warren's reasoning is sound. Shared, empirically derived knowledge necessarily operates through networks of trust with accepted methods for assaying knowledge in circulation: no single person can see everything with their own eyes, but must delegate authority to others

[51] Ibid., sig. C.3.*v*.

[52] George Warren, *An Impartial Description of Surinam upon the Continent of Guiana in America* (London, 1667), 20.

in order to use a much wider body of knowledge. For travellers in areas where nature departed most spectacularly from its operation at home, genuine eyewitness observation risked being thrown out with the claims of charlatans.

This challenge explains why Ralegh invokes multiple witnesses in service of his wondrous ethnography and thereby attempts to deflect the scepticism that had already adhered to his protestations of loyalty and claims about gold mines. He strives here to capitalize on the intrinsic credibility of tropical wonders. That Cecil did not remove the Amazons or the *Ewaipanoma* from the text suggests that Ralegh's approach was a reasonable one in the context of his audience. But while mapmakers and publishers were convinced by Ralegh's ethnography for a couple of decades, that credibility soon fell away.

How Jodocus Hondius read his Ralegh

As we saw in earlier chapters, Renaissance mapmakers practised visual exegesis: they analysed travel accounts in comparison with multiple textual traditions for explaining human diversity, and devised distinctive vignettes to characterize the peoples of different regions. At the end of the sixteenth century, the appeal of the Amazons and headless men whom Dutch mapmakers selected to represent Guiana was that these beings demonstrated the mapmakers' access to new sources and helped viewers to form a distinct mental picture of that region. The challenge these mapmakers faced was how to emblematize Guiana credibly through its most distinctive and memorable peoples when it was impossible to prove whether they were monstrous peoples rather than one-off monstrous individuals. As we shall see, mapmakers deployed distinctive forms of visual rhetoric in order to make convincing epistemological claims in a predominantly iconographical format.

Around 1598, the earliest surviving images of Guiana's *Ewaipanoma* and Amazons appeared on two maps by the Dutch cartographer Jodocus Hondius the Elder. Hondius's associate, Cornelis Claesz, printed a Dutch edition of Ralegh's *Discoverie* in the same year, with the same *Ewaipanoma* on the title page.[53] Hondius had spent around nine years in London c.1584–93, having fled Ghent around the time when it was captured by Spanish forces

[53] Sir Walter Ralegh, *Waerachtighe ende grondighe beschryvinge van . . . Guiana* (Amsterdam, 1598).

under the Duke of Parma.[54] Some of Hondius's cartographic activities had been sponsored by the merchant-adventurer William Sanderson, one of the investors in the Virginia expedition of 1584–6, which had been organized by Ralegh.[55] While there is no direct evidence that Hondius knew Ralegh, he continued to have associations with English mathematicians, mapmakers and those involved in voyages of exploration.[56]

The interplay between the various elements – title cartouche, ethnographic caption, topographical details, place names, human(oid) bodies and animals – on Hondius's map of Guiana build a powerful set of corroborations for the map's wondrous elements (Fig. 6.1). The layout – the staging, if you will, of Guiana's peoples – is in many ways highly original. Single-sheet maps of other New World regions had not previously contained this much writing. The map makes frequent references to its careful derivation from the testimony of individuals who participated in expeditions sponsored by Ralegh.

The title-cartouche announces this work as:

> [A] new map of the wondrous and gold-rich land [called] Guiana ... recently visited by Sir Walter Ralegh ... in the years 1594, 1595 and 1596. The coasts of this map have been drawn diligently. . .by a certain ship's mate who has sailed along them and visited them in the years noted previously. The interior provinces have been extracted with great difficulty from both booklets that have been published by and on order of the afore-mentioned Ralegh.[57]

Not only has the interior of Guiana been mapped here in accordance with Ralegh's *Discoverie* and (presumably) Lawrence Keymis's *A Relation of the Second Voyage to Guiana* (London, 1596), but the coastlines have been drawn by a sailor who had been there. Perhaps Hondius had access, through his contacts in London, to a sketch map. While Hondius has not drawn Guiana or its peoples from life – an epistemological claim that

54 For the move to London, see *MCN*, VIII, chap. II. 55 Ibid., 37.

56 For the English geographical context, see, e.g., Cormack, *Charting an Empire*.

57 Jodocus Hondius the Elder, *Nieuwe caerte van het wonderbaer ende goudrijcke landt Guiana* (Amsterdam, 1598): 'Nieuwe caerte van het wonderbaer ende goudrijcke landt Guiana ... nieuwelick besocht door Sir Water [sic] Ralegh Ridder van Engelandt, in het jaer 1594, –95 ende 1596. De Custen van dese caert, sijn seer vlietich geteekent op haere hooghten ende waere streckingen, door een seker stierman die dit selve beseilt ende besocht heest, inde jaren voornomt. De binnen Provincien, syn door groote moyte getrocken, uit beyde de boexkens, die door ende by laste van Ralegh voorseit, int licht gegeven sijn'; *MCN*, VIII, 257–8. Here and elsewhere, I have made minor revisions to the translation. For a description of the map, see *MCN*, VIII, 257–60 and facsimile 19.

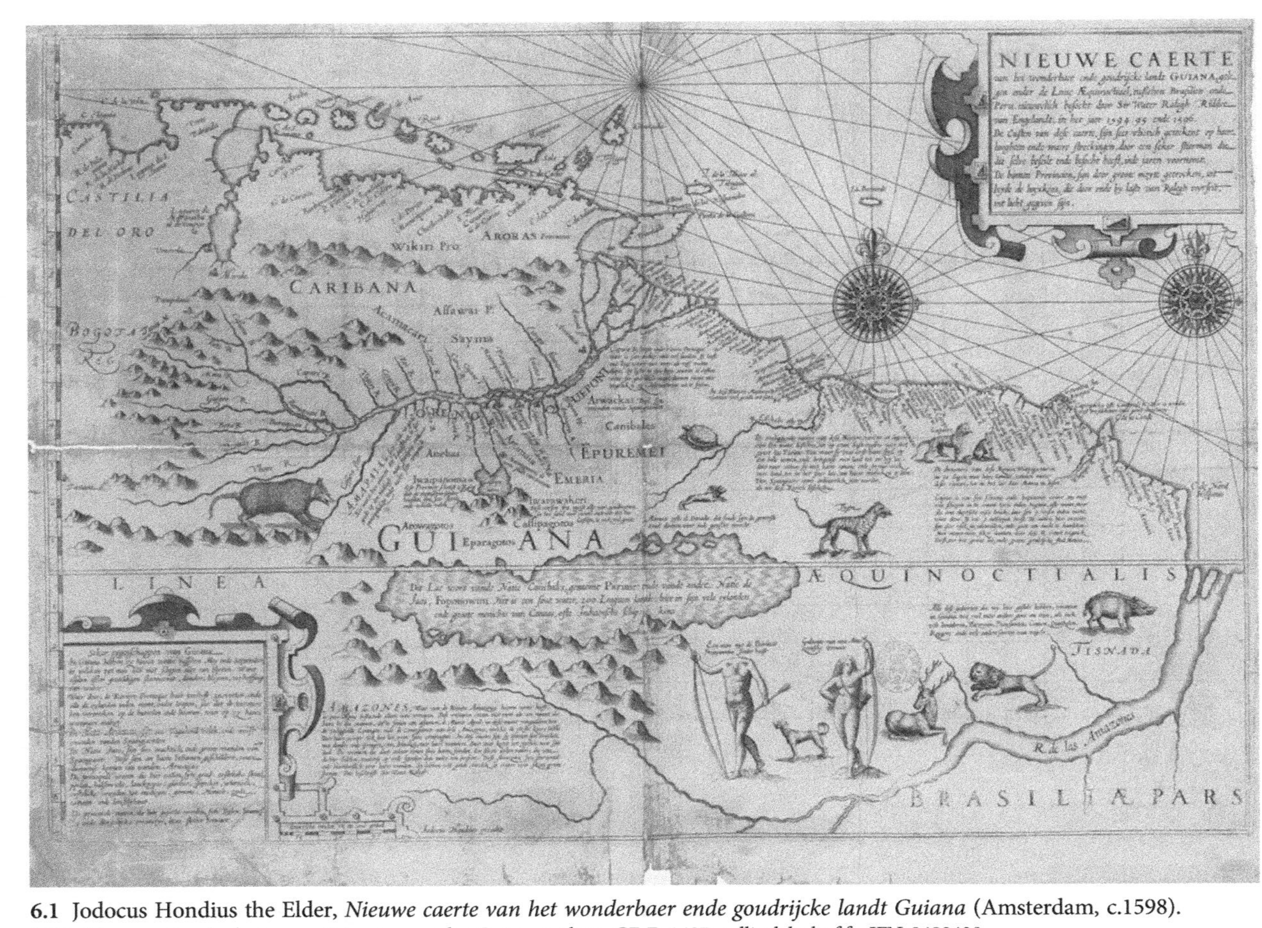

6.1 Jodocus Hondius the Elder, *Nieuwe caerte van het wonderbaer ende goudrijcke landt Guiana* (Amsterdam, c.1598). Bibliothèque nationale de France, Département des Cartes et plans, GE D 1437; gallicalabs.bnf.fr, IFN-8492438.

6.2 Jodocus Hondius the Elder, *Nieuwe caerte van het wonderbaer ende goudrijcke landt Guiana* (Amsterdam, c.1598), detail.
Bibliothèque nationale de France, Département des Cartes et plans, GE D 1437; gallicalabs.bnf.fr, IFN-8492438.

makers of printed and manuscript illustrations were not hesitant to use in this period – he had arguably done something just as useful by comparing and synthesizing the experiences of three witnesses. By embedding the testimony of multiple eyewitnesses in the map, Hondius imbued the map itself with what we might call an artefactual authority: an authority derived from the particularities of its form, sources and composition, and one distinct from and arguably greater than the authority of one of its sources.

Hondius wished for his readership of European scholars, nobles and merchants to believe that he had reliable information, and chose Ralegh – a European nobleman – as his ethnographic witness accordingly.[58] Two large figures appear in the centre of Guiana, identified as 'a man from the province of Iwaipanoma without a head'[59] and 'a figure of an Amazon woman' (Fig. 6.2).[60] A caption elaborates on the warrior women:

> Amazons, from where the Amazon River takes its name, is a nation consisting exclusively of women. These women do not spend more than one month a year with the men; as far as we can say, this is the month of April. In this month the surrounding kings meet with the queens of these Amazons, who have the first choice of mate. Afterwards, each chooses a

[58] See, e.g., the rhetoric of the map's lengthy title, discussed earlier in this chapter.
[59] 'Een man uyt de Provincie Iwaipanoma sonder hooft.'
[60] 'Gedaente van een Amazoensche vrouwe.'

> lot for their company. In this month they enjoy themselves greatly together with dancing and jumping, eating, drinking, according to their custom. Afterwards, each one returns to his or her land. The women who later bear a son send the same to the father; those who have a daughter raise her and send a present to the father. These Amazons are very cruel and bloodthirsty towards their enemies. They have much gold, which they obtain in exchange for certain green stones. This is described by Sir Walter Ralegh.[61]

This information follows Ralegh's account, which describes, in the same order, how the Guianian Amazons 'do accompanie with men but once in a yeere, and for the time of one moneth . . . in Aprill'; the first choice of mate going to the Amazon queens; the month-long revelry; the departure home; the return of male children to the father; the Amazons' bloodthirstiness; and their use of green stones.[62]A significant exclusion, however, is Ralegh's admission that his account of the Amazon was based solely on the testimony of native interlocutors. Readers of the inscription would no doubt have assumed that Ralegh had seen he what described – he had visited Guiana, after all. Similarly, in the description of headless men, there is no mention of Ralegh's indigenous informants; they have effectively been rendered invisible (or perhaps, inaudible)[63]: 'Iwaipanoma. In this province, as Ralegh writes, the people have no heads, [and] are very strong and cruel.'[64]

The map's illustrations of animals corroborate the images of people by reminding viewers of the almost incredible New World animals that could be seen in natural histories, menageries and cabinets of curiosities.[65] The dog and deer, combined with what we have been told about the

[61] 'Amazones; Waer van de Riviere Amazones haeren name heest, is eene Natie bestaende alleen van vrouwen. Dese vrouwen comen niet meer als een maent des Jaers by den mannen, dit is somen can afnemen, de Maent April in dese maent vergaderen hen de omliggende Coningen ende de Coninginnen van dese Amazones, welcke de eerste kuere hebben. Daer naer, werpt elck het lot, voor syne compaignie. In dese maent sijn sy tsamen seer vroylick met dansen ende springen, eten, drincken, naer haere manniere. Daer naer keert een ygelick naer sijn land. De vrouwen die daer achter eenen sone baren, seinden den selven anden vader; die eene dochter hebben, voedense op ende seynden den vader een present. Dese Amazones syn seer wreed ende bloetdorstich over haere vianden. Sy hebben vele goouds, twelck sy crigen voor sekere groene steenen. Dit beschrijft Sir Water [sic] Ralegh'; *MCN*, VIII, 260.

[62] Ralegh, *Discoverie*, 23.

[63] For a similar lack of information about first-hand witnesses, in geographical texts, see Johnson, 'Buying Stories', 440–1.

[64] 'Iwaipanoma in dese Provincie schrijft S. Raleg dat de meinschen sonder hoofden sijn, seer sterck ende wreedt volck.'

[65] Miguel Asúa and Roger French, *A New World of Animals: Early Modern Europeans on the Creatures of Iberian America* (Aldershot: Ashgate, 2005). For a survey of animals on maps, see Wilma George, *Animals in Maps* (London: Secker and Warburg, 1969).

characteristic hunting proficiency of the Amazons, brings to mind a life of hunting. Further afield, an armadillo appears in the northwestern reaches of the continent; a jaguar appears north of the human figures; and an animal resembling a tapir hovers in the northeast. Just as New World animals were not one-off monstrosities, so might the *Ewaipanoma* and Amazons in Guiana be indicators of monstrous peoples rather than monstrous individuals.

Despite the sober words and visual rhetoric of this elaborate map – and the intrinsic credibility of monstrous peoples in tropical climes – a group of roughly contemporary annotations in Dutch directly below the *Ewaipanoma* on the British Library's example shows that there were still problems with the use of *Ewaipanoma* and Amazons. An annotation below the *Ewaipanoma* reads: 'This I think is fabricated because no Dutchman ever saw it'.[66] A similar scepticism is evident in the annotation to the right of the Amazon: 'thus Ralegh'.[67] This seventeenth-century reader was presumably aware that subsequent Dutch voyages had not corroborated Ralegh's claims, and it was the ethical connection between the reader and the Dutch voyages that formed the basis of his or her scepticism and not any notion of *Ewaipanoma* being impossible in nature. While this is only one reader's view, it does bear out the continuing importance of the ethical status of a witness in relation to the judges of his/her testimony: the closer the ethical status of witness and judge, the more likely it was that the testimony would be believed.

The 1598 map of Guiana's textual commentaries, iconography and formal elements of style and design reveal the strategies through which their makers sought to make the map authoritative. By embedding the authority of the eyewitness into the map, the mapmakers also gave their workshop authority. The site where scholars and artisans had performed textual and visual hermeneutics on new sources in the light of established tradition was now, by implication, a place in which new knowledge that went beyond that of the eyewitness was made.

Yet the map of Guiana was not taken up by seventeenth-century Dutch atlas producers of the likes of Willem Blaeu, Gerard de Jode, and Abraham Ortelius.[68] This is surprising; mapmakers' businesses thrived on the

[66] 'Dit meen ick, is versiert mits noyt gene hollander gevonden'. [67] 'Sic[u]t ralegh'.

[68] See, e.g., the atlas map listings in Cornelis Koeman, *Atlantes Neerlandici. Bibliography of Terrestrial, Maritime and Celestial Atlases and Pilot Books, published in the Netherlands up to 1880*, 5 vols. (Amsterdam, 1967–71); Peter van der Krogt, *Koeman's Atlantes Neerlandici*, new edition, 4 vols. ('t Goy-Houten, 2000–2012).

acquisition of maps of new geographical regions which would demonstrate that an atlas was up-to-date, and that owners of previous atlases should buy a new one. One might well imagine that the hesitation of atlas producers to engrave maps of Guiana lay in the region's small size; maps of Peru and Brazil were already well-established, and a further map of a small corner of northeastern South America was unnecessary, although mapmakers did sometimes place sheets with some geographical overlap in their atlases. The absence of Amazons and *Ewaipanoma* on the illustrated borders of most wall maps, together with the lack of single-sheet maps of Guiana among the works of Hondius's competitors, suggest that Guiana had quickly become too contentious epistemologically to warrant a map of its own.

The rise and fall of the *Ewaipanoma*

A few Dutch maps from the turn of the seventeenth century illustrated the *Ewaipanoma* alongside other New World peoples. Analyzing the rhetoric of each map reveals how their makers picked carefully among eyewitness, artefactual and ethical modes of authority depending on whether they wished to bolster or to destroy credibility in these beings. Map viewers were also readers of travel accounts and encyclopedic geographies; each genre inflected their viewers' response to the others.

On Hondius's 1598 map of America, the New World peoples are arranged in a row along the top border in what one might call an ethnographic frieze. They appear in order of increasing difference from European viewers. This rendered the steps from civilized humanity and monstrosity visible, gradual and therefore more credible (Fig. 6.3). The physical aberration of the *Ewaipanoma* is visible to all, and stated unequivocally. The behavioural aberration of the next two figures, the cannibals Quoniambec and Tarizichus, is not visible, but would have been known to viewers who knew the works of André Thevet.[69] The next two figures, inhabitants of Florida, were not characterized as being monstrous in either texts or on maps.[70] The structure of the frieze minimizes the scepticism that might follow from too much difference between the viewer and the *Ewaipanoma*. As in Hondius's map of Guiana of the same year, it is Ralegh himself who is

[69] Discussed in Davies, 'Representations of Amerindians', chap. 4.

[70] The figures are taken from an engraving, *Americae Pars II*, plate XIIII. This identification was made in *MCN*, III, 162 in relation to Blaeu's 1608 map of America.

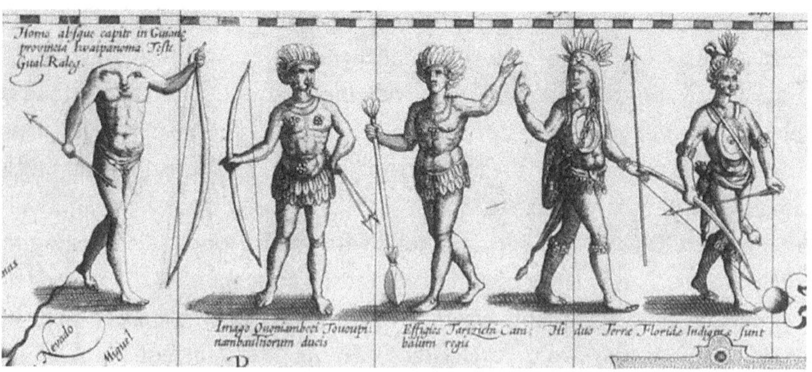

6.3 Jodocus Hondius the Elder, map of North America (Amsterdam, c.1598), detail. Courtesy of the New York Historical Society, NS3 M36 .1 .2.

implicitly credited as the witness of the *Ewaipanoma*, rather than his indigenous observers: the headless figure is 'a man without a head in the province of Guiana [called] Iwaipanoma, as Walter Ralegh testifies'.[71]

The ethnographic frieze was also adopted on a map of America from around 1602 by another Amsterdam printer and mapmaker, Cornelis Claesz, who often worked with Hondius (Fig. 6.4). Friezes across the map's top (Fig. 6.5) and centre (Fig. 6.6) illustrate peoples of North and South America respectively and derive from Hondius's 1598 maps, De Bry's *America* and Dutch travel journals.[72] These choices draw attention to Claesz's broader publishing interests, which included Dutch translations of travel accounts as well as topographical and navigational works.[73]

While Claesz's map reproduces four of the five figures on Hondius's frieze exactly, the *Ewaipanoma* figure has been redrawn. On Hondius's map (Fig. 6.3), his face is clearly below his shoulders. The map's inscription

[71] 'Homo absque capite in Guianae provincia Iwaipanoma. Teste Gual. Raleg.'

[72] Hondius's 1598 map, for which the lower sheets do not survive, contained North and South Americans along the top, so it is unlikely that it had a second frieze in the lower half of the map. A surviving example of a complete map that has just one frieze along the top, depicting both North and South Americans peoples, is Pieter van den Keere's map of 1619, to which we shall attend shortly. First published in 1609, the earliest surviving example of this map is *Nova orbis terrarum geographica ac hydrographica tabula* (Amsterdam, 1619).

[73] Many are listed in *MCN*, VII, 3–4. Ibid., 361, notes that prints from De Bry's *America* were often the models, but it does not list their plates or volumes. The upper frieze contains, from left to right, figures from *Americae Pars I*: plate V (first figure) and the title-page (second and third figures; the woman also appears on plate VIII); *Pars II*: plates XX (fourth figure), XIIII (fifth and sixth figures), frontispiece (seventh figure) and XXIII (eighth figure). The lower frieze contains four cannibals (see Chapter 4); the fifth figure is discussed below; and the sixth to eleventh figures, identified in *MCN*, III, 131 and VII, 362–3, are from Dutch travel journals.

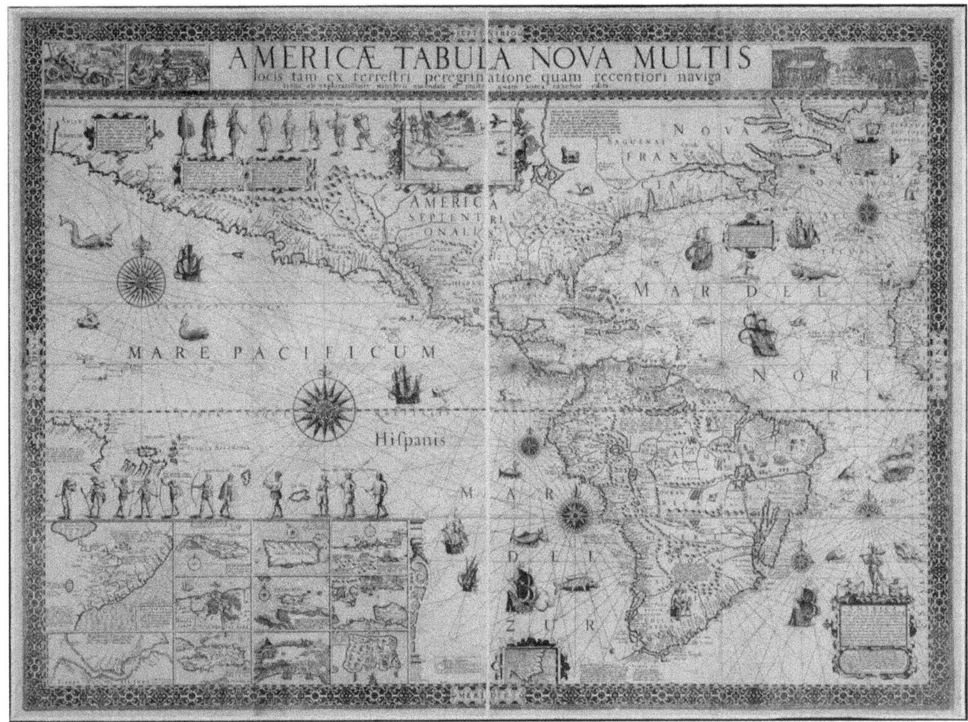

6.4 Cornelis Claesz, map of the Americas (Amsterdam, c.1602).
Bibliothèque nationale de France, Département des Cartes et plans, gallicalabs.bnf.fr, Rés GE B 1115 [Kl 560].

leaves us in no doubt that this is indeed a headless Guianian as Ralegh attests. On Claesz's map, the engraver changed this figure, even though he copied the two cannibal figures quite carefully (Fig. 6.6).[74] The Guianian still lacks a neck, but now has a head distinct from his chest as opposed to a face below his shoulders and no nipples. There was a medieval precedent for this: Isidore's *Etymologiae* had included beings lacking necks, although these had eyes in their shoulders.[75] Alternatively, someone in Claesz's workshop might have consulted the Popham letters printed at the end of Ralegh's *Discoverie*; Claesz's printing house did, after all, print a Dutch translation of Ralegh. One letter describes how Indians described to a Spanish expedition 'men [who] had the points of their shoulders higher then the crownes of their heades'.[76] The caption accompanying the map's

[74] By contrast, Claesz's edition of Keymis's account depicted Ralegh's headless man on the title-page.
[75] See Chapter 1, near n. 55.
[76] Ralegh, *Discoverie*, 109.

6.5 Cornelis Claesz, map of the Americas (Amsterdam, c.1602), detail of upper frieze. Bibliothèque nationale de France, Département des Cartes et plans, gallicalabs.bnf.fr, Rés GE B 1115 [Kl 560].

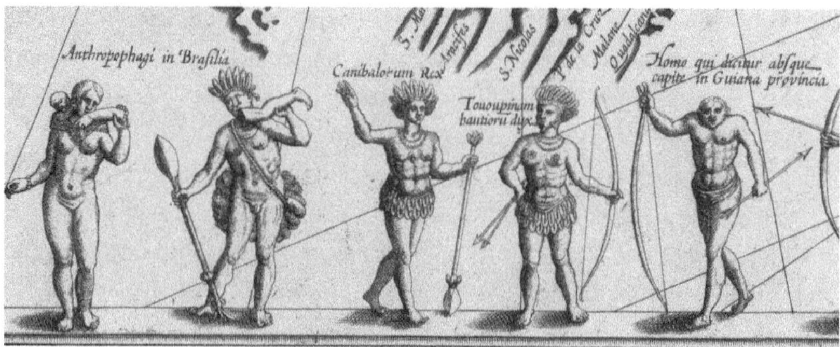

6.6 Cornelis Claesz, map of the Americas (Amsterdam, c.1602), detail of lower frieze. Bibliothèque nationale de France, Département des Cartes et plans, gallicalabs.bnf.fr, Rés GE B 1115 [Kl 560].

Ewaipanoma is equivocal, describing the figure as 'A man who is said [to be] without a head in Guiana province.'[77] Not only have we lost the statement of first testimony referring to Ralegh that had appeared on the earlier maps that showed the *Ewaipanoma*, but the illustration itself leads one to doubt the people's headlessness.

When Hondius published an illustrated world map in 1608, he chose not to include any images of *Ewaipanoma* or Amazons. Hondius, who had been part of a London group of cartographers, explorers and sponsors with interests in exploration and colonization ten years previously, might well have been aware that Ralegh's words on Guiana were now more suspect that they had been in 1596.[78] Second, Hondius probably knew that recent Dutch voyages had failed to corroborate Ralegh's report; his collaborator Claesz had printed some of these voyage accounts.[79]

A caption in northern South America still outlines some of what Ralegh had written about Guiana's inhabitants: [Ralegh] also affirms from the report of the indigenous inhabitants that 'in some places the people are vigorous but with an unheard-of appearance, that is, some are without heads or even have dogs' heads (which, however, I think is far-fetched)'.[80] Hondius engraved this map with his brother-in-law Pieter van den Keere, so we cannot be certain whose view this caption represents.[81] Nevertheless, it is the most explicit expression of doubt as to the existence of monstrous peoples in America that I have found on a printed map. Although Hondius had not mentioned indigenous testimony on his earlier map of Guiana of 1598, he must have been aware of it: as we saw earlier, he quoted a passage about Amazons, and referred to Ralegh's writing about *Ewaipanoma* while omitting mention of the native witnesses who abound in Ralegh's text. Hondius's 1608 map cites just such witnesses, revealing that Hondius was well aware of the part played by indigenous peoples in information about *Ewaipanoma*. Now, however, he casts doubt on these beings. One of the ways in which he does this is by removing his original

[77] 'Homo qui dicitur absque capite in Guiana provincia.'

[78] Ralegh, *Discoverie*, ed. Lorimer, xciv: Ralegh's own fortunes had nose-dived by this point. After the death of Elizabeth I in 1603, he was imprisoned in the Tower and tried for treason; he was suspected of being involved in a plot against James I.

[79] See *MCN*, VIII, for Claesz's works.

[80] 'homines quoque (nonnullis in locis) strenuos quidem, sed formae inauditae, ex indigenarum relatu, affirmat, scilicet absque capitibus nonnullos etiam caninis (quod tamen fabulosum existimo)'.

[81] For Van den Keere and his works, see *MCN*, VIII, part II.

6.7 Pieter van den Keere, *Nova orbis terrarum geographica ac hydrographica tabula* (Amsterdam, 1619), detail of upper frieze. Bibliothèque nationale de France, Département des Cartes et plans, Rés GE C 4931; gallicalabs.bnf.fr, IFN-720026.

citation of Ralegh and by deploying the hearsay of unnamed indigenous witnesses.[82]

Pieter van den Keere's 1619 world map is the latest map with an ethnographic frieze that includes an *Ewaipanoma* (Fig. 6.7).[83] The first five Amerindians from left to right appear in reverse order from that on Hondius's 1598 map (Fig. 6.3). Van den Keere did not, however, use the defiantly headless man from Hondius's map, but rather the less monstrous exemplar from Claesz's 1602 map (Fig. 6.6). The veracity of the multiple indigenous witnesses had, perhaps, fallen away in the face of multiple null results from subsequent travellers.

By the time Van den Keere's map appeared, Ralegh's fortunes had taken their final turn for the worse. In 1616, Ralegh had managed to negotiate his way out of the tower to lead another expedition to Guiana. During this expedition, his men attacked the Spanish outpost of San Tomé on the Orinoco River. On Ralegh's return to London, he was sentenced to death again; the sentence was carried out in 1618. As Mary Fuller has shown, neither Ralegh's geographical claims about discovering gold mines nor his

[82] Another reader of travel accounts who became more sceptical about Amazons over time was Gonzalo Fernández de Oviedo. For an analysis of Oviedo's writings on Amazons, most of which were not printed in the sixteenth century, see Kathleen Ann Myers, *Fernández de Oviedo's Chronicle of America: a New History for a New World* (Austin, TX: University of Texas Press, 2007), 90–6.

[83] The only similar case I have found is Giuseppe Rosaccio's world map, *Universale descrittione di tutto il mondo* (Venice, 1597), where images from New World travel accounts appear in other parts of the world; for an illustration, see Rodney W. Shirley, *The Mapping of the World: Early Printed World Maps 1472-1700* (Riverside, CT: Early World Press, 2001 [first published: 1984]), no. 205.

confessional ones about his intentions, actions and loyalty to the crown were believed.[84] What the cartographic archive shows is that Ralegh's claims about Guiana's wondrous ethnography were also coming under fire.

Collating monstrous evidence

Hondius's headless men were also disseminated via translations of Ralegh's *Discoverie*. A German version of Hondius's map of Guiana was devised for Theodor de Bry's *America* series, appearing in Latin and German translations of the *Discoverie* in 1599. In each case, the engraver went to great lengths to replicate Hondius's iconography.[85] Hondius's headless man also inspired engraved plates and map illustrations in the heavily abridged Latin and German translations of Ralegh's *Discoverie* printed by Levinus Hulsius at Nuremberg from 1599. Hulsius's travel books were cheaper, much abbreviated and smaller editions of works that had been printed by the De Brys.[86]

Benjamin Schmidt has shown how the Hulsius and De Bry firms, together with the Amsterdam publisher Cornelis Claesz, repackaged Ralegh's *Discoverie*, originally a text of Elizabethan proto-imperialism in new ways, into wonder picture book and *apologia* for Dutch colonization of Spanish imperial possessions.[87] The ways in which these publishers read and re-packaged Guiana's wondrous ethnography also allows us to track a broader engagement with the epistemology of Guiana's wondrousness. The iconography of the new maps and plates tell us something about paradigms of truth, tradition and observation at the turn of the seventeenth century.

Hulsius's books on Guiana were not Ralegh translations in the strict sense, but rather an emerging form of pamphlet in which illustrations taken from a travel account formed the point of departure for short texts which were selected and combined in order to explicate the images. Cornelis Claesz, for example, composed such a work out of De Bry's

[84] Fuller, *Voyages in Print*, 58. [85] For illustrations, see *Americae Pars VIII*, 256, 259–60.

[86] Levinus Hulsius, *Brevis & admiranda descriptio regni Guianae* . . . (Nuremberg, 1599); Levinus Hulsius, . . .*Kurtze wunderbare Beschreibung deß goldreichen Königreichs Guianae in America* . . . (Nuremberg, 1599). The map is entitled: 'Nova et exacta delineatio Americae partis australis'. For a discussion of German and Dutch editions of Ralegh's *Discoverie*, see Benjamin Schmidt, 'Reading Ralegh's America: Texts, Books, and Readers in the Early Modern Atlantic World' in Peter C. Mancall, ed., *The Atlantic World and Virginia, 1550–1624* (Chapel Hill, NC: University of North Carolina Press, 2007), 454–88, at 477–82. For the relationship between the two firms, see Michiel van Groesen, *Representations of the Overseas World*, 346–52.

[87] Schmidt, 'Reading Ralegh's America'.

engravings for Las Casas' *Brevisima relación*, and another from illustrations in Jan Huyghen van Linschoten's *Itinerario*.[88] These works are as much inscribed pictures as they are illustrated texts, the inscriptions encouraging closer comparative reading of the illustrations.

Each Hulsius edition comprised short sections of Ralegh's text, arranged in chapters in which each section of Ralegh was followed by extracts, in a smaller font, from corroborating authorities on, for example, Old World or New World headlessness or Amazons.[89] The structure of the pamphlets facilitated the analytical comparison of independent sources on the same phenomena, in much the same way as Ulisse Aldrovandi's *Monstrorum historia* did for the Patagonians in its section on giants.[90] This multitude of corroborating sources imbued Ralegh's ethnography with credibility, bringing to mind Ralegh's comments about the unlikelihood of great numbers of people telling the same lie.

The title-page reveals that Hulsius made ethnological extrapolations from his readings on the *Ewaipanoma* (Fig. 6.8):

> Concerning the Iwaipanoma province of the kingdom of Guiana, Lord Ralegh attests in the above-mentioned pamphlet (as Jodocus Hondius diligently records in a frequently mentioned geographical map) that in these places live a race of men, without a neck or heads, bearing eyes and the remaining parts of their face in their chest, who nevertheless are otherwise strong, loathsome and barbarous men.[91]

Here, the Guianians' physical abnormality is juxtaposed with a moral judgement that is absent in Ralegh's account. Such links were often drawn between physical difference and moral reprehensibility, most obviously in the discourse on black skin that took on new forms from the late seventeenth century.[92]

The headless figures and the Amazon bear enough similarities to the examples on Hondius's maps to have been inspired by them. No single

[88] For the Las Casas edition, see Chapter 7 of this book, near n. 64; for the Linschoten volume, see Chapter 8, near n. 76.

[89] Hulsius, *Descriptio regni Guianae*, 7–12. These include Pliny, St Augustine, Isidore of Seville, André Thevet's *Cosmographie* (tome IV, liure 22, cap. 2–3) and Oviedo's *Historia general de las Indias* (for extracts about the Orellana expedition).

[90] See Chapter 5 above.

[91] Hulsius, *Descriptio regni Guianae*, cap. VI, f. 11.*r*: 'De Provincia Ivvaipanoma regni Guianae . . . testatur Dominus Releghius, in supra allegato libello (ut Jodocus Hondius in saepe memorata tabula geographica diligenter refert) istis in locis vivere genus hominum sine collo et capita, oculos et reliquas faciei partes in pectore gerentes, qui tamen alias robusti, foedi et barbarici sint homines.'

[92] For these debates, see Curran, *Anatomy of Blackness*.

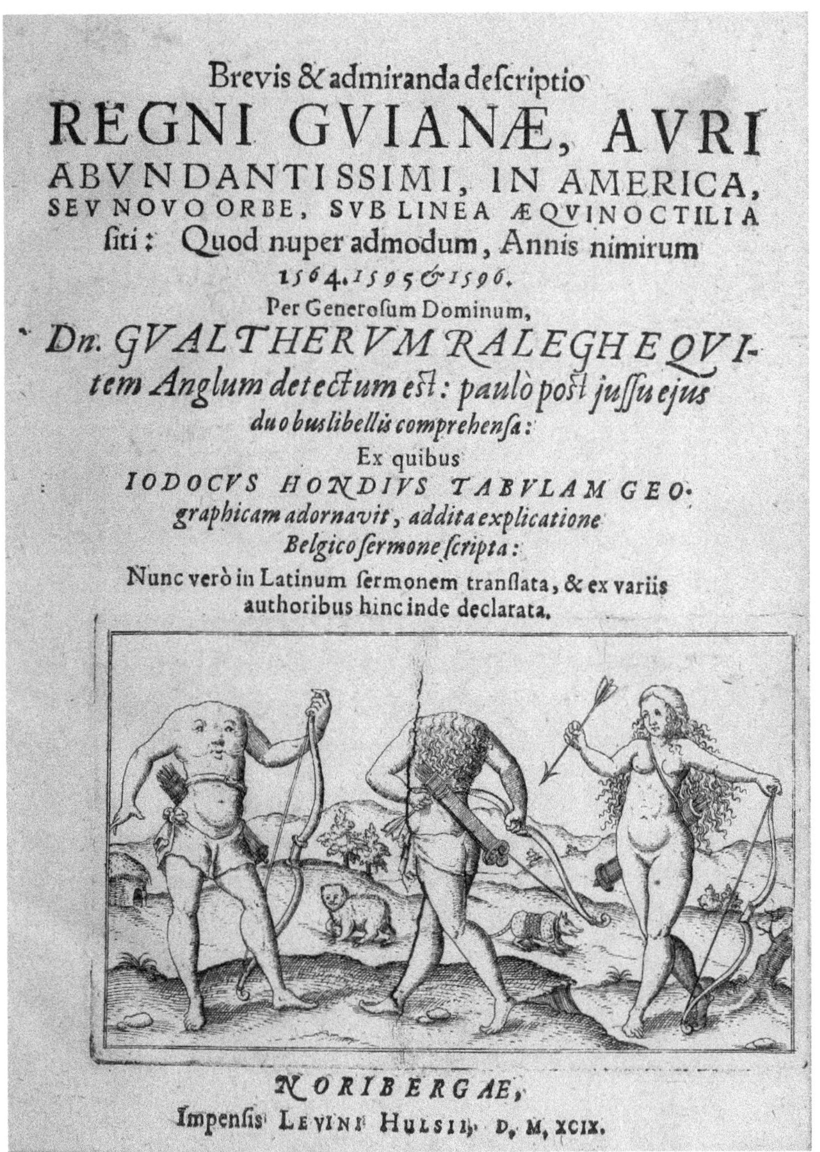

Brevis & admiranda deſcriptio
REGNI GVIANÆ, AVRI
ABVNDANTISSIMI, IN AMERICA,
SEV NOVO ORBE, SVB LINEA ÆQVINOCTILIA
ſiti: Quod nuper admodum, Annis nimirum
1564. 1595 & 1596.
Per Generoſum Dominum,
*Dn. GVALTHERVM RALEGH EQVI-
tem Anglum detectum eſt: paulò poſt juſſu ejus
duobus libellis comprehenſa:*
Ex quibus
*IODOCVS HONDIVS TABVLAM GEO-
graphicam adornavit, addita explicatione
Belgico ſermone ſcripta:*
Nunc verò in Latinum ſermonem tranſlata, & ex variis
authoribus hinc inde declarata.

NORIBERGAE,
Impenſis LEVINI HULSII, D. M. XCIX.

6.8 Sir Walter Ralegh, *Kurtze Wunderbare Beschreibung deß goldreichen Königreichs Guianae in America* . . . (Nuremberg, 1599), title page.
Courtesy of the John Carter Brown Library at Brown University, J Hulsius pt. 5 1599 1.

surviving source includes all these elements, although such a source may now be lost. In any case, Hulsius or his artist could have compared illustrations on several maps to devise the scene. The Amazon image had previously appeared only on Hondius's 1598 map of Guiana (Fig. 6.2).[93] The pair of headless figures later appeared in the South American interior of Claesz's c.1602 map, and might have appeared on the missing southern sheets of Hondius's 1598 world map (Fig. 6.3), one of the sources of Claesz's c.1602 world map. Alternatively, Hulsius might also have been inspired to show front and rear views of the *Ewaipanoma* by a monster compendium; such works often showed front and rear views of specimens; Ambroise Paré's *Monstres et prodiges* and Ulisse Aldrovandi's *Monstrorum historia* show front and back views of a figure without a head.[94]

The engraver has re-imagined the figures' costumes and accoutrements, exchanging elements between the two nations and adding a few embellishments. The *Ewaipanoma* now sport short cloth skirts tied at the waist; all the figures have more elaborate bows than those on Hondius's map. The Amazon bears aloft the stray arrow of Hondius's *Ewaipanoma*, and all three carry quivers. The *Ewaipanoma* on the left has his hand curved around his bow in the manner of Hondius's Amazon. With the centre figure the engraver has imagined how an *Ewaipanoma* might look from the rear, playfully bestowing upon him a mane of wavy hair in the manner of the nearby Amazon, which stops abruptly at his shoulders. This strategy compensates for the challenge of representing all sides of a three-dimensional object on a flat surface and draws attention to the missing head.

The figure at the centre of the image is iconographically a hybrid between the front-facing *Ewaipanoma* and the Amazon. Viewers might well have inferred, from the mirroring of body parts and postures, that these people were related. While some of the details, from the *contrapposto* stance to the elegantly muscled abdomens, were conventions of draftsmanship, they were freighted with meaning when read alongside Ralegh's *Guiana*. A viewer might well have wondered whether it is with the headless men that the Amazons conceive their children, keeping girls with heads attached, and giving headless boys to the *Ewaipanoma*.

93 The Amazon – if that is who this figure represents – in Claesz's edition of Ralegh's *Discoverie* does not resemble this.

94 Ambroise Paré, *Des Monstres et prodiges*, ed. Jean Céard (Geneva, 1971), 33; Aldrovandi, *Monstrorum historia*, 401.

The scene's composition draws on iconographical and rhetorical conventions for signalling subjects that were intended to be credible and that had been drawn from life. The central figure is in mid-stride with his weight balanced between the legs, left calf bulging at the moment of transferring weight to the right foot in front. His left hand, visible behind his back, grasps an arrow that he has presumably just removed from the sheaf on his back, perhaps for the purposes of hunting one of the animals in the middle distance. These animals include a sloth and an armadillo, two wondrous species that had been demonstrated to be real, and had already appeared in natural history compendia.[95]

While the *Ewaipanoma* and the Amazons both bore the characteristics of monstrous peoples in the Plinian sense, Hulsius's title-page challenges assumptions about the boundary between human and monstrous nations. The bows and arrows, loin coverings and small hut in the background all point to these peoples' ingenuity and at least partially civil lifestyles. Their stances suggest elegant burghers rather than savages; the musculature of the Amazon draws attention to her finely shaped body.

It was not inevitable that these would be the visual choices that the artist would make. The literature on monsters as divine portents and as anatomical deformities provided other modes that might have been chosen, but were not.[96] Further illustrations within the volume expand on this message of civility, showing *Ewaipanoma* and Amazons living in communities in well-built houses. Other engravings depict warfare and hunting, showing weaponry and stalking skills to great effect. These images – designed from Ralegh's account but not present in it – confirm that Hulsius editions transformed Ralegh's account from one promoting English imperialism into something altogether different – in this case, not a wonder book or even a justification of Dutch colonization, as Benjamin Schmidt has argued, but a statement on the multifarious forms of civil people.

Hulsius's words provide a direct insight into the reception of ethnographic illustrations on maps, revealing how they sometimes influenced depictions in books.[97] Hulsius informs us that a map by Hondius which depicted headless men was 'frequently mentioned' ('*saepe memorata*'). Such a map could not have appeared before the first, 1596 edition of Ralegh's *Guiana* at the very earliest; it may well have been Hondius's 1598 map of North America that raised great interest. The De Brys decided

[95] Asúa and French, *New World of Animals*.

[96] See Davies, 'The Unlucky, the Bad and the Ugly', 52–62.

[97] For a Patagonian example, see Chapter 6 above.

to print a German translation of the map, complete with monstrous illustrations, as part of their *America* series.[98]

Conclusion

Ralegh's and Keymis's descriptions of Guiana's ethnographic wonders derived not from their own observations, but from a medley of ancient authorities and contemporary observers who asserted that these beings existed. Ralegh attempted to reduce the distance between his readers and the eyewitnesses of these monsters: we learn, for example, that the son of an indigenous leader who knew of headless people was now in England, as were merchants who knew his Spanish witness. By contrast, Hondius's map of Guiana invoked just one witness: Ralegh himself, a 'knight of England' (*Ridder van Engelandt*). By omitting mention of Ralegh's informants and of classical and medieval authorities, Hondius's removed links in a chain of hearsay between Guiana and viewers of the map, thereby compensating for the addition of the mapmaker to this information relay. Attaching Ralegh's name to these monstrous peoples offered a more straightforward reason for believing in them – Ralegh's word – than Ralegh's own tortuous explanations.

Guiana's equatorial latitude made monstrous ethnography intrinsically credible. What may have 'really' existed could not be judged directly, since both mapmakers and viewers had to take the evidence on trust. As we saw in Chapter 5, some commentators did not consider that entire nations of monstrous peoples had been found. These sceptics included Sir Thomas Blundeville, with whom this chapter began, who described one of Plancius's maps (which was illustrated with cannibals and giants) and asserted that 'they are meere lies that are woont to be told of . . . people, that should haue their heads, their noses, their mouthes, and their eies in their breastes'. It was not that creatures with no heads was unlikely, but that monsters observed in distant regions could theoretically have been individual prodigies of the sort observed in Europe. For critics like Blundeville, it was not travellers' testimony (albeit of indigenous observers who had seen monstrous beings) that was suspect, so much as what had not observed: entire communities of peoples with their heads in their chests. In the light of Blundeville's reservations, Ralegh's uncertainty – and that of

[98] For cooperation and competition between the Hulsius and the De Bry firms, see Van Groesen, *Representations*, 346–52.

later mapmakers – might be read as pertaining to the prevalence of headlessness in Guiana as opposed to its very existence. As was shown in earlier chapters, map viewers expected mapmakers to illustrate people with characteristics that they had in common.

By the late sixteenth century, Dutch cartographers and travel publishers had acquired a reputation for printing the most recent information in high-quality editions before any of their competitors. The rhetoric of these works presented their compilers' aims as sober ones: the communication of synthesized knowledge about distant places after careful analysis of old and new sources about the wondrous east. Like Ralegh, these artisans needed to tack deftly between expections of monstrous peoples in distant places and the widespread awareness that travellers' testimony was problematic to verify and could be fabricated.

The printing houses of Hondius and Claesz may have rushed the Amazon and the *Ewaipanoma* material into production only to realize, a few years later, that they had not aged well. On later maps, Hondius, Claesz and Van den Keere displayed less confidence in the existence of headless people, and placed limited emphasis on Ralegh's testimony – indeed, a caption on Hondius's 1608 world map noted that Ralegh had recorded these creatures on the authority of indigenous observers. Not even Hondius's key competitor, Willem Blaeu, chose to incorporate them into his works. Mandeville, one of Ralegh's corroborating sources for the *Ewaipanoma*, was considered to be far less of an authority by the end of the sixteenth century than he had been at the start of it. Indeed, by 1611, the English translator and editor Edward Aston bemoaned the difficulty of telling a reliable travel witness from the 'multitude of Mandiuels that wander abroad in this pampletting age in the habite of sincere historiographers (like asses in lyons skins)'.[99]

It was not inevitable that headless men and Amazons would emblematize Guiana after Ralegh's *Discoverie* was printed. The De Bry firm, despite re-engraving Hondius's map for *Americae pars VIII*, the volume that contained Ralegh's *Discoverie*, produced a series of engravings that emphasized the indigenous metalworking practices, not physical monstrosity. And yet, Levinus Hulsius, who made a living out of producing simpler versions of the De Bry volumes, took the trouble to have a completely different set of

[99] Johannes Boemus, *The Manners, Lawes and Customes of All Nations* (London, 1611), f.3.*r*, Edward Aston's preface to the reader. The volume was originally published as *Omnium gentium mores, leges et ritus…* (Augsburg, 1520).

scenes of the daily life of Amazons and *Ewaipanoma* designed for his volumes.

Methods of textual and visual exegesis enabled a printer or other cultural arbiter without first-hand eyewitness knowledge of her/his own to generate authority. Hulsius's digest on headless men and Amazons from Ralegh alongside independent sources about such beings from different places and periods exemplifies this mode of crowd-sourcing testimony. For Hulsius, Guiana's wondrous ethnography lay just within the limits of credibility, and he packaged his volume in order to argue this case. Hondius's 'frequently mentioned' map, as Hulsius proclaimed on his title-page, was an authority that his audience would recognize as such on the subject.

Early modern ethnographic credibility, then, was a moving target. Ralegh's inclusion of distinctive, memorable ethnography for Guiana created a geographical region that was both previously undiscovered by Europeans and capable of being the location of the mythical El Dorado. *Ewaipanoma* and Amazons suggested that Ralegh had not merely read accounts of other regions but had actually been somewhere that was as yet free of Spanish dominion.

The path of the *Ewaipanoma* through texts and maps sheds light on how ethnological information helped establish the credibility not only of travellers but also of those cultural arbiters who analysed and incorporated them into other textual and visual forms. The headless men made Guiana distinctive from those New World regions that were already emblematized on maps by other motifs. Mapmakers pounced on the most distinctive elements of Ralegh's ethnography and trumpeted the knight's authority – as far as they wished to portray this as unproblematic knowledge. The ethnographic frieze format – a fleeting experiment – allowed mapmakers to contextualize that which was almost incredible. By choosing just the headless folk, and not the Amazons, for his larger maps, Hondius brought the iconography of Guiana's peoples in line with cartographic practices for other regions: one place, one people.

While the headless beings were not intrinsically incredible, the quality and quantity of witnesses affected credibility. The *Ewaipanoma* illuminate two co-existing epistemologies: that of the eyewitness, and that of the ethical relationship between eyewitness and audience. Ralegh wanted readers to believe that he had really gone to Guiana; simultaneously he offers eyewitnesses for something he himself has not seen, as mapmakers did, too. In an era in which information about distant lands grew at an ever-increasing rate, cultural arbiters decentred eyewitnesses even though they remained tethered to them as sources.

7 Civility, idolatry and cities in Mexico and Peru

Renaissance geographers and readers considered mental characteristics to be even more fundamental for classifying humans than physical ones. Since humans were embodied souls, one had to pin down the nature of the intellect and of the soul in order to establish whether a people's mental capacities placed them beyond the boundaries of the human. Both apologists for and critics of indigenous rights drew selectively from an ethno-geographical grab bag. For anyone who subscribed to the Augustinian tradition, a being descended from Adam was by definition fully rational, human and capable of salvation; and all rational beings *were* humans, regardless of their appearance. Neither the Plinian tradition of monstrous peoples, nor Hippocratic–Galenic humoral theory, nor Aristotelian traditions concerning civility and savagery enabled a clear separation between European minds, souls and bodies and those of peoples encountered in distant places.[1] The Americas were, however, so distant from Europe that new constellations studded the night skies; and since the heavens were deemed to affect bodies and temperaments, it was possible that New World peoples were fundamentally different. Physiognomy, the practice of predicting the aptitude and inclination of a person from external signs, offered another set of techniques for making knowledge about New World souls.[2]

An additional question raised by the colonial project was the extent to which persons of European lineage would also be shaped by New World environments and stars over time. The Spanish chronicler Gonzalo Fernández de Oviedo argued that the astral and environmental influences in the New World made its people 'shy and cowards'; the Franciscan friar Bernadino de Sahagún considered that creoles (persons of European ancestry born in the New World) showed evidence of degeneration and

[1] These traditions were outlined in Chapter 1.

[2] For physiognomy, see Van Deusen, *Global Indios*, 173–86; Nancy E. van Deusen, 'Seeing *Indios* in Sixteenth-Century Castile',. *William and Mary Quarterly*, 69:2 (2012), 205–34, at 208–214. For astrology's effects, see Cañizares-Esguerra, 'Patriotic Astrology'.

hence of the harmful effect of New World constellations.[3] While the Biblical tradition had posited a monogenetic human creation in which local environmental conditions lay at the root of human diversity across regions, the possibility that some populations had degenerated over time and passed this defect to their descendents was raised in various circles.[4]

Since mental capacity could only be assessed indirectly through behaviour (including language), interpreting the significance of cultural practices and artefacts lay at the core of the political, juridical and religious discourses through which the writing classes articulated issues of colonial administration.[5] Arguments about the mental faculties that Amerindians lacked were in essence exercises in what I shall term monstrification. These arguments rested on the premise that peoples who were enslaveable by nature lacked that intellective faculty of the soul which enabled humans to apply reason. This lack was taken to mean that such peoples deserved different legal rights because they were a different type of being.

In order to determine the quality of New World indigenous and creole souls, it was necessary to establish whether cultural and behavioural diversity had accidental causes in the physical or civic environment, or had innate ones. The inhabitants of the Mexica and Inca empires raised particular conundrums. While these peoples were ruled by organized, urban political structures that bore a certain resemblance to European nations and empires, observers found a number of customs, such as human sacrifice and what they termed idolatry and sodomy, abominable. Many arguments about the proper government of the Mexica and Inca peoples, modes for their evangelization, the legitimacy of Spanish claims to New World property rights, and the enslavement of indigenous peoples hinged on the ways in which observers interpreted indigenous customs and political organization.[6] At stake for Spain was the successful government and conversion of these peoples in the service of a commercially profitable empire.

Mapmakers' responses to the inhabitants of Brazil, Patagonia and Guiana emphasized their departure from those ideals for civil society and

3 Quoted in Cañizares-Esguerra, 'Patriotic Astrology', a work that contains numerous other examples.

4 For the continuation of this type of thinking into the eighteenth century, see Curran, *Anatomy of Blackness*.

5 In the Aristotelian tradition, language entailed certain kinds of beliefs, concepts, and ideas. There was a distinction between actual and potential mental capacity in this framework.

6 The literature is extensive. See, for example, Adorno, *Polemics of Possession*; MacCormack, *On the Wings of Time*; Pagden, *Fall of Natural Man*. For questions concerning property rights, see Pagden, *Spanish Imperialism*, chap. 1.

physiology long articulated by the classical tradition.[7] The choice of monstrous motifs, made from texts that also contained peaceful and 'normal' views of New World inhabitants, might suggest at first glance that the monstrification of Amerindians was an almost universal European approach on maps. Yet while early sixteenth-century travel accounts, chronicles, pamphlets and cosmographies about Mexico or Peru described human sacrifice, idolatry and sodomy, mapmakers tended not to design scenes detailing these practices.[8] Rather, they drew on admiring descriptions of Mexica and Inca cities, roads and architecture and devised images and commentaries that, in most cases, would have been read as evidence of the civility of these peoples and of the beneficial effects of their environment. While these iconographic selections helped viewers to distinguish one region from another, these emblematic summaries also intersected with a counternarrative against those colonists and scholars who argued that indigenous slavery was justified since native souls had only a limited capacity for improvement.

Aristotelianism and Spanish imperial philosophy

Spanish ethnological thinking about the viceroyalties of New Spain and Peru had two overarching approaches for determining the nature of the indigenous intellect. One was to consider human behaviour – including clothing, technology and social organization – as the key indicator. The other was to look for clues to mental capacities in local environmental conditions. From the earliest years of Spanish presence in the Americas, in the Caribbean islands, the Crown, the clergy and the colonists had distinct agendas in their engagement with the Amerindians. Spanish settlers depended on indigenous labour.[9] Settlers' practices were regularly questioned by Dominican and Franciscan priests, many of whom had travelled to the Indies for the purpose of peaceful evangelization.[10] The *encomenderos*, in turn, complained to officials in Spain, transforming

[7] See Chapters 3–6 of this book.

[8] The exceptions are a very small image relating to human sacrifice at the centre of the first map of Tenochtitlán, and an image of metalworkers in the Inca empire fashioning human figures that could be recognized by European viewers as idols.

[9] For the *encomienda* system, see Nestor Capdevila, *Las Casas: une politique de l'humanité* (Paris: Cerf, 1998), chap. 1.

[10] Patricia Seed, '"Are These Not also Men?" The Indians' Humanity and Capacity for Spanish Civilisation', *Journal of Latin American Studies*, 25 (1993), 629–52, at 634.

attacks on their implementation of the *encomienda* system of compulsory labour and tribute into a polemic against royal authority to colonize the Indies.[11] These groups disagreed about the Amerindians' level of intellect, their capacity to receive the Christian faith and even their humanity.[12] Such questions were crucial for legitimating colonial and missionary policy across the Spanish Indies.

The key theoretical framework within which jurists and clerics considered human variety in the global Spanish empire, and its implications for the colonial project, derived from Aristotle's definitions of civility and barbarism and his theory of natural slavery as articulated in his *Nicomachean Ethics* and his *Politics*.[13] Some scholars drawing on Aristotle considered barbarians to be enslaveable by their very nature; so, identifying a people as barbaric was justification for enslaving them or converting them by force. Spanish debates began to revolve around one question: did the Amerindians exhibit the characteristics of natural slaves as defined by Aristotle?[14]

Between 1513 and 1550, a string of disputations and university debates took place; royal and papal judgements attempted to limit the ill treatment of the Amerindians.[15] By the 1530s, questions were raised by missionaries, administrators and critics of Spanish imperial ambitions about the legality of their actions in the Americas. The Dominican theologian and humanist Francisco de Vitoria's lecture on the subject explored three issues: whether the Spaniards had the right to subject the Indians to their rule; the Spanish monarchy's power over the Indians; and the power of the monarchy and the Church over the Indians in spiritual matters.

In 1537, Pope Paul III issued the bull *Sublimis Deus* which declared that the Indians were not only men, but were both capable of and anxious to receive the true faith.[16] Charles V eventually suspended all conquests in America while a committee attempted to establish just methods for ruling

11 Pagden, *Fall*, 31.

12 See, e.g., Seed, '"Are These Not also Men?"'; Lewis Hanke, *The Spanish Struggle for Justice in the Conquest of America*, with new introduction by Susan Scafidi et al. (Dallas, TX: Southern Methodist University Press, 2002).

13 Lewis Hanke, *Aristotle and the American Indians: A Study in Race Prejudice in the Modern World* (Chicago, IL: H. Regnery, 1959); Pagden, *Fall*, 39, 47–50; G. L. Huxley, 'Aristotle, Las Casas and the American Indians', *Proceedings of the Royal Irish Academy*, 80 (1980), 57–68.

14 Huxley, 'Aristotle', 62–7; Pagden, *Fall*, 38–56; Hanke, *Aristotle*, 44–7, 53–5.

15 Huxley, 'Aristotle', 59–60.

16 Lewis Hanke, 'Pope Paul III and the American Indian', *The Harvard Theological Review*, 30 (1937), 65–102, at 72.

the colonies.[17] This meeting famously took place at Valladolid in 1550–1, in the form of a debate between the Dominican friar Bartolomé de las Casas and Charles V's chaplain, the jurist and chronicler Juan Ginés de Sepúlveda.[18]

The extent to which these arguments about civility, barbarism and natural slavery filtered down to the literate, but not always learned, milieu of mapmakers, travellers and readers is best determined through the study of printed vernacular texts. None of Sepúlveda's writings on the subject were published in the vernacular in this period.[19] Las Casas's shorter writings were widely disseminated in print and translated into various languages.[20] Up to 1624, his published works comprised nine tracts, eight of which, written in Spanish, were first printed in Seville in 1552–3.[21] The tracts often appeared together in subsequent editions and translations into French, Dutch, English and German.[22] They detail: the ill-treatment of the Amerindians; reasons why they should be freed, never again to be enslaved by the Spaniards in any way; instructions to the clergy to deny the sacraments to those who enslaved Amerindians; arguments for upholding these orders; and a summary of the statements made by Las Casas and Sepúlveda at Valladolid. By means of these tracts, readers across Europe became familiar with the main features of the theological–juridical debates concerning the nature of the Amerindians and their far-reaching political implications. Interpreted across Europe against a background of confessional conflict, they were influential in the formation of European ideas about the Amerindians' place in nature.

17 Hanke, *Aristotle*, 13.

18 For an overview, see Adorno, *Polemics of Possession*, chap. 3; Ángel Losada, 'The Controversy between Sepúlveda and Las Casas in the Junta of Valladolid', in *BLCH*, 279–307.

19 See Ángel Losada, 'Juan Ginés Sepúlveda: estudio bibliográfico', *Revista bibliográfica y documental*, 8 (1947), 315–93, at 323–57.

20 For publications to 1624, see Lewis Hanke and Manuel Giménez Fernández, *Bartolomé de las Casas, 1474–1566: bibliografía crítica* (Santiago de Chile: Fondo Histórico y Bibliográfico José Toribio Medina, 1954), *s.v.*; José Toribio Medina, *Biblioteca Hispano-Americana*, 7 vols. (Amsterdam: N. Israel, 1962), I and II, *s.v.*; *CCB*, nos 87–96; *BA*, III, nos 11227–93 and X, nos 39114–22; Thomas W. Field, *An Essay towards an Indian Bibliography* (New York, NY: Scribner, Armstrong & Co., 1873), 860–92.

21 See V. Afanasiev, 'The Literary Heritage of Bartolomé de Las Casas', in *BLCH*, 539–78, at 548–55; for critical editions, see Bartolomé de Las Casas, *Tratados de 1552 impresos por Las Casas en Sevilla*, ed. Ramón Hernández and Lorenzo Galmés, . . . *Obras completas*, 14 vols. (Madrid, 1988–99), X; for facsimiles of the tracts with facing-page transcriptions, see Bartolomé de Las Casas, *Tratados de 1552 impresos por Las Casas en Sevilla*, prologues by Lewis Hanke and Manuel Giménez Fernández;. See Field, *Indian Bibliography*, n. 870; *CCB*, 202, 213–15, no. 95: the ninth tract, written in Latin, was printed at Frankfurt and Tübingen, but never in Spain.

22 *CCB*, 198.

Many were used as propaganda in countries that were at war with Spain: England, France and the Low Countries.[23]

Las Casas's most widely published work was his *Brevíssima relación*, a catalogue of Spanish misdeeds organized by region in the order in which they were perpetrated.[24] Up to 1626 there were two editions in Spanish, together with one Italian, two English, two Latin, three German, five French and eleven Dutch translations.[25] These debates formed a context within which Dutch mapmakers interpreted New World peoples. The first illustrated edition was printed in Latin by the De Brys in 1598.[26]

Spanish approaches to new world religion – what the Christians called idolatry – were part of an older programme of viewing religious differences as evidence of physiological qualities and of the external forces that shaped them. The intellect was understood was a mental faculty that did not have access to the external world directly, but rather through the mediations of the bodily senses whose perceptions formed mental images called phantasms in the faculty of imagination. These phantasms were in turn interpreted by the intellect, which would draw also on other faculties such as memory to do so. The imagination, shaped by a person's inner condition, thus functioned differently in all individuals and varied with their health, emotional state and other conditions. In European scholarly investigations of the peoples of the Americas, the imagination's misapprehensions of sensory information were thought to explain religious and other cultural differences. Spanish and Hispanized clerics in the New World commonly considered the practice of idolatry to signal the work of the devil on a feeble mind.[27] As Sabine MacCormack has suggested, 'Christian European cognitive vocabulary was thus imperceptibly reformulated to explain not cognition but cultural hierarchy under the guise of cognition'.[28]

23 See, e.g., Schmidt, *Innocence Abroad*, 97–9; Afanasiev, 'Literary Heritage', 555–69; Benjamin Keen, 'Introduction: Approaches to Las Casas, 1535–1970', in *BLCH*, 3–63, at 7–11.

24 Bartolomé de Las Casas, *Brevissima relacion de la destruycion de las Indias* (Seville, 1552).

25 See Hanke and Giménez Fernández, *Bartolomé de las Casas*, 152.

26 Bartolomé de Las Casas, *Narratio regionum indicarum per Hispanos quosdam devastatarum verissima* (Frankfurt am Main, 1598). For the illustrations, see Tom Conley, 'De Bry's Las Casas', in *Amerindian Images and the Legacy of Columbus*, ed. René Jara and Nicholas Spadaccini (Minneapolis, MN and London: University of Minnesota Press, 1992), 103–31, at 107–26. For Dutch editions of the work, see also Chapter 5, near n. 102.

27 See, e.g., Kenneth Mills, *Idolatry and Its Enemies: Colonial Andean Religion and Extirpation, 1640–1750* (Princeton, NJ: Princeton University Press, 1997), chap. 7.

28 For a detailed treatment the Aristotelian traditions of the external and internal senses and of the ways in which they shaped interpretations of religious and cultural difference, see Sabine MacCormack, *Religion in the Andes: Vision and Imagination in Early Colonial Peru* (Princeton, NJ: Princeton University Press, 1991), chap. 1.

Not only did the body affect thoughts, but the converse was also true. Idolatry was believed to affect the blood and be passed on to one's descendents.[29] The Spanish Inquisition, set up to root out secret practitioners of Judaism and Islam, considered Jews, Muslims and those who converted from these religions to Christianity to lack 'purity of blood' (*limpieza de sangre*). In this case, not even conversion could wipe away the deformation, which would pass down through an individual's lineage. As Rebecca Earle put it, 'confessional identity was in part a physical condition', one that could be affected by the transmission of all manner of bodily fluids, and even by eating the wrong foods.[30] The concept of race (*raza*), first applied to horses to indicate pure blooded, desirable stock, was inverted in its usage in people to come to mean a pollutant or a deformation. The institutionally and legally driven persecution of New Christians that followed such arguments helped to legitimize the lineage of the nascent Spanish state.[31] Descriptions and illustrations of New World idolatry in the early accounts of New Spain and Peru were thus also potentially evidence of incorrigible idolatry.

Colonial administrators and clerics were concerned about the impact of climate on indigenous, creole and settler bodies. In the mid-sixteenth century, Las Casas prepared an extensive treatise, the *Apologetica historia*, on the healthful qualities of the Indies and its peoples. The treatise was underpinned by the assumptions that climate shaped bodies and consequently cultures, and that a body's physical characteristics were clues to the nature of its soul.[32] In the late sixteenth century, the cosmographers Alonso de Santa Cruz and Juan de Ovando devised sets of instructions and questionnaires for local officials in the Indies to complete and return. Some of the questions concerned the nature of the soil, the healthfulness of

[29] David Nirenberg, 'Race and the Middle Ages: The Case of Spain and Its Jews', in *Rereading the Black Legend: The Discourses of Religious and Racial Difference in the Renaissance Empires*, ed. Margaret T. Greer et al. (Chicago, IL and London: University of Chicago Press, 2007), 71–87.

[30] Earle, *Body of the Conquistador*, 205–13. For colonial anxieties about the transformative power of indigenous foodstuffs on creole religiosity, see Marcy Norton, *Sacred Gifts, Profane Pleasures: A History of Tobacco and Chocolate in the Atlantic World* (Ithaca, NY and London: Cornell University Press, 2008), chap. 6.

[31] Nirenberg, 'Race in the Middle Ages', 78–9; Kathryn Burns, 'Unfixing Race', in *Rereading the Black Legend: The Discourses of Religious and Racial Difference in the Renaissance Empires*, ed. Margaret T. Greer et al. (Chicago, IL and London: University of Chicago Press, 2007), 188–202, at 188–189.

[32] José Rabasa, 'Utopian Ethnology in Las Casas's *Apologética*', in *1492–1992: Re/Discovering Colonial Writing*, ed. Nicholas Spadaccini and René Jara (Minneapolis, MN: University of Minnesota Press, 1989), 263–89, at 265, 271. The work remained unpublished until the nineteenth century.

the location, and the relative health of the inhabitants.[33] On the questionnaire of 1577 devised by Juan de Ovando, the third of fifty questions inquired into 'the nature and quality' of the province, 'whether it is very cold, or hot, or humid, or dry', the quantity of water, and the strength, season and direction of the winds.[34]

By the mid-seventeenth century, the creole elites were sufficiently concerned about the negative associations being drawn in Europe between New World climates and stars and weak, lazy bodies and minds that they began drawing up arguments about the superiority of creole minds – Spanish bodies raised in New World environments – over both indigenous and peninsular Spanish intellects.[35] Arguments about how behaviour could affect bodies and their lineage further muddied the separation between nature and nurture. *Indio* and Spaniard were not impermeable categories: creoles of European parentage but born and raised in the Americas occupied a liminal, monstrous space that threatened to dissolve the difference between European and Amerindian. The Atlantic world prompted new versions of debates about essential human difference: travel and colonial settlement muddied the theoretical separation that textual traditions made between groups of different ancestry or environment.

Reading New World cities on maps

Readers from across Europe might well have thought about the inhabitants in the light of numerous writings on the importance of cities for the propagation of civil behaviour. Aristotelian views on the benefit of cities, outlined in Chapter 1 of this book, appeared in a range of texts. Particularly influential for later readers was the massive treatise by the French jurist, humanist and courtier Jean Bodin, *Six livres de la république* (1576). For Bodin as for many other authors, a city's most defining attribute was its inhabitants. Bodin asserted that 'it can be that the town may be well built

33 See Pardo-Tomás, 'Explanations of Native Mortality' for a discussion of these documents.

34 Juan López de Velasco, *Instrucción y memoria de las relaciones que se han de hacer para la descripción de las Indias, que Su Majestad manda hacer para el buen gobierno y ennoblecimiento de ellas* (1577): 'el temperamento y calidad de la dicha provincia, o comarca, si es muy fija, o caliente, o humeda, o seca'. Reprinted in *Relaciones geográficas del siglo XVI*, ed. René Acuña, 10 vols. (Mexico City: Universidad Nacional Autónoma de México, 1982–8), I, 73-8.

35 For numerous examples of creole, peninsular Spanish and European pronouncements on the impact of various elements of terrestrial and celestial phenomena on human minds and bodies, see Cañizares-Esguerra, 'Patriotic Astrology'.

and walled, and is also well populated, and nevertheless it is no city unless it has laws and magistrates to establish there a proper system of government'.[36] Bodin, writing against the backdrop of the French Wars of Religion, drew on but also diverged creatively from Aristotle to make arguments about the proper forms of government in various climatic regions. In his *Methodus* (1566), he expanded Aristotle's definition of a citizen beyond the inhabitants of cities to mean the inhabitants of a state; a citizen was thus 'one who enjoys the common liberty and the protection of authority'.[37]

Other authors emphasized the relationship between cities and optimum living conditions. The English clergyman and historian Peter Heylyn asserted that 'the magnificence of a citie' required three elements: 'a nauigable riuer or easie passage by the sea' for the facilitation of trade by 'all kinds of merchants, as now at Venice, Amsterdam, London, Constantinople'; a palace for a 'prince', for in the place where the court resides 'there wil continually be store of yong nobles to buy, and tradesmen to sell vsuall commodities'; and residences of the 'nobility' which 'raiseth cities with stately and beautifull buildings'.[38]

The absence of cities could explain why certain peoples languished in a state of barbarousness. In his treatise *Delle cause della grandezza e magnificenza delle città*, the former Jesuit Giovanni Botero portrayed the inhabitants of the New World as inhabiting a civic state beyond which Europeans had largely progressed. Botero recounted how people in Europe had first been scattered throughout the land, living 'a life little different from that of animals'.[39] A few people who possessed 'wisdom' ('la saviezza') and 'eloquence' (l'eloquenza') then declared 'to the rude masses' that living in one place as a group would be more profitable.[40]

[36] Jean Bodin, *Les Six Livres de la republique [1576]*, ed. Christiane Frémont et al., 6 vols. (Paris: Fayard, 1986), I, 119: 'il se peut faire que la ville sera bien bastie et muree. Et qui plus est remplie de peuple, et neantmoins ce n'est point cité, s'il n'y a loix, et magistrats pour y establir un droit gouvernement'. The translation is my own. For similar contemporary definitions of cities, see Richard L. Kagan and Fernando Marías, *Urban Images of the Hispanic World, 1493–1793* (New Haven, CT and London: Yale University Press, 2000), 10–11.

[37] Bodin, *Methods*, chap. VI, 158.

[38] Peter Heylyn, *Microcosmus, or A Little Description of the Great World* (Oxford, 1621), 6.

[39] Giovanni Botero, *Della ragion di stato libri dieci, con tre libri delle cause della grandezza, e magnificenza delle città* (Venice, 1589), 296: 'una vita poco differente dalle bestie'. My translations have derived elements from Giovanni Botero, *A Treatise, Concerning the Causes of the Magnificencie and Greatnes of Cities* ... (London, 1606), 2–3.

[40] Botero, *Della ragion di stato*, 296: 'alla roza moltitudine'; idem, *Magnificencie of Cities*, 2: 'the rude and barbarous multitude'.

Over time, these groups became villages, towns and finally cities. Botero compared this shift to what was currently taking place in Brazil:

> A similar thing is today continually practised in Brazil. These people live dispersed here and there and in caves or in huts made of branches and palm leaves rather than houses. And because of this manner of living in such a dispersed way, it happens that these people remain in their wildness of spirit and their rudeness of customs, and causes great difficulty to the preaching of the Gospel and to the conversion of the infidels and to their instruction by those who are converting them little by little, and to civil government. The Portuguese and the Fathers of the Society of Jesus have used the utmost diligence in bringing them together into certain suitable places, where living civilly, they are more easily instructed in the Faith by those Fathers, and governed by the officials of the king.[41]

Botero believed that the Brazilians' forms of habitation limited their potential for civility. By replacing their flimsy and isolated dwellings with permanent settlements, their conquerors were helping them to shed their savage mentality, in much the same way that a few people had once persuaded the inhabitants of Europe to embrace civic life. Botero clearly partook of the moral philosophy of Aristotle's *Ethics* and *Politics*: human perfection could only come through the practice of moral virtues for which the shared social life of the city was essential.

This form of social thinking also drove Spanish colonial policy in the Americas. Not only did Spanish friars attempt to reorganize indigenous Caribbean and Mesoamerican communities along urban lines, but, in the general resettlement instituted by viceroy Francisco de Toledo, the inhabitants of the Andean provinces were resettled in new towns with a uniform square grid, a central plaza and a church.[42]

[41] Botero, *Della ragion di stato*, 296–7: 'Vna simil cosa si practica hoggi continuamente nel Brasil. Habitano quei popoli sparsi quà, e là nelle spelonche, ò in capanne, anzi che case, composte di rami, e di foglie di palme: e perche questa maniera di uiuer cosi sparsamente, fa che quelle genti restino in quella loro saluatichezza d'animi, & asprezza di costumi e porta seco difficoltà grande alla predicatione dell Euangelio, alla conuersione de gl'infedeli, & all'instruttione di quei, che di mano in mano si van conuertendo, & al gouerno ciuile; i Portoghesi, & i Padri della Compagnia di Giesv vsano estrema diligentia in ridurli insieme in certi luoghi più opportuni; doue, viuendo ciuilmente, siano con più ageuolezza addottrinati nella Fede da quei Padri, e gouernati da gl'Vfficiali del Re.'

[42] Jeremy Ravi Mumford, *Vertical Empire: The General Resettlement of Indians in the Colonial Andes* (Durham, NC and London: Duke University Press, 2012).

Mapping cities and civility

New Spain was characterized in the sixteenth-century European imagination by a city, the ultimate cultural product: the Mexica capital of Tenochtitlán, today's Mexico City. Although maps of cities were not directly ethnographic, they contained implied judgements for viewers familiar with Aristotle's *Politics*. Such maps attributed to the regions' peoples a higher level of civility than was the case with map images of Patagonians – represented as giants dressed in animal skins – or of Brazilians – characterized by their predilection for human flesh.

Yet descriptions of idolatry, sacrifice and sodomy – practices that could be read as signs of irrational minds – also circulated in many texts that mapmakers used to derive information about Tenochtitlán.[43] A German pamphlet from 1522 expanded on the gory details in Peter Martyr's and Cortés's accounts of idolatry and human sacrifice. This and other vernacular German versions of these texts used images to associate the Amerindians of New Spain with alleged Jewish and Muslim practices, such as the myth of ritual blood sacrifice.[44] Since, in the 1520s, it was still assumed that the Apostles must have reached the New World, those who did not practice Christianity were those who, like the Jews, may well have heard the word of God but failed to apprehend it.[45]

Admiring accounts of Tenochtitlán and of the Aztec ruler Moctezuma began with the five letters that Hernán Cortés sent to Charles V between 1519 and 1526. In his second letter, Cortés observed that:

> 'in order to give an account ... of the magnificence, the strange and marvelous things of this great city of Temixtitan [Tenochtitlán] and of the dominion and wealth of this Mutezuma, its ruler, and of the rites and customs of the people, and of the order there is in the government of the capital as well as in the other cities of Mutezuma's dominions, I would need much time and many expert narrators. I cannot describe one hundredth part of all the things which could be mentioned...[46]

Cortés's version of his exploits also circulated in the histories of the humanist Peter Martyr and the chronicler and cleric Francisco López de

[43] For a discussion of these themes, see Johnson, *Cultural Hierarchy*, 33–6.

[44] This pamphlet is discussed in ibid., 41–8. [45] Ibid., 54.

[46] Hernán Cortés, *Letters*, *Letters from Mexico*, translated, edited, and with a new introduction by Anthony Pagden, with an introductory essay by J. H. Elliott (New Haven, CT: Yale Nota Bene / Yale University Press, 2001 [1986 revised ed.]), second letter, 101.

Gómara.[47] These in turn shaped reflections on European and New World civilizations in the writings of, for example, Michel de Montaigne.[48]

The 1524 Nuremberg edition of Cortés's second letter to Charles V contained the first European map of Tenochtitlán (Fig. 7.1). This anonymous woodcut combined elements from Cortés's accounts with European conventions for representing a city.[49] The caption draws the viewer to 'the famous city of Temixtitan [Tenochtitlán] and its diverse wonders', one of 'the many excellent cities of their provinces', some of which are depicted on the edge of the lake.

The centre of the map is a counternarrative from this attractive picture of civility, but one which legitimates Christian conquest and, in the context of cities, offers a good prognosis for the future of these subjects under Charles V. The temple quarter dominates the map: much exaggerated in size and placed at the centre of the woodcut, it draws the eye of the viewer and speaks for this place and its activities as the keys with which to remember and identify Mexico. The sacrificial temple, the heads of the victims and stone idols are labelled. At the centre is an idol, at whose feet rest the heads of sacrificial victims.[50] The fisheye perspective typically used to magnify the highlights that lie at the centre of a city have the effect, in this case, of emphasizing the city's monstrosities while placing its urban achievements at the periphery.[51]

Despite this plethora of idolatrous material, on subsequent printed maps from multiple centres of production, mapmakers tended to exclude idolatrous motifs while continuing to portray Tenochtitlán as Mexico's emblem.[52] The woodcut of Tenochtitlán that appears in the Venetian Benedetto Bordone's *Isolario* (1528) is one of the few maps to retain

[47] Pietro Martire d'Anghiera, *De orbo novo decades*; Francisco López de Gómara, *La historia general de las Indias y Nuevo Mundo* . . . (Saragossa, 1555).

[48] López de Gómara's work influenced subsequent writers, notably Montaigne; see, e.g., Tom Conley, 'Montaigne and the Indies: Cartographies of the New World' in *1492–1992: Re/Discovering Colonial Writing* (Minneapolis, MN: The Prisma Institute, 1989), ed. René Jara and Nicholas Spadaccini, 225–262, at 232–3, 243–50.

[49] Mundy, *Mapping of New Spain*, xii-xiii.

[50] For a discussion of the multiple geometric perspectives employed in this map, see ibid., xiii–xiv and 4–5. For detailed studies, see Barbara E. Mundy, 'Mapping the Aztec Capital: the 1524 Nuremberg Map of Tenochtitlan, its sources and meanings', *Imago Mundi*, 50 (1998), 11–33; Elizabeth Hill Boone, 'This New World Now Revealed: Hernán Cortés and the Presentation of Mexico to Europe', *Word & Image* 27:1 (2011), 31–46.

[51] For the fisheye perspective, see Padrón, *Spacious Word*, 128–9.

[52] The centres of printed map production to exclude idolatry included Antwerp and Amsterdam; surviving manuscript world maps and maps of the Americas from Normandy, Spain and Portugal did the same.

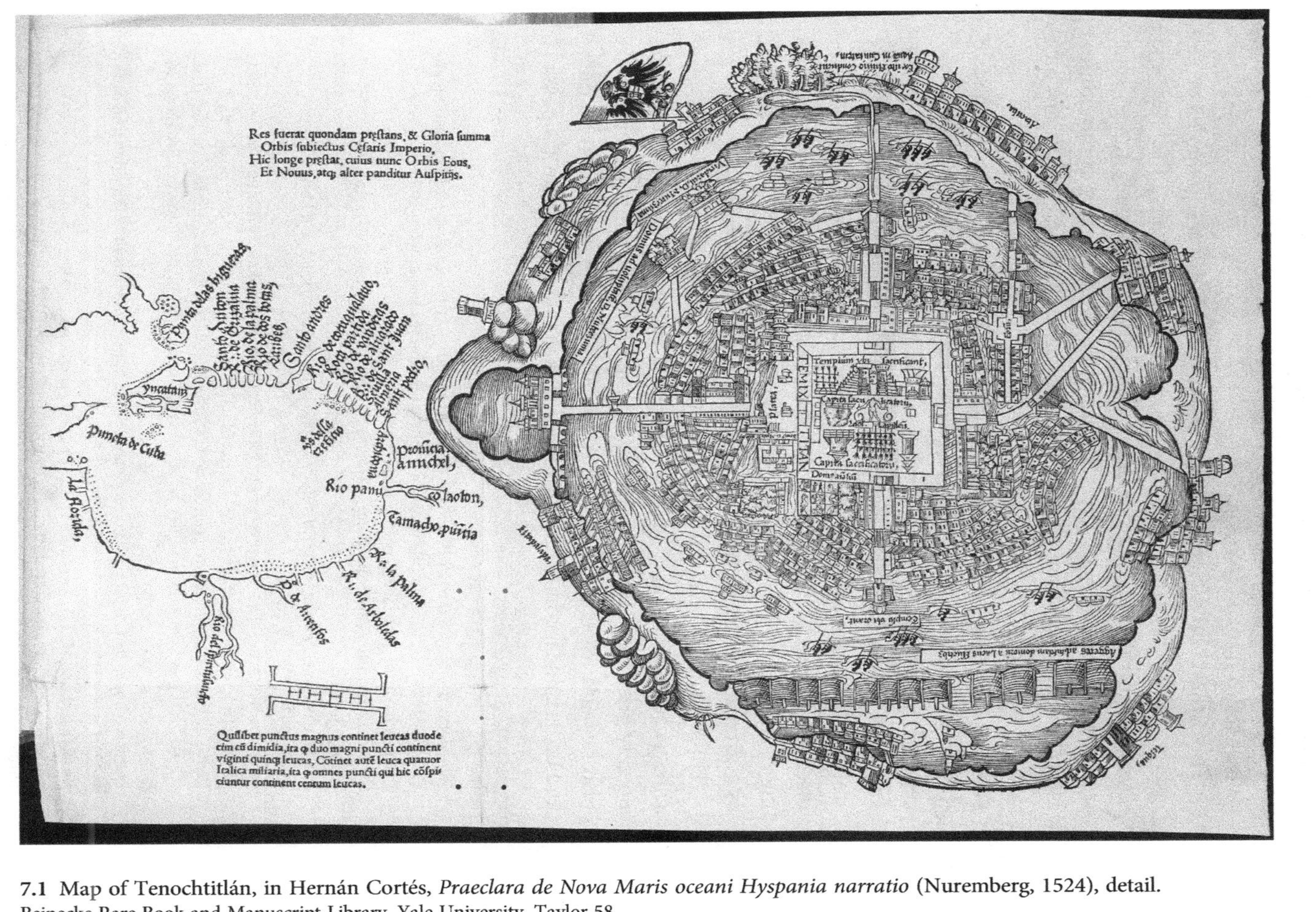

7.1 Map of Tenochtitlán, in Hernán Cortés, *Praeclara de Nova Maris oceani Hyspania narratio* (Nuremberg, 1524), detail. Beinecke Rare Book and Manuscript Library, Yale University, Taylor 58.

idolatrous practices in the Plaza Mayor.[53] By contrast, in Antoine du Pinet's *Plantz, pourtraitz et descriptions de plvsievres villes et forteresses*, a book of descriptions and views of cities and fortresses first printed in 1564, the map of central Tenochtitlán is slightly larger than it is on Cortés's map, and yet the central image has been excised of symbols of and references to human sacrifice.[54]

The earliest chroniclers interpreted Peru, like Mexico, through its urban spaces. Such chronicles outlined Inca power structures, the size and sophistication of the cities, evidence of technology (notably roads, spun clothing and metalwork), and the economic value of their commodities. Narratives of the conquest followed the conquistadors' travels to Inca centres of political and religious power.[55] Although the Spaniards' successes were largely due to the advantages of Old World pathogens and to the invaders' participation in local civil wars, their conquests were perceived by contemporaries as impressive military achievements for Spain and for Christendom. The conquistador and chronicler Cieza de León's story of the conquest, for example, relates how 'thirteen [Christians] ... discovered it with [Pizarro]...., [who] won it with 160 Spaniards, capturing Atahualpa'.[56] The impressive scale and organization of such Inca cities as Cuzco added lustre to the exploits of their conquerors.

Three Spanish travel narratives and two chronicles that dealt exclusively with Peru were printed in the sixteenth century. Subsequent writers, notably Francisco López de Gómara, mined these accounts for numerous histories and travel compendia.[57] While the number of texts, translations and geographical compendia produced means that it is not always possible

[53] Benedetto Bordone, *Libro di Benedetto Bordone nel qual si ragiona de tutte l'isole del mondo* (Venice, 1528), f. 10*r*. The title of some of the later editions began with 'Isolario'. For a discussion of the map, see David Y. Kim, 'Uneasy Reflections: Images of Venice and Tenochtitlán in Benedetto Bordone's "Isolario"', *Res: Anthropology and Aesthetics*, 49/50 (2006), 80–91.

[54] Antoine de Pinet, *Plantz, povrtraitz et descriptions de plvsievrs villes et forteresses* (Lyon, 1564), 297.

[55] See John Hemming, *The Conquest of the Incas* (London: Macmillan, 1970). For Inca society, politics, technology and religion, see Terence N. D'Altroy, *The Incas* (London: Blackwell, 2002).

[56] Pedro de Cieza de León, *Parte primera de la Chrónica del Perú* (Seville, 1553), sig. *iiii*r*: 'trezes [Cristianos] con el mismo marques ... lo descubieron.... con ciento y sesenta Españoles lo gano, prendiendo a Atabalipa'.

[57] Francisco López de Gómara, *La istoria general de las Indias, y conquista de Mexico* (Saragossa, 1552). I refer to this text as *Historia general*, following the spelling of subsequent Spanish editions. *EA*, I, 400–1 and II, 771, *s.v.*: by 1612, the *Historia general* portion had appeared in some 30 editions, issues and translations. For discovery narratives and their authors, see Francisco Esteve Barba, *Historiografía indiana*, 2a ed., rev. y aum. (Madrid: Editorial Gredos, 1992), 441–70.

to identify precisely which works were consulted by a particular mapmaker, we can establish which characterizations in original travel accounts ultimately informed particular map representations, compare the ways in which mapmakers selected and displayed information, and reflect on their likely impact on contemporary viewers.

The earliest two printed accounts of the conquest both appeared in 1534. An anonymous text printed in Spanish and Italian appeared in April; a French translation was printed in 1545.[58] The author was probably Cristóbal de Mena, a captain in Pizarro's fleet. He states that he joined Pizarro's forces in Panama in 1531 and witnessed the first European contact with the Inca empire and the execution of the Inca Atahualpa.[59] Another author, Francisco de Xérez, had accompanied Pizarro as his secretary on all three of his expeditions and produced an official account of the events from 1531–3. This narrative was first printed in Spanish in July 1534; by mid-1535 there were also two Italian editions.[60]

Augustín de Zárate, the Auditor of Accounts to Emperor Charles V, produced the next rendition of the conquest of Peru. Zárate was sent to Peru in 1543; he became embroiled in the ongoing war between Spanish factions and indigenous royal authority over Peru. He returned to Spain in 1545, bringing with him a large quantity of personal notes and official documents relating to the recent conflicts. His history of the conquest of Peru was printed at Antwerp in 1555. During the sixteenth century it went through several Spanish editions and was translated into Italian and English.[61]

Pizarro's secretary and army scrivener Pedro Sancho de Hoz wrote the fourth account of the conquest, one that included a lengthy description of the city of Cuzco. While no Spanish version survives, the text appeared

[58] *L'Histoire de la Terre Neuve du Peru en l'Inde Occidentale* (Paris, 1545). For editions, see Angel Delgado-Gómez, *Spanish Historical Writing about the New World, 1493–1700* (Providence, RI: John Carter Brown Library, 1992), 33; Giovanni Battista Ramusio, *Navigationi et viaggi, Venice 1563–1606*, ed. R. A. Skelton (Amsterdam: Theatrum Orbis Terrarum, 1970), 33; and [Cristóbal de Mena], *The Conquest of Peru as Recorded by a Member of the Pizarro Expedition [1534]*, trans. and annotations by Joseph H. Sinclair (New York, NY: New York Public Library, 1929), 45–7. This is a facsimile of *La conquista del Peru* (Seville, 1534).

[59] Francisco Esteve Barba, *Historiografía indiana*, 451. Note that the term 'Inca' is used to refer to the leaders as well as the empire.

[60] Esteve Barba, *Historiografía indiana*, 453–4; Delgado-Gómez, *Spanish Historical Writing*, 33; Alexander Pogo, 'Early Editions and Translations of Xérez: *Verdadera relacion de la conquista del Peru*', *Papers of the Bibliographic Society of America*, XXX (1936), 57–84, at 58. In ibid., 59–60, Pogo notes that there were two variants of the 1534 Spanish edition. I have used the 1534 II variant.

[61] Delgado-Gómez, *Spanish Historical Writing*; Ramusio, *Navigationi 1563–1606*, 32–3.

in the Venetian geographer and diplomat Giovanni Battista Ramusio's travel compendium, *Navigationi et viaggi*.[62] The most extensive sixteenth-century history was the work of Pedro de Cieza de León who, inspired by the sight of Inca treasures being unloaded in Seville in 1534, had left Spain for South America the following year, while still in his early teens. He participated in a variety of expeditions over the next fifteen years, keeping detailed notes of his experiences.[63] He wrote a four-part *Chronicle of Peru*, of which only the first volume was published in his lifetime, appearing in eleven editions printed at Seville, Antwerp, Rome and Venice between 1553 and 1556.[64] The third volume, covering the discovery and conquest of Peru, circulated throughout Spain in the sixteenth century via manuscript copies.[65] The official historian Antonio de Herrera y Tordesillas drew on Cieza de León's manuscripts for material for his *Historia general de los hechos de los castellanos en las Islas y Tierra Firme del Mar Océano* (Madrid, 1601–15).[66]

A paltry few world maps from the 1530s to 1550s contained ethnographic material on Peru, and this consisted of scenes of battle and siege that defined the region by its interactions with Europe. In the 1550s, a new model, the work of Venetian geographer Giacomo Gastaldi, emerged, and soon became the most influential early modern image of Peru on a map.[67] Gastaldi's city-view of the ancient Inca city of Cuzco inaugurated a tradition in which Peru was emblematized by a city worthy of admiration, thus putting indigenous ingenuity at the forefront of viewers' minds (Fig. 7.2). The Inca were now embedded in a narrative of civil and technological sophistication rather than of military defeat. By implication, these people also had the capacity to apprehend Christianity.

Gastaldi's map was one of several that were commissioned from him by Venetian humanist and geographer Giovanni Battista Ramusio. The maps

[62] Giovanni Battista Ramusio, *Delle navigationi et viaggi*, 3 vols. (Venice, 1550–59). According to Kagan and Marías, *Urban Images*, 68, n. 68, it was previously published as *Libro ultimo del summario delle indie occidentale* (Venice, 1534). For the work's publishing history, see Michael J. Schreffler, 'Inca Architecture from the Andes to the Adriatic: Pedro Sancho's Description of Cuzco', *Renaissance Quarterly*, 67:4 (2014), 1191–1223, at 1194–98.

[63] Cieza de León, *The Discovery and Conquest of Peru*, ed. and trans. Alexandra Parma Cook and Noble David Cook (Durham, NC and London: Duke University Press, 1998), 5–17.

[64] Cieza de León, *Parte primera*; *EA*, I, 370, *s.v.* For Cieza's sympathetic account of the Inca empire, and for the use of his published and unpublished writings by other authors, see MacCormack, *On the Wings of Time*, 39–100.

[65] Cieza de León, *Discovery and Conquest*, ed. Cook, 1.

[66] Ibid., 23.

[67] For Gastaldi, see Denis Cosgrove, 'Mapping New Worlds: Culture and Cartography in Sixteenth-Century Venice', *IM*, 44 (1992) 65–85, at 74–5. For Pero Sancho's description and its translation to cartographic form, see Schreffler, 'Inca Architecture'.

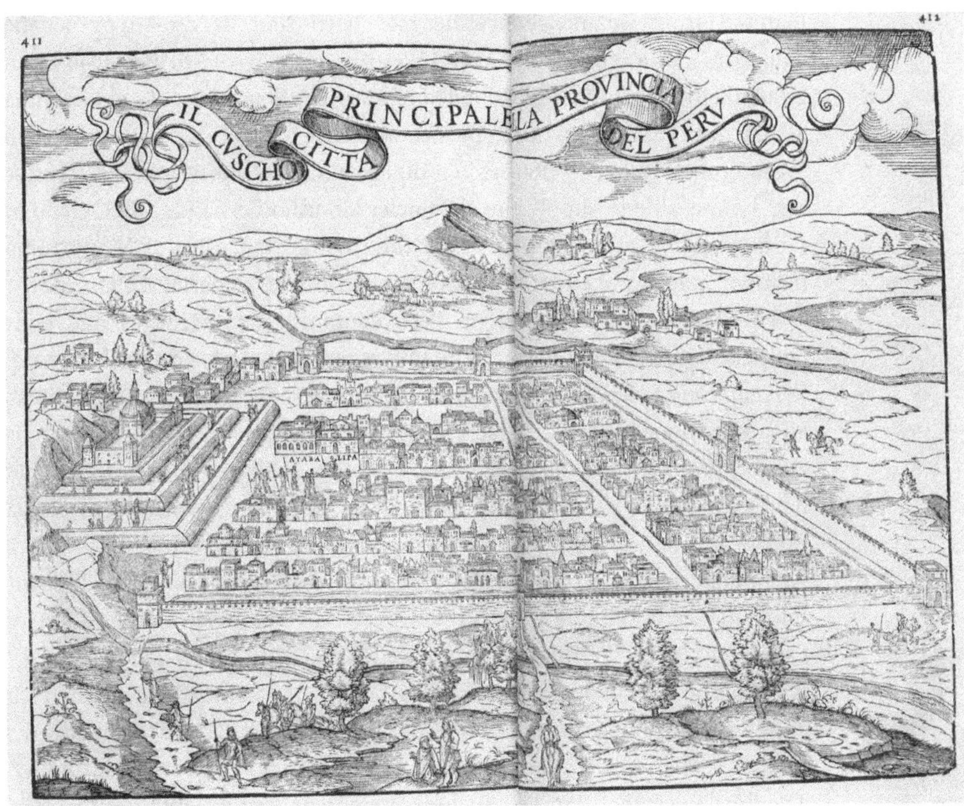

7.2 Giovanni Battista Ramusio, *Terzo volume delle nauigationi et viaggi* (Venice, 1565), 411–2, Giacomo Gastaldi's view of Cuzco.
Beinecke Rare Book and Manuscript Library, Yale University, 2001 +204 3.

appeared in Ramusio's *Navigationi et viaggi*, the first large-scale world travel compendium.[68] The gargantuan compendium, comprising around 1,000 pages in three quarto volumes, dwarfed its predecessors. Ramusio had worked in several positions in Venetian government. During the last fourteen years of his life, which encompassed the years in which the *Navigationi* volumes appeared, he was a secretary to the Council of Ten, the most senior governing body for the republic.[69] Through his official and personal contacts, which included the diplomat Andrea Navagero, he acquired a number of original French and Spanish travel manuscripts as well as printed editions fresh from their presses; Navagero sent him

[68] The third volume of the *Navigationi*, devoted, as noted on its title-page, to 'al Mondo Nuouo'. For an overview of the book and its maps, see Small, 'Displacing Ptolemy', 156–72.

[69] George B. Parks, 'Ramusio's Literary History', *Studies in Philology*, LII:2 (1955), 127–48, at 129.

material from Spain whence he had been sent as an envoy to the emperor.[70] In a letter from May 1526, Navagero wrote to Ramusio from Granada to report that he had failed to send 'the Spanish books about India affairs', but that he would 'collect as much as I can, then send you everything together'.[71] Ramusio's diplomatic contacts were so extensive that he was able to supply the chronicler Gonzalo Fernández de Oviedo in Hispaniola with information about the mythical ancestry of Montezuma from an Aztec source that he had obtained from an imperial ambassador.[72]

The *Navigationi*'s section on Peru contains three accounts and ends with Gastaldi's map of Cuzco. The first account, that of 'a Spanish captain' ('*vn capitano Spagnuolo*'), was one of the earliest accounts of the conquest, an anonymous text that first appeared in Spanish in April 1534.[73] Its author, probably Cristóbal de Mena, a captain in Pizarro's fleet, states that he joined Pizarro's forces in Panama in 1531 and witnessed the first European contact with the Inca empire and the execution of the Inca Atahualpa.[74] Ramusio himself is thought to have translated the work for the Italian edition that was printed in 1534.[75] Ramusio's translation of De Mena's text – the 1534 edition as well as the edition in the *Navigationi* – is a composite version that includes half as much material again from another text, Francisco de Xérez's 'La conquista del Peru, et Provincia del Cusco'.[76] The second account is the complete version of Xérez's account.[77] The third work that Ramusio includes here is an account of the conquest of Peru by Pedro Sancho de Hoz, Pizarro's secretary and army scrivener. Ramusio's is the only known surviving edition of Sancho's account.[78]

Gastaldi's view of Cuzco and, implicitly, of its people compared favourably with those of Europe. The view shows the city laid out with a fortress on the left, towards which armed guards carry Atahualpa – clearly labelled – on a palanquin. Pedro Sancho's account, which included a

70 Ibid., 130.

71 Ibid., 135, translated from Andreae Naugerii, … *Opera omnia minum editio II*, I 'Lettere' (Padua, 1739), 316.

72 Parks, 'Ramusio's Literary History', 142.

73 One earlier text is known: *Newe Zeutung aus Hispanien und Italien* ([Nuremberg?,] February 1534).

74 Francisco Esteve Barba, *Historiografía indiana*, 451.

75 Parks, 'Ramusio's Literary History', 137. *L'Histoire de la Terre Neuve du Peru en l'Inde Occidentale* (Paris, 1545). For editions, see Delgado-Gómez, *Spanish Historical Writing*, 33; Ramusio, *Navigationi et viaggi*, ed. Skelton, 33; and *Conquest of Peru*, ed. Sinclair, which contains a facsimile of *La conquista del Peru* (Seville, 1534).

76 Pogo 'Early Editions and Translations'.

77 Parks, 'Ramusio's Literary History', 137.

78 According to Kagan and Marías, *Urban Images*, 68, n. 68, it was previously published as *Libro ultimo del summario delle indie occidentale* (Venice, 1534).

'description of the city of Cuzco and of its wonderful fortress, and of the customs of its inhabitants', most likely inspired it (Fig. 7.2).[79] It describes the streets laid out at right angles, the largely stone houses, the stone gutter which ran down the middle of each street, and the stepped fortress with a tower at the centre, easily defensible due to its position at the edge of the mountain.[80] All these features are visible on Gastaldi's view.[81] We are told that the city 'is so full of beautiful things, and with so many buildings, that it would be noteworthy even in Spain'.[82] Its fortress equalled European architectural achievements. Moreover, the city was inhabited by the nobility, and there were 'houses and storehouses full of clothes, wool, weapons, metals, textiles and all the things that are grown or are made in the country'.[83] This description implied that these people had several of the features required for a city deemed to be civilized in the Aristotelian sense: wealthy people, an army, industry and agriculture.[84]

The artist of Gastaldi's map also added European elements such as wide streets (rather than the narrow ones described by Sancho), watch towers, Italianate houses, a perimeter wall and fortified gates, and moved the location of the (European-style) fortress to the site of the Inca's palace.[85] The city was not in fact square, but rather puma-shaped, with a grid of streets and a plaza in the centre rather than to one side.[86] Kagan and Marías have argued that the views of Cuzco and that of Tenochtitlán published in the 1520s were 'icons of civilization' that demonstrated that the Inca and Mexica were capable of building cities.[87] Michael J. Schreffler recently suggested that the map's European elements are likely signs of editorial intervention in the aftermath of the death of Sancho.[88]

79 Noted in Sabine MacCormack, 'Limits of Understanding: Perceptions of Greco-Roman and Amerindian Paganism in Early Modern Europe', in *America in European Consciousness, 1493–1750*, ed. Karen Ordahl Kupperman (Chapel Hill, NC and London: University of North Carolina Press, 1995), 79–129, at 80. Ramusio, *Navigationi*, III, 413*r*: 'Descrittione della città del Cusco, & della sua mirabil [sic] fortezza, & de costumi de suoi popoli'; Sancho, *Peru*, 153. Noted and discussed in Kagan and Marías, *Urban Images*, 68–9.

80 Ramusio, *Navigationi*, III, 413*r*.

81 Kagan and Marías, *Urban Images*, 69. For passages from Sancho's text that are reflected by the map, see also Schreffler, 'Inca Architecture', 1210.

82 Ramusio, *Navigationi*, III, 413*r*: 'è si grande & cosi bella, & con tanti edificii, che saria stata degna da veder in Spagna'; Sancho, *Peru*, 153. For this and further quotations, see Kagan and Marías, *Urban Images*, 69.

83 Ramusio, *Navigationi*, III 413: 'case ò fondachi piene di robbe, lane, armi, metalli & panni, & di tutte le cose che nascono, & si fanno nel paese'; Sancho, *Peru*, 158.

84 See Chapter 1, near n. 16.

85 MacCormack, *Limits*, 80; Kagan and Marías, *Urban Images*, 69.

86 Small, 'Displacing Ptolemy', 169.

87 Kagan and Marías, *Urban Images*, 69–70.

88 Schreffler, 'Inca Architecture', 1199–1200.

The creative synthesis of details from a travel account and elements of European civic architecture on the view of Cuzco suggests that Sancho's description had also succeeded in making Gastaldi, and perhaps Ramusio, see it as a thoroughly civilized city.

The map is not, however, a simple composite of one contemporary travel text and European symbols of civility. The human figures on the map indicate that the artist, or perhaps Gastaldi himself, examined a number of contemporary sources on Peru. Ramusio himself is the most likely source of these texts. The robed figures in the map's centre foreground may have been based on illustrations in Cieza de León's account.[89] The image of Atahualpa on a litter (Fig. 7.3), in the centre of the map, was inspired by the vignette that appears on the title-pages of Xérez's (Fig. 7.4) and Cristóbal de Mena's narratives.[90] This scene shows the first meeting of the emperor Atahualpa and Pizarro at Cajamarca. Xérez related how a friar preached to Atahualpa and gave him a Bible; Atahualpa threw the book to the ground, an action which precipitated the Spanish attack and Atahualpa's imprisonment. Despite the schematic character of the title-page woodcut, it contains subtle messages. The book in Atahualpa's hand stands out, as does the greater physical size of the Spaniards; both prefigure the ways in which the fateful meeting at Cajamarca would play out. Its appearance on both the title-page and the final page of the original edition of Cristóbal de Mena's account suggests that this moment was seen by that work's author, editor or printer as the most significant one of the encounter.[91] Gastaldi evidently consulted of a variety of sources on Peru – the very ones that Ramusio was editing.

The vignette of Atahualpa's litter is the only illustration from the three accounts of Peru in the *Navigationi* that was adapted for Gastaldi's map. Atahualpa's imminent response and Pizarro's subsequent order to his troops to attack would set in motion a chain of events which, in the eyes of some contemporaries, destroyed Atahualpa's world. Michel de Montaigne would end his essay 'De Coches' with a description of this incident, and the De Bry firm, as we shall see, devised an engraving of it.[92] Gastaldi's

[89] Cieza de León, *Primera parte*, ff. 46*r* and 107*v*.

[90] As noted at n. 51 above, Ramusio printed translations from both of these texts. The same illustration appeared on the title-pages to both the original editions.

[91] *Conquest of Peru*, ed. Sinclair, 32–3 and sig. A.iiii*v*.

[92] Lestringant, *Huguenot et le sauvage*, 383–4. For Montaigne's critique of the Spanish conquest through deception, see 'Des Coches' in Michel de Montaigne, *Brésil de Montaigne: Le Nouveau Monde des 'Essais' (1580–1592)*, introduction and notes, Frank Lestringant (Paris: Chandeigne, 2005), 146–50. For De Bry, see below.

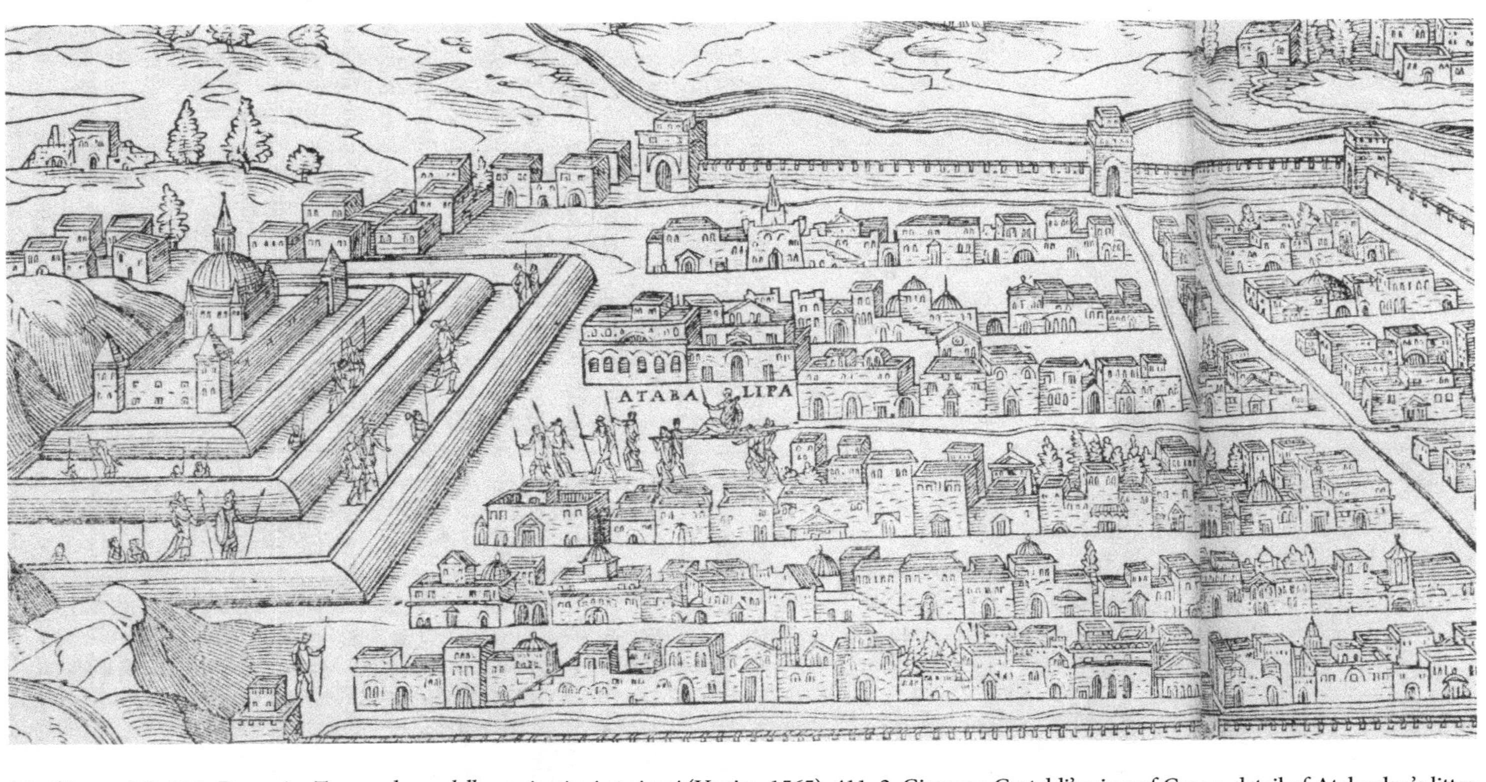

7.3 Giovanni Battista Ramusio, *Terzo volume delle nauigationi et viaggi* (Venice, 1565), 411–2, Giacomo Gastaldi's view of Cuzco, detail of Atahualpa's litter. Beinecke Rare Book and Manuscript Library, Yale University, 2001 +204 3.

7.4 Francisco de Xérez, *Verdadera relación de la conquista del Peru* . . . (Seville, 1534), title-page, detail.
Courtesy of the John Carter Brown Library at Brown University, B534 X61 /1-SIZE.

view of Cuzco also depicts a scene before another meeting, in the foreground. European figures on horseback and wearing helmets approach the city's walls; Atahualpa has yet to have the opportunity to handle – much less drop – a Bible.

Yet it was not inevitable that Gastaldi or his successors would choose to emblematize Peru with a city. Idolatry and human sacrifice had also been discussed by Zárate and by Francisco López de Gómara.[93] Cieza de León's account contained two woodcuts depicting these practices, which appeared several times in his *Primera parte*. One showed people consorting with a devil; the other, an idol on a pedestal and two sacrificial victims who had been hanged.[94] While an image from Cieza seems to have been the source for one of the figures in the foreground of Gastaldi's map, diabolical woodcuts from the same text have no place in it. In these early decades of the European Reformation, by avoiding imagery that would bring to the minds of viewers on both sides of the confessional divide the Eucharist and

[93] López de Gómara, *Historia general*, ff. lxviiv-lxviiir. Material on Inca beliefs and idolatry in Zárate, *Descubrimiento del Peru*, ff. 18*v*–22*r* (caps 10–12) was removed from the second Spanish edition (Seville, 1572); see Rubiés, 'New Worlds and Renaissance Ethnology', 191, n. 35.

[94] See, e.g., Cieza de León, *Primera parte*, ff. XVII*r* and XXII*r*, respectively. The former woodcut also appeared in Zárate, *Descubrimiento del Peru*, 19*v*.

the veneration of images, maps such as this argued implicitly for the evaluation of distant cultures via secular rather than religious criteria.

Mapmakers who copied the Gastaldi-Ramusio view of Cuzco for use in other works often changed the foreground scene. Antoine du Pinet copied the original very closely, adding only a French title outside the map border. Pinet's description of the city is flecked with admiring comparisons that translate the original Spanish text's sentiments, noting, for example, that Cuzco is so well situated and built that France should be proud to have its equal.[95]

In Georg Braun and Franz Hogenberg's six-part compendium on the world's cities known as *Civitates orbis terrarum* and published between 1572 and 1617, the tradition of emblematizing cities by their inhabitants achieved a gargantuan physical form.[96] The *Civitates*, printed in Latin, French and German editions, brought together cities from around the world on 363 plates depicting 543 town illustrations.[97] Each city or town received a half-page or more of descriptive text, a map, and images of its inhabitants in local costume. The map of Mexico (Fig. 7.5) shows a small being resembling a human-animal hybrid at the centre, but the text on the reverse page gives the reader no indication that this was the central sacrificial altar of the city – or, indeed, that human sacrifice or idolatry occurred here.

The map of Cuzco faces that of Mexico, facilitating comparison (Fig. 7.5). Viewers may have been struck by the differences in the overall structure of the cities: Mexico's symmetry was radial, the city lay on a lake; Cuzco's symmetry was along its horizontal and, to an extent, vertical axes. On the map of Cuzco, the mapmaker has replaced the figures in the foreground of Gastaldi's map with a palanquin. It is perhaps the litter that had faced the temple in Gastaldi's view, although the person on the litter is unnamed here. The accompanying text follows Sancho's description of Cuzco in Ramusio and summarizes the city's advantages:

> Cuzco is the metropolis and the principal city of this [region]; it is of a size, strength and magnificence that – with its impenetrable arched fortress, and multitude of thronging people, and the order and arrangement of the buildings, and the pleasant location – it can justly compete with even the most beautiful cities of France or Spain. . . .[98]

95 Pinet, *Plantz*, 294.

96 See Kagan and Marías, *Urban Images*, 95. Franz Braun and Georg Hogenberg, *Civitates orbis terrarum*, 3 vols. (Cologne, 1572–1617), I, plate 58.

97 Van der Krogt, *Koeman's Atlantes Neerlandici*, IV-I, 35.

98 Braun and Hogenberg, *Civitates*, I, f. 59*r*: 'Huius Metropolis, et praecipua est civitas Cuzco, ea amplitudine, fortitudine, et magnificentia, ut cum pulcherrimis etiam, vel Galliae, vel Hispaniae

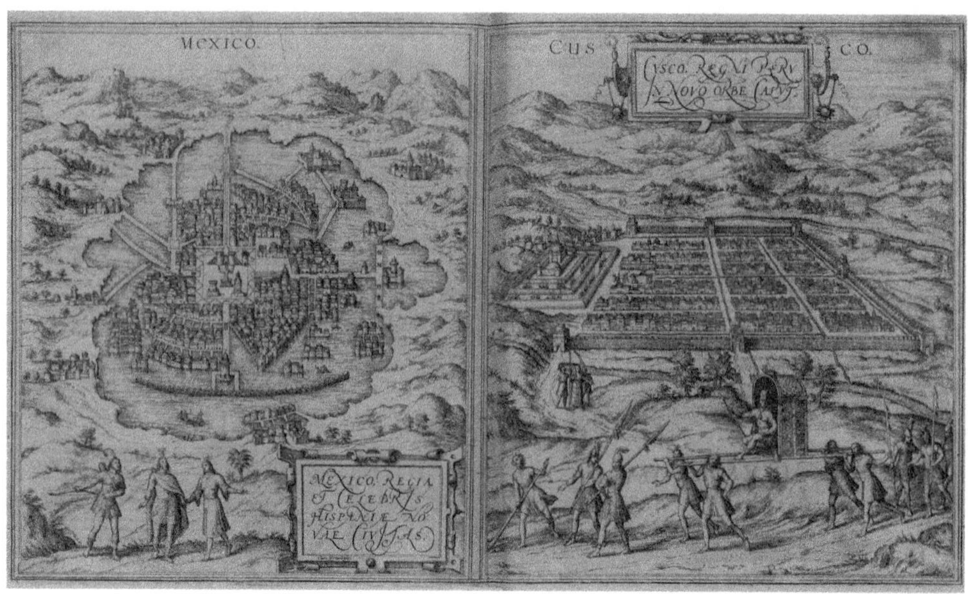

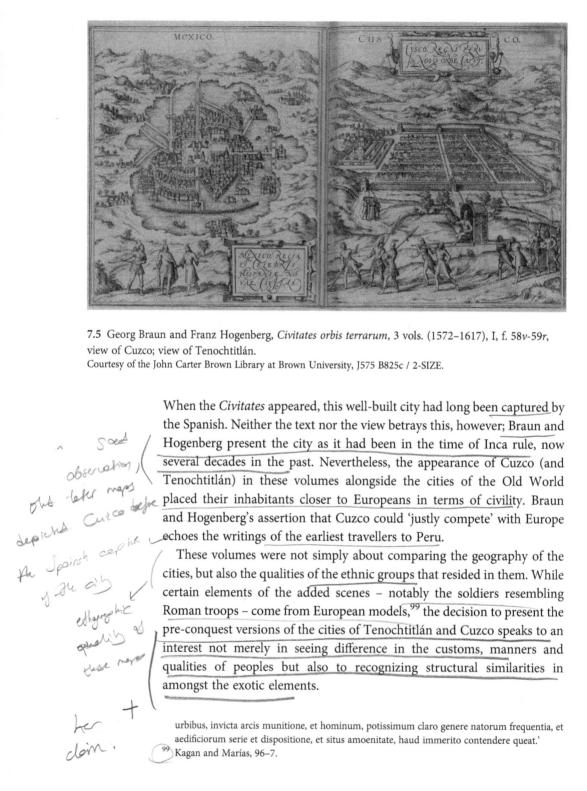

7.5 Georg Braun and Franz Hogenberg, *Civitates orbis terrarum*, 3 vols. (1572–1617), I, f. 58*v*-59*r*, view of Cuzco; view of Tenochtitlán.
Courtesy of the John Carter Brown Library at Brown University, J575 B825c / 2-SIZE.

When the *Civitates* appeared, this well-built city had long been captured by the Spanish. Neither the text nor the view betrays this, however; Braun and Hogenberg present the city as it had been in the time of Inca rule, now several decades in the past. Nevertheless, the appearance of Cuzco (and Tenochtitlán) in these volumes alongside the cities of the Old World placed their inhabitants closer to Europeans in terms of civility. Braun and Hogenberg's assertion that Cuzco could 'justly compete' with Europe echoes the writings of the earliest travellers to Peru.

These volumes were not simply about comparing the geography of the cities, but also the qualities of the ethnic groups that resided in them. While certain elements of the added scenes – notably the soldiers resembling Roman troops – come from European models,[99] the decision to present the pre-conquest versions of the cities of Tenochtitlán and Cuzco speaks to an interest not merely in seeing difference in the customs, manners and qualities of peoples but also to recognizing structural similarities in amongst the exotic elements.

urbibus, invicta arcis munitione, et hominum, potissimum claro genere natorum frequentia, et aedificiorum serie et dispositione, et situs amoenitate, haud immerito contendere queat.'

99 Kagan and Marías, 96–7.

In 1596, Theodor de Bry published a map of Cuzco in his *Americae pars VI*, a compendium of early accounts of Peru. As in the case of the previous volumes in this series, the firm commissioned high-quality engravings to illustrate the chronicles. In the German edition of 1597, twenty-eight numbered, half-page engravings appear at the end of the volume, each with a detailed caption. The majority of the engravings illustrate events and contexts from the encounters between the Inca and the Spanish: moments of communication and gesturing, audiences between the Inca Atahualpa and Francisco Pizarro, Inca subjects carrying gold objects to a storage room in order to pay the ransom for Atahualpa, and Atahualpa's eventual garrotting.

The volume's title page focuses not on this history of Inca-Spanish encounter, but on motifs of indigenous kingship, organization and technical industry (Fig. 7.6). At the centre is a vignette of the Inca Atahualpa carried on a litter preceded by musicians and followed by archers. The scene is reminiscent of descriptions of the meeting between Pizarro's forces and Atahualpa at the Inca city of Cajamarca, but may also have drawn on woodcuts of exotic processions, such as those produced by Hans Burgkmair and Wolf Traut.[100] In the background are vignettes of silver mining, a key activity that took place at Potosí and elsewhere. Despite the acknowledgement in the title to the Spaniards' conquest of Peru and capture of Atahualpa, the imagery offers a synoptic view of pre-conquest Peru that quietly effaces Spanish colonialism.

The city view of Cuzco, clearly derived from Gastaldi's view or from one of its derivatives, is similarly concerned with indigenous culture and industry before the arrival of the Spaniards (Fig. 7.7). The map's title announces that it depicts 'Cuzco, the most noble and opulent city situated in the western part of the kingdom of Peru, in which that great king Atahualpa lived, in whose time the Spanish appropriated that kingdom for themselves with their troops.'[101] In the right foreground are three figures carrying effigies of gods or devils[102]; the one on the far right is a

[100] See Chapter 4.

[101] 'Cusco urbs nobilissima et opulentissima Peruani regni in occidentali parte sita, in qua habitabat magnus ille Rex Atabaliba quo tempore Hispani regnum illud armis sibi vindicarunt', in *Americae Pars VI*, after 108. The location of the map varies in different copies; this and the rest of the plates follow the text pages.

[102] On Amerindian idolatry, see Fernando Cervantes, *The Devil in the New World: The Impact of Diabolism in New Spain* (New Haven, CT and London: Yale University Press, 1994). His discussion of De Bry's contribution is brief (pp. 6–7) and does not include either this map or other prints showing Indians with idols which appear in his editions.

7.6 Girolamo Benzoni and Nicolas Challeux, *Americae pars sexta, sive historiae ab Hieronymo Benzono Mediolanense scriptae, sectio tertia . . .*, ed. Theodor de Bry (Frankfurt am Main, 1596), title-page.
Beinecke Rare Book and Manuscript Library, Yale University, E159 +B79 6–9.

large bird. These were derived from figures in an engraving in the volume, which depicts barely clad men engaged in fashioning metal urns and idols from the gold and silver being melted down by their fellow workers

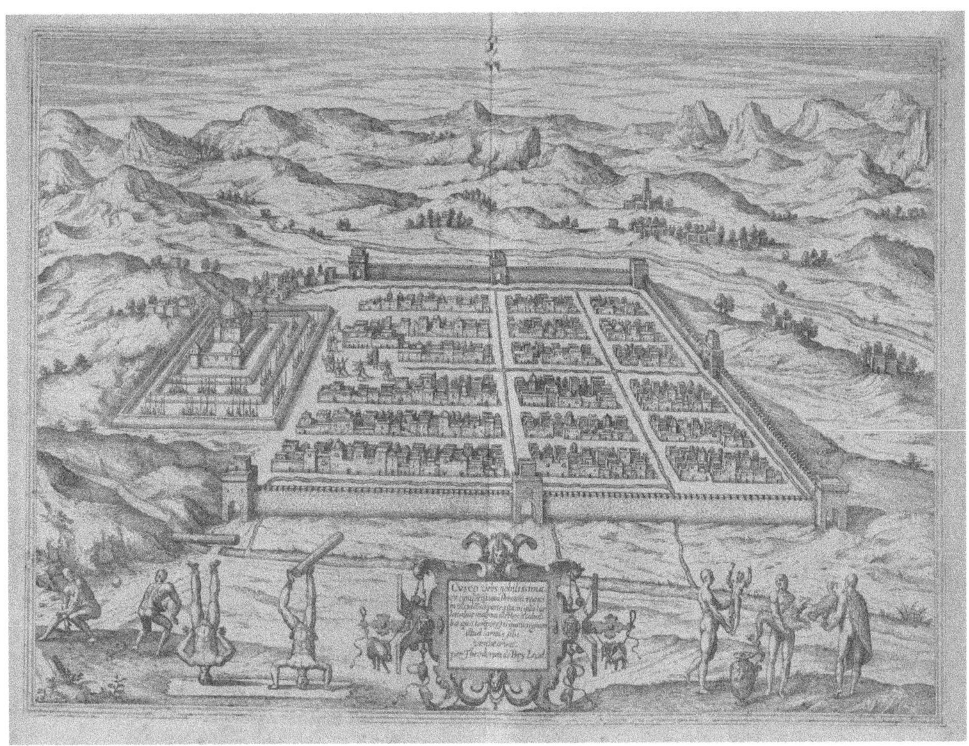

7.7 Girolamo Benzoni and Nicolas Challeux, *Americae pars sexta, sive historiae ab Hieronymo Benzono Mediolanense scriptae, sectio tertia . . .*, ed. Theodor de Bry (Frankfurt am Main, 1596), view of Cuzco.
Beinecke Rare Book and Manuscript Library, Yale University, 192 4–6.

(Fig. 7.8).[103] In the foreground of the latter, we see the human figurine from the map being made; the large, decorated ewer rests on a bench by the window of the workshop. The ewer's resemblance to a Greek amphora imbues the Inca with an element of classical civility that is somewhat at odds with the generally minimal attire and feather cape worn by the figures on the map and in the illustration.

The idols being worked here could have been read as signs of ingenuity. When worked goods from Mexico and Peru escaped the desecration of being melted down and reached Europe intact, their viewers met them with curiosity and wonder. Cortés sent Aztec treasure to the Holy Roman Emperor Charles V, and many artefacts were displayed around Europe with the itinerant royal court in, for example, Valladolid and Brussels. On a

[103] De Bry, *Americae Pars VI*, sig. G.ivr.

7.8 Girolamo Benzoni and Nicolas Challeux, *Americae pars sexta, sive historiae ab Hieronymo Benzono Mediolanense scriptae, sectio tertia . . .*, ed. Theodor de Bry (Frankfurt am Main, 1596), detail of metal-working, sig. G.4.*r*.
Courtesy of the Library of Congress, G159 .B7 pt. 6 F1442.

visit to Antwerp in 1520–1, Albrecht Dürer famously saw materials from Mexico on display in Brussels. These included:

> all sorts of wonderful things for different kinds of use, which is much nicer to see than objects of mere wonder (*wunderling*). These things were all too precious, for one valued them around one hundred thousand florins. And I have not seen anything in my whole life which pleased my heart as much. Because I saw in them wonderful artificial things (*wunderlich künstlich ding*) and have been amazed by the subtle ingenuity of the people in foreign lands.[104]

For Dürer, the Mexicans possessed the capacity to shape nature's bounty to their own purposes. Descriptions, inventories and admiring assessments of

[104] Quoted from Rublack, *Dressing Up*, 184.

Mexica treasure penned by humanists, chroniclers, ambassadors and others also circulated in print.[105]

Despite the contemporary confessional resonances of idolatry, the motif made only a brief appearance in the mapping of Peru. Michiel van Groesen has shown that the De Bry engravings consistently over-emphasized extra-European nudity and idolatry when compared to their source texts.[106] While De Bry's map of Cuzco illustrates both practices, neither it nor the rest of the plates in this volume contain highly graphic, savage elements.[107] Far more unpleasant images appeared in, for example, De Bry's source texts.

The two pairs of juggling figures to the left on the De Bry map of Cuzco derive from drawings by the artist Christoph Weiditz (1500–1559). Weiditz saw these games in 1529, when he visited the court of Charles V where Hernán Cortés was presenting inhabitants and treasures from Mexico.[108] Weiditz evidently felt admiration at many aspects of Mexica life that he saw at Charles V's court: the ingenuity of the performers who threw logs in the air; intricate feather dresses and jewellery; the artisanal skills required to make a wooden drinking jug; and their physical strength.[109] The figures circulated from 1555 as part of a set of 154 watercolours Weiditz made of the people he saw on his journey.[110]

Printed travel accounts had documented such games among the Mexica and Maya, but not the Inca or their subject peoples.[111] Pedro Sancho's text – the ultimate textual source for the city-view – had described neither

[105] Alessandra Russo, 'Cortés's Objects and the Idea of New Spain: Inventories as Spatial Narratives', *Journal of the History of Collections*, 23 (2011), 229–52, at 7.

[106] Van Groesen, *Representations*, 195–9, 233–42. A similar point is made in relation to this map in Kagan and Marías, *Urban Images*, 98.

[107] A small vignette on Blaeu's 1608 map of America includes De Bry's figures.

[108] Jean Michel Massing, 'Early European Images of America: The Ethnographic Approach', in *Circa 1492*, 515–20, nn. 45, 48. Theodor Hampe, *Das Trachtenbuch des Christoph Weiditz* (Berlin, 1927), 69: The court was travelling through Spain at the time, and Weiditz is believed to have followed it from Castile to Barcelona in 1529.

[109] Rublack, *Dressing Up*, 189.

[110] Daniel Defert, 'Un genre ethnographique profane au XVIe: les livres d'habits (essai d'ethno-iconographie)', in *Histoires de l'anthropologie: XVI-XIX siècles*, ed. Britta Rupp-Eisenreich (Paris: Klincksieck, 1984), 25–41, annexe, n. 13. The collection, which was arranged, cropped and mounted by a later owner, is known as Weiditz's *Trachtenbuch* or costume book (Nuremberg, Germanisches Nationalmuseum, Hs 22.494). Reproduced and described in Hampe, *Trachtenbuch*; for facsimile, see Christoph Weiditz, *Authentic Everyday Dress of the Renaissance: All 154 Plates from the 'Trachtenbuch'* (Mineola, NY: Dover, 1994). For discussion and bibliography, see Jean Michel Massing, 'Aztecs Playing Tlachtli', in *Circa 1492*, 572; Rublack, *Dressing Up*, 187–193.

[111] Kagan and Marías, *Urban Images*, 97.

pastimes nor pagan idolatry. De Bry may have been particularly keen to include indigenous activities on this map. By replacing the royal litter in the foreground with games and metalworkers, the engraver of the De Bry view introduced elements of exoticism and paganism to Gastaldi's predominantly civilized view of the Inca while remaining on the interpretative fence as to whether these peoples really were idolaters.[112]

Civility, environment and the problem of latitude

By the turn of the seventeenth century, Dutch mapmakers conceived of the inhabitants of different parts of the Americas in comparative perspective. Even though European conquest and colonialism had devastated and transformed indigenous societies, these maps continued to reflect the historic ethnicities of the earliest travel accounts to the region. The Amsterdam map publishers Cornelis Claesz and Clement de Jonghe printed several editions of a map of the Atlantic that placed of the inhabitants of Peru at the top of a hierarchy of civility. A large vignette of Atahualpa's procession appears on the four-sheet map of the Atlantic published by Clement de Jonghe in 1665 (Fig. 7.9).[113] The map was probably from the third edition of one listed in Cornelis Claesz's 1609 sale catalogue as a map of the region from the West Indies to Angola.[114] The vignette, closely resembling one of the De Bry engravings (Fig. 7.10),[115] shows Atahualpa on his litter. The scale of the illustration, whereby it is the largest scene in the Americas by some margin, shows off the size of Atahualpa's army; the grandeur of Cajamarca is visible

[112] While numerous maps printed at Antwerp and Amsterdam included small views of Cuzco, none that I have found includes the foreground figures on the left of the De Bry map. See, e.g., the following world maps and their derivatives: Ortelius 1564, Blaeu 1605 and 1607, De Jonghe's 1665 Atlantic map (no foreground figures); Plancius's map of southern South America (c. 1592–4) and De Jode's America map in his *Speculum orbis terrarum* (1578) show a horseman and a few European troops in the foreground; Hondius's world map of 1608 has a small view of Cuzco which includes the palanquin from the Braun and Hogenberg version (Fig. 7.5); Blaeu's 1608 America map includes the figures in the right-hand foreground on the De Bry map (Fig. 7.7).

[113] Clement de Jonghe, *Hydrographica planeque nova Indiae occidentalis, Guineae, regni Congo, Angolae, &c. delineatio* (Amsterdam, c.1665).

[114] De Jonghe's map reflects the contents of the earlier map, which no longer survives. *MCN*, VII, 302–5: Claesz's apprentice Michiel Colijn (1584–1637), who would later become a publisher and bookseller in his own right, is thought to have bought the map plates from an auction of the effects of Claesz's shop in 1610. The map's title shows that Colijn printed it in 1622. De Jonghe used these plates to produce his own map of 1665, which is therefore considered to be the third state of Claesz's map, and the only one for which a copy remains today.

[115] *Americae pars VI*, sig. G.iv.*r*. Noted in *MCN*, VII, 307.

7.9 Clement de Jonghe, *Hydrographica planeque nova Indiae occidentalis* . . . (Amsterdam, c.1665 [re-issue of map by Cornelis Claesz]), detail from northern South America. Bibliothèque nationale de France, Département des Cartes et plans, Ge DD 2987 [9637]; gallicalabs.bnf.fr, IFN-55005163.

in the background. A scene of cannibalism appears in Brazil, a stark contrast to the civility of Peru.

On this map, the key differences between Amerindian peoples were articulated in broadly Aristotelian terms: foodstuffs, religion, clothing and trade. The text panel asserts that 'the people there [in America] know nothing of wine, nor of wheat'.[116] Their levels of civility varied, but were generally low:

> there are those who are *Caribes*, that is, eaters of people; some worship the devil; others, the sun and the moon; others are totally devoid of religion, with no knowledge of good and bad. Gold, silver and pearls are of little value there, but they make much of some plumage of birds, which constitutes the greatest portion of their wealth.[117]

[116] 'les gens n'y cognoissoyent point le vin, ny le bled'.

[117] 'Il y en a qui sont *Caribes*, c'est-à-dire, mangeurs d'hommes: les uns adorent le diable, les autres le soleil & la lune, les autres sont du tout sans religion, sans connoissance du bien & du mal. or, argent, & perles y sont en petit estime; mais ils font grand cas de quelques plumes d'oiseaux, constituans en icelles la plus grande part de leurs richesses.'

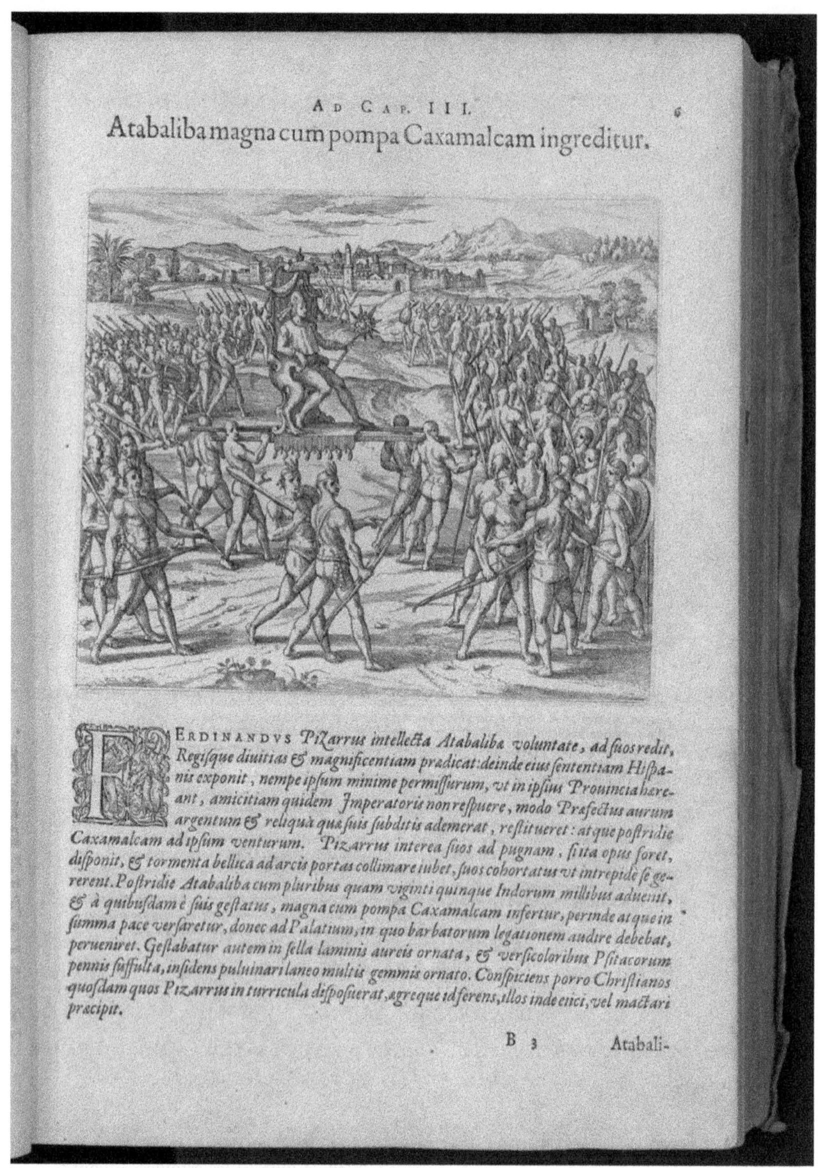

AD CAP. III.

Atabaliba magna cum pompa Caxamalcam ingreditur.

FERDINANDVS Pizarrus intellecta Atabaliba voluntate, ad suos redit, Regisque diuitias & magnificentiam prædicat: deinde eius sententiam Hispanis exponit, nempe ipsum minime permissurum, vt in ipsius Prouincia hæreant, amicitiam quidem Imperatoris non respuere, modo Præfectus aurum argentum & reliqua quæ suis subditis ademerat, restitueret: atque postridie Caxamalcam ad ipsum venturum. Pizarrus interea suos ad pugnam, si ita opus foret, disponit, & tormenta bellica ad arcis portas collimare iubet, suos cohortatus vt intrepide se gererent. Postridie Atabaliba cum pluribus quam viginti quinque Indorum millibus aduenit, & à quibusdam è suis gestatus, magna cum pompa Caxamalcam infertur, perinde atque in summa pace versaretur, donec ad Palatium, in quo barbatorum legationem audire debebat, perueniret. Gestabatur autem in sella laminis aureis ornata, & versicoloribus Psitacorum pennis suffulta, insidens puluinari laneo multis gemmis ornato. Conspiciens porro Christianos quosdam quos Pizarrus in turricula disposuerat, ægreque id ferens, illos inde eiici, vel mactari præcipit.

B 3 Atabali-

7.10 Girolamo Benzoni and Nicolas Challeux, *Americae pars sexta, sive historiae ab Hieronymo Benzono Mediolanense scriptae, sectio tertia* . . ., ed. Theodor de Bry (Frankfurt am Main, 1596*)*, detail of procession of Atahualpa, sig. B.3.*r*.
Courtesy of the Library of Congress, G159 .B7 pt. 6 F1442.

Renaissance missionaries, theologians and jurists frequently considered such differences in agriculture and religious habits as indications of varying but low levels of civility.[118]

The Claesz/Jonghe map presents the people of Virginia as more civilized than those of Brazil:

> The inhabitants are of medium height, good by nature, detesting injustice; they take particular pleasure from dances, [and] do not eat human flesh at all. They think there are many gods, but that there was only one before time began, who made the others in order to serve him in the creation of the world. They worship the sun, the moon and the stars, and go totally naked, except that they cover their private parts.[119]

The Virginia Algonquians' method of worship and sense of justice made them less reprehensible than the Caribs. Even more civilized, however, were the people of Peru, 'the noblest part of the New World'. De Jonghe relates that 'Cuzco, the flower of towns, [had] a great number of inhabitants'.[120] Mexico is also described in positive terms: 'it is considered the best in the New World.... The kingdom is so powerful that it could field 300,000 warriors.'[121] Moreover:

> Before the arrival of the Spanish, there were usually many merchants of diverse nations, who each had their place of trade, such that every day one saw there five markets well stocked with everything; furthermore, there were as many trades and types of merchandise as there were markets, so that law and order was enforced, which Xenophon said to be necessary for good government of the Republic.[122]

118 See, e.g., Botero, *Le relationi universali*, Introduction, near n. 14.

119 'Les habitans sont de moyenne hauteur, bons de leur naturel, haissans l'iniustice, & prenant plaisir singulierement aux dances, sans manger aucunement la chair des hommes. Ils tiennent qu'il y a plusieurs dieux: mais qu'il n'y en a qu'un devant tout temps, lequel a faict les autres pour s'en servir à la creation du monde: reuerent le soleil, la lune, & les estoilles; & vont tous nuds, hors mis qu'ils se couvrent les parties secrettes.' For the circulation in Europe of information about the inhabitants of Virginia, see Chapter 8, near n. 33.

120 'Peru qui est la plus noble partie du Nouveau Monde'; 'Cusco la fleur des villes a un grand nombre d'habitans'.

121 'La Province Mexicane ... est tenue pour la meilleure qui soit au Nouveau Monde. Ce Royaume a esté si puissant, qu'on en pouvoit tirer 300000. hommes de guerre.'

122 'Devant la venue des Espagnols il y avoit ordinairement plusieurs marchands de diverses Nations; lesquelles avoyent chasquune son lieu de trafique, en sorte qu'on y voyoit journellement cinq marchés bien garnis de toutes choses; qui plus est autant de mestiers & marchandises, autant de marchés y avoit il: de maniere qu'on y tenoit la Police & l'ordre, que disoit Xenophon estre necessaire au bon gouvernement de la Republique.'

For Claesz, the first printer of the caption (and presumably for De Jonghe and others who reprinted the map), the Inca, Mexica and Virginians were at least partly civilized within the Aristotelian framework.

Despite the abundance of evidence for the potential for Christianity and civility in the Inca empire, humoral theory had the potential to throw spokes in the wheels of attempts to conclude that the inhabitants of Peru were or could even become civil. While the urban wonders of Cuzco were widely praised, one of the counter-narratives against the purported civility of Peru was that the Equator passed through it, and that it was, therefore, in the torrid zone. This type of spatial thinking, ultimately derived from classical humoral theory and its vernacular iterations, was facilitated by the Ptolemaic gridding of world maps.

Moreover, spatial thinking did not merely occur in and through genres that contained maps, but also through textual, narrative geographies. As Margaret Small, Ricardo Padrón and others have argued, there were leading Renaissance geographers who preferred to deploy the narrative geographical mode to the cartographic one.[123] While updating the content of a map was a costly business, a new edition of a geographical compendium could simply have new pages inserted amongst the old. Nonetheless, narrative textual geographies were gridded with words which positioned latitudes, longitudes and other locational markers from mountains to rivers in relation to one another in order to create diagrammatic maps in the minds of viewers' minds. At times, this attention to the significance of location led to disjunctions between the ways in which the inhabitants of Mexico and Peru were emblematized in textual and cartographic geographies.

The *Description d'Amerique* (1622) by Petrus Bertius, a Flemish cartographer and sometime professor of philosophy and mathematics, contains just such disjunctions.[124] Analysing how Bertius distinguished between the inhabitants of Mexico and of Peru illuminates how some scholars continued to draw connections between latitude, environment and human behaviour in the early decades of the seventeenth century. Bertius, raised by a Reformed minister who had had to flee to England with his family, later developed Catholic sympathies. This led to the loss of his positions

[123] See, e.g., Margaret Small, 'Displacing Ptolemy? The Textual Geographies of Ramusio's *Navigazione e viaggi*', in *Mapping Medieval Geographies: Geographical Encounters in the Latin West and Beyond, 300–1600*, ed. Keith D. Lilley (Cambridge: Cambridge University Press, 2013), 152–72; Padrón, *Spacious Word.*

[124] Petrus Bertius, *Description d'Amerique, qui est le nouveau monde, tirée des 'Tableaux geographiques'* . . . (Amsterdam, 1622); also published in *Americae Pars XII.*

both as subregent of the theological college at Leiden and as professor at the university there, between 1615 and 1618. In 1620 he moved to Paris to become royal cosmographer to Louis XIII. He became a Catholic that year and was excommunicated by the Reformed church in 1621.[125]

The *Description* comprised a twenty-four page summary of the climate, landscape, people, flora and fauna of each part of America. It was one of several texts appended to a French translation of the Spanish official historian Antonio de Herrera y Tordesillas's *Descripcion de las Indias Occidentales*.[126] Bertius did not consider all Amerindians to be equally barbarous. The structure of the *Description* – with between one half and three pages devoted to each region, and similar information provided for each – invites the reader to make comparisons, even though Bertius does not himself do so. The descriptions of America's peoples demonstrate a general adherence to Aristotelian humoral thinking about human difference.

The *Description d'Amerique* was a work of textual geography, and one that was certainly known to mapmakers. The publisher of the work, Michiel Colijn, also printed maps, including at least one depicting Amerindian peoples, discussed in the previous section. Bertius had formerly used this text within an atlas, *Tabularum geographicarum libri septem*, published by Jodocus Hondius the Elder.[127] Bertius had worked closely with several mapmakers (Hondius, Cornelis Claesz and Pieter van den Keere)[128] whose works were copiously illustrated with Amerindian figures.

Bertius describes Mexicans in positive terms. In addition to Tenochtitlán, there were 'fifty towns each of 10,000 houses, in the service of which there are always 50,000 canoes for coming and going'.[129] In the *Libri*

[125] L. J. M. Bosch, *Petrus Bertius 1565–1629* (Meppel: [s.n.], 1979), 290–1.

[126] Antonio de Herrera y Tordesillas, *Description des Indes Occidentales* . . . (Amsterdam, 1622). First published as *Historia general de los hechos de los Castellanos* . . . (Madrid, 1601). The other additions to the 1622 volume were: Jacques le Maire's *Iournal & memoir de la navigation australe*; *Receuil et abbregé de tous les voyages, qui ont esté faicts devers le Destroit de Magallanes*; and *Particuliere description de l'Inde Occidentale*, extracted from Pedro Ordóñez de Ceballo's *Imagen del mundo* (Madrid, 1614). A preface to the additions states that they were intended to fill the gaps in Herrera's texts concerning the area around the Straits of Magellan.

[127] Petrus Bertius, *Tabularum geographicarum contractarum libri septem* . . . (Amsterdam, 1616); published by Jodocus Hondius the Younger. Each map was accompanied by several text pages; the atlas covered the whole world. For later editions and Bertius's other works, see Rodney W. Shirley, *Maps and Atlases in the British Library: A Descriptive Catalogue c. AD 850–1800*, 2 vols. (London: The British Library, 2004), I, T.Bert-1a to T.Bert-3a.

[128] Philip D. Burden, *The Mapping of North America: A List of Printed Maps*, 2 vols. (Rickmansworth: Raleigh Publications, 1996–2007), nos 183–6; Bosch, *Bertius*, 63–4.

[129] Bertius, *Description*, 240: '50 villes chascune environ de 10000 maisons; au service desquelles y a tousiours 50000 canoas pour aller & venir'.

septem, the text follows a map of Tenochtitlán based on the widely disseminated map by Cortés. Its houses, bridges and towers illustrate urban advantages.[130] We learn that: 'The inhabitants were once idolaters and eaters of men, and took many wives in marriage; but since they were baptized, these villanies gradually ceased to be popular.'[131] Not only did the Mexicans have urban spaces – superior environments for the practice of good living – but they were capable of moral improvement. Bertius's position differs from that of Montaigne, for whom the Amerindians' 'civility' did not require Christianity or European values.

One might assume that Bertius would believe that civil people inhabited Peru as well, particularly since he considered the region to be 'the noblest part of the New World'.[132] His assessment of Peru's inhabitants is, however, highly unflattering:

> They are simple and stupid by nature, held back by the past. They show this principally in trade, in which they exchange the most precious commodities of the world for worthless trifles, without awareness of the great gold and silver treasures which nature has lavished on them; for they only use them as unworked lumps, except that they take pleasure in gold and silver images and emblems, with which they decorate their temples and royal houses.[133]

Bertius focuses on the distinctly un-European ways in which the Incas used, valued and traded commodities. Such comments about commercial naivety were more common in writing about Brazilians.[134] Travel narratives about Peru had generally emphasized what the Incas had rather than what they lacked. Bertius's particular selections, however, allowed him to conclude that the Peruvians were simple and dim.

Bertius might equally have concentrated on the presence of cities[135] or on the gradual disappearance of idolatrous practices with the advance of Christianity, as he had with the Mexicans. The reason Bertius provides

[130] Bertius, *Libri septem*, 794, 796. For Cortés's map, see Fig. 5.13.

[131] Bertius, *Description*, 240–1: 'Les habitans estoyen iadis idolatres & mangeurs d'hommes; & prenoyent en mariage plusieurs femmes; mais depuis qu'ils ont receu le baptesme ces vilainies peu à peu cesserent d'avoir vogue'; Bertius, *Libri septem*, 797.

[132] Bertius, *Description*, 243: 'la plus noble partie du Nouveau Monde'.

[133] Ibid., 246: 'il sont de nature simples, stupides, lourdaux à l'antique: ce qu'ils demonstrent principalement en la marchandise, en ce qu'ils changent les plus nobles denrees du monde contre des brouilleries de nulle valeur, sans cognoistre les grands thresors d'or & argent que la nature richement leur a departy: car ils se servent seulement de leurs massues entieres sans les mettre en ouvrage, sinon quils prennent plaisir aux images & emblemes d'or & argent: dequoy ils vont orner les temples, & maisons royales.'

[134] See, e.g., Chapter 4 above.

[135] Mentioned briefly in Bertius, *Description*, 247.

for the different assessment of the Peruvians was Peru's latitude. Immediately after the passage above, we learn that

> Those who are closest to the Equator exceed the others in all vices and viciousness, [are] full of hypocrisy, mumbling between their teeth in the manner of the Jews, [and] are given excessively to luxury.[136]

The magnificence of the city of Quito and its numerous inhabitants is presented here as an exceptional characteristic due to its frigid temperature: 'It is almost right under the Equator, but the air is cold, rather than hot'.[137] Bertius may have been drawing on the writings of the Italian humanist Girolamo Cardano who argued that the height of a region above sea level determined its climate; Quito is at high elevation.[138] Bertius perceived a link between climate and human characteristics as Le Roy had done. This analysis was underpinned by a cartographical grammar in which the precise location of a people provided information about their capabilities and temperaments.

The people portrayed by Bertius as least civil were the Brazilians, another equatorial people who were 'cruels, sauvages, & barbares'.[139] They lacked many indicators of civility: religion, wine and villages, 'eating the flour made from a root in place of bread'.[140] Their very language betrayed their limitations; repeating an observation made by Thevet, Bertius asserted that 'they never use the three letters, F, L, R in speaking since they are totally without faith (foi), law (loi) and king (roi)'.[141] As if that were not enough, 'they are ungrateful beyond measure, bold and reckless, libidinous, vindicative, bloodthirsty and, in short, resemble brutal animals more than human beings'.[142] Curiously, the Brazilians are not said to be eaters of human flesh, a charge which Bertius levels at the inhabitants of 'the region of giants or Patagons', who are 'for the most

[136] Ibid., 246: 'Ceux qui approchent de plus pres la ligne equinoctiale surpassent les autres en tous vices & meschancetés, remplis d'hypocrisie, murmurants entre les dens à la façon des Iuifs, adonnés terriblement à luxure'.

[137] Ibid., 248: 'Elle gist quasi droictement desoubs la ligne equinoctiale, toutesfois la complexion de l'air y est plus tost froide, que chaude.'

[138] For Cardano, see Anthony Grafton, *Cardano's Cosmos: The Worlds and Works of a Renaissance Astrologer* (Cambridge, MA and London: Harvard University Press, 1999).

[139] Bertius, *Description*, 252.

[140] Ibid., 'mangeans au lieu de pain la farine d'une racine'.

[141] Ibid., 253: 'Iamais il n'usent en parlant de ces trois lettres F. L. R. comme estans du tout sans Foy, sans Loy, sans Roy.'

[142] Ibid., 'ils sont ingrats outre mesure, hardis & temeraires, libidineux, vindicatifs, sanguinaires, & pour abbreger plus aux bestes brutes, qu'aux hommes semblables'.

part cruel, barbarous, fierce and eaters of people',[143] and of New Galicia (part of New Spain), who were 'cruel and barbarous people, who are not afraid to eat human flesh'.[144]

Bertius's unusually negative account of Peru shows how individual peoples could be seen to have achieved very different levels of civility by different writers using a broadly Aristotelian framework. For Bertius, the key difference between the Peruvians and the Mexicans might ultimately have been their differing levels of convertibility to Christianity. And yet, representations of the six Amerindian groups most frequently illustrated on maps rarely contain indications that these people were pagan and sometimes idolaters. Nevertheless, we should remain alert to the fact that map viewers were likely to have been familiar with ethnological views derived from Christianity as well as from classical notions of civility and barbarism.

The mental gymnastics performed by Petrus Bertius and other northern geographers happened within a broader European debate about the proper way to treat the inhabitants of the Indies. In colonial Spanish America, creole literati were making claims for the relative sanguinity of New World climates while they also stressed their descent from Spaniards, rather than Indians.

Conclusion

Map imagery for Mexico and Peru gave little sense of these debates over blood and bodies. If anything, such imagery suggested that impressive intellects lay behind these cities. The presence of cities in Mexico and Peru did not simply suggest that the regions' inhabitants were intellectually proficient. That proficiency was the result of some combination of innate nature, the cultural setting and the natural environment – the Hippocratic trinity of airs, waters and places and the celestial configurations.

Tenochtitlán and the inhabitants of Mexico appear on world maps and atlases far less frequently than the scenes in Brazil, Patagonia, Peru or Virginia. One reason for this is a matter of scale: the Yucatán peninula was a smaller space on a map than the other regions; many images of Tenochtitlán on world maps are far too small to show much other than the simplest sketch of its insular geography. By representing

[143] Ibid., 254: 'La region des geans ou Patagons'; 'les habitans pour la plus part cruels, barbares, farouches, & mangeurs d'hommes'.

[144] Ibid., 240: 'les gens cruels & barbares, qui ne redoutent pas de manger chair humaine'.

pre-conquest Cuzco as a classically structured city, Giacomo Gastaldi and those who adopted his map effectively argued that there was nothing fundamentally wrong with either the climate or the bodies of the New World. Tracking the afterlife of Gastaldi's map in Pinet's *Pourtraictz*, Braun and Hogenberg's *Civitates orbis terrarum* and De Bry's *America pars VI* reveals that each intervention was an attempt to introduce more ethnographic information into Gastaldi's iconic vision. These maps showed that the inhabitants of Peru had both cities and leaders, two features that, since the time of Aristotle, had been seen by Europeans as key indicators of civility.

Comparing cartographic and narrative representations of the cities of Mexico and Peru across various centres and contexts reveals further that the exigencies of epistemological authority on a gridded map were subtly different from those of a geography that used words to conjure up the Ptolemaic grid and its ethnological implications. These differences led to the inhabitants of Peru being portrayed as significantly less civil in textual descriptions than on maps, something that was not the case for Mexico.

Several narrative geographies that did not contain maps had no compunction about censuring the inhabitants of Peru for their idolatry, alluding to the unhealthy equatorial climate of much of the region. For texts in this genre, descriptive spatial thinking by means of explicit lists of latitude and longitude helped to conjure up maps in their viewers' minds. Having done so, these maps, gridded as they were, led the geographers and their readers to make different ethnological judgements about the inhabitants of Mexico – some way north of the Equator – than they made about the inhabitants of Peru. While the ethnographic authority of a literal map lay in visibly distinctive imagery for peoples of different regions, the artefactual authority of the narrative geography lay in conjuring up the mental geographical map behind the text.

One might expect that, in an era of confessional strife, the representation of pagan peoples would vary on works produced in different centres of production. In fact, on world maps, atlases and maps of the Americas, the converse is generally true. The authority of these works rested on methods of synthesis rather than first-hand experience; their value lay in facilitating comparison. These factors may well have played a part in the widespread adoption of the city motifs for Mexico and Peru. In map printing centres, limiting references to culturally charged topics would also have facilitated wider sales. While Protestant polemic in print vilifying Papist idolatry flowed thick and fast from presses in the Dutch Republic and in parts of Germany, the Swiss Confederation and beyond, the De Bry firm made relatively few anti-Catholic critiques in its travel editions.[145]

The fact that mapmakers across multiple centres of production did not choose to emblematize Mexico or Peru with negative imagery argues against the commonplace that mapmakers chose the goriest elements in travel literature, or invented them wholesale, in order to appeal to their audiences' taste for the sensational images of exotic barbarism. Underlying mapmakers' iconographic decisions was a desire to show human difference across geographical space. Once Brazil was associated with the cannibal, other regions (with other climates) needed, by definition, to be represented differently in order to bolster the mapmakers' claims to authenticity. The region of Peru in particular needed an iconography that was distinct from that of anthropophagy. Thus we see, across the Americas, the selection of iconography to have been partly shaped by which motifs from the relevant travel accounts had not already been used elsewhere. When map illustrators reduced the diverse inhabitants to distinct motifs, they contributed to the emergence of a typology of indigenous peoples. Mapmakers paid careful attention to the travellers' accounts for particular areas for the derivation of their images. By selecting those motifs that had not been used before – that were new in the mapping of the Americas – they could claim for themselves the authority of their eyewitness source. Paradoxically, this meant that the cultural stereotypes, as a whole, contributed a sense of diversity across America's populations.

[145] Van Groesen, *Representations of the Overseas World*, 249.

8 | New sources, new genres and America's place in the world, 1590–1645

In the second half of the sixteenth century, mapmakers faced a proliferation of geographical modes describing the world's peoples. The genre of cosmography, multifarious in nature since antiquity, fissured into descriptive and geographical modes.[1] Other genres were highly illustrated, and offered new iconographic competition for the accolade of ideal synthetic works on human variety. The genre of the illustrated costume book emerged in the 1560s. The compendium of travel literature, arguably a type of descriptive cosmography, appeared in varied forms from Giovanni Battista Ramusio's three-volume *Navigationi* (1550–59) examined in the previous chapter, rich in text but with very few illustrations and maps, to the gargantuan, profusely illustrated twenty-three volumes devoted to *India orientalis* and *India occidentalis* by the De Bry family of printers in Frankfurt from the late sixteenth century. The 1590 publication of John White's watercolours of the Virginia Algonquians by the De Brys has often been viewed by scholars of cultural encounters as a seminal, even originary, iconographic moment in European ethnographic representations of New World peoples.[2]

Art historians, literary scholars and historians of cartography have focused on those Dutch wall maps that drew on De Bry's travel series. The illustrations on these maps set peoples in rectangular, frame-like boxes on map borders from the early seventeenth century, and have also been seen as a new epistemological moment in map illustration.[3] Although my analyses of Dutch wall maps builds on this work, I want to place these and other maps that drew on the De Bry engravings in a longer chronological arc of shifting modes of visual ethnography. As this book has shown, attempts to convey convincingly via map illustrations the essential nature of different peoples were not ushered in by the extensive models that were the De Bry engravings. Rather, the De Bry corpus of images was part of a far longer

[1] See, e.g., Cormack, *Charting and Empire*; Davies, 'America and Amerindians'.

[2] The literature on the De Bry family's *ouevre* is vast. For a thorough study of their *India orientalis* and *India occidentalis* (*America*) series, see Van Groesen, *Representations of the Overseas World.*

[3] See, e.g., Sutton, *Dutch Prints*; Traub, 'Mapping the Global Body'.

tradition that becomes visible when one considers map illustrations as diagrams, as we saw in the case of Jodocus Hondius the Elder's depictions of Guiana's headless folks and Amazons in Chapter 6, for example.

Another touchstone for the study of ethnography and Dutch visual culture is the artist Albert Eckhout's portraiture from seventeenth-century Dutch Brazil. Rebecca Parker Brienen noted that these ethnographic portraits showed 'that as early as the first decades of the seventeenth century, the process of creating visual racial stypes within a framework of established social hierarchies had already been set in motion.'[4] The present book pushes that story back by a century, also connecting it to a longer history from humanity's earliest representations to the present. Furthermore, the notion of naturalistic or lifelike representation, a culturally specific construct that articulates how well an image reproduces the optical experience of viewing the object itself, was not always the goal of representation. More importantly, it was not – and is not – a necessary condition of a convincing diagram, such as one devised to reveal the essential nature of a people rather than as a lifelike portrait of one individual.[5]

By treating a range of ethnographic modes together, this chapter illuminates why Dutch wall maps of the world with decorated borders were not the beginning of attempts at ethnographic verisimilitude on maps, but were rather the culmination of the cartographic genre's claim for ethnographic authority based on an epistemology that was at once artefactual, cartographical and exegetical. By the mid-seventeenth century, the mode of the ethnographically encyclopedic wall map collapsed under its own weight and shifted its focus, at least explicitly, to other types of content and visual subjects. The excessiveness of the maps' size and detail, and the ways in which they struggle to do the work upon which their makers pinned their knowledge claims, brings to mind Johann Huizinga's classic argument that the Renaissance was the final flourish of the mentalities of the Middle Ages.[6] Dutch wall maps with decorated borders rich in depictions of peoples constitute the last gasp of a body of artisanal

[4] Rebecca Parker Brienen, *Visions of Savage Paradise: Albert Eckhout, Court Painter in Colonial Dutch Brazil: Albert Eckcourt, Court Painter in Colonial Dutch Brazil, 1637–1644* (Amsterdam, 2006).

[5] For an account of how epistemological priorities, and the scientific images that practitioners make to serve them, vary over time, see Lorraine Daston, 'Epistemic Images', in *Vision and its Instruments: Art, Science, and Technology in Early Modern Europe*, ed. Alina Payne (University Park, PA: Pennsylvania State University Press), 13–35.

[6] Johan Huizinga, *The Waning of the Middle Ages* (New York, NY: Doubleday, 1954 [Dutch 1st ed.: 1919]).

and scholarly geographical practitioners who had sought authority for their artefacts not through their own direct experience of the regions depicted on them, but by virtue of the epistemological rigour of their visual exegetical practices and the geographical grammar through which they had articulated the peoples of the world.

This chapter explores some of the experiments that geographers, illustrators and mapmakers undertook with their depictions of distant peoples in response to this proliferation in modes of what we might call ethnographic geography. It has three complementary and sometimes overlapping concerns: first, non-cartographic modes of mapping New World peoples visually, namely costume books and illustrated travel books; second, Virginia, a region whose inhabitants were first emblematized through these new visual and cartographic ones modes; and finally, a region of production: the Antwerp–Amsterdam axis. We shall see how mapmakers experimented with new visual layouts and arguments. These endeavours culminated in the multi-sheet wall maps printed in Amsterdam in the early seventeenth century, in which emblematic representations of each part of the world were arranged and discussed in direct comparison to one another. By analyzing the ethnological evaluations on these maps of Europe, Africa, Asia and the Americas in the setting of the other modes that also compared inhabitants from the different parts of the world – loosely what we call continents today – this chapter dissolves the edges of the genre of the map into those closely related modes of writing and picturing the world's peoples which were underpinned by a cartographical grammar. At the turn of the seventeenth century, a comparative ethnology based on a historical rather than geographical grammar provided the rationale for placing America's peoples at the lowest run of the hierarchy of civility, an unhappy distinction they would, to a great extent, lose, by the end of that century, to the peoples of Africa.[7]

Costume books

The mid-sixteenth century saw the emergence of the illustrated costume book, or handbook on the clothing of different ranks of society or peoples from various regions of Europe and the wider world. The costume book was a genre with the potential to compete with illustrated maps in the sphere of ethnographic illustration. These books offered engraved full-

7 One exception was the inhabitants of Tierra del Fuego, described as late as the nineteenth century as the most abject peoples on earth. See Qureshi, *Peoples on Parade*, chap. 1.

length portraits showing the diversity of the world's peoples, portraits that would shape subsequent iconography on maps.[8] The major publishers of Dutch wall maps drew extensively on costume book illustrations from the turn of the sixteenth century and, as we shall see later in this chapter, re-thought the genre of the illustrated wall map in order to incorporate images in a format that more closely resembled that of these books.

In Renaissance and early modern Europe, clothing, choices of bodily ornament and physical appearance were taken to explicate identity, to offer evidence of deeper characteristics, and even to change the wearer.[9] At the same time, commentators recognized that these surface elements could be manipulated, thus throwing into uncertainty interpretations made by observing a person's appearance.[10]

According to François Deserps, the author of the earliest exemplar, within the pages of such a work you would find 'realistic portraits of women, girls and men; gesture, and clothing; of nakedness, in our present time'.[11] These figures were devised for comparative purposes, allowing the viewer to 'clearly recognize that people make extraordinary garments which differ one from the other'.[12] To this end, Deserps illustrated 'the diversity of clothing' ('*la diuersité des habits*') in Europe, Asia, Africa and the New World. Although Deserps's avowed focus was the sartorial aspect of 'habit', his models are no mere human coat-hangers. His writing reveals his opinions about the customs and moral status of the people he characterized by their clothing; America is here relegated to the status of unnamed 'islands of savages and barbarism' ('*isles des sauvages et barbarie*').[13]

The earliest costume books were relatively free with geographical structure and the boundaries of humanity. In Deserps's influential *Recueil des*

[8] Defert, 'Un genre ethnographique', 25. For a recent study, see Rublack, *Dressing Up*, 146–65.

[9] Ann Rosalind Jones and Peter Stallybrass, *Renaissance Clothing and the Materials of Memory* (Cambridge: Cambridge University Press, 2000); Rublack, *Dressing Up*, 138.

[10] Michael Gaudio, 'The Truth in Clothing: The Costume Studies of John White and Lucas de Heere', in *European Visions: American Voices*, ed. Kim Sloan (London: British Museum, 2009), 24–32, at 25–8.

[11] François Deserps, *Recueil de la diuersité des habits qui sont de present en usaige tant es pays d'Europe, Asie, Affrique et Illes sauvages, le tout fait apres le naturel* (Paris, 1562). Deserps, *A Collection of the Various Styles of Clothing Which Are Presently Worn in Countries of Europe, Asia, Africa, and the Savage Islands, All Realistically Depicted*, ed. Sara Shannon (Minneapolis, MN: University of Minnesota Press, 2001), 24–5:'de femmes, filles & hommes, plusieurs pourtraicts, le geste, & vestement, du naturel, en ce temps ou nous sommes'. I have made minor amendments to the translation.

[12] Deserps, *Collection of Styles*, 24–5: 'cognoistras les habits clairement, qui les humains font l'un de l'autre estrange'.

[13] Ibid., 28–9.

La Picarde.
Voy ceste femme auec son Bauolet,
C'est la Picarde esueillée & honneste,
Son parler plait, son maintien n'est pas laid
Mais bien souuent elle à mauuaise teste.

8.1 François Deserps, *Receuil de la diuersité des habits* (Paris, 1562), unpaginated, a Picardy woman.
Houghton Library, Harvard University, Typ 515.64.734.

habits, pages are dedicated to men and women from the different ranks of French society and regions of the country – 'Le Docteur', 'Le laboureur', 'La Picarde' and 'La rustique françoyse', for example – and interspersed with pages on people from other parts of Europe, like 'Le Venetien', and the other parts of the world (Fig. 8.1). The inhabitants of Asia and Africa appear in graceful clothing that covers their bodies; the costumes and coiffures of the women of Asia are said to be beyond reproach, even for Venetians. Scotland contains both civil and wild people, and is represented by two figures in standard European clothing – L'escossoys and L'escossoyse – and by 'La sauuage d'Escosse' who wears animal skins to guard against the cold (*froidure*).

The lands found west of the Atlantic are noted on the title-page as mere afterthoughts, being as they are 'isles sauuages'. Nevertheless, they receive a number of pages.[14] Even quasi-human animals and monsters (a monkey standing on his hind legs while wearing a cloak and carrying a club, and a cyclopes) appear (Figs. 8.2 and 8.3).

[14] Two images are discussed in Chapter 4, at 130–2.

Le ſinge debout.
Pres le Peru par effect le voit-on,
Dieu a donné au Singe telle forme,
Veſtu de ionc, ſ'apuiant d'vn baſton,
Eſtant debout choſe aux hõmes cõforme.

8.2 François Deserps, *Receuil de la diuersité des habits* (Paris, 1562), unpaginated, a monkey.
Houghton Library, Harvard University, Typ 515.64.734.

Costume books, like other Renaissance genres, were not hermetically sealed from other modes of writing and picturing, and neither were their authors and illustrators. The diplomat Nicolas de Nicolay, author of *Les quatre premiers livres des navigations et peregrinations orientales*, an account of his travels through the Ottoman empire, identified himself on the title-page of the 1568 edition as 'dauphinoys, seigneur d'Arfeuille, varlet de chambres, & geographe ordinaire du Roy', which the 1585 English translation would render as 'chamberlaine and geographer ordinarie to the king of Fraunce'.[15] The book blends personal narrative, costume and descriptive geography and includes, for example, descriptions of the costumes and rites of peoples of the Ottoman lands, notes on architectural highlights, and full-page illustrations of individual subjects, from a 'Grand

[15] Nicolas de Nicolay, *Les qvatre premiers livres des navigations et peregrinations Orientales, de N. de Nicolay Dauphinoys, seigneur d'Argeuille, varlet de chambre, & Geographe ordinaire du Roy. Auec les figures au naturel tant d'hommes que de femmes selon la diuersité des nations, & de leur port, maintien, & habitz* (Lyon, 1568), title-page; Nicolas de Nicolay, *The nauigations, peregrinations and voyages, made into Turkie by Nicholas Nicholay* (London 1585). The work was first printed in 1567 and subsequently reprinted and translated widely.

Le Ciclope.
De Polipheme & des Siclopiens,
Font mention poetes anciens:
On dit encor que ce lignage dure,
Auec vn œil ſelon ceſte figure.

8.3 François Deserps, *Receuil de la diuersité des habits* (Paris, 1562), unpaginated, a cyclopes.
Houghton Library, Harvard University, Typ 515.64.734.

Dame Turque' to a 'Gentilhomme Persien'.[16] As Chandra Mukerji has argued, the book functioned as a primer of the visual indicators of Ottoman social hierarchies and consequent moral relationships, valuable information for European travellers seeking to navigate the social geography of the empire.[17] While Mukerji connected Nicolay's decision to illustrate his account with costume to the concurrent rise in interest among European mapmakers for displaying costumed figures on their maps, Nicolay's immediate source was most likely Deserps's costume book. Nicolay's title-page and the extended commentaries on subsequent versions of the text reveal that he was responding directly to the preface of Deserps's book.

[16] Nicolas de Nicolay, *Navigations et peregrinations*, facing 66.

[17] Chandra Mukerji, 'Costume and Character in the Ottoman Empire: Dress as Social Agent in Nicolay's *Navigations*', in *Early Modern Things: Objects and Their Histories, 1500–1800*, ed. Paula Findlen (London and New York, NY: Routledge, 2013), 151–69, 153: Nicolay had also collected strategic geographical information, but subsequent military developments most likely led Nicolay not to print this material.

Versions of Deserps's and Nicolays' costume books inspired numerous new costume books with different peoples, illustrations and commentaries. The genre was not restricted to printed examples. A 600-page manuscript book of the peoples of the Philippines is preserved in the Lilly Library at Indiana University-Bloomington.[18] At the opposite end of the geographical spectrum but anticipating the mode of the costume book, a 'Book of Clothes' in watercolours commissioned in 1526 by the twenty-nine year-old Mathäus Schwarz, head accountant of the Fugger mercantile firm, showed Schwarz himself in various outfits; the portraits began, retrospectively, with Schwarz's infancy, and continued to be painted until he was sixty-three.[19]

The designers of costume books, like mapmakers, expected their readers to consult their works alongside travel accounts. The dedicatory epistle to the 1585 English translation of Nicolay's *Navigations* observes that the narrative falls within the bounds of credibility since 'thinges no lesse straunge and true are remembred, then eyther Christopherus Colonus noteth in his voyage to the Indies, or Petrus Martyr de Angleria mentioneth of the West Ocean ylands, or Gonzalus Ferdinandus Ouiedus specifieth of the occidentall Indies, or Ludouicus Wertomannus rehearseth of Arabia, Aegypt, Syria, Aethiopia, &c. or Maximilian Transiluan recordeth of the wonderful nauigation of the Spaniards about the worlde'.[20] Like maps, then, costume books functioned as visual reference works that collated and elaborated ethnographic information from travel accounts.

Allegory and comparative ethnology

Another new mode for picturing humanity in the sixteenth century was the allegorical personification of a geographical region. Personifications shared the attributes of local inhabitants, animals and commodities. The cannibal motifs on early sixteenth-century maps influenced cosmographies and prints to such an extent that they would come to personify the Americas as a whole. In 1570, the Antwerp cartographer Abraham Ortelius published an atlas entitled *Theatrum orbis terrarum* and prefaced by a title-page, probably devised by Ortelius himself, which depicted the earliest

[18] Bloomington, IN, Indiana University, Lilly Library, Boxer mss. II. Sino-Spanish codex (Boxer codex), c.1590.

[19] Discussed in Rublack, *Dressing Up*, chap. 2.

[20] Nicolay, *Nauigations*, sig.3.*v*.

8.4 Abraham Ortelius, *Theatrum orbis terrarum* (Antwerp, 1570), title-page. Courtesy of the Library of Congress, Geography and Map Division, G1006 .T5 1570b.

known printed personifications of the parts of the world (Fig. 8.4).[21] This gave an influential visual form to the notion that America was less civilized than the regions of the Old World. An accompanying Latin poem by the jurist and Hellenist Adolphus Mekerchus explained to viewers the significance of its constituent elements.[22]

The poem and the title-page served to underline the superior civility of Europe in comparison to the other continents.[23] Europe's position is

[21] Abraham Ortelius, *Theatrum orbis terrarum* (Antwerp, 1570). For overviews and bibliography, see Van der Krogt, *Koeman's Atlantes Neerlandici*, III; Marcel R. van den Broecke, 'Introduction to the Life and Works of Abraham Ortelius (1527–1598)', in *Abraham Ortelius and the First Atlas: Essays Commemorating the Quadricentennial of His Death, 1598–1998*, ed. Marcel R. van den Broecke (Utrecht: HES, 1998), 29–54. For studies of the title-page, see Elizabeth McGrath, 'Humanism, Allegorical Invention, and the Personification of the Continents', in *Concept, Design & Execution in Flemish Painting (1550–1700)*, ed. Hans Vlieghe et al. (Turnhout: Brepols, 2000), 43–71; Werner Waterschoot, 'The Title-Page of Ortelius's *Theatrum Orbis Terrarum: A Comment*', *Quaerendo*, 9 (1979), 43–68. The engraver is unknown, but Waterschoot suggests either Maarten de Vos or Filips Galle; Ortelius knew them both.

[22] This was translated into the vernacular for the French and Dutch editions. For a transcription and translation of the Latin and Dutch versions, see Waterschoot, 'Title-Page', Appendix I and II.

[23] Ibid., 48–9; Ernst van den Boogaart, 'The Empress Europe and Her Three Sisters: The Symbolic Representation of Europe's Superiority in the Low Countries 1570–1655', in *America, Bride of*

indicated, for instance, by her place at the top of the image: she holds a sceptre and a rudder (*clavus*) shaped like a crucifix with which she guides the world. Africa holds a sprig of balsam; Asia, dressed in rich fabrics, a lighted censer. Naked America, by contrast, holds a club and bears aloft a severed human head. A fifth continent, Magellanica, considered to be still largely undiscovered, does not even have a full body, much less signs of a civilized populace.[24]

Scholars have noted that Ortelius relied on the account of Hans Staden's captivity for details of American cannibalism,[25] but considering the sources that Ortelius knew but chose not to use when designing the frontispiece is also illuminating. The text page accompanying the map of the New World lists such authors as Hernán Cortés and Francisco de Xérez, who had described the Mexica and Inca empires in admiring tones.[26] Despite this, just as Martin Waldseemüller had chosen cannibalism to represent Brazil from a range of possibilities, Ortelius selected it to symbolize the whole of America some fifty years later.

The *Theatrum* grew with successive editions. The texts accompanying new maps of America described its natural riches and sophisticated civilizations. A particularly striking example is the description of Peru that appeared in the 1584 edition:

> These few [arguments] among many others demonstrate [this] to be the richest in gold among all regions of the world. Francisco Xérez writes that in *Cuzco* there was a house whose courtyard, walls and roof were completely covered with gold plates. Girava relates that the inhabitants of the province of Anzerma are always armed for battle in gold from head to toe: cuirasses, breastplates and shin-covers are all made of gold. The same author says that there are goldmines near Quito where more gold is dug up than earth. Those that have written the story of Atahualpa, last king of the Incas, agree that he offered as much gold to the Spaniards for his ransom as could be held in the room where he was being held captive.... When the Spanish first entered this region, they shod their horses with gold and silver.[27]

the Sun: 500 Years, Latin America and the Low Countries (Ghent and Brussels: Antwerp Royal Museum of Fine Arts, 1992), 120–8, at 123.

[24] For a description, see Van den Boogaart, 'The Empress Europe and Her Three Sisters', 121–3.

[25] Waterschoot, 'Title-Page', 52–3. [26] For these works, see Chapter 7.

[27] Ortelius, *Theatrum*, 1584, fol. 8*r*.: 'Auri ditissimam inter omnes totius orbis regiones esse, arguunt inter multa, haec pauca. Scribit Franciscus Xeresius in Cusco aedes fuisse, cuius area, parietes, & tectum, undique aureis laminis erant inductae. Tradit Girava incolas Anzermae provinciae ab im[m]o calcaneo ad cervicem, auro ad proelia armari: loricas, thoraces, tibialia, omnia ex auro fabricari. Idem auctor est, circa Quito auri fodinas esse, unde, plus auri quam

A people such as this who could build, work metal and organize armies could not be inferred from Ortelius's title-page or Mekerchus's poem. And yet the same title-page, with no revisions, continued to appear in all editions of the *Theatrum* up to 1612[28] – despite the fact that the plate wore out and was replaced at least three times.[29] From the 1590s, the equally distinctive peaceful images of the Virginia Algonquians and Florida Timucua, both widely known through De Bry's *America*, had been appearing on maps. Nevertheless, allegorical personifications of America in other media had been set and continued to emphasize Brazilian-style motifs, such as feather costumes and cannibalism, in a phenomenon that William Sturtevant dubbed the *tupinambization* of distant peoples.[30]

Between 5,600 and 12,000 copies of Ortelius's title-page circulated in various editions and translations of the *Theatrum*.[31] Its influence continued via print-makers who drew on it when designing their own personifications, and whose prints were in turn the inspiration for subsequent maps, prints and other artefacts. The most popular model for mapmakers devising personifications of the parts of the world was a series of prints by Adriaen Collaert after drawings by Maarten de Vos.[32] The background of Collaert's America print includes the popular cannibal motifs of a limb being turned on a spit and an indigenous figure butchering a body on a table.[33] These and

terrae effodiatur. Qui historiam Atabalipae ultimi Ingarum regis litteris tradidere, in eo consentiunt, eum Hispanis pro sua redemtione obtulisse tantum auri, quantum locus, quo ipse captivus detinebatur, capere posset. . . .. Hispanos quum primum hanc regionem occupassent, equorum soleas ex auro et argento formasse. . . .' Ortelius's sources were probably Xérez, *Verdadera relación* and Gerónimo Girava, *Dos libros de cosmographia* (Milan, 1556).

28 Rodney W. Shirley, 'The Title Pages to the *Theatrum* and *Parergon*', in *Ortelius*, ed. Van den Broecke, 161–9, at 164; for a list of the editions, see Van der Krogt, *Atlantes*, IIIA, 33–244.

29 Waterschoot, 'Title-Page', 46.

30 William C. Sturtevant, 'La "tupinambisation" des Indiens d'Amérique du Nord', in *Figures de l'Indien*, ed. Gilles Thérien (Montreal: Typo, 1995), 345–61.

31 Van den Boogaart, 'The Empress Europe and Her Three Sisters', 124.

32 For map personifications based on prints by De Vos, as well as by Jan Sadeler, Filips Galle and Gerard van Groeningen, see *MCN*, V, 22–9, where the De Vos prints are identified as a source for the following world maps: Plancius 1594; Josua van den Ende 1604; Harmen and Maarten Jansz, 1610 (BNF-Cartes, Rés. Ge A 1048); and Visscher 1639. Additional examples I have found are Arnold Floris and Henricus van Langren 1596; Hondius the Elder 1608 and Evert Gijsbertsz 1599. For other print series, especially the series by Sadeler after designs by Dirck Barendsz, see Schmidt, *Innocence Abroad*, 123–38. Cannibal motifs also symbolized America in later prints by Jost Amman and Crispijn de Passe; for illustrations, see *MCN*, V, 24, and Honour, *European Vision*, 87–8; for prints produced in the Low Countries, see also Sabine Poeschel, *Studien zur Ikonographie der Erdteile in der Kunst des 16.-18. Jahrhunderts* (Augsburg, 1985), 78–87.

33 These were incorporated into interiors of the American continent on maps by published by Petrus Plancius, Arnold van Langren, Cornelis Claesz, Michiel Colijn and Clement de Jonghe.

other anthropophagous personifications of America and their continuing appearance on maps indicate that the images of Carib anthropophages had more impact than any other Amerindian representation, well into the seventeenth century.

Illustrated travel books and the natural historical mode: De Bry's voyages

The 1590s saw the emergence of a new printed visual archive for America's peoples upon which mapmakers in Antwerp, Amsterdam and England would draw. The *India Occidentalis* or *America* series published by Theodor de Bry and his sons, comprising thirteen volumes published between 1590 and 1634, comprised editions of travel and historical literature that contained engravings of the highest quality.[34] The first volume of De Bry's *America* combined the *Briefe and True Report of the New Found Land of Virginia* by astronomer and surveyor Thomas Harriot with engravings after the artist John White's seventy-five watercolour drawings of life among the North Carolina Algonquians, which White had made in 1585–6.[35] Published in Latin, German, French and English editions, the engravings of Algonquian life combined draftsmanly quality, aesthetic appeal, quantity and first-hand authority. This helped them to become the essential model for North American Indians until the nineteenth century.[36] As late as 1812, Thomas Jefferson suggested to John Adams, a former president of the United States, that he could learn about the Indians from De Bry's *America*; Jefferson himself owned three volumes, which he had bought via an Amsterdam auction in 1788.[37]

The drawings, perhaps the most iconic series of images of native peoples of North America, are the earliest known eyewitness images of Amerindians to have been produced by a trained European artist. Their sheer number

34 See Van Groesen, *Representations of the Overseas World*, Appendix 1 for the firm's publications.

35 Thomas Harriot, *A Briefe and True Report of the New Found Land of Virginia* (Frankfurt am Main, 1590). British Museum, Department of Prints & Drawings, 1906, 0509. John White, watercolour drawings of Virginia, 1585–6.

36 The Latin and German editions were particularly successful and influential; later volumes of the *America* series were published only in these languages; see Peter Stallybrass, '*Admiranda narratio*: A European Best Seller' in Thomas Harriot, *A Briefe and True Report…: The 1590 Theodor de Bry Latin Edition* (Charlottesville, VA: Published for the Library at the Mariners' Museum by the University of Virginia, 2007), 9–30.

37 Gaudio, *Engraving the Savage*, xiii. Van Groesen, *Representations of the Overseas World*, 1–4.

and variety, comprising individual portraits, village life, flora and fauna, made them the first systematic visual record of the natural history of the New World. The images fall broadly into three types: portraits, scenes of everyday life and views of two Algonquian villages, Pomeiooc and Secotan.[38] Their high level of detail and sympathetic rendering of ethnographic difference have traditionally been considered as evidence that White tried to reproduce precisely what he saw; the drawings have been characterized as a landmark in the history of English natural sciences.[39]

Scholars have traditionally approached the Harriot and White material as Ur-moments in writing and painting others, whether that be in the form of foundational English responses, 'naturalistic' or sympathetic representations, or iconic and influential images. The preceding chapters of this book, ranging as they have across earlier European textual and visual traditions for representing peoples of the Americas, and across cartographic motifs and comparative epistemologies, argue for the de-centering of the Harriot–White material here and its re-contextualization within broader representational trends in ethnography, cartography and natural history.

The first edition of Harriot's *Briefe and True Reporte* on Virginia was printed in London in 1588 as an inexpensive, unillustrated 25-page pamphlet.[40] The work was brought to the attention of Theodor de Bry by the geographer and Anglican minister Richard Hakluyt the Younger, arguably the most vocal supporter of English overseas colonization in the sixteenth century.[41] Hakluyt encouraged De Bry to publish Harriot's report as the first volume of his *America* series, and helped De Bry to acquire White's watercolours which De Bry and his sons turned into ambitious, high-quality copper engravings, with captions supplied (in Latin) by Harriot.[42] De Bry's editions were printed in 1590 in English, French, German and Latin, with the first printed illustrations of the Algonquians,[43] and immediately began

[38] For the watercolours as a coherent series, see Ernst van den Boogaart, 'Serialized Virginia: The Representational Format for Comparative Ethnology c.1600', in *European Visions: American Voices*, 113–19.

[39] David Beers Quinn, *The Roanoke Voyages*, 2 vols. (London: The Hakluyt Society, 1955), I, 35.

[40] Thomas Harriot, *A Briefe and True Report of the New Found Land of Virginia* (London, 1588).

[41] In 1589, Hakluyt included the *Briefe Report* in his *The Principall Navigations, Voyages and Discoveries of the English Nation* (London, 1589), a collection of English voyages. In 1598, Hakluyt reprinted the *Briefe Report* in an enlarged edition of his compendium.

[42] Peter Mancall, *Hakluyt's Promise: An Elizabethan's Obsession for an English America* (New Haven, CT and London: Yale University Press, 2007), 196.

[43] Thomas Harriot, *A Briefe and True Report of the New Found Land of Virginia* (Frankfurt am Main, 1590). Hereafter, *Briefe Report* will refer to De Bry's 1590 edition.

shaping European perceptions.[44] The success of the German and Latin editions of the *Briefe Report* was such that subsequent volumes of the series were published solely in these languages.

In many ways, the De Bry edition of Harriot's *Brief Reporte* is significantly different from Harriot's first edition. De Bry's selection of distant peoples as the most important material to illustrate, over 'marchantable commodities' or animals for which White had also made numerous watercolours, is one that might well have been prompted by sixteenth-century illustrated maps; mapmakers had made the same iconographic choice since the beginning of the sixteenth century. Although Harriot's text is preserved – albeit with some unusual spellings courtesy of Frankfurt's German-speaking typesetters – everything around it contrives to change the focus of the volume. The title-page visually announces that Virginia's inhabitants would be central to its contents (Fig. 8.5). Five figures from within the book adorn a classical portico structure. Since title-pages were commonly displayed loose in printing-shops, as advertisements, this page would have attracted prospective buyers interested in the customs and manners of distant peoples.[45] The title is a compressed version of the original, which had given much more weight to the commodities. By adding Algonquian engravings after John White and supplementary ethnographic material, but not engravings of flora and fauna after other watercolours in White's Virginia archive, the De Bry firm turned Harriot's pamphlet into an illustrated travel account whose focus was ethnographic rather than economic.

The first dedication in the Frankfurt edition is De Bry's to Sir Walter Ralegh, the central organizer, promotor and sponsor of the Virginia voyages. With it, De Bry appropriated Harriot's text for his own purpose. De Bry writes that, in order to demonstrate that he remained Ralegh's 'most humble servant', he has taken 'the paines to cott in copper . . . the figures which doe leuelye represent the form and maner of the Inhabitants of the same countrye with theirs ceremonies, sollemne, feastes, and the manner and situation of their Townes, or Villages'. Excepting the title-page, this is

[44] John W. Shirley, *Thomas Harriot: A Biography* (Oxford, 1983), 143–5; Quinn, *Roanoke Voyages*, 39. For De Bry's transformations of White's watercolours, see Gaudio, *Engraving the Savage*; Ute Kuhlemann, 'Between Reproduction, Invention and Propaganda: Theodor de Bry's Engravings after John White', in Sloan et. al., *New World*, 79–92; and Christian F. Feest, 'The Virginia Indian in Pictures, 1612–1624', *The Smithsonian Journal of History*, 2 (1967), 1–30. For De Bry's travel publications, see Susanna Burghartz, ed., *Staging New Worlds: De Brys' Illustrated Travel Reports, 1590–1630* (Basle, 2004).

[45] For a similar point, see Kuhlemann, 'Between Reproduction, Invention and Propaganda', 84.

A briefe and true report
of the new found land of Virginia:
of the commodities and of the nature and manners of the naturall inhabitants. Discouered by
the English Colony there seated by Sir Richard
Greinuile Knight In the yeere 1585. Which Remained Vnder the gouernement of twelue monethes,
At the speciall charge and direction of the Honourable SIR WALTER RALEIGH Knight lord Warden
of the stanneries Who therein hath beene fauoured
and authorised by her MAIESTIE
and her letters patents:
This fore booke Is made in English
BY Thomas Hariot seruant to the abouenamed
Sir WALTER, a member of the Colony, and there
imployed in discouering
CVM GRATIA ET PRIVILEGIO CÆS. MA^TIS SPECIA^LI

FRANCOFORTI AD MOENVM
TYPIS IOANNIS WECHELI, SVMTIBVS VERO THEODORI
DE BRY ANNO CIϽ IϽ XC.
VENALES REPERIVNTVR IN OFFICINA SIGISMVNDI FEIRABENDII

8.5 Thomas Harriot, *A Briefe and True Report of the New Found Land of Virginia* (Frankfurt am Main, 1590), title-page.
Beinecke Rare Book and Manuscript Library, Yale University, Taylor 194.

the first reference to the volume's contents, and it gives the copper engravings made by the house of De Bry as its *raison d'être.* He continues thus:

> I ... haue thincke that the aforesaid figures wear of greater commendation, If somme Histoire which traitinge of the commodites and

8.6 Thomas Harriot, *A Briefe and True Report of the New Found Land of Virginia* (Frankfurt am Main, 1590), facing p. 51, image of a Pict.
By permission of the Folger Shakespeare Library, STC 12786.

> fertillitye of the said countrye weare Ioyned with the same, therfore haue I serue miselfe of the rapport which Thomas Hariot hath lattely sett foorth, and haue causse them booth togither to be printed.[46]

De Bry's words reveal that Harriot's text was an afterthought for De Bry, and it is not surprising that De Bry should seek to emphasize his own contribution in his dedication. Since it is the twenty-three engravings of Algonquians that have been foregrounded, not Harriot's report, viewers are invited to look at the report merely as contextual apparatus for the engravings. Indeed, the *Briefe and True Reporte* is not the only commentary on the engravings. Each image is now accompanied by a descriptive text. Harriot wrote these descriptions, and they were translated for the English, French and German editions. Thus Harriot himself participated in providing material that changed the emphasis of his original report.

As if the addition and foregrounding of the engravings after John White were not enough meddling with the book that was still called the *Briefe and True Reporte*, the images are followed by a supplement of five engravings of ancient British Picts, each with a facing-page commentary (Fig. 8.6).

[46] Harriot, *Briefe Report*, dedication.

The point of the Algonquians' innate perfectibility is made more strongly in the preface to the material on Picts. Harriot writes that he 'wold well sett [these figures] to the ende of thees first figures, for to showe how that the inhabitants of the great Bretannie haue bin in times past as sauuage as those of Virginia'.[47] As the ancient Britons had forsaken their 'sauuage' dress and customs, so too might the Virginians, under the tutelage of the English settlers. These illustrations were not initially associated with Harriot's report, but were only added to it in the De Bry edition. De Bry writes that White provided them, out of an 'olld English chronicle', 'to showe how that the Inhabitants of the great Bretannie haue bin in times past as sauuage as those of Virginia'. In other words, what the early modern reader held in his or her hands was not merely Harriot's *Brief Reporte* but a work of comparative ethnology *avant la lettre*, focusing on the Algonquians, with comparative material about Picts, and some background information on Virginia.

Renaissance English antiquarians had recently constructed the conception of the ancient Picts as the barbarous but noble ancestors of the inhabitants of Britain.[48] White's Picts are regal and muscular, like pictures of classical gods; they stand in *contrapposto*, a pose that gave them dignity by association.[49] These Picts – who were even more savage than the Algonquians – had the capacity to be civilized, and thus, by analogy, so did the Algonquins whose present state resembled them. Indeed, the Algonquians are cast as being more tractable and capable of being civilized than the Picts. The Latin edition of the *Briefe and True Reporte* included a brief 'Interpres/lectori', or a note from the translator to the reader. This contains material from classical sources on the warlike Picts, their battles with Roman forces and their appearance. No Algonquian warrior brandishes a scalp, whereas one of the Pictish warriors carries a severed human head.[50]

Paul Hulton has argued that White's Picts are a combination of stylistic clichés and 'aboriginal' elements that White had observed in New World Algonquians.[51] I would argue that once the Algonquians were accepted as resembling Britons of an earlier age from the point of view of their customs, they became reasonable models for the Picts, and that some of the standard forms of artistic artifice were intended to communicate deeper meanings.

[47] Ibid., title-page following plate XXIII.

[48] Sam Smiles, 'John White and British Antiquity: Savage Origins in the Context of Tudor Historiography', in *European Visions, American Voices*, 109–15, at 111–114.

[49] For this point, see ibid., 110. [50] Ibid., 107–8.

[51] See Hulton, 'Realism and Tradition', 23–4.

Transferring information from a drawing to an engraving also brought about – indeed, necessitated – a certain amount of invention. It is well known that the De Bry engravings are careful responses to the watercolours, incorporating subtle changes in style and content such as consistently classicized postures in cases where White had tried to preserve their otherworldliness. Nevertheless, the edition participated in a wider discourse on the nature of America's inhabitants, implying that their state of relative savagery in comparison to Europe was merely a temporary condition, and that they had the potential for conversion to Christianity. The addition of the engravings and commentary on the Picts reinforced Harriot's textual argument that the Algonquians could be 'brought to civilitie' by signalling that what separated them from European viewers of these engravings was time and space, not the civil human essence.

The De Bry edition constituted an important departure from the 1588 London edition of the *Briefe and True Reporte*: while the lion's share of Harriot's text (in both the original and the De Bry editions) was dedicated to Virginia's 'marchantable commodities', the De Bry edition re-oriented the conversation around its inhabitants. More broadly, the edition opened up the field for ethnographic images to be the primary subject of a book in which travel narrative served as supporting apparatus. This division of labour had been already been effected in large, illustrated maps at small scales, where geographical erudition played a supporting role to the iconographic content, and its application in De Bry may well have been spurred by such maps.

Mapmakers and Algonquians: De Jode's map of North America, 1593

In 1593, the Antwerp cartographer Cornelis de Jode published a map of North America containing copious captions on the history of the region's exploration. The illustrations, like those on most illustrated maps of the sixteenth century, depict the region's inhabitants rather than its flora or fauna. It shows only the peoples of one region, Virginia (Fig. 8.7), using Algonquian images after De Bry's engravings. The first figure, 'an image of a lord', had previously appeared on Johann de Bry's map.[52] The next is a 'noblewoman from Secota', one of the villages visited by White and

[52] 'Reguloi [sic] typus'. It also appeared on Harriot, *Brief Report*, plate III.

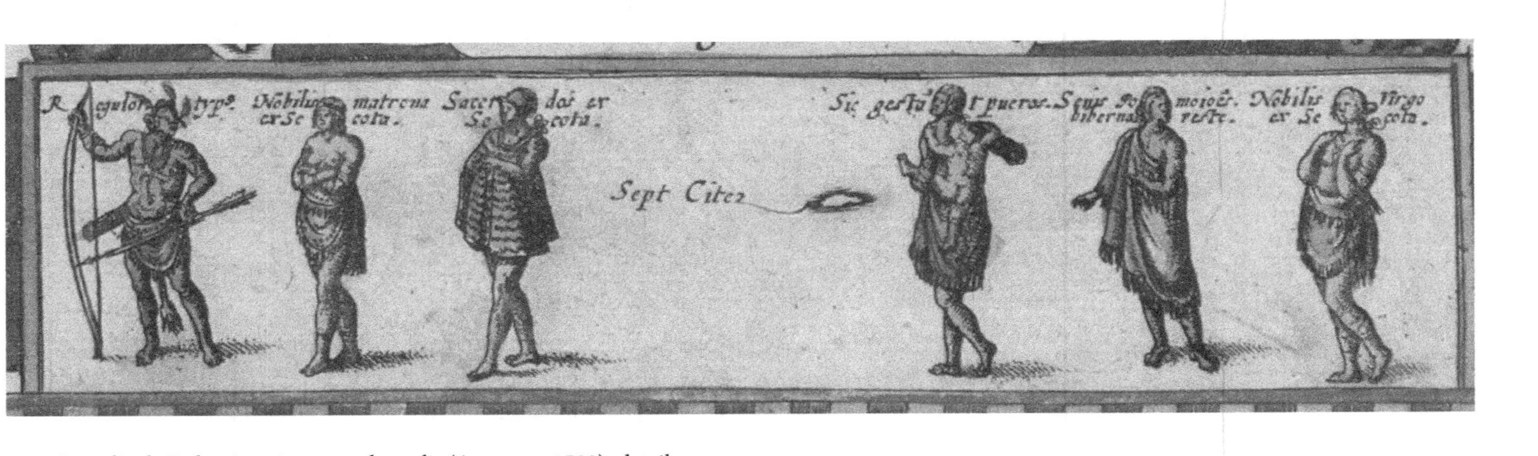

8.7 Cornelis de Jode, *Americae pars borealis* (Antwerp, 1593), detail.
From Phillips Academy, Andover MA, *The Sidney R. Knafel Map Collection.*

Harriot.[53] The third is a priest of Secota.[54] The fourth shows the Algonquian manner of carrying their children.[55] The fifth shows an old man of Pomeiooc in his winter clothing.[56] The last is a young woman of noble birth.[57] Admittedly, North American exploration had been limited up to this point, and visual models for the continent's other peoples were scarce. Visual material relating to Mexico was, however, available, and mapmakers did at times devise images directly from written descriptions, as they had done for the Patagonian giant. Nevertheless, De Jode chose to focus on the Algonquians, and gave them an overarching relevance for the whole continent by placing them in a compartment on the map's border, rather than within the landmass of Virginia.

The figures on De Jode's map constituted a significant departure from the majority of previous representations of Amerindians on maps. By using many illustrations of the same people, De Jode's map made the Algonquians emblematize all of the region's peoples. The portraits chosen would have suggested to early modern readers that the Algonquians had some form of government, religion, and a social hierarchy, with a leader, nobility and priests. The map's captions, however, contain anecdotes that paint a far less welcoming picture of North America. One inscription informs us that, somewhere between Canada and Florida, the Florentine explorer Giovanni da Verrazzano was captured, struck down, roasted and devoured.[58] This observation is reduced to an isolated caption on a busy map on which the most prominent ethnographic elements are the peaceful engravings of Algonquians. As such, the tale feels more like a random mishap than an important feature of North America.

While Martin Waldseemüller's choice of cannibal iconography, analysed in Chapter 3, had helped to fix the spectre of cannibalism onto European visions of Brazil, the White/De Bry images of Algonquians imprinted North America with images of peaceful inhabitants with 'goodly bodies'. Neither

[53] 'Nobilis matrona ex Secota'. Taken from ibid., plate IV.

[54] 'Sacerdos ex Secota'. Ibid., plate V. [55] 'Sic gestant pueros'. Ibid., plate X.

[56] 'Senis Pomoiocens hiberna veste'. Ibid., plate IX.

[57] 'Nobilis virgo ex Secota'. Ibid., plate VI. In something of a circular path of transmission, these six figures reappear in a later travel account, De Bry's *Americae Pars XIII*, plate CXX, along with three other portrait groups from the engravings in De Bry's edition of Harriot's *Briefe Report*. The plate had previously appeared in an abridgement of the *America* series published by Johann Theodor de Bry: Philipp Ziegler, *America, Das ist, Erfindung und Offenbahrung der Newen Welt* (Frankfurt am Main, 1617), 230, illustrated in Kuhlemann, *Reproduction, Invention and Propaganda*, 88.

[58] 'Verazano [sic] ... inter Canadam et Floridam, a Barbaris captus, occiditur, assatur, et devoratur.'

was a full answer to the question, 'what are the people over there like?' As Algonquian-English relations during the first century of Virginia voyages would show, the Algonquians were fully capable of eradicating the early settlements, even though they rarely chose to do so. De Jode's imagery was as much a selective invention as Waldseemüller's cannibal scenes from 1516.

William Hole's map of Virginia, 1612

One of the challenges for mapmakers and artists wishing to illustrate peoples, plants or animals was how to choose between depicting representative, unusual, and superlative examples of their subjects, and between subjects at different points in their life cycles. Two maps of Virginia that appeared in Captain John Smith's account of attempts to settle a region further north, in Jamestown, each show English mapmakers using multiple solutions to this challenge on the same map. Smith's 1612 account of Virginia contains a map engraved by William Hole with two vignettes (Fig. 8.8). Smith had been captured by Pamunkey Indians while reconnoitring; his two companions were killed in the skirmish. Smith was delivered to Powhatan, leader of the Algonquian tribes loosely banded together in a confederacy, by Powhatan's brother, the Pamunkey chief Opechancanough. Smith would famously be 'rescued' from death by Powhatan's daughter Pocahontas, although her part in the events was not recorded until Smith's later account of 1624. The vignette in the map's top left-hand corner contains several elements that are faithful to Smith's account. It shows the chief Powhatan, who 'held this state & fasion when Capt[ain] Smith was deliuered to him prisoner, 1607'. The viewer is thus instructed to take this scene as a representation of a specific historical moment. A woman sits on each side of Powhatan, as described in Smith's text.[59] The building in which the figures are seated, however, was inspired by De Bry's engraving after John White of *The Tombe of their Werowans.*[60]

The second illustration exhibits a more complicated relationship to Smith's text and the White/De Bry engravings. It too shows a leader, and is captioned: 'The Sasquesahanougs are a Gyantlike people & thus atired.' Smith's text refers the reader to 'the picture of the greatest of them [which] is signified on the mappe'; it was clearly was meant to be read alongside the

the status of the example

[59] Smith, *Description of Virginia*, 38: '. . .when he sitteth, one [woman] sitteth on his right hand and another on his left.'

[60] Discussed and identified in Gaudio, *Engraving the Savage*, 92–3, Figs 45, 47; the source is Harriot, *Briefe Report*, plate X.

8.8 William Hole, 'Virginia' map in John Smith, *A Map of Virginia, with a Description of the Covntrey, the Commodities, People, Government and Religion* (Oxford, 1612).
Beinecke Rare Book and Manuscript Library, Yale University, Vanderbilt +145.

map tipped between its pages.[61] By implication, the text would show how the details on the map illustration related to features observed and recorded *in situ*. Smith describes the chief Sasquesahanoug, presumably 'the greatest of them', thus:

> The calfe of whose leg was 3 quarters of a yard about, and all the rest of his limbes so answerable to that proportion, that he seemed the goodliest man that euer we beheld. His haire, the one side was long, the other shore close with a ridge over his crown like a cocks combe. His arrows were fiue quarters long, headed with flints or splinters of stones, in forme like a heart, an inch broad, and an inch and a halfe or more long. These hee wore in a woolues skinne at his backe for his quiver, his bow in the one hand and his clubbe in the other, as is described.[62]

[61] Smith, *Description of Virginia*, 9. [62] Ibid.

The map figure does indeed exhibit the characteristics that Smith describes: long hair with a ridge in the centre; an animal skin over his body with arrows behind him, as if the skin had been fashioned into a sack; a bow and club. Smith's description of the chief is immediately preceded by one of an ordinary Sasquesahanock:

> Their attire is the skinnes of Beares, and Woolues, some haue Cassacks made of Beares heades and skinnes that a mans necke goes through the skinnes neck, and the eares of the bear fastned to his shoulders behind, the nose and teeth hanging downe his breast, and at the end of the nose hung a Beares Pawe, the halfe sleeues comming to the elbowes were the neckes of Beares and the armes through the mouth with pawes hanging at their noses. One had the head of a Woolfe hanging in a chaine for a Iewell. . . .[63]

The figure on the map, then, drew on elements of the costume common to the chiefs and ordinary men and on the hairstyle, weaponry and 'goodly' body described in the text about the leader, or 'great lorde'.

Yet this man is not quite what he seems. Underneath the 'woolues skinne' cape, the thick necklace bearing a lupine ornament, the thick, flowing locks and the heavy club is a familiar figure – a 'great Lorde' of Virginia from De Bry's *America* of 1590 (Fig. 8.9).[64] Hole's man stands, bow in right hand, in *contrapposto*. While Hole might simply have used this stance because he had been trained to depict it (and, moreover, because it was the stance of his model), one wonders whether the narrative itself might have encouraged Hole to retain these elements of the chief's bearing. Smith's description suggests a perfectly proportioned man who 'seemed the goodliest man that euer we beheld' – presenting a subtly positive message to European eyes.

The differences in costume between the chief on Hole's 1612 map and De Bry's figure, which bring the former more into line with Smith's text, effectively presented a new image. Although Hole copied the De Bry figure's body, he took the trouble to change the man's costume, hair, armaments and ornaments to bring them in line with the text he was illustrating. That the faces, postures and general composition of the bodies

[63] Ibid., 8.

[64] Plate III. This source was identified by Feest, 'Virginia Indian', 7–8, who says he 'will not go into ethnographic details here' and identifies only the following differences: the figure's left hand holds an arrow in De Bry's image, a club in Hole's; only the De Bry figure has a puma-like tail emerging from the back of his costume; the figure's hair is adorned with feathers in De Bry's image, but is unadorned and long in Hole's.

8.9 Thomas Harriot, *A Briefe and True Report of the New Found Land of Virginia* (Frankfurt am Main, 1590), plate III, detail.
Courtesy of the John Carter Brown Library, J590 B915v GV-E.l [F] / 2-SIZE.

were similar did not necessarily indicate a lack of originality at a time when clothing played a greater part in defining differences between people than physical features such as skin colour. In early modern Europe there was a sense in which you were what you wore.[65] It is the Sasquehanock chief's 'woolues skinne' garment and 'iewell' that mark the significant differences between his people – whom he represents – and others. As Karen Ordahl Kupperman has argued, English colonists in this period were most concerned with recording those aspects of appearance that could be changed. These elements conveyed information about self-fashioned and socially imposed identities, and allowed one to distinguish between ordinary and high-status individuals.[66]

[65] See, e.g., Jones and Stallybrass, *Renaissance Clothing*, 4–5; Defert, 'Un genre ethnographique', 28; Rublack, *Dressing Up*.

[66] Karen Ordahl Kupperman, *Settling with the Indians: The Meeting of English and Indian Cultures in America, 1580–1640* (London, 1980), 33–8.

Wall maps with decorated borders

By the late sixteenth century, Dutch printers and illustrators were responding to, and contributing to, a large array of geographical and ethnographical modes as well as to new and old traditions of ethnographic representation on maps. For Cornelis Claesz, a printer whose output ranged from illustrated travel books to large, illustrated wall maps, the relationship between travel accounts and maps was not so much of competition but of mutual reinforcement, or what Elizabeth Sutton has characterized as a symbiotic arrangement.[67] Studies of Dutch wall maps do not tend to stray far beyond them, except to introduce earlier maps and images as a brief prelude or as sources for individual illustrations. In fact, not only did Dutch mapmakers innovate in other genres, but the very structure of their works also changed in response to them.

Devising images of the peoples of the parts of the world involved grappling with several issues: what was the genealogy of these peoples? What were their relative levels of civility? How might one select a representative personification from the myriad peoples of each part ? Devising allegorical personifications of the continents was the next step in emblematizing peoples of the world for mnemonic purposes.

There were late medieval precedents for placing peoples on the edges of maps. On the thirteenth-century Psalter map, this edge is partially separated off from the geographical space, as is the case on Dutch maps with illustrated borders (Fig. 1.2).[68] Nevertheless, this edge-space is populated exclusively by peoples who live at the edge of mapped region. A map with monstrous peoples along the border famously appeared in the *Nuremberg Chronicle* map of 1493.[69] The strip of peoples was not, however, connected to the map with which it shares folio space, but rather was a run-on from the previous folio of text and illustration.[70] Moreover, while this was a map of the *oikoumene* or the entirety of the known inhabited world, the peoples at the border related only to those peoples believed to live in those parts most distant from Europe. In other words, the border was not a space in which to depict peoples dwelling across the whole region of the map. Before the late sixteenth century, there was no pre-existing tradition in cartographic media for placing, in a border outside the geographical space of a map, examples of human diversity from across the geographical board.

[67] Sutton, *Dutch Prints*, 161. [68] Discussed in Chapter 1, near n. 50.
[69] Discussed in Chapter 1, near n. 89. [70] Leitch, *Mapping Ethnography*, 26.

In the late Middle Ages, when world maps began to be projected using broadly Ptolemaic systems, distinctive inhabitants were devised to emblematize specific locales and places in those locales, and, in so doing, to advance their makers' knowledge claims, as has been shown earlier. Why, then, did late sixteenth-century Dutch mapmakers give up the geographically positioned 'hic sunt...' paradigm upon which mapmakers had based their epistemological and ethnographic authority for a century? I would argue that there were two reasons, one epistemological and the other commercial. In the end, however, the decision would be to the detriment of both needs.

Cornelis Claesz and the *icones*

By the time the Amsterdam mapmaker Cornelis Claesz began to publish maps with decorative borders, he had already established his reputation as a printer of Dutch translations of navigational and other works, and of innovative travel editions.[71] In 1596 Claesz printed Jan Huygen van Linschoten's *Itinerario*, an account of the regions of Asia engaged in maritime trade combined with shorter sections on West Africa, America and sailing directions for navigators. Linschoten had travelled to India in 1583, and his book summarized knowledge about the East for anyone who wished to challenge Hispano-Lusitanian trade and influence in the region. Early in 1595, Cornelis Claesz rushed the quires on sailing directions through the presses, giving them to the first Dutch fleet to sail to the East Indies that April. Claesz published the rest of the book in Dutch in 1596, and collaborated in the publication of a Latin edition at The Hague in 1599. The De Bry family published another translation into Latin, also in 1599, and there were translations into English and French.[72]

In 1604, Claesz devised and printed an illustrated digest of Linschoten's *Itinerario* entitled *Icones, habitus gestusque Indorum ac Lusitanorum per Indiam viventium etc.*[73] As we have seen, this was a mode that Claesz also used in one of his translations of Las Casas' *Brevissima relacion*.[74] Claesz's *Icones* volume comprised a new title-page and thirty of the *Itinerario*'s

[71] *MCN*, VII.

[72] This overview of the *Itinerario*'s printing history is based on Ernst van den Boogaart, *Civil and Corrupt Asia: Images and Text in the 'Itinerario' and the 'Icones' of Jan Huygen van Linschoten* (Chicago, IL: University of Chicago Press, 2003), 1.

[73] For a facsimile and study, see ibid. [74] See Chapter 5.

thirty-six plates. The brief captions on the original plates were replaced with lengthier ones excerpted from the *Itinerario*. The engravings laid out the customs, costumes, social hierarchies, gender relations and technological capabilities of a range of Asian peoples. The regions of China, Goa, Ballagate and Malabar receive lengthier consideration; peoples discussed more briefly include those of Java and Mozambique. Ernst van den Boogaart has shown how the images were composed to invite comparisons between societies, and to argue for a hierarchy of civility in Asia: the northernmost peoples, the Chinese, were the most civil; the southernmost peoples from Malabar, Mozambique and Java, were the least civilized. Linschoten considered that it was not climate that drove these differences, but rather the lifestyle choices of individual peoples. He used a range of indicators to classify peoples in a hierarchy of civility, of which costume was particularly important. The form of a people's dress offered clues to their levels of modesty, technical skill and wealth.[75]

Europe on the map

Dutch maps with illustrated borders combined aspects of these ethnographic modes within a distinctive cartographic format. Unlike a costume book, a De Bry *America* edition or the *Icones* volume, the range of human diversity could be taken in almost at a glance a map; images of numerous peoples could be quickly compared against one another without any page turning. The map was a taxonomic device that located the habitats of each people, making it easier to contemplate possible correlations between geography, latitude, climate and human difference.

In 1570, the Elizabethan polymath John Dee noted the usefulness of maps for comparing 'the large dominion of the Turke, the wide empire of the Moschouite, and the litle morsel of ground, where Christendome (by profession) is certainly knowen'.[76] While we might quibble with Dee's diminution of the size of Iberian empires – driven, perhaps by a reluctance to acknowledge the achievements of heretics – his nod to the importance of empires that lay to the east reminds us that western European self-perceptions of superiority began not in the spheres of technology or empire, but in that of faith. What we know of Dee's reading patterns from the surviving books from his library and his annotation in them

75 Ernst van den Boogaart, *Civil and Corrupt Asia*, 10–14. 76 See Chapter 2, 56.

illuminates his close reading of works of Spanish geography.[77] In the same year, Abraham Ortelius's *Theatrum orbis terrarum* personified the parts of the world in such a way as to overtly claim legitimate European imperial rule over the world.

On Dutch world maps of the early seventeenth century, mapmakers re-orienting their emblems for the world rather than for parts of individual continents shifted their selections of customs, achievements and appearance to offer distinctive representations for Europe, Asia, Africa and America. In so doing, they consistently placed America at the bottom of their system of cultural hierarchy.

The earliest surviving example of a Dutch wall map of the world to feature complete borders with figures is the twenty-sheet map in two hemispheres published by Willem Blaeu in 1605.[78] Claes Jansz Visscher probably etched the decorative borders, and Josua van den Ende engraved the map itself.[79] Just one copy of the original edition, in poor condition and lacking its lower border, survives today.[80] After Blaeu's death, Jodocus Hondius the Younger purchased the plates and published a second edition in 1624.[81] Two partial copies of the 1624 edition survive.[82] From the close correspondence of these sheets to what remains of the 1605 edition, we can deduce that the latter had a very similar, if not identical, illustrative

[77] For Dee's knowledge of the New World, see, for example, William H. Sherman, *Used Books: Marking Readers in Renaissance England* (Philadelphia, PA: University of Pennsylvania Press, 2008), chap. 6.

[78] See the facsimile edition: Günter Schilder, *The World Map of 1624 by Willem Jansz. Blaeu & Jodocus Hondius* (Amsterdam: N. Israel, 1977), 4. The map was printed on three rows of six sheets and two extra sheets which, when cut up, made the lower border. Each sheet was 513 × 397 mm.

[79] Ibid., 12. In addition to the 1605 and 1624 editions, there were two others after my cut-off date of 1624: see ibid., 13–14. The map's designer is unknown.

[80] Ibid., 3. For illustrations, see Willem Jansz. Blaeu, *World Map of 1605*, introduction by Edward Luther Stevenson (New York, NY: Hispanic Society of America, 1914); for bibliographical details, see ibid., 51–9.

[81] Günter Schilder, *Three World Maps by François van den Hoeye of 1661, Willem Janszoon (Blaeu) of 1607, Claesz Janszoon Visscher of 1650* (Amsterdam: N. Israel, 1981), 23. According to Schilder, *World Map of 1624*, 3–4, this edition included revisions reflecting the discovery of the Le Maire Strait south of Patagonia and alterations to the dedication and publisher's name, but was otherwise unchanged from Blaeu's original map. In the absence of the lower border from the 1605 edition, however, we cannot know for certain that changes were not also made to this area.

[82] Schilder says that between them we have 'a *complete second edition of Willem Jansz. Blaeu's map of the world of 1605*' (ibid., 4, Schilder's italics). His facsimile, however, contains inconsistencies that run counter to this claim: for instance, two Amerindian figures examined below survive only as disembodied heads. Shirley, *Mapping*, n. 310, repeats Schilder's assertion; Shirley mentions the borders in particular, which he claims 'are complete in the 1624 state'.

8.10 Willem Blaeu, world map, 1605 [1624 edition by Jodocus Hondius the Younger], detail of inhabitants of Greenland and Florida.
Bibliothèque nationale de France, Département des Cartes et plans, GE DD 5161; gallicalabs.bnf.fr, IFN-55005078.

programme of map borders decorated with people and towns, and rulers filling the spaces between the hemispheres and the borders.[83]

Blaeu's 1605 wall map was innovative in its visual epistemology. In the individual roundels, the map breaks new ground by combining in the same roundel peoples who did not live in the same region and composing scenes in which they interacted with one another. In the top left-hand roundel, an Inuit group taken from Dionyse Settle's account has been recomposed (Fig. 8.10). The image appears to be the earliest one on which the woman's stance has been altered so that the two Inuit adults face each other. More radically, they are joined here by a Floridan, identifiable by the plate on his chest.[84] The three adults have been positioned so that they appear to be scrutinizing the baby. Other roundels also combine peoples from different parts of the Americas.[85]

By devising the roundels thus, the designer gave up the positional specificity upon which mapmakers had grounded their synoptic authority.

[83] See Schilder, *World Map of 1624*, 5, for descriptions of the illustrations in the map's interior; for a list of the contents of the borders on the 1624 map and the geographical contents, see 5–10. Amerindian figures are not discussed.

[84] Floridian Warriors wear such plates in *Americae pars II*.

[85] For source identification and discussion, see Davies, 'Representations of Amerindians', chap. 11.

Why make such a move when the visual language of Renaissance maps depended on a cartographical grammar? The gain in epistemological authority of this strategy was a more explicit rhetoric of eyewitnessing and a new visual paradigm for verisimilitude, one that appropriated the rhetoric of the De Bry engravings that showed distant peoples going about their daily lives. The roundels showing people in conversation give this impression of eyewitnessing even though some of the subjects were taken from costume books, themselves derivative works in most cases.[86]

While the roundels provide frozen moments of (hypothetical) eyewitness experience at the expense of using the coding of the gridded map to arrange inhabitants carefully by their geographical positions, the map's depictions of leaders of different nations make arguments about the hierarchy of civilizations. The corners and spandrels of the map each contain an Old World ruler displaying his majesty by appearing on horseback: the king of Spain, the Holy Roman emperor, the Turkish emperor, the kings of China, Abyssinia and Persia, the Great Khan of the Tartars and the Grand Duke of Moscow. No such leader has been chosen for the Americas, although Motecuhzoma and Atahualpa were two well-known examples for whom European iconographic traditions were already in place, and whose empires were represented on this map by city views of Tenochtitlán and Cuzco. Blaeu's dedicatory cartouche provides an explanation, for here we learn that he has provided 'pictures of the eight most powerful princes ruling the entire world in our era'.[87] New World figures who might pass for leaders on account of being of a similar size to the Old World rulers do appear on the map in North America (Fig. 8.11). Only one of the figures is female, the usual sex of geographical personifications. Two figures in similar costumes – this time, both female – appeared on Blaeu's 1619 map and its later editions and are labelled North and South America, so the figures on the 1605 map may also have been intended to be viewed that way.

The nearby inscriptions celebrate European explorers rather than instructing the reader on the Amerindian figures whose seat on an

[86] The 1605 map is one of the earliest maps on which ethnographic imagery has been taken from a costume book rather than a travel narrative. A second roundel combines a Chilean from an illustration in Van Noort's journal with a Peruvian from Jost Amman's costume book, *Im Frauenzimmer wirt vermeldt von allerley schönen Kleidungen unnd Trachten* (Frankfurt am Main, 1586), but gives no indication of a distinction in the designer's mind between first-hand and derivative information.

[87] '. . . octo potentissimorum principum, qui toti terrarum orbi nostro hoc saeculo imperant, effigies'.

8.11 Willem Blaeu, world map, 1605 [1624 edition by Jodocus Hondius the Younger], detail of personifications of America.
Bibliothèque nationale de France, Département des Cartes et plans, GE DD 5161; gallicalabs.bnf.fr, IFN-55005078.

ox-hide rather than on equine mounts and lack of royal or imperial attire gives them a different status from the rulers of the Old World. Instead, these emblematic Amerindians served to signify the scantily clothed peoples discovered and conquered by Columbus and Vespucci (whose portraits appear below them) and by those who followed in their footsteps.

In 1607, Blaeu published another wall map of the world, expanding the number of rulers on the upper border to include the kings of France and England. The layout of the map broadly mirrors that of the 1607 map, but with the inclusion of a large new vignette in the region of the southern oceans, which is reproduced here from a 1619 world map by Pieter van den Keere (Fig. 8.12). This image comprises an allegorical group of figures. Europe receives gifts from Asia, Africa and America. The accompanying legend by Richardus Lubbaeus articulates the group's significance:

> To whom do the Mexicans and the Peruvians offer brilliant gold necklaces and shining silver jewels? To whom does the armadillo bring skins, sugar cane and spices? To Europe, enthroned on high, the supreme ruler with the world at her feet: most powerful on land and at sea through war and enterprise, she owns a wealth of all goods. Oh Queen, it is to you that the fortunate Indian brings gold and spices, while the Arabs bring balsamic resin; the Russian sends furs, his eastern neighbour embellishes your dress with silk. Finally, Africa offers you costly spices and fragrant

8.12 Pieter van den Keere, *Nova orbis terrarum geographica ac hydrographica tabula* (Amsterdam, 1619), detail of personifications of the parts of the world.
Bibliothèque nationale de France, Département des Cartes et plans, Rés GE C 4931; gallicalabs.bnf.fr, IFN-720026.

> balsam, and also enriches you with bright white ivory, to which the dark coloured people of Guinea add a great weight of gold.[88]

Here, in contrast to John Dee's view of the world's empires, even China (the source of silk) and the Ottoman and Russian empires are portrayed as vassals of a Europe whose power is legitimized by military might. While all parts of the world are exemplified by their natural resources, Europe is known only for its prowess in grasping them. The sixteenth century had been a period of sharpening of confessional boundaries within Christendom as well as of cultural and religious conflicts at its anxious and shifting edges.[89] In this context, the portrayal of the Ottomans in particular as vassals rather than as rivals and adversaries with whom one engaged through military endeavours or diplomacy at once suggested Europe's superiority to its traditional foe and reduced the cultural distance between them.

This relationship between Europe and the other parts of the world is that of an emperor and his vassals, rather than one that is overtly racial in the sense of dehumanizing others on the basis of physical features. Lubbaeus and the artist of this vignette may have been inspired by triumphal entries

[88] 'Cui Mexicana et Peruana fulgidas / Auro catenas splendidasque argenteo / Nitore gemmas offerunt? Cui Vellera, / Et saccarum, atque aromata Armadilla fert? / Europae in alta constitutae sede, que / Regina tanquam summa calcat totius / Pedibus globum orbis: Marte et arte praepotens / Terra marique, est dives omnibus bonis. / Regina foelix Indus aurum et aromata, Sed balsamum Arabes advehunt tibi; vellera / Moscus remittit. Accola Eôi mars / Vestes tuas Bombycino filo expalit. / Preciosa tandem aromata offert Aphrica / Cum balsam fragrante tibi, te et candido / Puroque ebore ditat, cui atropollice / Guinaea gens adiungit auri pondera.' See *MCN*, V, 29–30, for the translation of the legend and further cartographic examples of Europe receiving homage from the other continents.

[89] Johnson, *Cultural Hierarchy*, chap. 7.

from the early sixteenth century, in which representatives from different parts of the world paid homage to a European ruler. In 1522 Hans Burgkmair had produced a series of woodcuts for a *Triumphal Procession* designed by the Holy Roman Emperor Maximilian I in order to promote his public image.[90] One scene was devoted to Indian, African and American peoples. The accompanying verse made clear the nature of the Emperor's relationship with these people:

> The Emperor in his warlike pride
> Conquering nations far and wide
> Has brought beneath our Empire's yoke,
> The far-off Calicuttish folk.
> Therefore we pledge him with our oath
> Lasting obedience and troth.[91]

Here, as in the case of Lubbaeus's poem, the inhabitants of far-off parts of the world pay tribute to a European leader. Such claims to universal rule, made on the basis of an idea of the superior religious truth of Christianity, had been made since the time of Emperor Constantine in the fourth century CE.[92]

The text border of the 1645/6 edition of this Blaeu map articulates this view of comparative human diversity, but also makes clear the precise status assigned to the Amerindians. Lengthy inscriptions in this border established a variety of levels of civility among the world's peoples. A description of the continents begins with Europe:

> Although Europe may be the smallest [part of the world], it surpasses the other learned nations by far in dignity, excellence, power, fame, in its multitude of magnificently built cities, in its inhabitants most skilled in every type of art and in its virtue and knowledge of the divine will (which is more powerful than all the treasures and riches of the world).[93]

[90] For this series, see Larry Silver, *Marketing Maximilian: The Visual Ideology of a Holy Roman Emperor* (Princeton, NJ: Princeton University Press, 2008), 93–9; Ulinka Rublack, *Dressing Up*, 178–80; Leitch, *Mapping Ethnography*, 152–4.

[91] Translated in Stanley Appelbaum, ed., *The Triumph of Maximilian I* (New York, NY: Dover, 1964), at 19; see also Massing, *Studies in Imagery* II, 103. The term 'Calicuttish' appears in German sources in this period to refer to a variety of distant peoples.

[92] Silver, *Marketing Maximilian*, 80.

[93] *MCN*, III, 319: 'Europa, licet aliarum sit minima, eas tamen dignitate, praestantia, potentia, nominis celebritate, multitudine urbium magnifice extructarum, populis in omni artium genere exercitatissimis, virtuteque et divini numinis cognitione (quae omnibus mundi thesauris ac divitiis potior est) prae aliis nationibus instructis longe superat.' Translations from this map are my own, but I have consulted the transcription and translation cited in *MCN*, III, Appendix.

The text expands on the riches of Europe through short descriptions of the advantages of its principal countries: the fertility of the land; the military achievements of the peoples of Spain and France; the mining wealth and printing trade of Germany; the ports and ships of the Netherlands.[94] In short, Europeans were skilled in the military, artistic, technological and commercial endeavours that characterized great civility. Asia and Africa, by contrast, contain both civil and savage peoples. Asia 'surpasses Europe and Africa, as well as the other continents, not only in size, but also in wealth, in its abundance of spices and precious stones and in its pre-eminence in other things.'[95] China had long possessed printing and the mechanical arts of warfare;[96] nevertheless a part of this 'second part of the ancient world' was 'under the despotic rule of the Turks'.[97] The migratory Tartars, moreover, 'live not in cities, communities or edifices, but in groups, called hordes in their language'.[98] Asia's best characteristics, then, were commodities and technical arts, but the political and social incivilities of some blotted its copy-book. Africa's notable attributes included pyramids, but it was also the home of simple and rustic inhabitants lacking European customs.[99] No specific mention is made of differences in their religions, perhaps because they were predominantly non-Christian, and therefore wrong.

The verses accompanying each of the rulers at the top of the map offered another comparative view. The Amerindians are included, after a fashion, as subjects of Philip III of Spain. Philip is urged to continue his support of the pope and to send his troops to aid the Holy Roman Emperor Rudolf II in his struggle against the Ottomans, 'for not only does Spain obey your laws, but all of those out of sight in the New World serve you with bent neck.[100] This scheme brings to mind Burgkmair's plan for Maximilian's *Procession*. One section contained a group of prisoners 'from all nations', and men carrying winged victories. A caption declared that: 'The members

94 Ibid., 320–3.

95 Ibid., 323: 'Europam et Africam, ut et alias mundi partes, non solum amplitudine, verum etiam divitiis, aromatum, pretiosarumque gemmarum copia, ac aliarum rerum praestantia antecellit'.

96 Ibid.; for other examples, see 324–6.

97 Ibid., 323: 'secunda pars antiqui orbis'; 'subjecta est . . . Turcarum tyrannidi'.

98 Ibid., 324: 'In nullis urbibus, pagis aut aedificiis habitant, [sed congregationes], proprio idiomate Horda, dictas'.

99 Part of the text on Africa is destroyed; I have indicated these lacunae with parentheses. Ibid., 326: 'Inc[olae sim]plices sunt et agrestes, neq[ue. . .] nostros mores habentes, neque [. . ..]' ('The inhabitants are simple and rustic, having neither our customs nor [. . ..]').

100 Ibid., portfolio, map 2.3–4: 'nam tuis non sola Hispania paret statutis, sed novo quotquot latent in orbe tibi cervice plexa serviunt'.

of this captive band / Are prisoners from every land / Where Maximilian waged war – / The battles were all shown before. / Marching in this Triumph now, / To his Imperial will they bow.[101]

The Blaeu map's scenes of leaders on horses are also reminiscent of triumphal processions. The designers of the map's iconographic programme appear to have perceived the world's peoples within a discourse of the righteous might of imperial Christianity. Several other verses on the map revolve around cultural and religious conflict, particularly with the Ottoman Empire.[102] Here too there is a parallel with Maximilian's self-presentation as the leading defender of Christendom against the threat of the Turks, and of a leader of successful military activities.[103]

A description of New Spain along the bottom of the map focuses on the idolatry of the region's inhabitants, especially their predeliction for human sacrifice and the ritual consumption of victims. The conclusion is damning: 'The inhabitants of this and the other American countries were prey to idolatrous superstitions, contrary to all piety and humanity, until 1519, when they were first brought under the dominion of the king of Spain by the bravery of the most illustrious hero Hernán Cortés.'[104] In 1622, the Catholic geographer Petrus Bertius had noted that the Mexicans had given up such practices.[105] Blaeu's 1645/46 map painted the Spanish conquest as bringing about this welcome transformation.[106] In contrast to the position of many non-Spanish commentators, Blaeu considered the conquest of Mexico and other regions to have been beneficial, insofar as the Spaniards had attempted to stamp out idolatry. Indeed, the reader is left with the impression that the Mexicans were savages, much like the typical view of Brazilians that we find on Blaeu's description on this map:

[101] For discussion and quotation, see Silver, *Marketing Maximilian*, 95; for translation, see Appelbaum, *Triumph*, 15.

[102] Henri IV of France is praised for bringing peace to his country; Emperor Rudolph II is urged to protect Germany and the Papal See from the Ottomans; the Persians and Russians are praised for resisting them. The Ottoman emperor is reprimanded for his attempts to destroy Rome. Similar verses appeared on Blaeu's 1605 map; for a transcription and translation from the 1624 edition, see Schilder, *World Map of 1624*, 17.

[103] Silver, *Marketing Maximilian*, 114–9, and chap. 5 for presentations of Maximilian as a military leader.

[104] *MCN*, III, 327: 'Huiusmodi idolatricis superstitionibus, cum omni piet[ate] humanitateque pugnan[tibus] incolae huius et aliarum [Ame]ricanarum regionum [dediti(?)] fuere, ad illud usque te[mpus], quo primum virtute illustrissimi Herois Ferdinandi Cortesii, anno 1519, sub potestate Regis Hispaniae sunt redacti.'

[105] See Chapter 7, near n. 131.

[106] This may also have been the case on the 1619 edition (whose borders do not survive) and on its source, Blaeu's 1607 map (of which no copy remains).

> All these nations are wild and most cruel *anthropophagi*, that is, man-eaters. The male sex as well as the female go naked. They adorn their bodies with plumage and pegs. They pierce their lips, into which they set small precious stones or little bones. They are devoid of all government and religion. They neither worship nor venerate the gods; nevertheless, they acknowledge the immortality of the soul.[107]

Readers were, nevertheless, supposed to interpret all these peoples as capable of becoming Christians, rather than as incorrigible idolaters, physically monstrous beings or irrational animals.

Jodocus Hondius the Elder's 1608 world map makes the common genealogy and humanity of the world's peoples even more visible.[108] The map depicts such content as monarchs, peoples and cities; some of these images had appeared on Blaeu's 1605 map.[109] Blaeu had included portraits of the first four circumnavigators on his 1607 map, and Hondius now added their itineraries. Hondius's map was therefore a direct response to the earlier ones of Blaeu, extending some of the information that they had provided.[110] The letterpress beneath the map includes brief descriptions of the peoples and regions of the world, focusing mainly on commodities.

This map's ethnological innovation consists of illustrations and discussions of the sons of Noah: Shem, Ham and Japhet. Although these figures had appeared on the world map in the *Nuremberg Chronicle* of 1492, they did not re-appear on maps that also depicted peoples of the Americas in the sixteenth century. At the top left-hand corner is a table of several generations of Noah's progeny. Their link to the peoples of the contemporary world is explained in the cartouches. The people of Europe are said to be Japhet's descendants: his son Tubal, for instance, is described as the

[107] *MCN*, III, 328: 'quae gentes omnes, sunt silvestres et crudelissimi antrωpofagoi [sic], id est hominum devoratores, tam masculinus hic quam foemininus sexus nude procedunt, corpus plumis pennisque ornant, labia transforant, quibus indunt lapillos pretiosos aut ossicula. Sunt expertes omnis politiae atque religionis; Deos nullos adorant aut reverentur, nihilominus animarum immortalitatem fa[t]entur.'

[108] Jodocus Hondius, *Nova et exacta totius orbis terrarum descriptio geographica et hydrographica* (Amsterdam, 1608). An inscription at the bottom states: 'Jodocus Hondius excudit et una cum affine Petro Kaerio caelavit' ('Jodocus Hondius printed and engraved [this] with Pieter van den Keere, a relative'.) For a description of the map, see *MCN*, III, 71–5.

[109] Most were mirror images of portraits in Plancius's 1607 world map, now lost.

[110] Jodocus Hondius the Elder, *The Map of the World on Mercator's Projection . . . Amsterdam 1608, from the Unique Copy in the Collection of the Royal Geographical Society*, memoir by Edward Heawood (London, 1927), 13–14: the similarities between such pictorial elements on both maps strongly suggest that Hondius's was designed to outdo its rival. Blaeu's 1605 map, in turn, may have been inspired by earlier maps by Hondius, now lost. For Hondius's use of maps by Mercator and Plancius for geographical content, see ibid., 10–13.

ancestor of the Spaniards.[111] The people of Africa are descended from Cham (Ham), whose grandson Ludum is listed next to the 'Libyi'.[112] The Amerindians are incorporated into this schema thus:

> What father America might have had is very uncertain. Arias Montanus and other learned men identify Ophir, from which gold was brought in the time of Solomon, with Peru. And so they make Ophir, the great-great-great-grandson of Sem, the father [of America], and this from some play on the name.[113] But it is more plausible that this region began to be populated from the northern parts of Europe or Asia (with which America is contiguous or at any rate separated from them by a narrow strait); but by whom or when is most uncertain.[114]

The Jesuit scholar José de Acosta had argued that America had been populated from Europe and Asia, and had refuted the view that Ophir was Peru.[115] Not only were the Amerindians descended from Noah, but America had been peopled by the ancient inhabitants of Europe itself. The effect of both Acosta's text and Hondius's map was to reduce the difference between Amerindians and Europeans. While sixteenth-century Rhenish maps such as Waldseemüller's 1516 *Carta Marina* had presented America as a 'most cruel nation of anthropophages', thus perhaps leaving the reader to wonder whether they were Plinian monstrous peoples rather than regular people, Hondius's map clearly argued that Amerindians and Europeans had a shared genealogy.[116]

111 'Tubal, cultor Hispaniae' ('Tubal, the founder of Spain'). According to Braude, 'Sons of Noah', from the 15th century, Noah's sons began to be identified with specific parts of the Old World: Shem with Asia, Ham with Africa and Japhet with Europe. Prior to this, the identification varied.

112 The map is too fragile for clear reproduction of the personifications and descendents of Noah, but their general shape can be made out on the facsimile: Hondius, *Map of the World*, portfolio, sheets 1 and 6.

113 Zur Shalev, 'Sacred Geography: Antiquarianism and Visual Erudition: Benio Arias Montano and the Maps in the Antwerp Polyglot Bible', *Imago Mundi*, 55 (2003), 56–80, at 71: the identification of Peru with Ophir was given 'philological proof' in Benito Arias Montano, *Antiquitatum Iudicarum libri IX, in quis, praeter Iudaeae, Hierosolymorum, et Templi Salomonis accuratam delineationem, praecipui sacri ac profani gentis ritus describuntur … Adiectis formis aeneis* (Leiden, 1593), sig. 4a.

114 Hondius, *Map of the World*, portfolio, sheet 2: 'America quem patrem habuerit admodum incertum est. Arias Montanus aliique viri docti, Ophir, Peru interpretantur, unde tempore Salomonis aurum adferebutur. Et ita Ophir Atnepotem [recte: adnepotem] Sem, huius Patrem constituunt idque ex quadam nominis allusione verum credibilius est hanc regionem a Septentrionalibus Europae vel Asiae partibus (ubi America vel contigua vel saltem ab hi[s] exiguo freto separatur) inhabitari caeptam a quo vero vel quando incertissimum est.' Here and elsewhere I have consulted the translations in idem, *Map of the World*, but made my own.

115 José de Acosta, *Historia natural y moral delas Indias* (Seville, 1590), chaps 13 and 20.

116 Of course, St Augustine had hesitantly suggested that one could be both monstrous and descended from Adam; see Chapter 1, near n. 13.

Among the map's numerous other illustrations, the largest and most prominent are its personifications of the continents accompanied by explanatory verses.[117] Europe is presented as the ruler of the other continents: 'Renowned Europe adorned with the empress's crown ... has subjugated the world on which she sits ... to herself by the power of her sword.'[118] Asia too has its advantages: 'Like Europe, she triumphs by her valour and her men; she alone rightly bears the palm for her beautiful women.'[119] We are told that Africa comes third (*tertia*) – another indicator that the continents were arranged in a hierarchy. Nevertheless: 'she stands out for the wondrous novelty of her possessions and takes the first place for the massive structures of her everlasting pyramids'.[120] America is described last, characterized by its gold deposits and the cannibalism of its inhabitants: 'Made hugely and widely famous in a short time by her gold mines, depraved America, hiding away the entrails of men within her own, holds out a deadly club.'[121] The verses present the reader with a comparative précis of the continents; its selection of New World information made the Amerindians appear markedly less civil than the inhabitants of the Old World continents. Hondius's 1608 map and, to a lesser extent, Blaeu's 1605 map, show America at the bottom of an ethnographic hierarchy. Nevertheless, there had been cities in some areas prior to the discovery of the New World by Europeans, as the maps city viewed showed. Finally, as descendants of Noah, their humanity was established, even though their civility was not.

Conclusion

Pre-modern genres of comparative ethnology (and arguably modern genres as well) were structured by a geographical grammar that inflected how readers interpreted empirical evidence. The costume book and the

[117] For analysis of the rest of the illustrations, see Davies, 'Representations of Amerindians', chap. 11. The map survives in a single, highly damanged copy. The images and the verses are based on prints by Maarten de Vos.

[118] Hondius, *Map of the World*, portfolio, sheet 7: 'Induperatrici decorata Europa corona, orbem quo sedet ... valido sibi subdidit inclyta ferro.'

[119] Ibid., sheets 6–7: 'Quae virtute velut Europa virisque triumphat, Femineis merito palmam fert unica formis.'

[120] Ibid., sheet 6: 'rerum praestans novitate stupenda, Primas pyramidum fert molibus aeternarum'.

[121] Ibid., sheet 2: 'Facta brevi auriferis late celeberrima venis, Visceribus scelerata suis humana recondens Viscera feralem praetendit America clavam.'

illustrated travel book were not hard and fast genres in the sense of there being a disjunction between 'just a book with a few illustrations' and a finely and profusely illustrated one, or between a costume book that examined many parts of the world and provided one or more illustrations for each, and the outliers like Nicolas de Nicolay's book that focused on the peoples in one empire. Nevertheless, these modes do signal a departure from previous approaches to representing diversity. They were not merely distinctive in terms of content and layout, but were also different rhetorical modes that argued for the reliability of their contents in different ways. The costume book made its claims to authority by virtue of its makers' powers of synthesis and comparison. By contrast, the illustrated travel book with richly detailed engravings of what one might call action scenes in the field deployed the rhetoric of the eyewitness.

This characterization had wide-ranging implications for colonial administration: in the eyes of many Europeans, cannibalism justified conquest and subjugation. The practice was also seen by some as indications of a limited capacity for apprehending Christianity, and thus, of a people's inability to become full members of a Christian empire. The invention of the cannibal – by which I mean the collective processes of observation and interpretation of New World peoples that led to this motif being chosen over others – constituted the construction of a people/beings that European viewers could interpret as being radically different from themselves.

Claesz and his close associate Hondius the Elder began to add peoples along the edges of their maps at the turn of the seventeenth century, and established the peoples of the Americas at the lowest rung of a hierarchy of civility. Within a decade, their competitor Willem Blaeu would join the fray. The resulting iconographical arms race resulted in a clutch of world and continental maps that were some 2m across, with extra border sheets that (for a price) could be obtained to frame their edges, and were rich in descriptive text that helped the viewer to contemplate the relationship between the world's peoples and the genealogy of humanity.

But, despite the mnemonic and interpretative value of the visual format, these maps became increasingly impractical. Because of their size, reading the captions, consulting the iconographic detail and viewing the whole map on a wall to see the geographical relationship between regions requires the viewer to adopt multiple body positions. In the Bibliothèque Nationale in Paris, for example, a number of Dutch wall maps backed in cloth now hang, in the manner of theatre backcloths, at the back of a basement area called *le théâtre*. In order to consult them, I was presented with a ladder and a very hot lamp that I could rest on the steps as I climbed up and down to examine the iconography and transcribe captions. Making transcriptions while standing on the ladder and looking at a caption was far from straightforward. In the Royal Geographical Society, the sole surviving and decidedly grubby and damaged copy of Hondius's 1608 world map hangs on a wall in a glass frame; dirt and reflections obscure many details. Ladders, dedication and eyesight must be tested in order to study the genealogy of Noah articulated in text and image here. Framed maps that are not on walls can still be impractical, be they printed or manuscript; Ribeiro's 1529 manuscript world map in the Vatican Library is almost immovable, interred in a basement from which its size prevents its escape, and had to be consulted in its caged vault. Even those wall maps that were mounted on rolls that can be consulted flat are not straightforward to study, as sufficiently large table space in a research library requires negotiation, and many portions are difficult to reach through any combination of bodily contortion and map rolling.

While the mental, visual and physical acrobatics required to study large maps do embed certain insights in the body of the viewer, for potential buyers making decisions about books and maps to purchase for multiple purposes, the giant ethno-geographic creations of early seventeenth-century Amsterdam map workshops were not the most practical way to gain insights about humanity. Just as, in the sixteenth century, the genre of cosmography had fissured into descriptive and mathematical genres, in the seventeenth century the illustrated wall map began to fail as an epistemologically valuable artefact with which to think about human diversity. The explosion of new information about a myriad of different cultures, giddying when displayed on even an enormous map, was better served by illustrated books. When new peoples were found, new books could be bought without the old ones becoming obsolete in quite the same way as a wall map.

Epilogue

> I have seen no more evident monster or miracle in the world than myself.
>
> (Michel de Montaigne, *Essays*, 'Les Boyteaux'.)

Renaissance mapmakers designed ethnographic motifs to service their readers' interests in both distant wonders and accurate, first-hand knowledge. These needs were not necessarily in opposition: since marvels were expected at the edges of the earth, accounts of man-eating tribes and giants were, *de facto*, credible. Just as a culture's discourse on madness is revelatory of its assumptions about rationality,[1] a culture's discussions about monsters reveal – and indeed help to *create* – the stress fractures in its assumptions about the nature of living beings. A history of representations of Amerindians on maps is therefore also a history of European conceptions of what it meant to be human, and of the ways in which scholars and artisans constructed and policed the boundaries between human and monstrous peoples. The logical conclusion of wonders being expected at the edges of the earth was that wonders expanded the concept of the human.

During the sixteenth century, accurate information became pertinent to practical affairs of colonization and empire rather than remaining in the theoretical sphere of the contemplation of God and his universal powers. Mapmakers' selections of ethnographic material – from headless men to images of impressive Inca cities – came from travel accounts that expressed wonder, a cognitive passion stimulated by the presence of something that transgressed the boundaries of everyday, explicable nature. The challenges of particular characterizations – such as the Patagonian giant – show how New World wonders drew contrasting emotional and intellectual responses as readers evaluated them in relation to the ethnological frameworks of civility, Christianity, humoral theory and monstrosity. The conception of the human was of great political significance in the colonial Americas: should any of those beings resembling human form turn out to be monsters rather than humans, that would permit, legitimate and, indeed, *necessitate* a different colonial policy.

[1] Clark, *Vanities of the Eye*, 5.

Sixteenth-century illustrated map traditions were changing at a time when the notion of monstrous peoples in distant lands was being contested in new ways. Reading publics had long associated maps with images of monstrous peoples, but these characterizations were increasingly coming under fire as the veil separating humans of different appearance and the notion of monstrous peoples began to tear. Against this backdrop, mapmakers fond themselves on the horns of a dilemma: should they sensationalize their imagery to appeal to the voyeuristic aspects of their readers' psyches, or to speak to their need for what they considered to be accurate information? And what if there were indeed marvellous beings in the Americas? So many marvels had been brought back that commentators including Sir Walter Ralegh and Jean de Léry argued that Pliny the Elder and John Mandeville appeared, with hindsight, to be more credible rather than less so. Mapmakers thus had to tack deftly between different agendas. These epistemological negotiations led to particular iconographic decisions being taking for different peoples.

The authors and amenuenses of travel accounts came from a range of social circles, from knights and ambassadors to sailors and adventurers from much further down the social pecking order. As Julia Schleck has reminded us, not only did such groups have mixed credibility to the reading public, but travel itself was a problematic way in which to garner knowledge; a popular proverb warns that travellers might lie with authority since few could test their claims. Travellers sought to bolster their authority through the generic and physical forms and rhetoric of written accounts.[2] What the incorporation of such material on a map suggested to its viewers was that a composite social group whose credit depended on both the artisanal skills and the intellectual prowess of its members, and who had not compromised this credit by wandering abroad, had evaluated all available accounts (which could differ), and presented the best knowledge for the viewer's consumption. A map, then, allowed its viewers to have their epistemological cake and eat it: new and multiple forms of knowledge from distant parts of the world but collected by unknown and potentially tricksy witnesses had been synthesized by the sober minds of those who had never travelled.

It is a commonplace of comparative histories that artefacts and ideas produced in different contexts vary. Each centre of cartographic production catered to distinct audiences; the manuscript maps of the sixteenth

[2] Schleck, *Telling True Tales*, 21–22.

century often catered to individual patrons audiences, while printed maps were aimed at a broader, pan-European viewing public. Despite this, the iconography for individual peoples of the Americas as produced in different settings were similar in important ways. Even though there were small differences between, for example, images of giants on different maps, they were still giants. The differences are illustrative of a common concern for going back to the sources, where possible, and extrapolating creatively from them. Map makers needs often transcended those of their local audiences where the ethnographic iconography was concerned. It was more important to show broadly the same activity in a region as previous maps from various centres had done, but to demonstrate thoughtful engagement with the appropriate travel accounts and introduce small details, than to devise a completely different motif.

The long sixteenth century was a period that witnessed a shift in the contents of illustrated world maps. The wide range of wonders seen on the late medieval Fra Mauro, Hereford and Ebstorf maps became restricted; information about the customs and manners of the world's peoples began to dominate textual and iconographic data on world maps. In other words, the long sixteenth century was a period in which the map became the genre *nonpareil* for disseminating world views of human diversity. Even though early voyages of exploration were primarily about finding spices and other commodities (and only incidentally about finding new souls to save), European reading publics were captivated by the peoples they encountered. Mapmakers' choices to show people, not commodities, was an invention and re-orientation of the most pressing reasons to go to and/or possess the Americas. This invention was the diametric opposite of the one effected by Alexander von Humboldt three centuries later when, as Mary Louise Pratt put it, he 'reinvented South America first and foremost as nature. . .. a nature that dwarfs humans, commands their being, arouses their passions, defies their powers of perception'.[3]

The comparative ethnology of illustrated maps drew relatively little from notions of food and local atmospheric conditions as influences on human bodies and polities. With the notable exception of cannibalism, foodstuffs do not play a part in the motifs characterizing peoples. One reason for this might be that it was difficult to tell different foodstuffs apart via illustrations. Given the general obsession with trade and 'marchantable commodities', this might appear to be somewhat surprising. It is,

[3] Pratt, *Imperial Eyes*, 118.

however, explicable if we bear in mind mapmakers' concerns for making each motif as different as possible from the others.

To what extent did mapmakers try to create knowledge that, to paraphrase Lorraine Daston and Peter Galison, bore no trace of the viewer? Daston and Galison have argued that scientists only started searching for this in the mid-nineteenth century.[4] They outlined three codes of epistemic virtue: 'truth-to-nature, mechanical objectivity, and trained judgement'. They examined scientific atlases, or 'those select collections of images that identify a discipline's most significant objects of inquiry',[5] from the early eighteenth to the mid-twentieth century. Although geographical atlases are not part of Daston and Galison's account, mapmakers also sought to reproduce, with their illustrations, 'the characteristic, the essential, the universal, the typical'.[6] In order to do so, these artisans and scholars distilled iconic characteristics that allowed viewers to distinguish between peoples, as the present study has shown. We must beware of mistakenly judging these images unfavourably by silently comparing them to photographs. Just as a diagram of a molecule or an electrical circuit in the latest issue of *Nature* does not replicate what the human eye sees (and at what magnification, anyway?), a representation of a monstrous person on a map should be read as a diagram of a category-disrupting observation, not as a substitute for 'real' knowledge with the visual impact of a failed *trompe l'oeil* painting.

What, then, was the 'technology of scientific sight implicating author, illustrator, production, and reader' in Renaissance images of Amerindians on maps?[7] What were the epistemic codes of making ethnographic knowledge via maps? Throughout the sixteenth century, mapmakers strove to place peoples within the landmasses they inhabited. This coding began to break apart at the turn of the seventeenth century. The De Bry volumes prompted a new paradigm: detailed images of daily life around the borders of a map. Rather than picking ways of distinguishing between peoples and emphasizing their locational specificity, Dutch map images began to focus on everyday life and costume. A new epistemic virtue for maps had emerged, one that stressed the universal humanity of peoples at the expense of demonstrating the geographical and thus environmental influences on bodies and temperaments.

The illustrated sheet map or atlas functioned as a display space – a theatre – upon which the mapmaker choreographed an ethnographic

[4] Lorraine Daston and Peter Galison, *Objectivity* (New York, NY: Zone Books, 2007), 17.
[5] Ibid., 17–18. [6] Ibid., 20. [7] Ibid., 18.

parade in the manner of a seventeenth-century fairground huckster. There was, however, a crucial difference: mapmakers gained customers and credibility not merely by selling the sensational, but also by peddling what their punters would interpret as sober, synthesized summaries of the state of the world and its peoples. In this way, a mapmaker was akin to a princely collector arranging his treasures, with the map functioning as a two-dimensional cabinet of the curiosities of travel. Like a collector, a mapmaker decided what examples to keep, and how to arrange them in order to best reveal his knowledge as well as the order of nature.

In Renaissance Europe, for a claim to be accepted as true, it needed to be both intrinsically and extrinsically plausible. This book has shown how distinctive cultural stereotypes emerged as the epistemologies of wonder and eyewitnessing intermingled in a genre that encouraged the viewer to compare and classify peoples. The ethnographic material on an illustrated wall map or map of a continent was the result of a distinctive type of exercise in synthetic, visual exegesis that could not be fully replicated in any other genre. The boundaries between human, monster and animal, and the relationship between wonder and knowledge, were redrawn through the processes of making knowledge about places that were theoretically expected to contain marvels, but were now being reached and explored by multiple witnesses.

Bibliography

PRIMARY SOURCES

Manuscript Sources

Barcelona

Universitat de Barcelona, CRAI Biblioteca de Reserva

MS 1557. Sebastián Fernández de Medrano. Guia Geografica y Hidrografica, 17th century.

Bloomington, IN

Indiana University Bloomington, Lilly Library

Boxer mss. II. Sino-Spanish codex (Boxer codex), c.1590.

Chicago, IL

Newberry Library

Greenlee MS map 26. Sebastian Lopes Atlas, c.1565.

The Hague

Koninklijke Bibliotheek

**MS 129 A 24. Hague (Vallière) Atlas, c.1545.

London

The British Library, Department of Manuscripts

Add. MS. 5413. Harleian (Dauphin) chart, c.1547.

Add. MS. 5415.a. Diogo Homem, 'Queen Mary Atlas', 1558.

Add. MS. 57555. Sir Walter Ralegh's notebook.

** Consulted via digital facsimile.

Add. MS. 21592. Portolan Atlas, Italian, 16th century.
Add. MS. 24065. Pierre Desceliers, 'Mappemonde', 1550.
Add. MS. 28681, fol. 9*r*. Psalter Map, c.1265.
Add. MS. 27303. Lopes North Atlantic map, 1558.
Add. MS. 31317. Vaz Dourado Atlas, 1575.
Egerton MS. 1513. Portolan Atlas, 1587.
Harley MS. 3954. Travels of John Mandeville. East Anglia, c.1430.
Royal MS. 20.E.IX. Jean Rotz, Rotz Atlas, 1542.

The British Museum, Department of Prints and Drawings
BM P&D 1906, 0509. John White, watercolour drawings of Virginia, 1585–6.

Lambeth Palace Library
Sir Walter Ralegh, 'Sir Wallter Ralleghes Dyscourse: of his first voyadg to Guiana', 1595, MS 250.

Royal Geographical Society
mr 6.G.10 (0). Edward Luther Stevenson, 'Atlas of Nicolas Vallard, 1547' (unpublished typescript, 1927).

Manchester

John Rylands Library, Special Collections
French MS 1*. Rylands (Henri II) planisphere, 1546.

Munich

Bayerische Staatsbibliothek, Abteilung für Handschriften und Alte Drucke
Cod. icon. 133. 'Kunstmann Map', c.1502–1506.
Cod. Hisp. 12. Diego Ribero [Diogo Ribeiro], 'Libro de la navegacion de la India de Portugal', 1524.

New York City, NY

Pierpont Morgan Library
MS 461. 'Livre des merveilles du monde', France, possibly Angers, c.1460.
MS M.506. Pierre Desceliers, 'Portolan Atlas', c.1546.
MS 3900. 'Histoire Naturelle des Indes', 1586. (The Drake Manuscript).

Paris

Bibliothèque Nationale de France, Département des Cartes et plans
Rés. Ge A 1048. Harmen and Marten Jansz, 'Nova orbis terrarum geographica ac hydrographica tabula', 1610.

Ge C 5086 (RES). Diogo Homem, 'Universa ac navigabilis totius terrarum orbis descriptio', c.1558.

Rés. Ge C 5007. Jacques de Vau de Claye, 'Le vrai pourtraict de Geneure et du Cap de Frie', 1579.

Rés. Ge D 13871. Jacques de Vau de Claye, 'Les côtes du brésil', 1579.

Rés. Ge DD. 683 and Rés. Ge AA 640. Miller Atlas, 1519.

S.H. Archives no.6. Pierre de Vaulx, 'L'ocean Atlantique', 1613.

Bibliothèque Nationale de France, Département des Manuscrits

MS. français 19 112. Guillaume Le Vasseur, 'Traicté de la geodrographie ou art de naviguer', 1608.

MS. français 24269. Jean Cordier, 'S'ensuyt le langaige du Brésil et du françoys'.

MS. espagnol 30. Abraham Cresques[?], Catalan Atlas, c.1375.

Providence, RI

John Carter Brown Library

Codex Latin 1. Henricus Glareanus, 'De geometriae principiis ad sphaerae astronomicae noticiam necessariis', c.1513.

Codex Sp 7 1-size. Juan López de Velasco, 'Demarcacion y division de las Yndias', 1575.

San Marino, CA

Henry E. Huntington Library

HM 29. Vallard Atlas, c.1547.

Vatican City

Biblioteca Apostolica Vaticana

MS Borgiano III. Diogo Ribeiro, 'Carta uniuersal . . .', 1529.

Vienna

Österreichische Nationalbibliothek, Kartensammlung

** K I 99.416. Sancho Gutiérrez, world map, 1551.

Vincennes

Château de Vincennes, Service historique de l'armée de terre

Archives du Dépôt de la guerre, D.2.z.14. Guillaume Le Testu, 'Cosmographie universelle selon les navigateurs, tant ancien que modernes', 1555 [1556 n.s.].

Printed Sources

Acosta, José de, *Historia natural y moral delas Indias* (Seville, 1590).

Natural and Moral History of the Indies, trans. by Frances López-Morillas, ed. Jane Mangan and commentary Walter Mignolo (Durham, NC and London: Duke University Press, 2002).

Ailly, Pierre d', *Sexta figura. Hec figura servit nono capitulo pro divisione terre per climata.[right] Septima figura. Hec figura servit xiiii. capitulo pluribus aliis pro divisione terre in tres partes* . . . in Pierre d'Ailly, [Ymago Mundi], ([Louvain?], [1483?]).

Albertus Magnus, *De natura locorum*, in *Opera omnia*, ed. Auguste Borgnet, 38 vols. (Paris: apud Ludovicum Vivès, 1890–5) IX.

Aldrovandi, Ulisse, *Monstrorum historia* (Bologna, 1642).

Amman, Jost, *Im Frauenzimmer wirt vermeldt von allerley schönen Kleidungen unnd Trachten* (Frankfurt am Main, 1586).

Anghiera, Pietro Martire d', *Opera, Legatio babylonica, Oceani decas, Poemata, Epigrammata* (Seville, 1511).

De orbe novo . . . decades octo (Alcalá de Henares, 1530).

Selections, ed. and trans. Geoffrey Eatough (Turnhout: Brepols, 1998).

Anon., *Cursor mundi*, ed. Richard Morris et al. (London: Published for the Early English Text Society by N. Trubner, 1874–93 [first circulated: late thirteenth-century]).

Appelbaum, Stanley, ed., *The Triumph of Maximilian I* (New York: Dover, 1964).

Aristotle, *The Nicomachean Ethics*, trans. H. Rackham (London: William Heinemann, 1926).

Politics, trans. H. Rackham (Cambridge, MA: Harvard University Press, 1932).

Meteorologia, ed. and trans. H. D. P. Lee (London: William Heinemann; Cambridge, MA: Harvard University Press, 1952).

On the Soul, English trans. by W. S. Hett (London: William Heinemann; Cambridge, MA: Harvard University Press, 1957).

Generation of Animals, trans. by A. L. Peck (London and Cambridge, MA: Harvard University Press, 1963).

Augustine, Saint, *The City of God Against the Pagans*, trans. by Eva Matthews Sanford and William McAllen Green, 7 vols. (London and Cambridge, MA: Harvard University Press, 1965).

Benzoni, Girolamo, *Americae pars quarta. Sive, insignis et admiranda historia de reperta primum Occidentali India a Christophoro Columbo anno MCCCCXCII*, ed. Theodor de Bry (Frankfurt am Main, 1594).

Das vierdte Buch von der neuwen Welt, ed. Theodor de Bry (Frankfurt am Main, 1594).

Americae pars quinta. Nobilis et admiratione plena Hieronymi Benzoni Mediolanensis, secundae sectionis Historia, ed. Theodor de Bry (Frankfurt am Main, 1595).

Benzoni, Girolamo and Nicolas Challeux, *Americae pars sexta, sive historiae ab Hieronymo Benzono Mediolanense scriptae, sectio tertia*, ed. Theodor de Bry (Frankfurt am Main, 1596).

Bertius, Petrus, *Tabularum geographicarum contractarum libri quatuor* (Amsterdam, 1600).

Tabularum geographicarum contractarum libri septem (Amsterdam, 1616).

Description d'Amerique, qui est le nouveau monde, tirée des 'Tableaux geographiques' (Amsterdam, 1622).

Best, George, *A Trve Discovrse of the Late Voyages of Discouerie, for the finding of a passage to Cathaya, by the Northvveast, vnder the conduct of Martin Frobisher* (London, 1578).

Blaeu, Willem Jansz., *World Map of 1605*, Introduction by Edward Luther Stevenson (New York: Hispanic Society of America, 1914).

Nova et exacta terrarum orbis tabula geographica ac hydrographica (Amsterdam, 1604).

Nova totius Americae sive novi orbis tabula (Amsterdam, 1608).

Blundeville, Thomas, *Exercises* (London, 1594).

Bodin, Jean, *Les Six Livres de la republique [1576]*, ed. Christiane Frémont et al., 6 vols. (Paris: Fayard, 1986).

Method for the Easy Comprehension of History, trans. Beatrice Reynolds (New York: Columbia University Press, 1945).

Methodus ad facilem historiarum cognitionem [1566] (Aalen: Scientia, 1967).

Boemus, Johannes, ... *Omnium gentium mores, leges et ritus*... (Augsburg, 1520).

Omnium gentium mores, leges et ritus (Antwerp and Venice, 1542).

The Manners, Lawes and Customes of All Nations (London, 1611).

Boone, Elizabeth Hill, 'This New World Now Revealed: Hernán Cortés and the Presentation of Mexico to Europe', *Word & Image*, 27:1 (2011), 31–46.

Bordone, Benedetto, *Libro di Benedetto Bordone nel qual si ragiona de tutte l'isole del mondo* (Venice, 1528).

Botero, Giovanni, *Della ragion di stato libri dieci, con tre libri delle cause della grandezza, e magnificenza delle città* (Venice, 1589).

Relationi universali ... (Brescia, 1599)

A Treatise, Concerning the Causes of the Magnificencie and Greatnes of Cities (London, 1606).

Braun, Georg and Franz Hogenberg, *Civitates orbis terrarum*, 3 vols. (Cologne, 1572–1617).

Theatre des principales villes de tout l'vniuers, 6 vols. (Cologne, 1579–1625).

Browne, Thomas, *Pseudodoxia Epidemica: or, Enquiries into Very Many Received Tenets, and Commonly Presumed Truths* (London, 1646).

Bulwer, John, *Anthropometamorphosis: Man Transform'd; or, the Artificial Changeling* (London, 1650).

Burton, Robert, *The Anatomy of Melancholy* (Oxford, 1621).

Cabot, Sebastian, [*Mappemonde*] (Antwerp, 1544).

Cabral, Pedro Álvares and Pedro Vaz de Caminha, *The Voyage of Pedro Álvares Cabral [1500] to Brazil and India*, ed. and trans. William Brooks Greenlee (London: Hakluyt Society, 1938).

Carvajal, Gaspar de, *Relación* . . ., ed. José Toribio Medina and Julio F. Guillén Tato (Madrid: Consejo de la Hispanidad, 1944 [first published: 1894]).

Carvajal, Gaspar de and Francisco de Orellana, *The Discovery of the Amazon*, ed. José Toribio Medina, trans. Bertram T. Lee (New York: Dover, 1988).

Cicero, *De senectute; De amicitia; De divinatione*, trans. by William Armistead Falconer (London: William Heinemann; / Cambridge, MA: Harvard University Press, 1971).

Cieza de León, Pedro de, *Parte primera de la Chrónica del Perú* (Seville, 1553).

The Travels . . . Contained in the First Part of His Chronicle of Peru, ed. and trans. Clements R. Markham (London: Hakluyt Society, 1864).

Obras completas. La crónica del Perú. Las guerras civiles peruanas, ed. Carmelo Sáenz de Santa Maria, 2 vols. (Madrid: Consejo Superior de Investigaciones Científicas, Instituto Gonzalo Fernández de Oviedo, 1984–85).

The Discovery and Conquest of Peru, ed. and trans. Alexandra Parma Cook and Noble David Cook (Durham, NC and London: Duke University Press, 1998).

Claesz, Cornelis, *Americae tabula nova* (Amsterdam, c.1602).

Columbus, Christopher, *Epistola . . . de su gran descubrimiento . . .* (Barcelona, 1493).

Juan Gil and Consuelo Varela, eds., *Cartas de particulares a Colón y relaciones coetáneas* (Madrid: Alianza, 1984).

Letters from America: Columbus's First Accounts of the 1492 Voyage, ed. and trans. B. W. Ife (London: King's College, London, 1992).

A Synoptic Edition of the Log of Columbus's First Voyage, ed. Francesca Lardicci (Turnhout: Brepols, 1999).

Cortés, Hernán, *Praeclara de Nova Maris oceani Hyspania narratio* (Nuremberg, 1524).

Cortés, Hernán, *Letters from Mexico*, translated, edited, and with a new introduction by Anthony Pagden, with an introductory essay by J. H. Elliott (New Haven, CT: Yale Nota Bene / Yale University Press, 2001 [1986 revised ed.]).

Cortés, Martín, *Breue compendio de la sphera y de la arte de nauegar, con nuevos instrumentos y reglas, exemplificado con muy subtiles demonstraciones* (Seville, 1551).

Covarrubias, Sebastián de, *Tesoro de la lengua castellana, o española* (Madrid, 1611).

Coyer, Gabriel François, *Letter to Dr Maty . . . containing an abstract of the relations of travellers of different nations, concerning the Patagonians* (London, 1767).

Dee, John, *The Elements of Geometrie of Euclide* (London, 1570).

Desceliers, Pierre, *Autotype Facsimiles of Three Mappemondes: 1: The Harleian, or Anonymous, Mappemonde, c.1536*, ed. C. H. Coote ([Aberdeen: privately printed], 1898).

Autotype Facsimiles of Three Mappemondes: 2: The Mappemonde by Desceliers of 1546, ed. C. H. Coote ([Aberdeen: privately printed], 1898).

Autotype Facsimiles of Three Mappemondes: 3: The Mappemonde of Desceliers of 1550, ed. C. H. Coote ([Aberdeen: privately printed], 1898).

Die Weltkarte des Pierre Desceliers von 1553, herausgegeben von Eugene Oberhummer (Vienna: Geographische Gesellschaft, 1924).

The World for a King: Pierre Desceliers' Map of 1550, ed. and trans. Chet Van Duzer (London: The British Library, 2015).

Deserps, François, *Recueil de la diuersité des habits qui sont de present en usaige tant es pays d'Europe, Asie, Affrique et Illes sauvages, le tout fait apres le naturel* (Paris, 1562).

A Collection of the Various Styles of Clothing Which Are Presently Worn in Countries of Europe, Asia, Africa, and the Savage Islands, All Realistically Depicted, ed. Sara Shannon (Minneapolis, MN: University of Minnesota Press, 2001).

Doesborgh, Jan van, *De novo mondo. Antwerp, Jan van Doesborch [about 1520]. A Facsimile of a Unique Broadsheet*, ed. and trans. Maria Elizabeth Kronenberg (The Hague: M. Nijhoff, 1927).

Of the Newe Landes and of ye People founde by the Messengers of the kynge of Portyngale named Emanuel ([Antwerp], c.1520).

Duverger, Erik, *Antwerpse kunstinventarissen uit de zeventiende eeuw* (Brussels: AWLSK, 1984).

Die Ebstorfer Weltkarte: Kommentierte Neuausgabe in zwei Bänden, herausgegeben von Hartmut Kugler, 2 vols. (Berlin: Akademie, 2007).

Ende, Josua van den, *Nova et exacta terrarum orbis tabula geographica ac hydrographica* (Amsterdam, 1604).

L'entrée de Henri II à Rouen, 1550: A Facsimile, introduction by Margaret McGowan (Amsterdam: Theatrum Orbis Terrarum, 1973).

Elyot, Thomas, *The Boke Named the Gouernor* (London, 1531).

Fries, Lorenz, *Uslegung der mercarthen, oder Carta Marina* (Strasbourg, 1527).

...Carta Marina universalis, 1530 ... (Munich: L. Rosenthal, 1926).

Garcia de Palacio, Diego, *Instruccion nautica para navegar [1587] prologue*, Julio F. Guillén Tato (Madrid: Instituto de Cultura Hispánica, 1944).

Garcia, José Manuel, *O descobrimento do Brasil nos textos de 1500 a 1571* (Lisbon: Calouste Gulbenkian Foundation, 2000).

Ghadessi, Touba, 'Inventoried Monsters: Dwarves and Hirsutes at Court', *Journal of the History of Collections*, 23:2 (2011), 267–81.

George Warren, *An Impartial Description of Surinam upon the Continent of Guiana in America* (London, 1667), 20.

Gesner, Konrad, *Historiae animalium ...*, 5 vols. (Zurich, 1551).

Gómara, Francisco López de, *La istoria general de las Indias, y conquista de Mexico* (Saragossa, 1552).

La historia general de las Indias y Nuevo Mundo ... (Saragossa, 1555).

Guinnard, Auguste, *Trois Ans chez les patagons: Le récit de captivité d'Auguste Guinnard (1856–1859)*, introduction & dossier historique de Jean-Paul Duviols (Paris: Chandeigne, 2009).

Gutiérrez, Diego, *Americae sive quartae orbis partis nova et exactissima descriptio* (Antwerp, 1562).

Hakluyt, Richard, *The Principall Navigations, Voyages and Discoveries of the English Nation* (London, 1589).

The Principal Navigations, Voyages and Discoveries of the English Nation, 8 vols. (Glasgow: Maclehose, 1903–5).

Harriot, Thomas, *A Briefe and True Report of the New Found Land of Virginia* (London, 1588).

Admiranda narratio, fida tamen: de commodis et incolarum ritibus Virginiae [ed. Theodor de Bry] (Frankfurt am Main, 1590).

A Briefe and True Report of the New Found Land of Virginia [ed. Theodor de Bry] (Frankfurt am Main, 1590).

Herrera y Tordesillas, Antonio de, *Description des Indes Occidentales* (Amsterdam, 1622).

Herrera y Tordesillas, Antonio de, Pedro Ordóñez de Cevallos [and Petrus Bertius], *Novi orbis pars duodecima. Sive descriptio Indiae Occidentalis*, ed. Johannes Theodor de Bry (Frankfurt am Main, 1624).

Heylyn, Peter, *Microcosmus, or a Little Description of the Great World* (Oxford, 1621).

Cosmographie in foure bookes containing the Chorographie and Historie of the whole World (London, 1657).

L'Histoire de la Terre Neuve du Peru en l'Inde Occidentale (Paris, 1545).

Homem, Diogo, *Atlas universal*, introduction Alfredo Pinheiro Marques and Ludmila Kildushevskaya, trans. Anne Barton de Mayor (Barcelona: M. Moleiro Editor, 2002).

Hondius the Elder, Jodocus, *America noviter delineata* (Amsterdam, 1590).

Nieuwe caerte van het wonderbaer ende goudrijcke landt Guiana (Amsterdam, c.1598).

Virginiae item et Floridae Americae provinciarum, nova descriptio (Amsterdam, 1606).

America Septentrionalis (Amsterdam, 1606).

Nova et exacta totius orbis terrarum descriptio geographica et hydrographica (Amsterdam, 1608).

America noviter delineata (Amsterdam, 1618).

Nova Virginiae tabula (Amsterdam, 1618).

The Map of the World on Mercator's Projection … Amsterdam 1608, from the Unique Copy in the Collection of the Royal Geographical Society, memoir by Edward Heawood (London: Royal Geographical Society, 1927).

Hondius the Younger, Jodocus, *America noviter delineata* (Amsterdam, 1623).

Hulsius, Levinus, *Brevis & admiranda descriptio regni Guianae …* (Nuremberg, 1599).

. . . *Kurtze wunderbare Beschreibung deß goldreichen Königreichs Guianae in America* . . . (Nuremberg, 1599).

Huttich, Johann, *Novus orbis regionum ac insularum veteribus incognitarum, una cum tabula cosmographica, et aliquot aliis consimilis argumenti libellis* . . ., preface, Simon Grynaeus (Basle and Paris, 1532).

Isidore of Seville, *Etymologiarum sive originum libri xx*, ed. W. M. Lindsay, 2 vols. (Oxford: Clarendon Press, 1962).

The Etymologies of Isidore of Seville, ed. and trans. Stephen A. Barney et al. (Cambridge: Cambridge University Press, 2006).

Jode, Cornelis de, *[South America]* (Antwerp, 1576).

Speculum orbis terrae (Antwerp, 1593).

Americae pars borealis (Antwerp, 1593).

Jode, Gerard de, *Speculum orbis terrarum* (Antwerp, 1578).

Jonghe, Clement de, *Hydrographica planeque nova Indiae occidentalis, Guineae, regni Congo, Angolae, &c. delineatio* (Amsterdam, 1665).

Keere, Pieter van den, *Americae nova descriptio* (Amsterdam, 1614).

Nova orbis terrarum geographica ac hydrographica tabula (Amsterdam, 1619).

Keymis, Lawrence, *A Relation of the Second Voyage to Guiana* (London, 1596).

Waerachtighe ende grondighe beschryvinge vande tweede Zeevaert der Engelschen nae Guiana (Amsterdam, 1598).

Kunstmann, Friedrich, Karl Spruner von Merk and Georg Martin Thomas, eds., *Atlas zur Entdeckungsgeschichte Amerikas. Aus Handschriften der K. Hof- und Staats-Bibliothek, der K. Universitaet und des Hauptconservatoriums der K. B. Armee* (Munich: In commission bei A. Asher, 1859).

Langren, Arnold van, *Delineatio omnium orarum totius Australis partis Americae* (Amsterdam, 1596).

Las Casas, Bartolomé de, *Brevissima relacion de la destruycion de las Indias* (Seville, 1552).

Tyrannies et cruautez des espagnols, perpetrées és Indes Occidentales (Antwerp, 1579).

The Spanish Colonie, or Briefe Chronicle of the Acts and Gestes of the Spaniardes in the West Indies (London, 1583).

Narratio regionum indicarum per Hispanos quosdam devastatarum verissima (Frankfurt am Main, 1598).

Den Spieghel vande Spaensche Tyrannie beeldelijcken afgemaelt (Amsterdam, 1609).

Le Miroir de la tyrannie espagnole perpetrée aux Indes Occidentales (Amsterdam, 1620).

A Short Account of Destruction of the Indies, ed. and trans. Nigel Griffin (London: Penguin, 1991).

Tratados de 1552 impresos por Las Casas en Sevilla, ed. Ramón Hernández and Lorenzo Galmés, . . . *Obras completas*, 14 vols. (Madrid: Alianza, 1988–99), X.

Laudonnière, René de, Jacques Le Moyne de Morgues, et al., *Brevis narratio eorum quae in Florida Americae provincia Gallis acciderunt .... Quae est secunda pars Americae...*, ed. Theodor de Bry (Frankfurt am Main, 1591).

Leonardo de Argensola, Bartolomé, *Conqvista de las islas Malvcas* (Madrid, 1609).

Le Roy, Louis, *De la vicissitude ou variété de choses in l'vnivers* (Paris, 1579).

Of the Interchangeable Course, or Variety of Things in the Whole World (London, 1594).

Le Testu, Guillaume, *Cosmographie universelle selon les navigateurs tan anciens que modernes [1555]*, ed. Frank Lestringant ([Paris]: Arthaud, 2012).

Léry, Jean de, *Histoire d'un voyage fait en la terre du Bresil* (La Rochelle, 1578).

Histoire d'un voyage faict en la terre du Bresil (Geneva, 1580).

Histoire d'un voyage fait en la terre du Brésil [1580], ed. Jean-Claude Morisot (Geneva: Droz, 1975).

History of a Voyage to the Land of Brazil, Otherwise Called America, trans. Janet Whatley (Berkeley, CA: University of California Press, 1990).

Libro segundo de Palmerin que trata los grandes fechos de Primaleón (Salamanca, 1512).

Linschoten, Jan van Huygen van, *Itinerario. Voyage ofte Schipvaert* (Amsterdam and The Hague, 1596).

La historia general de las Indias y Nuevo Mundo ... (Saragossa, 1555).

Magnus, Olaus, *Historia de gentibus septentrionalibus* (Rome, 1555).

Mandeville, John, *[Itinerarium]* (Westminster, 1499) (Cambridge University Library, Inc.5.d.1.2 [4140]).

The Voyages and Trauailes (London, 1618).

The Travels ... trans. and introduction by C. W. R. D. Moseley (London: Penguin, 2005).

Mapamundi, the Catalan Atlas of the Year 1375, ed. and with commentary by Georges Grosjean (Dietikon-Zurich: Urs Graf, 1978).

Marees, Pieter de, *Beschryvinghe ende historische verhael van het Gout Koninckrijck van Guinea* (Amsterdam, 1602).

Description and Historical Account of the Gold Kingdom of Guinea (1602), trans. and ed. Albert van Dantzig and Adam Jones (Oxford: Oxford University Press, 1987).

Maximilianus Transylvanus, *De Moluccis insulis* (Rome, 1523).

Mena, Cristóbal de, *The Conquest of Peru as Recorded by a Member of the Pizarro Expedition [1534]*, with a trans. and annotations by Joseph H. Sinclair (New York: New York Public Library, 1929).

Mercator, Gerard and Jodocus Hondius the Elder, *Atlas sive cosmographicae meditationes de fabrica mundi et fabricati figura* (Amsterdam, 1606).

Montaigne, Michel de, *The Complete Essays*, trans. and ed. M. A. Screech (London: Penguin, 2003).

Le Brésil de Montaigne: Le Nouveau Monde des 'Essais' (1580–1592), introduction and notes, Frank Lestringant (Paris: Chandeigne, 2005).

Montalboddo, Fracanzano da, *Paesi novamente retrovati & novo mondo da Alberico Vesputio Florentino intitulato* (Vicenza, 1507).
Paesi novamente retrovati (Milan, 1508).
Itinerarium Portugallensium (Milan, 1508).
Newe vnbekanthe Landte (Nuremberg, 1508).
Itinerarium Portugallensium, ed. Luís de Matos (Lisbon Fundação Calouste Gulbenkian, 1992).
Münster, Sebastian, *Typus cosmographicus universalis* (Basle, 1532).
Geographia universalis, vetus et nova, complectens Claudii Ptolemaei Alexandrini enarrationis libros VIII (Basle, 1540).
Cosmographiae. Beschreibung aller lender (Basle, 1544).
Cosmographiae. Beschreibung aller lender (Basle, 1545).
Cosmographia universalis (Basle, 1550).
Nicolay, Nicolas de, *Les qvatre premiers livres des navigations et peregrinations Orientales* (Lyon, 1568).
The nauigations, peregrinations and voyages, made into Turkie by Nicholas Nicholay (London 1585).
Noort, Olivier van, *Beschryvinghe van de Voyagie om den geheelen Werelt Cloot* (Amsterdam, 1602).
Ortelius, Abraham, *Theatrum orbis terrarum* (Antwerp, 1570).
Theatrum orbis terrarum (Antwerp, 1571).
Nova totius terrarum orbi . . . descriptio (Antwerp, 1564).
Nova totius terrarum orbi . . . descriptio (Antwerp, 1584).
Oresme, Nicolas, *Nicole Oresme and the Marvels of Nature: A Study of his De causis mirabilium with Critical Edition, Translation, and Commentary*, ed. Bert Hanson (Toronto, ON: Pontifical Institute of Mediaeval Studies, 1985).
Paré, Ambroise, *Les Oeuvres d'Ambroise Paré* (Paris, 1579).
Des Monstres et prodiges, ed. Jean Céard (Geneva: Droz, 1971).
Parmentier, Jean and Raoul Parmentier, *Voyage à Sumatra en 1529. Journal de bord* (Clermont-Ferrand: Paleo, 2001).
Pepys, Samuel, *The Diary of Samuel Pepys: A New and Complete Transcription*, ed. Robert Latham and William Matthews (London: HarperCollins, 2000 [reissue of 1970–83 ed.]).
Pigafetta, Antonio, *Le Voyage et navigation faict par les Espaignolz es isles de Mollucques* (Paris, c.1525).
The Voyage of Magellan: The Journal of Antonio Pigafetta . . . from the edition in the William L. Clements Library, University of Michigan, Ann Arbor, trans. Paula Spurlin Paige (Englewood Cliffs, NJ: Prentice Hall, 1969).
Magellan's Voyage: A Narrative Account of the First Circumnavigation, ed. and trans. R. A. Skelton (New York: Dover, 1994).
The First Voyage Around the World, 1519–1522: An Account of Magellan's Expedition, ed. Theodor J. Cachey Jr (Toronto: University of Toronto Press, 2007).

Pigafetta, Antonio and Maximilianus Transylvanus, *First Voyage Around the World . . . and 'De Moluccis insulis' . . .*, ed. Carlos Quirino (Manila: Filipiniana Book Guild, 1969).

Pinet, Antoine de, *Plantz, povrtraitz et descriptions de plvsievrs villes et forteresses* (Lyon, 1564).

Plancius, Petrus, *Haec pars Peruvianae, regiones Chicam & Chilem complectitur, & Regionum Patagonum* (Amsterdam, c.1592–4).

Orbis terrarum typus de integro multis in locis emendatus (Amsterdam, 1594).

Pliny the Elder, *Natural History*, trans. H. Rackham, 10 vols. (Cambridge, MA: Harvard University Press, 1969).

Polo, Marco, *The Travels. . .*, trans. and intro., Ronald Latham (Harmondsworth, 1958).

Polo, Marco et al., *Livre des merveilles . . .reproduction des 265 miniatures . . .*, 2 vols. (Paris: Bibliothèque nationale de France, 1907).

Ptolemy, Claudius, . . . *Geographiae opus* (Strasbourg, 1513).

. . . *Opus geographiae* (Strasbourg, 1522).

Claudii Ptolomaei Geographicae enarrationis libri octo (Strasbourg, 1525).

Ptolemy's Geography: *An Annotated Translation of the Theoretical Chapters*, eds. and trans. J. Lennart Berggren and Alexander Jones (Princeton, NJ and Oxford: Princeton University Press, 2000).

Purchas, Samuel, *Microcosmus or The Historie of Man* (London, 1619).

Hakluytus Posthumus or Purchas his Pilgrimes, 20 vols. (Glasgow: Maclehose, 1905–7).

Ralegh, Sir Walter, *The Discoverie of the Large, Rich, and Bewtifvl Empyre of Guiana* (London, 1596).

Waerachtighe ende grondighe beschryvinge van het groot ende Goudt-rijck Coninckrijck van Guiana (Amsterdam, 1598).

Waerachtighe ende grondighe beschryvinge van . . . Guiana (Amsterdam, 1598).

The Discoverie of the Large, Rich, and Bewtiful Empyre of Guiana by Sir Walter Ralegh, transcribed, annotated and introduced by Neil L. Whitehead (Norman, OK: University of Oklahoma Press, 1997).

. . . *Discoverie of Guiana*, ed. Joyce Lorimer (Aldershot, Hants and Burlington, VT: Ashgate, 2006).

Ramusio, Giovanni Battista, *Navigationi et viaggi*, 3 vols. (Venice, 1550–59).

Navigationi et viaggi, Venice 1563–1606, ed. R. A. Skelton (Amsterdam: Theatrum Orbis Terrarum, 1970).

Relaciones geográficas del siglo XVI, ed. René Acuña, 10 vols. (Mexico City: Universidad Nacional Autónoma de México, 1982–8).

Rodríguez de Montalvo, Garci, *Amadis of Gaul*, trans. Edwin B. Place and Herbert C. Behm, 2 vols. (Lexington, KY: University of Kentucky Press, 1974).

Rosaccio, Giuseppe, *Universale descrittione di tutto il mondo* (Venice, 1597).

Rotz, Jean, *The Maps and Text of the Boke of Idrography presented by Jean Rotz to Henry VIII now in The British Library*, ed. Helen Wallis (Oxford: Roxburghe Club, 1981).

Ruysch, Johannes, *Universalior cogniti orbis tabula ex recentibus confecta observationi* (Rome, 1507).

Sancho, Pedro, *An Account of the Conquest of Peru*, trans. Philip Ainsworth Means (New York: Cortes Society, 1917).

Schedel, Hartmann, *Chronicle of the World: The Complete and Annotated Nuremberg Chronicle of 1493*, introduction and appendix by Stephan Füssel (Cologne and London: Taschen, 2001).

Scillacio, Nicolò, *De insulis meridiani atque Indici maris ... nuper inventis* (Pavia, 1494).

Sensuyt le nouveau monde & navigations faictes par Emeric de Vespuce (Paris, 1515).

Settle, Dionyse, *De Martini Frobisseri Angli navigatione in regiones occidentis et septentrionis narratio historica* (Nuremberg, 1580).

Shakespeare, William, *Othello* ed. Kenneth Muir (London: Penguin, 1996).

Smith, John, *A Map of Virginia, with a Description of the Covntrey, the Commodities, People, Government and Religion* (Oxford, 1612).

The Complete Works, ed. Philip L. Barbour, 3 vols. (Chapel Hill, NC: University of North Carolina Press, 1986).

Burgkmair, Hans, *Some Woodcuts by Hans Burgkmair, printed as an appendix to the fourth part of Le Relationi Vniversali di Giovanni Botero, 1618*, introduction by Walter Oakeshott (Oxford: Roxburgh Club, 1960).

Springer, Balthasar, *Die Merfart und erfarung nüwer Schiffung* (s.l., 1509).

Staden, Hans, *Warhaftige Historia und Beschreibung eyner Landschafft der Wilden, Nacketen, Grimmigen Menschfresser Leuthen, in der Newenwelt America gelegen* (Marburg, 1557).

Staden, Hans, Jean de Léry and Nicolas Barré, *Americae tertia pars memorabile provinciae Brasiliae historiam*, ed. Theodor de Bry (Frankfurt am Main, 1592).

Dritte Buch Americae, darinn Brasilia ... ass eigener erfahrung in Teustsch beschrieben, ed. Theodor de Bry (Frankfurt am Main, 1593).

... True History: An Account of Cannibal Captivity in Brazil, ed. and trans. Neil L. Whitehead and Michael Harbsmeier (Durham, NC: Duke University Press, 2008).

Warhaftige Historia. Zwei Reisen nach Brasilian (1548–1555), ed. Franz Obermeier (Kiel, 2007).

The True History of His Captivity, 1557, ed. Malcolm Letts (London: Routledge, 1928).

Swift, Jonathan, *On Poetry: A Rapsody* [1733] in *Eighteenth-Century Literature*, ed. Geoffrey Tillotson et al. (New York: Routledge, 1969).

Symcox, Geoffrey, ed., *Italian Reports on America, 1493–1533: Letters, Dispatches, and Papal Bulls* (Turnhout: Brepols, 2001).

Symcox, Geoffrey and Luciano Formisano, eds., *Italian Reports on America, 1493–1533: Accounts by Contemporary Observers* (Turnhout: Brepols, 2002).

Syria, Pedro de, *Arte de la verdadera navegacion* (Valencia, 1602).

Trevisano, Angelo, *Libretto de tutta la navigatione de re de Spagna de le isole et terreni nuouamente trouati* (Venice, 1504).

Libretto de tutta la nauigatione de re de spagna de le isole et terreni nouamente trouati: A Facsimile, introduction by Lawrence C. Wroth (Paris: Durand, 1929).

Thacher, John Boyd, *Christopher Columbus: His Life, His Work, His Remains, as revealed by Original Printed and Manuscript Records*, 3 vols. (New York: Knickerbocker Press, 1903).

Thevet, André, *Les Singularitez de la France Antarctique* (Paris, 1557).

La Cosmographie universelle (Paris, 1575).

Les Vrais Portraits et vies des hommes illustres (Paris 1584).

André Thevet's North America: A Sixteenth-Century View, ed., trans., notes and intro., Roger Schlesinger and Arthur P. Stabler (Kingston and Montreal: McGill-Queen's University Press, 1986).

Le Brésil d'André Thevet. Les Singularités de la France Antarctique, ed. Frank Lestringant (Paris: Chandeigne, 1997).

Histoire . . . de deux voyages par luy faits aux Indes Australes, et Occidentales, ed. Jean-Claude Laborie and Frank Lestringant (Geneva: Droz, 2006).

Vaughan, William, *The Newlanders Cure* (London, 1630).

Vecellio, Cesare, *Habiti antichi et moderni di tutto il mondo* (Venice, 1598).

Vespucci, Amerigo, *Albericus Vesputius Laurentio Petri Francisci de Medicis salutem plurimam dicit* (Paris, 1503).

De ora antarctica per regem Portugallie pridem inventa (Strasbourg, 1505).

De novo mundo (Rostock, 1505).

Lettera . . . delle isole nuovamente trovate (Florence, 1505).

Van den nyge[n] Insulen und landen (Magdeburg, 1506).

Diss büchlin saget wie die zwen durchlüchtigsten herren . . . haben . . . funden vil insulen vnnd ein Nüwe welt von wilden nackenden Leuten vormals vnbekant (Strasbourg, 1509).

Letters from a New World: Amerigo Vespucci's Discovery of America, ed. and with introduction by Luciano Formisano (New York: Marsilio Pub, 1992).

[Writings], ed. Ilaria Luzzana Caraci, 2 vols. (Rome: Istituto poligrafico e Zecca dello Stato, 1996–99).

Le Voyage de Gonneville (1503–1505) & la découverte de la Normandie par les Indiens du Brésil, étude & commentaire de Leyla Perrone-Moisés (Paris: Chandeigne, 1995).

Waldseemüller, Martin, *Carta Marina* ([Strasbourg?], 1516).

The Cosmographiae introductio in Facsimile, ed. Charles George Herbermann, introduction by Joseph Fischer and Franz von Wieser (Freeport, NY: Books for Libraries Press, 1969 [first published 1907]).

Waldseemüller, Martin and Matthias Ringmann, *Cosmographie introductio cum quibusdam geometriae [ac] astronomiae principiis ad eam rem necessariis* (St. Dié, 1507).

Cosmographie introductio quibusdam geometriae [ac] astronomiae principiis ad eam rem necesariis (St. Dié, 1507).

Waterhouse, Edward, *A Declaration of the State of the Colony in Virginia [1622]* (Amsterdam and New York: Theatrum Orbis Terrarum, 1970).

Weiditz, Christoph, *Authentic Everyday Dress of the Renaissance: All 154 Plates from the 'Trachtenbuch'* (Mineola, NY: Dover, 1994).

Weigel, Hans, *Trachtenbuch* (Nuremberg, 1577).

Wytfliet, Cornelius, *Histoire vniverselle des Indes Occidentales et Orientales, et de la conversion des Indiens* (Douai, 1611).

Xérez, Francisco de, *Reports on the Discovery of Peru*, ed. and trans. Clement R. Markham (London: Hakluyt Society, 1872).

Verdadera relación de la conquista del Peru . . . (Seville, 1534).

Verdadera relación de la conquista del Peru . . . (Seville, 1535).

Zárate, Augustín de, *Historia del descubrimiento y conquista del Peru* (Antwerp, 1555).

The Discovery and Conquest of Peru: A Translation of Books I to IV of Augustín de Zárate's History of these Events, supplemented by Eye-witness Accounts of Certain Incidents . . ., ed. and trans. J. M. Cohen (London: The Folio Society, 1981).

SECONDARY LITERATURE

Abulafia, David, *The Discovery of Mankind: Atlantic Encounters in the Age of Columbus* (New Haven, CT and London: Yale University Press, 2008).

Adorno, Rolena, *The Polemics of Possession in Spanish American Narrative* (New Haven, CT and London: Yale University Press, 2007).

Aiello Leslie C., 'Five Years of *Homo floresiensis*', *American Journal of Physical Anthropology*, 142 (2010), 167–79.

Afanasiev, V., 'The Literary Heritage of Bartolomé de Las Casas', in *Bartolomé de Las Casas in History: Toward an Understanding of the Man and His Work*, ed. Juan Friede and Benjamin Keen (DeKalb, IL: Northern Illinois University Press, 1971), 539–80.

Akbari, Suzanne Conklin, *Idols in the East: European Representations of Islam and the Orient, 1100–1450* (Ithaca, NY and London: Cornell University Press, 2009).

Alden, John, and D. C. Landis, eds., *European Americana: A Chronological Guide to Works printed in Europe relating to the Americas, 1493–1776*, 6 vols. (New York: Readex Books, 1980–1997).

Alegria, Maria Fernanda et al., 'Portuguese Cartography in the Renaissance', in *The History of Cartography Volume 3: Cartography in the European Renaissance*, ed. David Woodward, 2 vols. (Chicago, IL and London: University of Chicago Press, 2007), I, 975–1068.

Alpers, Sveltana, *The Art of Describing: Dutch Art in the Seventeenth Century* (Chicago, IL: University of Chicago Press, 1983).

Altroy, Terence N. d', *The Incas* (London: Blackwell, 2002).

Amaral, Joaquim Ferreira do, ed., *Atlas Miller* (Barcelona: M. Moleiro Editor, 2006).

Anderson, Benedict, *Imagined Communities: Reflections on the Origin and Spread of Nationalism* (London: Verso, 1991).

Anthiaume, A., *Cartes marines, constructions navales, voyages de découverte chez les normands, 1500–1650*, 2 vols. (Paris: Ernest Dumont, 1916).

Arens, William, *The Man-Eating Myth: Anthropology and Anthropophagy* (New York: Oxford University Press, 1979).

'Rethinking Anthropophagy', in *Cannibalism and the Colonial World*, ed. Francis Barker et al. (Cambridge: Cambridge University Press, 1998), 39–62.

Armitage, David, 'What's the Big Idea? Intellectual History and the *Longue Durée*', *History of European Ideas*, 38:4 (2012), 593–607.

Arnold, David, 'Introduction: Tropical Medicine before Manson', in *Warm Climates and Western Medicine: The Emergence of Tropical Medicine, 1500–1900*, ed. David Arnold (Amsterdam and Atlanta, GA: Rodopi, 1996), 1–19.

Ashworth, William B., 'Remarkable Humans and Singular Beasts', in *The Age of the Marvelous*, ed. Joy Kenseth (Hanover, NH: Hood Museum of Art, Dartmouth College, 1991), 103–44.

Astengo, Corradino, 'The Renaissance Chart Tradition in the Mediterranean', in *The History of Cartography Volume 3: Cartography in the European Renaissance*, ed. David Woodward, 2 vols. (Chicago, IL and London: University of Chicago Press, 2007), I, 174–262.

Asúa, Miguel and Roger French, *A New World of Animals: Early Modern Europeans on the Creatures of Iberian America* (Aldershot: Ashgate, 2005).

Bagrow, L. and R. A. Skelton, *The History of Cartography*, 2nd ed. (Chicago, IL: University of Chicago Press, 1985).

Barber, Peter, 'Visual Encyclopedias: The Hereford and other Mappae Mundi', *The Map Collector*, 48 (1989), 2–8.

The Queen Mary Atlas: Commentary (London: Folio Society, 2005).

'Mapmaking in England, ca. 1470–1650', in *The History of Cartography Volume 3: Cartography in the European Renaissance*, ed. David Woodward, 2 vols. (Chicago, IL and London: University of Chicago Press, 2007), II, 1589–669.

Barrera-Osorio, Antonio, *Experiencing Nature: The Spanish American Empire and the Early Scientific Revolution* (Austin, TX: University of Texas Press, 2006).

Bartra, Roger, *Wild Men in the Looking Glass: The Mythic Origins of European Otherness*, trans. Carl T. Berrisford (Ann Arbor, MI: University of Michigan Press, 1997).

Baxandall, Michael, *The Limewood Sculptors of Renaissance Germany* (New Haven, CT and London: Yale University Press, 1980).

Beer, Anna R., *Sir Walter Ralegh and His Readers in the Seventeenth Century* (Basingstoke: Macmillan, 1997).

Belyea, Barbara, 'Images of Power: Derrida/Foucault/Harley', *Cartographica*, 29 (1992), 1–9.

Benedict, Barbara M., *Curiosity: A Cultural History of Early Modern Inquiry* (Chicago, IL: University of Chicago Press, 2001).

Bernheimer, Richard, *Men in the Middle Ages: A Study in Art, Sentiment, and Demonology* (Cambridge, MA: Harvard University Press, 1952).

Bethell, Leslie, ed., *The Cambridge History of Latin America*, 11 vols. (Cambridge: Cambridge University Press, 1984–2008).

Bethencourt, Francisco, 'Race Relations in the Portuguese Empire', in *Encompassing the Globe: Portugal and the World in the 16th & 17th Centuries. Essays*, ed. Jay A. Levenson (Washington, D.C.: Arthur M. Sackler Gallery, Smithsonian Institution, 2007), 45–53.

Bethencourt, Francisco and Diogo Ramada Curto, eds., *Portuguese Oceanic Expansion, 1400–1800* (Cambridge: Cambridge University Press, 2007).

Biagioli, Mario, *Galileo, Courtier: The Practice of Science in the Culture of Absolutism* (Chicago, IL and London: University of Chicago Press, 1993).

Galileo's Instruments of Credit: Telescopes, Images, Secrecy (Chicago, IL and London: University of Chicago Press, 2006).

Bishop, Louise M., 'The Myth of the Flat Earth', in ed. Stephen J. Harris and Bryon L. Grigsby, *Misconceptions about the Middle Ages* (London and New York: Routledge, 2008), 97–101.

Blair, Ann M., *Too Much to Know: Managing Scholarly Information Before the Modern Age* (New Haven, CT and London: Yale University Press, 2010).

The Theater of Nature: Jean Bodin and Renaissance Science (Princeton, NJ: Princeton University Press, 1997).

Bleichmar, Daniela, *Visible Empire: Botanical Expeditions and Visual Culture in the Hispanic Enlightenment* (Chicago, IL: University of Chicago Press, 2012).

Bolens-Duvernay, Jacqueline, 'Les Géants patagons ou l'espace retrouvé. Les débuts de la cartographie américaniste', *L'Homme*, XXVIII (1988), 156–73.

Bosch, L. J. M., *Petrus Bertius 1565–1629* (Meppel: [s.n.], 1979).

Braham, Persephone, 'The Monstrous Caribbean', in *The Ashgate Research Companion to Monsters and the Monstrous*, ed. Asa Simon Mittman (Farnham and Burlington, VT: Ashgate, 2012), 17–47.

Braude, Benjamin, 'The Sons of Noah and the Construction of Ethnic and Geographical Identities in the Medieval and Early Modern Periods', *William and Mary Quarterly*, 54:1 (1997), 103–42.

Braudel, Fernand, *Civilisation and Capitalism, 15th-18th Century*, 3 vols., trans. Siân Reynolds (London: Fontana, 1985).

Brienen, Rebecca Parker, *Visions of Savage Paradise: Albert Eckhout, Court Painter in Colonial Dutch Brazil: Albert Eckcourt, Court Painter in Colonial Dutch Brazil, 1637–1644* (Amsterdam: Amsterdam University Press, 2006).

Brunelle, Gayle K., *The New World Merchants of Rouen, 1559–1630* (Kirksville, MI: Sixteenth Century Journal Publishers, 1991).

'The Images of Empire: Francis I and his Cartographers', in *Princes and Princely Culture, 1450–1650*, ed. Martin Gosman et al., 2 vols. (Leiden and Boston, MA: Brill, 2003–5), 81–102.

Bucher, Bernadette, *Icon and Conquest: A Structural Analysis of the Illustrations of de Bry's Great Voyages*, trans. Basia Miller Gulati (Chicago, IL and London: University of Chicago Press, 1981).

Buisseret, David, ed., *Monarchs, Ministers and Maps: The Emergence of Cartography as a Tool of Government in Early Modern Europe* (Chicago, IL and London: University of Chicago Press, 1992).

Burden, Philip D., *The Mapping of North America: A List of Printed Maps*, 2 vols. (Rickmansworth: Raleigh Publications, 1996–2007).

Burghartz, Susanna, ed., *Staging New Worlds: De Brys' Illustrated Travel Reports, 1590–1630* (Basle: Schwabe, 2004).

Burke, Peter, *A Social History of Knowledge from Gutenberg to Diderot* (Cambridge: Polity Press, 2000).

Eyewitnessing: The Uses of Images as Historical Evidence (London: Reaktion, 2001).

'Translating Knowledge, Translating Cultures', in Michael North, ed., *Kultureller Austausch in der Frühen Neuzeit* (Cologne: Böhlau, 2009), 69–77.

Burns, Kathryn, 'Unfixing Race', in *Rereading the Black Legend: The Discourses of Religious and Racial Difference in the Renaissance Empires*, ed. Margaret T. Greer et al. (Chicago, IL and London: University of Chicago Press, 2007), 188–202.

Butler, Diane S. 'Of Bodies and Borders: Images of Africans on Early Modern Maps', PhD diss., Cornell University, 2004.

Campbell, Mary Baine, *Wonder and Science: Imagining Worlds in Early Modern Europe* (Ithaca, NY and London: Cornell University Press, 1999).

'Travel Writing and Its Theory', in *The Cambridge Companion to Travel Writing*, ed. Peter Hulme and Tim Youngs (Cambridge: Cambridge University Press, 2002), 261–78.

The Witness and the Other World: Exotic Eastern Travel Writing 400–1600 (Ithaca, NY and London: Cornell University Press, 1988).

Campbell, Tony, 'Egerton MS 1513: A Remarkable Display of Cartographical Invention', *Imago Mundi*, 48 (1996), 93–102.

Cañizares-Esguerra, Jorge, 'New World, New Stars: Patriotic Astrology and the Invention of Indian and Creole Bodies in Colonial Spanish America, 1600–1650', *American Historical Review*, 104:1 (1999), 33–68.

How to Write the History of the New World: Historiographies, Epistemologies, and Identities in the Eighteenth-Century Atlantic World (Stanford, CA: Stanford University Press, 2001).

Capdevila, Nestor, *Las Casas: une politique de l'humanité* (Paris: Cerf, 1998).

Cattaneo, Angelo, *Fra Mauro's Mappa Mundi* (Turnhout: Brepols, 2011).

Céard, Jean, *La Nature et les prodiges: l'insolite au XVIe siècle en France* (Geneva: Droz , 1977).

Cerezo Martínez, Ricardo, *La cartografía náutica española en los siglos XIV, XV, y XVI* (Madrid: CSIC, 1994).

'Los padrones reales del primer cuarto del siglo XVI', in *La casa de la contratación y la navegación entre España y las Indias*, ed. Antonio Acosta Rodríguez et al. (Seville: Universidad de Sevilla, Consejo Superior de Investigaciones Científicas, 2003), 605–37.

Cervantes, Fernando, *The Devil in the New World: The Impact of Diabolism in New Spain* (New Haven, CT and London: Yale University Press, 1994).

Chaplin, Joyce E., 'Natural Philosophy and an Early Racial Idiom in North America: Comparing English and Indian Bodies', *William and Mary Quarterly*, Third Series, 54 (1997), 229–52.

Subject Matter: Technology, the Body, and Science on the Anglo-American Frontier, 1500–1676 (Cambridge, MA and London: Harvard University Press, 2001).

'Ogres and Omnivores: Early American Historians and Climate History', *William and Mary Quarterly*, 72:1 (2015), 25–32.

Chiappelli, Fredi et al., eds., *First Images of America: The Impact of the New World on the Old*, 2 vols. (Berkeley, CA and London: University of California Press, 1976).

Clarke, G. N. G., 'Taking Possession: The Cartouche as Cultural Text in Eighteenth-Century Maps', *Word and Image*, 4 (1988), 455–74.

Clark, Stuart, *Vanities of the Eye: Vision in Early Modern European Culture* (Oxford: Oxford University Press, 2009).

Clifford, James and George E. Marcus, *Writing Culture: The Poetics and Politics of Ethnography* (Berkeley, CA: University of California Press, 1986).

Cohen, Jeffrey Jerome, *Hybridity, Identity and Monstrosity in Medieval Britain: On Difficult Middles* (New York: Palgrave Macmillan, 2006).

Of Giants: Sex, Monsters, and the Middle Ages (Minneapolis, MN and London: University of Minnesota Press, 1999).

'Green Children from Another World, or the Archipelago in England', in *Cultural Diversity in the British Middle Ages: Archipelago, Island, England*, ed. Jeffrey Jerome Cohen (New York: Palgrave Macmillan, 2008), 75–94.

Cohen, Jeffrey Jerome, ed., *Monster Theory: Reading Culture* (Minneapolis, MN: University of Minnesota Press, 1996).

Cole, George Watson, *A Catalogue of Books Relating to the Discovery and Early History of North and South America Forming a Part of the Library of E. D. Church*, 5 vols. (New York: Dodd, Mead & Co., 1907).

Colin, Susi, 'The Wild Man and the Indian in Early 16th-Century Book Illustration', in *Indians and Europe: An Interdisciplinary Collection of Essays*, ed. Christian F. Feest (Aachen: Edition Herodot, 1987), 5–36.

Das Bild des Indianers im 16. Jahrhundert (Idstein: Schulz-Kirchner, 1988).

'Woodcutters and Cannibals: Brazilian Indians as seen on Early Maps', in *America: Early Maps of the New World*, ed. Hans Wolff (Munich: Prestel, 1992), 175–81.

Conley, Tom, 'Montaigne and the Indies: Cartographies of the New World' in *1492–1992: Re/Discovering Colonial Writing* (Minneapolis, MN: The Prisma Institute, 1989), ed. René Jara and Nicholas Spadaccini, 225–62.

'De Bry's Las Casas', in *Amerindian Images and the Legacy of Columbus*, ed. René Jara and Nicholas Spadaccini (Minneapolis, MN and London: University of Minnesota Press, 1992), 103–31.

'The Essays and the New World', in *Cambridge Companion to Montaigne*, ed. Ullrich Langer (Cambridge: Cambridge University Press, 2005), 74–95.

Cook, Harold, *Matters of Exchange: Commerce, Medicine, and Science in the Dutch Golden Age* (New Haven, CT and London: Yale University Press, 2007).

Cormack, Lesley B., 'Maps as Educational Tools in the Renaissance', in *The History of Cartography Volume 3: Cartography in the European Renaissance*, ed. David Woodward, 2 vols. (Chicago, IL and London: University of Chicago Press, 2007), I, 622–36.

Charting an Empire: Geography at the English Universities, 1580–1620 (Chicago, IL: University of Chicago Press, 1997).

Cortesão, Armando, *Cartografia e cartógrafos portugueses dos séculos XV e XVI*, 2 vols. (Lisbon, 1935).

Cortesão, Armando and Avelino Teixeira da Mota, *Portugaliae Monumenta Cartographica*, 6 vols. (Lisbon, 1960).

Cosgrove, Denis, 'Mapping New Worlds: Culture and Cartography in Sixteenth-Century Venice', *Imago Mundi*, 44 (1992), 65–85.

ed., *Mappings* (London: Reaktion, 1999).

Apollo's Eye: A Cartographic Genealogy of the Earth in the Western Imagination (Baltimore, MD and London: The Johns Hopkins University Press, 2001).

Geography and Vision: Seeing, Imagining and Representing the World (London: I. B. Tauris, 2008).

Crawford, Julie, *Marvelous Protestantism: Monstrous Births in Post-Reformation England* (Baltimore, MD and London: The Johns Hopkins University Press, 2005).

Cummins, Tom, 'De Bry and Herrera: "Aguas Negras" or The Hundred Years War over an Image of America', in *Arte, historia e identidad en América: visiones comparativas*, ed. Gustavo Curiel et al. (Mexico: Universidad Nacional Autónoma de México, Instituto de Investigaciones Estéticas, 1994), 17–31.

Curran, Andrew S., *The Anatomy of Blackness: Science and Slavery in an Age of Enlightenment* (Baltimore, MD: Johns Hopkins University Press, 2011).

Dackerman, Susan, ed., *Prints and the Pursuit of Knowledge in Early Modern Europe* (Cambridge, MA, New Haven, CT and London: Yale University Press, 2011).

Darby, Graham, ed., *The Origins and Development of the Dutch Revolt* (London: Routledge, 2001).

Darnton, Robert, *The Great Cat Massacre and Other Episodes in French Cultural History* (New York: Basic Books, 1984).

Daston, Lorraine, 'Epistemic Images', in *Vision and its Instruments: Art, Science, and Technology in Early Modern Europe*, ed. Alina Payne (University Park, PA: Pennsylvania State University Press), 13–35.

Daston, Lorraine and Peter Galison, *Objectivity* (New York: Zone Books, 2007).

Daston, Lorraine and Katharine Park, 'Unnatural Conceptions: The Study of Monsters in Sixteenth- and Seventeenth-Century France and England', *Past and Present*, 92 (1981), 20–54.

Wonders and the Order of Nature, 1150–1750 (New York: Zone Books, 1998).

Davies, Surekha, 'The Navigational Iconography of Diogo Ribeiro's 1529 Vatican Planisphere', *Imago Mundi*, 55 (2003), 103–12.

'Representations of Amerindians on European Maps and the Construction of Ethnographic Knowledge, 1506–1642', Ph.D. dissertation, 2 vols. (University of London: Warburg Institute, 2009).

'America and Amerindians in Sebastian Münster's *Cosmographiae universalis libri VI* (1550)', *Renaissance Studies*, 25:3 (2011), 351–73.

'The Wondrous East in the Renaissance Geographical Imagination: Marco Polo, Fra Mauro and Giovanni Battista Ramusio' in *History and Anthropology*, 23:2, (2012), 215–34.

'The Unlucky, the Bad and the Ugly: Categories of Monstrosity from the Renaissance to the Enlightenment', in *Ashgate Research Companion to Monsters and the Monstrous*, ed. Asa Simon Mittman with Peter Dendle (Farnham and Burlington, VT: Ashgate, 2012).

'Depictions of Brazilians on French Maps, 1542–1555', *The Historical Journal*, 55:2 (2012), 217–48.

'Science, New Worlds, and the Classical Tradition: An Introduction', in *Journal of Early Modern History* 18 (2014), 1–13.

Davis, Natalie Zemon, *The Gift in Sixteenth-Century France* (Oxford: Oxford University Press, 2000).

Defert, Daniel, 'Un genre ethnographique profane au XVIe: les livres d'habits (essai d'ethno-iconographie)', in *Histoires de l'anthropologie: XVI-XIX siècles*, ed. Britta Rupp-Eisenreich (Paris: Klincksieck, 1984), 25–41.

Delano Smith, Catherine, 'Map Ownership in Sixteenth-Century Cambridge: The Evidence of Probate Inventories', *Imago Mundi*, 47 (1995), 67–86.

Delgado-Gómez, Angel, *Spanish Historical Writing about the New World, 1493–1700* (Providence, RI: John Carter Brown Library, 1992).

Denis, Ferdinand, *Une Fête Brésilienne célébrée à Rouen en 1550* (Paris: J. Techener, 1850).

Destombes, Marcel, *La Mappemonde de Petrus Plancius gravée par Josua van den Ende, 1604* (Hanoi: Société de Géographie de Hanoi, 1944).

Destombes, Marcel and D. Gernez, 'Un Atlas nautique du XVIème siècle à la Bibliothèque Royale de la Haye (Pays-bas)', *Congresso Internacional de História dos Descobrimentos: Actas*, II (1961), 151–61.

Delbourgo, James and Nicholas Dew, eds., *Science and Empire in the Atlantic World* (New York and London: Routledge, 2008).

Dickason, Olive Patricia, 'The Brazilian Connection: A Look at the Origin of French Techniques for Trading with Amerindians', *Revue française d'histoire d'outre-mer*, LXXI (1984), 129–46.

The Myth of the Savage and the Beginnings of French Colonialism in the Americas (Edmonton: University of Alberta Press, 1984).

Disney, A. R., *A History of Portugal and the Portuguese Empire* 2 vols. (New York: Cambridge University Press, 2009).

Doege, Heinrich, 'Die Trachtenbücher des 16. Jahrhunderts', in *Beiträge zur Bücherkunde und Philologie*, ed. August Wilmanns (Leipzig: O. Harrassowitz, 1903), 229–44.

Deusen, Nancy E. van, 'Seeing *Indios* in Sixteenth-Century Castile', *William and Mary Quarterly*, 69:2 (2012), 205–34.

Global Indios: The Indigenous Struggle for Justice in Sixteenth-Century Spain (Durham, NC and London: Duke University Press, 2015).

Dudley, Edward and Maximillian E. Novak, eds., *The Wild Man Within: An Image in Western Thought from the Renaissance to Romanticism* (Pittsburgh, PA: University of Pittsburgh Press, 1972).

Duvernay-Bolens, Jacqueline, *Les Géants patagons: voyage aux origines de l'homme* (Paris: Éditions Michalon, 1995).

Duviols, Jean-Paul, 'The Patagonian 'Giants', in *Patagonia: Natural History, Prehistory and Ethnography at the Uttermost End of the Earth*, ed. Colin McEwan and Luis A. Borrero (Princeton, NJ: Princeton University Press, 1997), 127–39.

Duzer, Chet Van, 'A Northern Refuge of the Monstrous Races: Asia on Waldseemüller's 1516 Carta Marina', *Imago Mundi*, 62:2 (2010), 221–31.

'*Hic sunt dracones*: The Geography and Cartography of Monsters', in *The Ashgate Research Companion to Monsters and the Monstrous*, ed. Asa Simon Mittman with Peter J. Dendle (Farnham and Burlington, VT: Ashgate, 2012), 385–433.

Sea Monsters on Medieval and Renaissance Maps (London: The British Library, 2013).

Edney, Matthew H., *Mapping an Empire: The Geographical Construction of British India, 1765–1843* (Chicago, IL and London: University of Chicago Press, 1997).

Earle, Rebecca, *The Body of the Conquistador: Food, Race and the Colonial Experience in Spanish America, 1492–1700* (Cambridge: Cambridge University Press, 2012).

Edson, Evelyn, *The World Map, 1300–1492: The Persistence of Tradition and Transformation* (Baltimore, MD: The Johns Hopkins University Press, 2007).

Eisenstein, Elizabeth L., *The Printing Press as an Agent of Change: Communications and Cultural Trannsformations in Early-Modern Europe* (Cambridge: Cambridge University Press, 1979).

Divine Art, Infernal Machine: The Reception of Printing in the West from First Impressions to the Sense of an Ending (Philadelphia, PA and Oxford: University of Pennsylvania Press, 2011).

Eliav-Feldon, Miriam et al., *The Origins of Racism in the West* (Cambridge: Cambridge University Press, 2009).

Elliott, J. H., *The Old World and the New, 1492–1650* (Cambridge: Cambridge University Press, 1972).

Spain, Europe, and the Wider World, 1500–1800 (New Haven, CT and London: Yale University Press, 2009).

Esteve Barba, Francisco, *Historiografía indiana*, 2a ed., rev. y aum. (Madrid: Editorial Gredos, 1992).

Eyffinger, Arthur, *Huygens Herdacht. Catalogus bij de tentoonstelling in de Koninklijke Bibliotheek ter gelegenheid van de 300ste sterfdag van Constantijn Huygens* (The Hague: De Bibliotheek, 1987).

Falchetta, Piero, *Fra Mauro's World Map* (Turnhout: Brepols, 2006).

Febvre, Lucien and Henri-Jean Martin, *The Coming of the Book: The Impact of Printing, 1450–1800*, trans. David Gerard (London: Foundations of History Library, 1976).

Feest, Christian F., 'The Virginia Indian in Pictures, 1612–1624', *The Smithsonian Journal of History*, 2 (1967), 1–30.

Feest, Christian F., ed., *Indians and Europe: An Interdisciplinary Collection of Essays* (Aachen: Edition Herodot, 1987), 37–60.

Felton, D., 'Rejecting and Embracing the Monstrous in Ancient Greece and Rome', in *The Ashgate Research Companion to Monsters and the Monstrous*, ed. Asa Simon Mittman with Peter J. Dendle (Farnham and Burlington, VT: Ashgate, 2012), 103–31.

Fernández-Armesto, Felipe, *So You Think You're Human?* (Oxford: Oxford University Press, 2004).

Amerigo: The Man Who Gave His Name to America (London: Weidenfeld & Nicolson, 2006).

'Maps and Exploration in the Sixteenth and Early Seventeenth Centuries', in *The History of Cartography Volume 3: Cartography in the European Renaissance*, ed. David Woodward, 2 vols. (Chicago, IL and London: University of Chicago Press, 2007), I, 738–70.

Ferro, Gaetano et al., *Columbian Iconography*, trans. Luciano F. Farina and Carla Onorato Wysokinski (Rome: Istituto poligrafico e Zecca dello Stato, 1992).

Field, Thomas W., *An Essay towards an Indian Bibliography* (New York: Scribner, Armstrong & Co., 1873).

Findlen, Paula, ed., *Early Modern Things: Objects and Their Histories, 1500–1800* (London and New York: Routledge, 2013).

Fiorani, Francesca, *The Marvel of Maps: Art, Cartography and Politics in Renaissance Italy* (New Haven, CT and London: Yale University Press, 2005).

Fischer, S. J. and R. Wieser, *The Oldest Map with the Name America of the Year 1507 and the Carta Marina of the Year 1516* (Innsbruck: Wagner'sche Universitäts-Buchhandlung, 1903).

Floyd-Wilson, Mary, *English Ethnicity and Race in Early Modern Drama* (Cambridge and New York: Cambridge University Press, 2003).

Ford, Thayne R., 'Stranger in a Foreign Land: José de Acosta's Scientific Realizations in Sixteenth-Century Peru', *Sixteenth-Century Journal*, 29 (1998), 19–33.

Forsyth, Donald W., 'Three Cheers for Hans Staden: The Case for Brazilian Cannibalism', *Ethnohistory*, 32:1 (1985), 17–36.

Fox, Robert, ed., *Thomas Harriot: An Elizabethan Man of Science* (Aldershot: Ashgate, 2000).

Friede, Juan and Benjamin Keen, eds., *Bartolomé de Las Casas in History: Toward an Understanding of the Man and His Work* (DeKalb, IL: Northern Illinois University Press, 1971).

Friedman, John Block, 'Cultural Conflicts in Medieval World Maps', in *Implicit Understandings: Observing, Reporting, and Reflecting on the Encounters between Europeans and Other Peoples in the Early Modern Era*, ed. Stuart B. Schwartz (Cambridge: Cambridge University Press, 1994), 64–95.

The Monstrous Races in Medieval Art and Thought, 2nd ed. (Syracuse, NY: Syracuse University Press, 2000).

Frisch, Andrea, *The Invention of the Eyewitness: Witnessing and Testimony in Early Modern France* (Chapel Hill, NC: University of North Carolina Press, 2004).

Fuller, Mary C., 'Ralegh's Fugitive Gold: Reference and Deference in *The Discoverie of Guiana*', *in New World Encounters*, ed. Stephen Greenblatt (Berkeley, CA: : University of California Press, 1993), 218–40.

Voyages in Print: English Travel to America, 1576–1624 (Cambridge: Cambridge University Press, 1995).

Gaffarel, Paul, *Histoire du Brésil français au seizième siècle* (Paris: Maisonneuve, 1878).

Ganong, W. F., *Crucial Maps in the Early Cartography and Place-Nomenclature of the Atlantic Coast of Canada* (Toronto: University of Toronto Press, 1964).

Gaudio, Michael, *Engraving the Savage: The New World and Techniques of Civilization* (Minneapolis, MN: University of Minnesota Press, 2008).

'The Truth in Clothing: The Costume Studies of John White and Lucas de Heere', in *European Visions: American Voices*, ed. Kim Sloan (London: British Museum, 2009), 24–32.

Gautier Dalché, Patrick, 'The Reception of Ptolemy's *Geography* (End of the Fourteenth to Beginning of the Sixteenth Century)', in *The History of Cartography Volume 3: Cartography in the European Renaissance*, ed. David Woodward, 2 vols. (Chicago, IL and London: University of Chicago Press, 2007), I, 285–364.

George, Wilma, *Animals in Maps* (London: Secker and Warburg, 1969).

Gillies, John, 'The Figure of the New World in *The Tempest*', in '*The Tempest' and Its Travels*, ed. Peter Hulme and William H. Sherman (London, 2000), 180–200.

Ginzburg, Carlo, *The Cheese and the Worms: The Cosmos of a Sixteenth-Century Miller* (Baltimore, MD and London: The Johns Hopkins University Press, 1980).

Glacken, Clarence J., *Traces on the Rhodian Shore: Nature and Culture in Western Thought from Ancient Times to the End of the Eighteenth Century* (Berkeley, and Los Angeles, CA: University of California Press, 1967).

Gliozzi, Giuliano, *Adam et le Nouveau Monde. La naissance de l'anthropologie comme idéologie coloniale: des généalogies bibliques aux théories raciales (1500–1700)*, trans. Arlette Estève and Pascal Gabellone (Lecques: Théétète, 2000).

Goetz, Rebecca Anne, *The Baptism of Early Virginia: How Christianity Created Race* (Baltimore, MD: Johns Hopkins University Press, 2012).

Goldberg, Jonathan, *Sodometries: Renaissance Texts, Modern Sexualities* (New York: Fordham University Press, 2010).

Gow, Andrew, 'Gog and Magog on *Mappaemundi* and Early Printed World Maps: Orientalizing Ethnography in the Apocalyptic Tradition', *Journal of Early Modern History*, 2 (1998), 61–88.

'Fra Mauro's World View: Authority and Empirical Evidence on a Venetian Mappamundi', in *The Hereford World Map: Medieval World Maps and Their Context*, ed. P. D. A. Harvey (London: The British Library, 2006), 405–414.

Grafton, Anthony, *Defenders of the Text: The Traditions of Scholarship in an Age of Science, 1450–1800* (Cambridge, MA: Harvard University Press, 1991).

Cardano's Cosmos: The Worlds and Works of a Renaissance Astrologer (Cambridge, MA and London: Harvard University Press, 1999).

'The Jewish Book in Christian Europe: Material Texts and Religious Encounters', in Andrea Sterk and Nina Caputo, eds., *Faithful Narratives: Historians, Religion, and the Challenge of Objectivity* (Ithaca, NY and London: Cornell University Press, 2014), 96–114.

Grafton, Anthony and Lisa Jardine, "Studied for action': how Gabriel Harvey read his Livy', *Past and Present*, 129 (1990), 30–78.

et al., *New Worlds, Ancient Texts: The Power of Tradition and the Shock of Discovery* (Cambridge, MA and London: Belknap Press of Harvard University Press, 1992).

Greenblatt, Stephen, *Marvelous Possessions: The Wonder of the New World* (Oxford: Clarendon Press, 1991).

Greenblatt, Stephen, ed., *New World Encounters* (Berkeley, CA: University of California Press, 1993).

Greer, Margaret R., et al., *Rereading the Black Legend: The Discourses of Religious and Racial Difference in the Renaissance Empires* (Chicago, IL: University of Chicago Press, 2007).

John A. Walter and Ronald E. Grim, eds., *Images of the World: The Atlas through History* (Washington, DC: Library of Congress, 1997).

Groesen, Michiel van, *The Representations of the Overseas World in the De Bry Collection of Voyages (1590–1634)* (Leiden and Boston, MA: Brill, 2008).

Grosshaupt, Walter, '*Commercial Relations between Portugal and the Merchants of Augsburg and Nuremburg*', ed. Jean Aubin (Paris: Fondation Calouste Gulbenkian, 1990).

Guénin, Eugène, *Ango et ses pilotes d'après des documents inédits* (Paris: Imprimerie National, 1901).

Gundersheimer, Werner L., *The Life and Works of Louis Le Roy* (Geneva: Droz, 1966).

Haase, Wolfgang and Meyer Reinhold, eds., *The Classical Tradition and the Americas* (Berlin and New York: Walter de Gruyter, 1994).

Hampe, Theodor, *Das Trachtenbuch des Christoph Weiditz* (Berlin: Walter de Gruyter, 1927).

Hamy, E.-T., 'Le Bas-relief de l'Hôtel du Brésil au Musée Départmental d'Antiquités de Rouen', *Journal de la Société des Américanistes de Paris, Nouvelle série* (1907), 1–6.

Hanafi, Zakiya, *The Monster in the Machine: Magic, Medicine, and the Marvelous in the Time of the Scientific Revolution* (Durham, NC: Duke University Press, 2000).

Hanke, Lewis, *The First Social Experiments in America: A Study in the Development of Spanish Indian Policy in the Sixteenth Century* (Cambridge, MA: Harvard University Press, 1935).

'Pope Paul III and the American Indian', *The Harvard Theological Review*, 30 (1937), 65–102.

Aristotle and the American Indians: A Study in Race Prejudice in the Modern World (Chicago, IL: H. Regnery, 1959).

All Mankind is One: A Study of the Disputation between Bartolomé de Las Casas and Juan Ginés de Sepúlveda in 1550 on the Intellectual and Religious Capacity of the American Indians (DeKalb, IL: Northern Illinois University Press, 1974).

The Spanish Struggle for Justice in the Conquest of America, with new introduction by Susan Scafidi et al., (Dallas: Southern Methodist University Press, TX, 2002).

Hanke, Lewis and Manuel Giménez Fernández, *Bartolomé de las Casas, 1474–1566: bibliografía crítica* (Santiago de Chile: Fondo Histórico y Bibliográfico José Toribio Medina, 1954).

Haring, Clarence Henry, *Trade and Navigation between Spain and the Indies in the Time of the Hapsburgs* (Cambridge, MA: Harvard University Press, 1918).

Harley, J. B., 'Maps, Knowledge and Power', in *The Iconography of Landscape: Essays on the Symbolic Representation, Design and Use of Past Environments*, ed. Denis Cosgrove and Stephen Daniels (Cambridge: Cambridge University Press, 1988), 277–312.

'Deconstructing the Map', *Cartographica*, 26 (1989), 1–19.

'Maps and the Invention of America', *The Map Collector*, 58 (1992), 8–12.

'New England Cartography and the Native Americans', in *American Beginnings: Exploration, Culture and Cartography in the Land of Norumbega*, ed. Harald

E. Prins (Baltimore, MD and London: The Johns Hopkins University Press, 1994), 287–313.

'Deconstructing the Map', in *The New Nature of Maps*, ed. Paul Laxton (Baltimore, MD and London: The Johns Hopkins University Press, 2001), 150–68.

The New Nature of Maps: Essays in the History of Cartography, ed. Paul Laxton (Baltimore, MD and London: The Johns Hopkins University Press, 2001).

Harley, J. B. and David Woodward, eds., *The History of Cartography Volume 1: Cartography in Prehistoric, Ancient and Medieval Europe and the Mediterranean* (Chicago, IL: University of Chicago Press, 1987).

Harrison, Mark, *Climates & Constitutions: Health, Race, Environment and British Imperialism in India* (Delhi: Oxford University Press, 2002).

Medicine in an Age of Commerce and Empire: Britain and its Tropical Colonies, 1660–1830 (New York: Oxford University Press, 2010).

Harrisse, Henry and Carlos Sanz, *Bibliotheca Americana vetustissima: A Description of Works Relating to America, Published between the Years 1492 and 1551* (New York: G. P. Philes, 1866).

Harvey, P. D. A., ed., *The Hereford World Map: Medieval World Maps and Their Context* (London: The British Library, 2006).

Haudrère, Philippe, *L'Empire des rois, 1500–1789* (Paris: Denoël, 1997).

Headley, John M., 'Geography and Empire in the Late Renaissance: Botero's Assignment, Western Universalism and the Civilizing Process', *Renaissance Quarterly*, 53 (2000), 1119–55.

Hébert, John R., *The 1562 Map of America by Diego Gutiérrez* (Washington, DC: Library of Congress, 1999).

Helms, Mary W., *Ulysses' Sail: An Ethnographic Odyssey of Power, Knowledge and Geographical Distance* (Princeton, NJ: Princeton University Press, 1988).

Hemming, John, *The Conquest of the Incas* (London: Macmillan, 1970).

'The Indians of Brazil in 1500', in *The Cambridge History of Latin America*, ed. Leslie Bethell, 11 vols. (Cambridge: Cambridge University Press, 1984–2008), I, 119–43.

Red Gold: The Conquest of the Brazilian Indians (London : Pan Macmillan, 2004).

Henige, David, *In Search of Columbus: The Sources for the First Voyage* (Tucson, AZ: University of Arizona Press, 1991).

Hessler, John W., *The Naming of America: Martin Waldseemüller's 1507 World Map and the 'Cosmographiae introductio'* (London: GILES, 2008).

Hessler, John W. and Chet Van Duzer, *Seeing the World Anew: The Radical Vision of Martin Waldseemuller's 1507 & 1516 World Maps* (Delray Beach, FL: Levenger Press in association with the Library of Congress, 2012).

Hiatt, Alfred, *Terra Incognita: Mapping the Antipodes before 1600* (London and Chicago, IL: The British Library, 2008).

Higgins, Iain Macleod, *Writing East: The "Travels" of Sir John Mandeville* (Philadelphia, PA: University of Pennsylvania Press, 1997).

Hirsch, Rudolf, 'Printed Reports on the Early Discoveries and Their Reception', in *First Images of America: The Impact of the New World on the Old*, ed. Fredi Chiappelli et al., 2 vols. (Berkeley, CA and London: University of California Press, 1976), II, 537–60.

Hodgen, Margaret, *Early Anthropology in the Sixteenth and Seventeenth Centuries* (Philadelphia, PA: University of Philadelphia Press, 1964).

Hofmann, Catherine, 'Publishing and the Map Trade in France, 1470–1670', in *The History of Cartography Volume 3: Cartography in the European Renaissance*, ed. David Woodward, 2 vols. (Chicago, IL and London: University of Chicago Press, 2007), II, 1569–88.

Holt, Mack P., *The French Wars of Religion, 1562–1629* (Cambridge: Cambridge University Press, 2005).

Honour, Hugh, *The New Golden Land: European Images of America from the Discoveries to the Present Time* (London: Allan Lane, 1975).

Hoogvliet, Margriet, *Pictura et scriptura: textes, images et herméneutique des 'mappae mundi' (XIIIe-XVIe siècles)* (Turnhout: Brepols, 2007).

Hostetler, Laura, *Qing Colonial Enterprise: Ethnography and Cartography in Early Modern China* (Chicago, IL and London: University of Chicago Press, 2001).

Huet, Marie-Hélène, *Monstrous Imagination* (Cambridge, MA: Harvard University Press, 1993).

'Monstrous Medicine', in *Monstrous Bodies / Political Monstrosities in Early Modern Europe*, ed. Laura Lunger Knoppers and Joan B. Landes (Ithaca, NY and London: Cornell University Press, 2004), 127–47.

Huizinga, Johan, *The Waning of the Middle Ages* (New York: Doubleday, 1954 [Dutch 1st ed.: 1919]).

Hulme, Peter, *Colonial Encounters: Europe and the Native Caribbean, 1492–1797* (London and New York: Methuen, 1992).

'Introduction: The Cannibal Scene', in *Cannibalism and the Colonial World*, ed. Francis Barker et al. (Cambridge: Cambridge University Press, 1998), 1–38.

'Postcolonial Theory and Early America', in *Possible Pasts: Becoming Colonial in Early America*, ed. Robert Blair St George (Ithaca, NY: Cornell University Press, 2000), 33–48.

Hulton, Paul, *The Work of Jacques Le Moyne de Morgues: A Huguenot Artist in France, Florida and England*, 2 vols. (London: British Museum, 1977).

'Realism and Tradition in Ethnological and Natural History Imagery of the 16th Century', in *The Natural Sciences and the Arts: Aspects of Interaction from the Renaissance to the 20th Century* (Stockholm: Almqvist and Wiksell International, 1985), 18–31.

Husband, Timothy, *The Wild Man: Medieval Myth and Symbolism* (New York: Metropolitan Museum of Art, 1980).

Huxley, G. L., 'Aristotle, Las Casas and the American Indians', *Proceedings of the Royal Irish Academy*, 80 (1980), 57–68.

Isaac, Benjamin et al., 'Introduction', in *The Origins of Racism in the West*, ed. Miriam Eliav-Feldon et al. (Cambridge: Cambridge University Press, 2009), 1–31.

Ilg, Ulrike, 'The Cultural Significance of Costume Books in Sixteenth-Century Europe', in *Clothing Culture, 1350–1650*, ed. Catherine Richardson (Aldershot: Ashgate, 2004), 29–47.

Israel, Jonathan, *The Dutch Republic: Its Rise, Greatness, and Fall, 1477–1806* (Oxford: Clarendon Press, 1998).

Jacob, Christian, 'Towards a Cultural History of Cartography', *Imago Mundi*, 48 (1996), 191–8.

The Sovereign Map: Theoretical Approaches in Cartography throughout History, trans. Tom Conley, ed. Edward H. Dahl (Chicago, IL: University of Chicago Press, 2006).

Jacquot, J. and L. Konigson, eds., *Les Fêtes de la Renaissance* (Paris: Éditions du CNRS, 1975).

Johns, Adrian, *The Nature of the Book: Print and Knowledge in the Making* (Chicago, IL and London: University of Chicago Press, 1998).

Johnson, Carina L., *Cultural Hierarchy in Sixteenth-Century Europe: The Ottomans and Mexicans* (New York: Cambridge University Press, 2011).

Johnson, Christine R., 'Renaissance German Cosmographers and the Naming of America', *Past & Present*, 191 (2006), 3–43.

'Buying Stories: Ancient Tales, Renaissance Travelers, and the Market for the Marvelous', *Journal of Early Modern History*, 11 (2007), 405–46.

The German Discovery of the World: Renaissance Encounters with the Strange and Marvelous (Charlottesville, VA and London: University of Virginia Press, 2008).

Johnson, Hildegard Binder, *Carta Marina: World Geography in Strassburg, 1525* (Minneapolis, MN: University of Minnesota Press, 1963).

'Portuguese Settlement, 1500–1580', in *Colonial Brazil*, ed. Leslie Bethell (Cambridge: Cambridge University Press, 1987), 1–38.

Julien, Charles André, *Les Débuts de l'expansion et de la colonisation françaises (XVe-XVIe siècles)* (Paris: Presses universitaires de France, 1947).

Les Voyages de découverte et les premiers établissements (XVe-XVIe siècles) (Paris: Gerard Monfort, 1948).

Justo Guedes, Max and Gerald Lombardi, eds., *Portugal-Brazil: The Age of Atlantic Discoveries* (New York: Brazilian Cultural Foundation, 1990).

Kagan, Richard L. and Fernando Marías, *Urban Images of the Hispanic World, 1493–1793* (New Haven, CT and London: Yale University Press, 2000).

Karrow, Robert T., *Mapmakers of the Sixteenth Century and Their Maps: Bio-Bibliographies of the Cartographers of Abraham Ortelius* (Winnekta, IL, 1993).

Keen, Benjamin, 'Introduction: Approaches to Las Casas, 1535–1970', in *Bartolomé de Las Casas in History: Toward an Understanding of the Man and His*

Work, ed. Juan Friede and Benjamin Keen (DeKalb, IL: Northern Illinois University Press, 1971), 3–63.

Kelsey, Harry, 'The Planispheres of Sebastian Cabot and Sancho Gutiérrez', *Terrae Incognitae*, XIX (1987), 41–61.

'American Discoveries noted on the Planisphere of Sancho Gutiérrez', in *Early Images of the Americas: Transfer and Invention*, ed. Jerry M. Williams and Robert E. Lewis (Tucson, AZ and London, 1993), 247–61.

Kenseth, Joy, ed., *The Age of the Marvelous*, (Hanover, NH: Hood Museum of Art, Dartmouth College, 1991), 103–44.

Keuning, Johannes, 'Pieter van den Keere', *Imago Mundi*, XV (1960), 66–72.

Kim, David Y., 'Uneasy Reflections: Images of Venice and Tenochtitlán in Benedetto Bordone's "Isolario"', *Res: Anthropology and Aesthetics*, 49/50 (2006), 80–91.

Kleinschmidt, Harald, *Ruling the Waves: Emperor Maximilian I, the Search for Islands and the Transformation of the European World Picture c.1500* (Utrecht: 't Goy-Houten, 2008).

Kline, Naomi Reed, *Maps of Medieval Thought: The Hereford Paradigm* (Woodbridge: Boydell Press, 2001).

'Alexander Interpreted on the Hereford Mappamundi', in *The Hereford World Map: Medieval World Maps and Their Context*, ed. P. D. A. Harvey (London, 2006), 167–83.

Knecht, R. J., *The Rise and Fall of Renaissance France, 1483–1610* (London: Fontana, 1996).

Koeman, Cornelis, *Atlantes Neerlandici. Bibliography of Terrestrial, Maritime and Celestial Atlases and Pilot Books, published in the Netherlands up to 1880*, 5 vols. (Amsterdam, 1967–71).

'Life and Works of Willem Janszoon Blaeu: New Contributions to the Study of Blaeu, Made during the Last Hundred Years', *Imago Mundi*, XXVI (1972), 9–16.

Koeman, Cornelis et al., 'Commercial Cartography and Map Production in the Low Countries, 1500-ca.1672', in *The History of Cartography Volume 3: Cartography in the European Renaissance*, ed. David Woodward, 2 vols. (Chicago, IL and London: University of Chicago Press, 2007), II, 1296–393.

Kohl, Karl-Heinz, ed., *Mythen der Neuen Welt: zur Entdeckungsgeschichte Lateinamerikas* (Berlin: Frölich & Kaufmann, 1982).

Korhonen, Anu, 'Washing the Ethiopian White: Conceptualising Black Skin in Renaissance England', in *Black Africans in Renaissance Europe*, ed. K. J. P. Lowe and T. F. Earle (Cambridge: Cambridge University Press, 2005), 94–112.

Koyré, Alexandre, *Du Monde clos à l'univers infinit* (Paris: Gallimard, 1973).

Krautheimer, Richard, *Studies in Early Christian, Medieval and Renaissance Art* (New York: New York University Press; /London: University of London Press, 1969).

Krogt, Peter van der, *Koeman's Atlantes Neerlandici*, new edition, 4 vols. ('t Goy-Houten, 2000-).

Kuhlemann, Ute, 'Between Reproduction, Invention and Propaganda: Theodor de Bry's Engravings after John White', in *A New World: England's First View of America* (London: British Museum, 2007), 79–92.

Kupcík, Ivan, ... *Munich Portolan Charts: "Kunstmann I - XIII" and Ten Further Portolan Charts* (Munich and Berlin: Deutcher Kunstverlag, 2000).

Kupperman, Karen Ordahl, *Settling with the Indians: The Meeting of English and Indian Cultures in America, 1580–1640* (London: Dent, 1980).

'Fear of Hot Climates in the Anglo-American Colonial Experience', *William and Mary Quarterly*, 3rd ser., 41 (1984), 215–40.

ed., *America in European Consciousness, 1493–1750* (Chapel Hill, NC and London: University of North Carolina Press, 1995).

Indians and English: Facing Off in Early America (Ithaca, NY and London: Cornell University Press, 2000).

'Roanoke's Achievement', in *European Visions, American Voices*, ed. Kim Sloan (London: British Museum, 2009), 3–12.

Kusukawa, Sachiko, 'Leonard Fuchs on the Importance of Pictures', *Journal of the History of Ideas*, 58 (1997), 403–27.

Picturing the Book of Nature: Image, Text, and Argument in Sixteenth-Century Human Anatomy and Medical Botany (Chicago, IL and London: University of Chicago Press, 2012).

Kusukawa, Sachiko and Ian Maclean, eds., *Transmitting Knowledge: Words, Images and Instruments in Early Modern Europe* (Oxford: Oxford University Press, 2006).

Landau, David and Peter Parshall, *The Renaissance Print, 1450–1550* (New Haven, CT and London: Yale University Press, 1994).

Lane, Kris, 'Africans and Natives in the Mines of Spanish America', in *Beyond Black and Red: African-Native Relations in Colonial Latin America*, ed. Matthew Restall (Albuquerque, NM: University of New Mexico Press, 2005), 159–84.

Langer, Ullrich, 'Montaigne's Political and Religious Context', in *Cambridge Companion to Montaigne*, ed. Ullrich Langer (Cambridge: Cambridge University Press, 2005), 9–26.

Lecouteux, Claude, *Les Monstres dans la littérature allemande du Moyen Age* (Göppingen: Kümmerle, 1982).

Leitch, Stephanie, *Mapping Ethnography in Early Modern Germany: New Worlds in Print Culture* (New York: Palgrave MacMillan, 2010).

Lestringant, Frank, 'The Myth of the Indian Monarchy: An Aspect of the Controversy between Thevet and Léry (1575–1585)', in *Indians and Europe: An Interdisciplinary Collection of Essays*, ed. Christian F. Feest (Aachen: Edition Herodot, 1987), 37–60.

'La Flèche du patagon ou la preuve des lointains: sur un chapitre d'André Thevet', in *Voyager à la Renaissance*, ed. Jean Céard and Jean-Claude Margolin (Paris: Maisonneuve et Larose, 1987), 468–96.

André Thevet: cosmographe des derniers Valois (Geneva: Droz, 1991).

Mapping the Renaissance World: The Geographical Imagination in the Age of Discovery, trans. David Fausett (Berkeley and Los Angeles, CA: University of California Press, 1994).

Cannibals: The Discovery and Representation of the Cannibal from Columbus to Jules Verne, trans. Rosemary Morris (Cambridge: Polity Press, 1997).

Le Huguenot et le sauvage: L'Amérique et la controverse coloniale, en France, au temps des guerres de Religion (1555–1589), 3ème éd. revue et augmentée (Geneva: Droz, 2004).

'Les Patagons de la carte (1520–1620)', in *Patagonie: images du bout du monde*, ed. Christine Maine (Paris: Musée du quai Branly; Arles: Actes Sud, 2012), 12–27.

Levenson, Jay A., ed., *Circa 1492: Art in the Age of Exploration* (New Haven, CT and London: Yale University Press, 1991).

Encompassing the Globe: Portugal and the World in the 16th & 17th Centuries. Reference Catalogue (Washington, DC: Smithsonian Institution, 2007).

Encompassing the Globe: Portugal and the World in the 16th & 17th Centuries. Essays (Washington, DC: Smithsonian Institution, 2007).

Langfur, Hal, *The Forbidden Lands: Colonial Identity, Frontier Violence, and the Persistence of Brazil's Eastern Indians, 1750–1830* (Stanford, CA: Stanford University Press, 2006).

'Introduction: Recovering Brazil's Indigenous Pasts', in *Native Brazil: Beyond the Convert and the Cannibal, 1500–1900*, ed. Hal Langfur (Albuquerque, NM: University of New Mexico Press, 2014), 1–28.

Lanfgur, Hal and Maria Leônia Chaves de Resende, 'Indian Autonomy and Slavery in the Forests and Towns of Colonial Minas Gerais', in *Native Brazil: Beyond the Convert and the Cannibal, 1500–1889*, ed. Hal Langfur (Albuquerque, NM: University of New Mexico Press, 2014), 132–65.

ed., *Native Brazil: Beyond the Convert and the Cannibal, 1500–1900* (Albuquerque, NM: University of New Mexico Press, 2014).

Lawrance, Jeremy, 'Black Africans in Renaissance Spanish Literature', in *Black Africans in Renaissance Europe*, ed. K. J. P. Lowe and T. F. Earle (Cambridge: Cambridge University Press, 2005), 70–93.

Lewis, Martin W. and Kären E. Wigen, *The Myth of Continents: A Critique of Metageography* (Berkeley, CA and London: University of California Press, 1997).

Lewis, Rhodri, 'William Petty's Anthropology: Religion, Colonialism, and the Problem of Human Diversity, *Huntington Library Quarterly*, 74:2 (June 2011), 261–88.

Lira, Margarita, 'La representación del Indio en la cartografía de América', *Revista Chilena de Antropologia Visual*, 9 (2007), 86–102 at http://www.rchav.cl/2004_4_art06_lira.html (last accessed 13/12/15).

Livingstone, David N., *Adam's Ancestors: Race, Religion, and the Politics of Human Origins* (Baltimore, MD: The Johns Hopkins University Press, 2008).

Losada, Ángel, 'Juan Ginés Sepúlveda: estudio bibliográfico', *Revista bibliográfica y documental*, 8 (1947), 315–93.

'The Controversy between Sepúlveda and Las Casas in the Junta of Valladolid', in *Bartolomé de Las Casas in History: Toward an Understanding of the Man and His Work*, ed. Juan Friede and Benjamin Keen (DeKalb, IL: Northern Illinois University Press, 1971), 279–306.

Lowe, K. J. P., 'The Stereotyping of Black Africans in Renaissance Europe', in *Black Africans in Renaissance Europe*, ed. K. J. P. Lowe and T. F. Earle (Cambridge: Cambridge University Press, 2005), 17–47.

Lozovsky, Natalia, *"The Earth is Our Book": Geographical Knowledge in the Latin West, ca. 1400–1000* (Ann Arbor, MI: University of Michigan Press, 2000).

Lugt, Maaike van der, 'Les maladies héréditaires dans la pensée scolastique (XIIe-XVIe siècles)', in *L'hérédité entre Moyen Âge et Époque modern. Perspectives historiques*, ed. Maaike van der Lugt and Charles de Miramon (Florence: Sismel/Edizioni del Galluzzo, 2008), 273–320.

MacCormack, Sabine, *Religion in the Andes: Vision and Imagination in Early Colonial Peru* (Princeton, NJ: Princeton University Press, 1991).

'Limits of Understanding: Perceptions of Greco-Roman and Amerindian Paganism in Early Modern Europe', in *America in European Consciousness, 1493–1750*, ed. Karen Ordahl Kupperman (Chapel Hill, NC and London: University of North Carolina Press, 1995), 79–129.

On the Wings of Time: Rome, The Incas, Spain, and Peru (Princeton, NJ: Princeton University Press, 2007).

Magaña, Edmundo, 'Note on Ethnoanthropological Notions of the Guiana Indians', *Anthropologica*, XXIV (1982), 215–33.

'Hombres salvajes y razas monstruosas de los Indios Kaliña de Surinam', *Journal of Latin American Lore*, 8 (1982), 63–114.

Magaña, Edmundo, ed., *Les monstres dans l'imaginaire des Indiens d'Amérique latine* (Paris: Lettres modernes, 1988).

Magaña, Edmundo and Peter Mason, eds., *Myth and the Imaginary in the New World* (Amsterdam and Dordrecht: Centrum voor Studie en Documentatie van Latijns Amerika, 1986).

Magasich-Airola, Jorge and Jean-Marc de Beer, *America Magica: When Renaissance Europe Thought It Had Conquered Paradise*, trans. Monica Sander (London: Anthem Press, 2000).

Maine, Christine, ed., *Patagonie: images du bout du monde* (Paris: Musée du quai Branly / Arles: Actes Sud, 2012).

Mancall, Peter C., *Hakluyt's Promise: An Elizabethan's Obsession for an English America* (New Haven, CT and London: Yale University Press, 2007).

Mancall, Peter C. ed., *The Atlantic World and Virginia, 1550–1624* (Chapel Hill, NC: University of North Carolina Press, 2007).

Manuel Garcia, José and Max Justo Guedes, *Tesouros da cartografia portuguese* (Lisbon: Edições Inapa, 1997).

March, Kathleen N. and Kristina M. Passman, 'The Amazon Myth and Latin America', in *The Classical Tradition and the Americas*, ed. Wolfgang Haase and Meyer Reinhold (Berlin and New York: Walter de Gruyter, 1994), 285–338.

Marchant, Alexander, *From Barter to Slavery: The Economic Relations of Portuguese and Indians in the Settlement of Brazil, 1500–1580* (Baltimore, MD: The Johns Hopkins University Press, 1942).

Margócsy, Dániel, *Commercial Visions: Science, Trade, and Visual Culture in the Dutch Golden Age* (Chicago, IL: University of Chicago Press, 2014).

Marques, Alfredo Pinhiero, 'Nautical Cartography . . .', in *Atlas Miller*, ed. Joaquim Ferreira do Amaral (Barcelona: M. Moleiro Editor, 2006), 55–102.

'The Outstanding Artistic Value of the Atlas Miller . . .', in *Atlas Miller*, ed. Joaquim Ferreira do Amaral (Barcelona: M. Moleiro Editor, 2006), 137–216.

Martín Merás, Luisa, *Cartografía marítima hispana. La imagen de América* (Barcelona: Lunwerg Editores, 1993).

'La cartografía de los descubrimientos en la época de Carlos V', in *Carlos V: La náutica y la navegación* (Barcelona: Lunwerg Editores, 2000), 75–94.

Mason, Peter, *Deconstructing America: Representations of the Other* (London: Routledge, 1990).

Infelicities: Representations of the Exotic (Baltimore, MD and London: The Johns Hopkins University Press, 1998).

The Lives of Images (London: Reaktion, 2001).

Massa, Jean-Marie, 'Le mond luso-brésilien dans la joyeuse entrée de Rouen', in *Les Fêtes de la Renaissance*, études réunies et présentées par J. Jacquot and L. Konigson (Paris: Éditions du CNRS, 1975), 105–16.

Massing, Jean Michel, 'Aztecs Playing Tlachtli', in *Circa 1492: Art in the Age of Exploration*, ed. Jay A. Levenson (New Haven, CT and London: Yale University Press, 1991), 572.

'Early European Images of America: The Ethnographic Approach', in *Circa 1492: Art in the Age of Exploration*, ed. Jay A. Levenson (New Haven, CT and London: Yale University Press, 1991), 515–20.

'Observations and Beliefs: The World of the *Catalan Atlas*', in *Circa 1492: Art in the Age of Exploration*, ed. Jay A. Levenson (New Haven, CT and London: Yale University Press, 1991), 27–33.

'Hans Burgkmair's Depiction of Native Africans', *Res: Anthropology and Aesthetics*, 27 (1995), 39–51.

'La Mappemonde de Pierre Desceliers de 1550', in *Henri II et les arts*, ed. Hervé Oursel and Julia Fritsch (Paris: École du Louvre, 2003), 231–48.

'The Image of Africa and the Iconography of Lip-Plated Africans in Pierre Desceliers's World Map of 1550', in *Black Africans in Renaissance Europe*, ed. K. J. P. Lowe and T. F. Earle (Cambridge: Cambridge University Press, 2005), 48–69.

'From Marco Polo to Manuel I: The European Fascination with Chinese Porcelain', in *Encompassing the Globe: Portugal and the World in the 16th & 17th Centuries. Essays*, ed. Jay A. Levenson (Washington, DC: Arthur Sackler Gallery, Smithsonian Institution, 2007), 222–34.

Studies in Imagery, 2 vols. (London: Princeton, 2007).

Matos, Luís de, *Les Portugais en France au XVIe siècle. Études et documents* (Coimbra: Por ordem da Universidade, 1952).

Mauss, Marcel, *The Gift: The Form and Reason for Exchange in Archaic Societies* (London and New York: Routledge, 1990).

McLean, Matthew, *The Cosmographia of Sebastian Münster: Describing the World in the Reformation* (Aldershot: Ashgate, 2007).

Malkiel, María Rosa Lida de, 'Para la toponimia argentina: Patagonia', *Hispanic Review*, XX (1952), 321–3.

McGrath, Elizabeth, 'Humanism, Allegorical Invention, and the Personification of the Continents', in *Concept, Design & Execution in Flemish Painting (1550–1700)*, ed. Hans Vlieghe et al. (Turnhout: Brepols, 2000), 43–71.

McIntosh, Gregory C., *The Piri Reis Map of 1513* (Athens, GA: University of Georgia Press, 2000).

Medina, José Toribio, *Biblioteca Hispano-Americana*, 7 vols. (Amsterdam: N. Israel, 1962).

Metcalf, Alida C., 'The Society of Jesus and the First *Aldeias* of Brazil', in Hal Langfur, ed., *Native Brazil: Beyond the Convert and the Cannibal, 1500–1900* (Albuquerque, NM: University of New Mexico Press, 2014), 29–61.

Go-Betweens and the Colonization of Brazil, 1500–1600 (Austin, TX: University of Texas Press, 2005).

Meurer, Peter H., 'Cartography in the German Lands, 1450–1650', in *The History of Cartography Volume 3: Cartography in the European Renaissance*, ed. David Woodward, 2 vols. (Chicago, IL and London: University of Chicago Press, 2007), II, 1172–245.

Mignolo, Walter D., *The Darker Side of the Renaissance: Literacy, Territoriality, and Colonization* (Ann Arbor, MI: University of Michigan Press, 1995).

Mills, Kenneth, *Idolatry and Its Enemies: Colonial Andean Religion and Extirpation, 1640–1750* (Princeton, NJ: Princeton University Press, 1997).

Mittman, Asa Simon, *Maps and Monsters in Medieval England* (New York and London: Routledge, 2006).

'Introduction: The Impact of Monsters and Monster Studies', in *The Ashgate Research Companion to Monsters and the Monstrous*, ed. Asa Simon

Mittman with Peter J. Dendle (Farnham and Burlington, VT: Ashgate, 2012), 1–14.

Mittman, Asa Simon with Peter Dendle, eds., *The Ashgate Research Companion to Monsters and the Monstrous* (Farnham and Burlington, VT: Ashgate, 2012).

Mollat du Jourdin, Michel, *Le Commerce maritime normand à la fin du Moyen Âge* (Paris: Plon, 1952).

'Premières relations entre la France et le Brésil: des Verrazani à Villegaignon', *Cahiers de l'Institut des hautes études de l'Amérique latine*, 6 (1964), 59–74.

Sea Charts of the Early Explorers, trans. L. le R. Dethan (New York: Thames & Hudson, 1984).

Mollat du Jourdin, Michel and Jacques Habert, *Giovanni et Girolamo Verrazano, navigateurs de François 1er: dossiers de voyages* (Paris: Imprimerie Nationale, 1982).

Montaigne, Jean-Marc, *Le Trafiq du brésil: navigateurs normands, bois-rouge et cannibales pendant la renaissance* (Rouen: ASI Communication, 2000).

Monteiro, John, 'The Crises and Transformations of Invaded Societies: Coastal Brazil in the Sixteenth Century', in *Cambridge History of the Native Peoples of the Americas*, ed. Frank Salomon and Stuart B. Schwartz (Cambridge: Cambridge University Press, 1999), 3 vols., III:i, 973–1023.

Morán, J. M. and F. Checa, *El Coleccionismo en España: De la cámara de maravillas a la galería de pinturas* (Madrid: Cátedra, 1985).

Morison, Samuel Eliot, *The European Discovery of America: The Northern Voyages, A.D. 500–1600* (New York and Oxford: Oxford University Press, 1971).

The European Discovery of America: The Southern Voyages AD 1492–1616 (New York, NY and Oxford: Oxford University Press, 1974).

Mukerji, Chandra, 'Costume and Character in the Ottoman Empire: Dress as Social Agent in Nicolay's *Navigations*', in *Early Modern Things: Objects and Their Histories, 1500–1800*, ed. Paula Findlen (London and New York: Routledge, 2013), 151–69.

Mumford, Jeremy Ravi, *Vertical Empire: The General Resettlement of Indians in the Colonial Andes* (Durham, NC and London: Duke University Press, 2012).

Mundy, Barbara E., *The Mapping of New Spain: Indigenous Cartography and the Maps of the Relaciones Geográficas* (Chicago, IL: University of Chicago Press, 1996).

'Mapping the Aztec Capital: the 1524 Nuremberg Map of Tenochtitlan, its sources and meanings', *Imago Mundi*, 50 (1998), 11–33.

Myers, Kathleen Ann, *Fernández de Oviedo's Chronicle of America: A New History for a New World* (Austin, TX: University of Texas Press, 2007).

Nash, Gary B., 'The Image of the Indian in the Southern Colonial Mind', in *The Wild Man Within: An Image in Western Thought from the Renaissance to Romanticism*, ed. Edward Dudley and Maximillian E. Novak (Pittsburgh, PA: University of Pittsburgh Press, 1972), 55–86.

Niccoli, Ottavia, *Prophecy and People in Renaissance Italy*, trans. Lydia G. Cochrane (Princeton, NJ: Princeton University Press, 1990).

Nirenberg, David, *Communities of Violence in the Middle Ages* (Princeton, N.J.: Princeton University Press).

'Race and the Middle Ages: The Case of Spain and Its Jews', in *Rereading the Black Legend: The Discourses of Religious and Racial Difference in the Renaissance Empires*, ed. Margaret T. Greer et al. (Chicago, IL and London: University of Chicago Press, 2007), 71–87.

Norton, Marcy, *Sacred Gifts, Profane Pleasures: A History of Tobacco and Chocolate in the Atlantic World* (Ithaca, NY and London: Cornell University Press, 2008).

O'Doherty, Marianne, *The Indies and the Medieval West: Thought, Report, Imagination* (Turnhout: Brepols, 2013).

O'Gorman, Edmundo, *La invención de América* (Mexico City: Fondo de Cultura Económica, 1977).

Oxford Dictionary of National Biography: From the Earliest Times to the Year 2000, ed. H. C. G. Matthew and Brian Harrison, 61 vols. (Oxford: Oxford University Press, 2004).

Padrón, Ricardo, *The Spacious Word: Cartography, Literature and Empire in Early Modern Spain* (Chicago, IL and London: University of Chicago Press, 2004).

'"The Indies of the West": Or the Tale of how an Imaginary Geography Circumnavigated the Globe', in *Western Visions of the Far East in a Transpacific Age* (Aldershot, Hants, Burlington, VT: Ashgate, 2012), 19–42.

Pagden, Anthony, *The Fall of Natural Man: The American Indian and the Origins of Comparative Ethnology*, reprinted with corrections and additions (Cambridge: Cambridge University Press, 1986).

'The Impact of the New World on the Old: A History of an Idea', *Renaissance and Modern Studies*, 30 (1986), 1–11.

European Encounters with the New World: From Renaissance to Romanticism (New Haven, CT: Yale University Press: Yale University Press, 1993).

Palencia-Roth, Michael, 'The Cannibal Law of 1503', in *Early Images of the Americas: Transfer and Invention*, ed. Jerry M. Williams and Robert E. Lewis (Tucson, AZ and London: University of Arizona Press, 1993), 21–64.

Pardo-Tomás, José, '"Antiguamente vivían más sanos que ahora": Explanations of Native Mortality in the *Relaciones Geográficas de Indias*', in *Medical Cultures of the Early Modern Spanish Empire*, ed. John Slater et al. (Farnham and Burlington, VT: Ashgate, 2014), 41–65.

Park, Katharine, 'The Organic Soul', in *The Cambridge History of Renaissance Philosophy*, ed. Charles B. Schmitt et al. (Cambridge: Cambridge University Press, 1988), 464–84.

'The Intellective Soul', in *The Cambridge History of Renaissance Philosophy*, ed. Charles B. Schmitt et al. (Cambridge: Cambridge University Press, 1988), 485–534.

Parks, George B., 'Ramusio's Literary History', *Studies in Philology*, LII:2 (1955), 127–48.

Pellegrin, Nicole, 'Vêtements de peau(x) et de plumes: la nudité des indiens et la diversité du monde au XVIe siècle', in *Voyager à la Renaissance*, ed. Jean Céard and Jean.-Claude Margolin (Paris: Maisonneuve, 1987), 509–30.

Pero, Alejandra, 'The Tehuelche of Patagonia as Chronicled by Travelers and Explorers in the Nineteenth Century', in *Archaeological and Anthropological Perspectives on the Native Peoples of Pampa, Patagonia, and Tierra del Fuego to the Nineteenth Century*, ed. Claudia Briones and José Luis Lanata (Westport, CT and London: Bergin & Garvey, 2002), 103–19.

Pigeonneau, H., *Histoire du commerce de la France*, 2 vols. (Paris: Léopold Cerf, 1889).

Poeschel, Sabine, *Studien zur Ikonographie der Erdteile in der Kunst des 16.-18. Jahrhunderts* (Augsburg: Scaneg, 1985).

Pogo, Alexander, 'Early Editions and Translations of Xérez: *Verdadera relacion de la conquista del Peru*', *Papers of the Bibliographic Society of America*, XXX (1936), 57–84.

Popper, Nicholas, 'An Ocean of Lies: The Problem of Historical Evidence in the Sixteenth Century', *Huntington Library Quarterly*, 74:3 (2011), 375–400.

Walter Ralegh's History of the World and the Historical Culture of the Late Renaissance (Chicago, IL: University of Chicago Press, 2012).

Portuondo, María M., *Secret Science: Spanish Cosmography and the New World* (Chicago, IL and London: University of Chicago Press, 2009).

Pratt, Mary Louise, *Imperial Eyes: Travel Writing and Transculturation* (London: Routledge, 1992 [2008 printing]).

Pratt, Stephanie, 'From the Margins: The Native American Personage in the Cartouche and the Decorative Borders of Maps', *Word & Image*, 12 (1996), 349–65.

'Truth and Artifice in the Visualization of Native Peoples: From the time of John White to the Beginning of the 18th Century', in *European Visions: American Voices*, ed. Kim Sloan (London: British Museum, 2009), 33–40.

Prieto, Alfredo, 'Patagonian Painted Cloaks: An Ancient Puzzle', in *Patagonia: Natural History, Prehistory and Ethnography at the Uttermost End of the Earth*, ed. Colin McEwan et al. (Princeton, NJ: Princeton University Press, 1997), 173–85.

Proctor, Robert, *Jan van Doesborgh, Printer at Antwerp: An Essay in Bibliography* (London: Bibliographical Society, 1894).

Quinn, David Beers, *The Roanoke Voyages*, 2 vols. (London: Hakluyt Society, 1955).

'The Americas in the Rotz Atlas of 1542', in *European Approaches to North America, 1450–1640*, ed. David Beers Quinn (Aldershot: Ashgate, 1998), 69–92.

Qureshi, Sadiah, *Peoples on Parade: Exhibitions, Empire, and Anthropology in Nineteenth-Century Britain* (Chicago, IL and London: University of Chicago Press, 2011).

Rabasa, José, *Inventing America: Spanish Historiography and the Formation of Eurocentrism* (Norman, OK and London: University of Oklahoma Press, 1993).

'Utopian Ethnology in Las Casas's Apologética', in *1492–1992: Re/Discovering Colonial Writing*, ed. Nicholas Spadaccini and René Jara (Minneapolis, MN, 1989), 263–89.

Ravenstein, E. G., *Martin Behaim: His Life and His Globe* (London: George Philip & Son, 1908).

Relaño, Francesc, *The Shaping of Africa: Cosmographic Discourse and Cartographic Science in Late Medieval and Early Modern Europe* (Aldershot: Ashgate, 2002).

Reske, Christoph, ... *The Production of Schedel's Nuremberg Chronicle* (Wiesbaden: Harrassowitz, 2000).

Richardson, Catherine, ed., *Clothing Culture, 1350–1650* (Aldershot: Ashgate, 2004).

Rivera Novo, Belén and Luisa Martín-Merás, *Quatro siglos de cartografía en América* (Madrid: Mapfre, 1992).

Roberts, Sean, *Printing a Mediterranean World: Florence, Constantinople, and the Renaissance of Geography* (Cambridge, MA: Harvard University Press, 2013).

Robinson, A. H., 'It was the mapmakers who really discovered America', *Cartographica*, 29 (1992), 31–6.

Romm, James, 'Continents, Climates, and Cultures: Greek Theories of Global Structure', in *Geography and Ethnography: Perceptions of the World in Pre-Modern Societies*, ed. Kurt A. Raaflaub and Richard J. A. Talbert (Chichester, 2010), 215–35.

Roncière, Charles de La, *Histoire de la marine française*, 6 vols. (Paris: Plon, 1899–1932).

Ronsin, Albert, 'L'Amérique du Gymnase vosgien de Saint-Dié-des-Vosges', in *La France-Amérique (XVIe-XVIIIe siècles)*, ed. Frank Lestringant (Paris: H. Champion, 1998), 37–64.

Rosen, Mark, *The Mapping of Power in Renaissance Italy: Painted Cartographic Cycles in Social and Intellectual Context* (New York: Cambridge University Press, 2015).

Rosselló Verger, Vinceç, 'Cartes i atles portolans de les col•lections espanyoles', in *Portolans procedents de col•lecions espanyoles, segles XV-XVII*, ed. Vincenç Rosselló Verger and M. Carme Montaner i Garcia (Barcelona: Institut Cartogràfic de Catalunya, 1995), 9–59.

Rouse, Irving, *The Tainos: Rise and Decline of the People who Greeted Columbus* (New Haven, CT: Yale University Press, 1992).

Rublack, Ulinka, *Dressing Up: Cultural Identity in Renaissance Europe* (Oxford: Oxford University Press, 2010).

Rubiés, Joan-Pau, 'New Worlds and Renaissance Ethnology', *History and Anthropology*, 6 (1993), 157–97.

Travel and Ethnology in the Renaissance: South India through European Eyes, 1250–1625 (Cambridge: Cambridge University Press, 2000).

'Travel Writing as a Genre: Facts, Fictions and the Invention of a Scientific Discourse in Early Modern Europe', *Journeys*, 1 (2000), 5–35.

'Travel Writing and Ethnography', in *The Cambridge Companion to Travel Writing*, ed. Peter Hulme and Tim Youngs (Cambridge: Cambridge University Press, 2002), 243–60.

'Travel Writing and Humanistic Culture: A Blunted Impact?', *Journal of Early Modern History*, 10 (2006), 131–68.

Travellers and Cosmographers: Studies in the History of Early Modern Travel and Ethnology (Aldershot: Ashgate, 2007).

'Imagen mental e imagen artística en la representación de los pueblos no europeos: salvajes y civilizados, 1500–1650', in *La historia imaginada. Construcciones visuales del pasado en la edad moderna*, ed. Joan Lluís Palos and Diana Carrió-Invernizzi (Madrid: Centro de Estudios Europa Hispánica, 2008), 327–57.

'Texts, Images, and the Perception of 'Savages' in Early Modern Europe: What we can Learn from White and Harriot', in *European Visions, American Voices*, ed. Kim Sloan (London: British Museum, 2009), 123–33.

Russo, Alessandra, 'Cortés's Objects and the Idea of New Spain: Inventories as Spatial Narratives', *Journal of the History of Collections*, 23 (2011), 229–52.

Sabin, Joseph, *Bibliotheca Americana: A Dictionary of Books Relating to America*, 19 vols. (New York: Joseph Sabin, 1868–1936).

Sacks, David Harris, 'Discourses of Western Planting: Richard Hakluyt and the Making of the Atlantic World', in *The Atlantic World and Virginia, 1550–1624*, ed. Peter C. Mancall (Chapel Hill, NC: University of North Carolina Press, 2007), 410–53.

Safier, Neil, *Measuring the World: Enlightenment Science and South America* (Chicago, IL: University of Chicago Press, 2008).

Said, Edward W., *Orientalism* (New York: Pantheon Books, 1978).

Culture and Imperialism (London: Vintage, 1993).

Sandman, Alison, 'Mirroring the World: Sea Charts, Navigation, and Territorial Claims in Sixteenth-Century Spain', in *Merchants & Marvels: Commerce, Science and Art in Early Modern Europe*, ed. Pamela H. Smith and Paula Findlen (New York and London: Routledge, 2004), 83–109.

'An Apologia for the Pilots' Charts: Politics, Projections and Pilots' Reports in Early Modern Spain', *Imago Mundi*, 56 (2004), 7–22.

'Spanish Nautical Cartography in the Renaissance', in *The History of Cartography Volume 3: Cartography in the European Renaissance*, ed. David Woodward, 2 vols. (Chicago, IL and London: University of Chicago Press, 2007), I, 1095–142.

'Controlling Knowledge: Navigation, Cartography, and Secrecy in the Early Modern Spanish Atlantic', in *Science and Empire in the Atlantic World*, ed. James Delbourgo and Nicholas Dew (New York and London: Routledge, 2008), 31–51.

Sandman, Alison and Eric S. Ash, 'Trading Expertise: Sebastian Cabot between Spain and England', *Renaissance Quarterly*, 57 (2004), 813–46.

Scafi, Alessandro, *Mapping Paradise: A History of Heaven on Earth* (London: The British Library, 2006).

Schilder, Günter, *The World Map of 1624 by Willem Jansz. Blaeu & Jodocus Hondius* (Amsterdam: N. Israel, 1977).

'Willem Jansz. Blaeu's Wall Map of the World on Mercator's Projection 1606–7, and its Influence', *Imago Mundi*, 31 (1979), 36–54.

The World Map of 1611 by Pieter van den Keere (Amsterdam: N. Israel, 1980).

Three World Maps by François van den Hoeye of 1661, Willem Janszoon (Blaeu) of 1607, Claesz Janszoon Visscher of 1650 (Amsterdam: N. Israel, 1981).

'Jodocus Hondius, Creator of the Decorative Map Border', *Map Collector*, 32 (1985), 40–3.

Monumenta Cartographica Neerlandica (Alphen aan den Rijn: Uitgeverij Canaletto, 1986–2013).

Schilder, Günter and Marco Van Egmond, 'Maritime Cartography in the Low Countries during the Renaissance', in *The History of Cartography Volume 3: Cartography in the European Renaissance*, ed. David Woodward, 2 vols. (Chicago, IL: University of Chicago Press, 2007) II, 1384–432.

Schleck, Julia, *Telling True Tales of Islamic Lands: Forms of Mediation in English Travel Writing, 1575–1630* (Selinsgrove, PA: Susquehanna University Press, 2011).

Schmidt, Benjamin, *Innocence Abroad: The Dutch Imagination and the New World, 1570–1670* (Cambridge: Cambridge University Press, 2001).

'Reading Ralegh's America: Texts, Books, and Readers in the Early Modern Atlantic World' in Peter C. Mancall, ed., *The Atlantic World and Virginia, 1550–1624* (Chapel Hill, NC: University of North Carolina Press, 2007), 454–88.

Schuller, Rudolf, 'The Oldest Known Illustration of the South American Indians', *Journal de la Société des Americanistes de Paris*, N. S., 16 (1924), 111–18.

Juergen Schulz, 'Jacopo de' Barbari's View of Venice: Map Making, City Views, and Moralized Geography before the Year 1500', *The Art Bulletin*, 60 (1978), 425–74.

Schottmüller, Kurt, 'Reiseindrücke aus Danzig, Lübeck, Hamburg und Holland 1636. Nach dem neuentdeckten II Teil von Charles Ogiers Gesandtschaftstagebuch', *Zeitschrift des westpreussischen Geschichtsverein*, 52 (1910), 199–273.

Schwartz, Stuart B., 'Indian Labor and New World Plantations: European Demands and Indigenous Responses in Northeastern Brazil', *American Historical Review*, 83:1 (1978), 73–79.

'Brazilian Ethnogenesis: *Mestiços*, *Mamelucos*, and *Pardos*', in *Le Nouveau Monde, Mondes Nouveaux: L'expérience américaine*, ed. Serge Gruzinski and Nathan Wachtel (Paris: Recherche sur les civilisations : Ecole des hautes études en sciences sociales, 1996), 7–27.

'New Peoples and New Kinds of People: Adaptation, Readjustment, and Ethnogenesis in South American Indigenous Societies (Colonial Period)', in *Cambridge History of the Native Peoples of the Americas*, ed. Frank Salomon and Stuart B. Schwartz (Cambridge: Cambridge University Press, 1999), 443–501.

Schwartz, Stuart B., ed., *Implicit Understandings: Observing, Reporting, and Reflecting on the Encounters between Europeans and Other Peoples in the Early Modern Era* (Cambridge: Cambridge University Press, 1994).

Schwartz, Stuart B. and Hal Langfur, 'Tapahuns, Negros da Terra, and Curibocas: Common Cause and Confrontation between Blacks and Natives in Colonial Brazil', in *Beyond Black and Red: African-Native Relations in Colonial Latin America*, ed. Matthew Restall (Albuquerque, NM: University of New Mexico Press, 2005), 81–114.

Schwartz, Seymour I., *Putting 'America' on the Map: The Story of the Most Important Graphic Document in the History of the United States* (Amherst, NY: Prometheus, 2007).

Sebastián, Santiago, *Iconografía del indio americano, siglos XVI-XVII* (Madrid: Ediciones Tuero, 1992).

Seed, Patricia, '"Are These Not also Men?": The Indians' Humanity and Capacity for Spanish Civilisation', *Journal of Latin American Studies*, 25 (1993), 629–52.

Shalev, Zur, 'Sacred Geography: Antiquarianism and Visual Erudition: Benio Arias Montano and the Maps in the Antwerp Polyglot Bible', *Imago Mundi*, 55 (2003), 56–80.

Shapin, Steven, 'Pump and Circumstance: Robert Boyle's Literary Technology', *Social Studies of Science* 14 (1984), 481–520.

A Social History of Truth: Civility and Science in Seventeenth-Century England (Chicago, IL and London: University of Chicago Press, 1994).

Shapin, Steven and Simon Schaffer, *Leviathan and the Air-Pump: Hobbes, Boyle, and the Experimental Life* (Princeton, N. J.: Princeton University Press, 1985).

Shapiro, Barbara J., *Probability and Certainty in Seventeenth-Century England: A Study of the Relationships between Natural Science, Religion, History, Law and Literature* (Princeton, NJ: Princeton University Press, 1983).

A Culture of Fact: England, 1550–1720 (Ithaca, NY and London: Cornell University Press, 2000).

Sherman, William H., *Used Books: Marking Readers in Renaissance England* (Philadelphia, PA: University of Pennsylvania Press, 2008).

Shirley, John W., *Thomas Harriot: A Biography* (Oxford: Oxford University Press, 1983).

Shirley, Rodney W., 'The Title Pages to the *Theatrum* and *Parergon*', in *Abraham Ortelius and the First Atlas: Essays Commemorating the Quadricentennial of his Death, 1598–1998*, ed. Marcel P. R. Van den Broecke (Utrecht: HES, 1998), 161–9.

The Mapping of the World: Early Printed World Maps, 1472–1700 (Riverside, CT: Early World Press, 2001 [first published: 1984]).

Maps and Atlases in the British Library: A Descriptive Catalogue c. AD 850–1800, 2 vols. (London: The British Library, 2004).

Silver, Larry, *Marketing Maximilian: The Visual Ideology of a Holy Roman Emperor* (Princeton, NJ: Princeton University Press, 2008).

Siraisi, Nancy G., *Medieval and Early Renaissance Medicine: An Introduction to Knowledge and Practice* (Chicago, IL and London: University of Chicago Press, 1990).

Skelton, R. A., 'A Contract for World Maps at Barcelona, 1399–1400', *IM*, 22 (1968), 107–13.

Sloan, Kim et al., *A New World: England's First View of America* (London: British Museum, 2007).

ed., *European Visions: American Voices* (London: British Museum, 2009).

Small, Margaret, 'Displacing Ptolemy? The Textual Geographies of Ramusio's *Navigazione e viaggi*', in *Mapping Medieval Geographies: Geographical Encounters in the Latin West and Beyond, 300–1600*, ed. Keith D. Lilley (Cambridge: Cambridge University Press, 2013), 152–72.

Smiles, Sam, 'John White and British Antiquity: Savage Origins in the Context of Tudor Historiography', in *European Visions, American Voices*, ed. Kim Sloan (London: British Museum, 2009), 109–15.

Smith, Pamela H., *The Body of the Artisan: Art and Experience in the Scientific Revolution* (Chicago, IL: University of Chicago Press, 2004).

'Science on the Move: Recent Trends in the History of Early Modern Science', *Renaissance Quarterly*, 69:2 (2009), 345–75.

Smith, Pamela H. and Paula Findlen, eds., *Merchants & Marvels: Commerce, Science and Art in Early Modern Europe* (New York and London: Routledge, 2002).

Smith, Pamela H. and Benjamin Schmidt, eds., *Making Knowledge in Early Modern Europe: Practices, Objects, and Texts, 1400–1800* (Chicago, IL and London: University of Chicago Press, 2007).

Spinks, Jennifer, *Monstrous Births and Visual Culture in Sixteenth-Century Germany* (London: Pickering & Chatto, 2009).

Stagl, Justin and Christopher Pinney, 'Introduction: From Travel Literature to Ethnography', *History and Anthropology*, 9 (1996), 121–5.

Stallybrass, Peter, '*Admiranda narratio*: A European Best Seller' in Thomas Harriot, *A Briefe and True Report...: The 1590 Theodor de Bry Latin Edition*

(Charlottesville, VA: Published for the Library at the Mariners' Museum by the University of Virginia, 2007), 9–30.

Stallybrass, Peter and Ann Rosalind Jones, *Renaissance Clothing and the Materials of Memory* (Cambridge: Cambridge University Press, 2000).

Steel, Karl, 'Centaurs, Satyrs, and Cynocephali: Medieval Scholarly Teratology and the Question of the Human', in *The Ashgate Research Companion to Monsters and the Monstrous*, ed. Asa Simon Mittman with Peter J. Dendle (Farnham and Burlington, VT: Ashgate, 2012), 257–74.

Stepan, Nancy Leys, *Picturing Tropical Nature* (London: Reaktion, 2001).

Stephens, Walter, *Giants in Those Days: Folklore, Ancient History, and Nationalism* (Lincoln, NE and London: University of Nebraska Press, 1989).

Sturtevant, William C., 'First Visual Images of Native America', in *First Images of America: The Impact of the New World on the Old*, ed. Fredi Chiappelli et al., 2 vols. (Berkeley, CA and London: University of California Press, 1976), I, 417–54.

'La "tupinambisation" des Indiens d'Amérique du Nord', in *Figures de l'Indien*, ed. Gilles Thérien (Montreal: Typo, 1995), 345–61.

Sutton, Elizabeth A., *Early Modern Dutch Prints of Africa* (Farnham and Burlington, VT: Ashgate, 2012).

Texeira da Mota, Avelino, 'Some Notes on the Organization of Hydrographical Services in Portugal Before the Beginning of the Nineteenth Century', *Imago Mundi*, 28 (1976), 51–60.

Tolias, George, 'Maps in Renaissance Libraries and Collections', in *The History of Cartography Volume 3: Cartography in the European Renaissance*, ed. David Woodward, 2 vols. (Chicago, IL and London: University of Chicago Press, 2007), I, 637–60.

Tomlinson, Regina, *The Struggle for Brazil: Portugal and 'The French Interlopers' (1500–1550)* (New York: Las Americas Publishing, 1970).

Toulouse, Sarah, 'L'art de naviguer: hydrographie et cartographie marine en Normandie, 1500–1650', 2 vols., thèse doctorat, École Nationale des Chartes, Université de Paris, 1994.

'Marine Cartography and Navigation in Renaissance France', in *The History of Cartography Volume 3: Cartography in the European Renaissance*, ed. David Woodward, 2 vols. (Chicago, IL and London: University of Chicago Press, 2007), II, 1550–68.

Traub, Valerie, 'Mapping the Global Body', in *Early Modern Visual Culture: Representation, Race, and Empire in Renaissance England*, ed. Peter Erickson and Clark Hulse (Philadelphia, PA: University of Pennsylvania Press, 2000), 44–97.

Turnbull, David, 'Cartography and Science in Early Modern Europe: Mapping and the Construction of Knowledge Spaces', *Imago Mundi*, 40 (1996), 5–23.

Turner, Henry S., 'Literature and Mapping in Early Modern England, 1520–1688', in *The History of Cartography Volume 3: Cartography in the European*

Renaissance, ed. David Woodward, 2 vols. (Chicago, IL and London: University of Chicago Press, 2007), 412–26.

Tzanaki, Rosemary, *Mandeville's Medieval Audiences: A Study on the Reception of the 'Book' of Sir John Mandeville (1371–1550)* (Aldershot: Ashgate, 2003).

Van den Boogaart, Ernst, 'The Empress Europe and Her Three Sisters: The Symbolic Representation of Europe's Superiority in the Low Countries 1570–1655', in *America, Bride of the Sun: 500 Years, Latin America and the Low Countries* (Ghent and Brussels: Antwerp Royal Museum of Fine Arts, 1992), 120–8.

Civil and Corrupt Asia: Images and Text in the 'Itinerario' and the 'Icones' of Jan Huygen van Linschoten (Chicago, IL: University of Chicago Press, 2003).

'Serialized Virginia: The Representational Format for Comparative Ethnology c.1600', in *European Visions: American Voices*, ed. Kim Sloan (London: British Museum, 2009), 113–19.

Van den Broecke, Marcel P. R., 'Introduction to the Life and Works of Abraham Ortelius (1527–1598)', in *Abraham Ortelius and the First Atlas. Essays Commemorating the Quadricentennial of his Death, 1598–1998*, ed. Marcel P. R. Van den Broecke (Houten: HES, 1998), 29–54.

Vaughan, Alden T., 'Trinculo's Indian: American Natives in Shakespeare's England', in *'The Tempest' and its Travels*, ed. Peter Hulme and William H. Sherman (London: Reaktion, 2000), 48–59.

Transatlantic Encounters: American Indians in Britain, 1500–1776 (New York: Cambridge University Press, 2006).

Vigneras, L. A., 'The Cartographer Diogo Ribeiro', *Imago Mundi*, 16 (1962), 76–83.

Vila Llonch, Elisenda, *Beyond El Dorado: Power and Gold in Ancient Colombia* (London: British Museum, 2013).

Vitet, L., *Histoire des anciennes villes de France. Première série. Haute-Normandie. Dieppe* (Paris: Alexandre Mesnier, 1833).

Wallis, Helen, 'Sixteenth-Century Maritime Manuscript Atlases for Special Presentation', in *Images of the World: The Atlas through History*, ed. John A. Walter and Ronald E. Grim (Washington, DC: Library of Congress, 1997), 3–29.

Waterschoot, Werner, 'The Title-Page of Ortelius's *Theatrum Orbis Terrarum*. A Comment', *Quaerendo*, 9 (1979), 43–68.

Weil-Garris, Kathleen and John d'Amico, 'The Renaissance Cardinal's Ideal Palace: A Chapter from Cortesi's *De cardinalatu*', *Memoirs of the American Academy in Rome*, 35 (1980), 45–123.

Weinstock, Jeffrey Andrew. 'Vision, Horror, and Contemporary Culture', in *The Ashgate Research Companion to Monsters and the Monstrous*, ed. Asa Simon Mittman with Peter J. Dendle (Farnham and Burlington, VT: Ashgate, 2012), 273–287.

Westrem, Scott D., *The Hereford Map: A Transcription and Translation of the Legends with Commentary* (Turnhout: Brepols, 2001).

Wey Gómez, Nicolás, *The Tropics of Empire: Why Columbus Sailed South to the Indies* (Cambridge, MA and London: MIT Press, 2008).

Wheeler, Roxann, *The Complexion of Race: Categories of Difference in Eighteenth-century British Culture* (Philadelphia, PA: University of Pennsylvania Press, 2000).

White, Hayden, 'The Forms of Wildness: Archaeology of an Idea', in *The Wild Man Within: An Image in Western Thought from the Renaissance to Romanticism*, ed. Edward Dudley and Maximillian E. Novak (Pittsburgh: University of Pittsburgh Press, 1972), 3–38.

Tropics of Discourse: Essays in Cultural Criticism (Baltimore, MD and London: The Johns Hopkins University Press, 1984).

Whitehead, Neil L., 'Carib Cannibalism: The Historical Evidence', *Journal de la société des Americanistes de Paris*, LXX (1984), 53–74.

'The Historical Anthropology of text: The Interpretation of Ralegh's *Discoverie of Guiana*', *Current Anthropology*, 36 (1995), 53–74.

'The Crises and Transformations of Invaded Societies: The Caribbean (1491–1580)', in *Cambridge History of the Native Peoples of the Americas*, ed. Frank Salomon and Stuart B. Schwartz (Cambridge: Cambridge University Press, 1999), 864–903.

'Hans Staden and the Cultural Politics of Cannibalism', *Hispanic American Historical Review*, 80 (2000), 721–51.

'Arawak Linguistic and Cultural Identity through Time: Contact, Colonialism, and Creolization', in *Comparative Arawakan Histories: Rethinking Language Family and Culture Area in Amazonia*, ed. Jonathan D. Hill and Fernando Santos-Granero (Urbana, IL and Chicago, IL: University of Illinois Press, 2002), 51–73.

'Black Read as Red: Ethnic Transgression and Hybridity in Northeastern South America and the Caribbean', in *Beyond Black and Red: African-Native Relations in Colonial Latin America*, ed. Matthew Restall (Albuquerque, NM: University of New Mexico Press, 2005), 223–43.

'Guayana as Anthropological Imaginary: Elements of a History', in *Anthropologies of Guayana: Cultural Spaces in Northeastern Amazonia*, ed. Neil L. Whitehead and Stephanie W. Alemán (Tucson, AZ: University of Arizona Press, 2009), 1–20, at 4–5.

Of Cannibals and Kings: Primal Anthropology in the Americas (University Park, PA: Pennsylvania State University Press, 2011).

Wieder, F. C., *Monumenta Cartographica*, 5 vols. (The Hague: M. Nijhoff, 1925–33).

Wiesner-Hanks, Merry, *The Marvelous Hairy Girls: The Gonzales Sisters and Their Worlds* (New Haven, CT and London: Yale University Press, 2009).

Wintroub, Michael, 'Civilizing the Savage and Making a King: The Royal Entry Festival of Henri II (Rouen, 1550)', *Sixteenth Century Journal*, 29 (1998), 465–94.

A Savage Mirror: Power, Identity and Knowledge in Early Modern France (Stanford, CA: Stanford University Press, 2006).

Wittkower, Rudolf, 'Marvels of the East: A Study in the History of Monsters', *Journal of the Warburg and Courtauld Institutes*, 5 (1942), 159–97.

'Marco Polo and the Pictorial Tradition of the Marvels of the East', in *Oriente Poliano* (Rome: Istituto italiano per il Medio e Estremo Oriente, 1957), 155–72.

Wolff, Hans, ed., *America: Early Maps of the New World* (Munich: Prestel, 1992).

'Martin Waldseemüller: The Most Important Cosmographer in a Period of Dramatic Scientific Change', in *America: Early Maps of the New World*, ed. Hans Wolff (Munich: Prestel, 1992), 111–26.

'America – Early Images of the New World', in *America: Early Maps of the New World*, ed. Hans Wolff (Munich: Prestel, 1992), 16–102.

'The Munich Portolan Charts: Past and Present', in *America: Early Maps of the New World*, ed. Hans Wolff (Munich: Prestel, 1992), 127–44.

Woodward, David, 'Medieval *Mappaemundi*', in *History of Cartography Volume 1: Cartography in Prehistoric, Ancient and Medieval Europe and the Mediterranean*, ed. J. B. Harley and David Woodward (Chicago, IL: University of Chicago Press, 1987), 286–370.

ed., *Art and Cartography: Six Historical Essays* (Chicago, IL: University of Chicago Press, 1987).

Maps as Prints in the Italian Renaissance: Makers, Distributors and Consumers (London: The British Library, 1996).

'Geography', in *The Cambridge History of Science: Volume 3: Early Modern Science*, ed. Katharine Park and Lorraine Daston (New York: Cambridge University Press, 2006), 548–68.

'Techniques of Map Engraving, Printing and Coloring in the European Renaissance', in *The History of Cartography Volume 3: Cartography in the European Renaissance*, ed. idem, 2 vols. (Chicago, IL and London: University of Chicago Press, 2007), I, 591–610.

et al., *11è curs plantejaments i objectius d'una història universal de la cartografia / Approaches and Challenges in a Worldwide History of Cartography* (Barcelona: Institut Cartogràfic de Catalunya, 2001).

Worms, Laurence, 'The London Map Trade to 1640', in *The History of Cartography Volume 3: Cartography in the European Renaissance*, ed. David Woodward, 2 vols. (Chicago, IL and London: University of Chicago Press, 2007), II, 1693–721.

Zamora, Margarita, *Reading Columbus* (Berkeley, CA: University of California Press, 1993).

Zandvliet, Kees, *Mapping for Money: Maps, Plans and Topographic Paintings and their Role in Dutch Overseas Expansion during the 16th and 17th Centuries* (Amsterdam: Batavian Lion International, 1998).

'Mapping the Dutch World Overseas in the Seventeenth Century', in *The History of Cartography Volume 3: Cartography in the European Renaissance*, ed. David Woodward, 2 vols. (Chicago, IL and London: University of Chicago Press, 2007), II, 1433–62.

Zerubavel, Eviatar, *Terra Cognita: The Mental Discovery of America* (New Brunswick, NJ: Rutgers University Press, 1992).

Index

CPSIA information can be obtained
at www.ICGtesting.com
Printed in the USA
LVHW01s2343080418
572690LV00017B/1257/P